BEN WILSON

Ben Wilson is the author of five critically acclaimed books, including *What Price Liberty?*, for which he received the Somerset Maugham Award; the *Sunday Times* bestseller *Empire of the Deep*; and, most recently, *Heyday: The Dawn of the Global Age*. Born in London in 1980, he has worked in television, broadcast on the radio in several countries, and writes regularly for publications such as *The Times*, *Daily Telegraph* and *Prospect*.

ALSO BY BEN WILSON

Heyday: The Dawn of the Global Age

*Empire of the Deep: The Rise and Fall of the
British Navy*

*What Price Liberty?: How Freedom Was Won and
Is Being Lost*

*Decency and Disorder: The Age of Cant,
1789–1837*

*The Laughter of Triumph: William Hone and the
Fight for the Free Press*

BEN WILSON

Metropolis

A History of the City, Humankind's
Greatest Invention

VINTAGE

1 3 5 7 9 10 8 6 4 2

Vintage is part of the Penguin Random House
group of companies whose addresses can be found at
global.penguinrandomhouse.com

Penguin
Random House
UK

First published in Vintage in 2021
First published in hardback by Jonathan Cape in 2020

penguin.co.uk/vintage

A CIP catalogue record for this book is available from the
British Library

ISBN 9781784707521

Printed and bound in Great Britain by Clays Ltd, Elcograf S.p.A.

The authorised representative in the EEA is Penguin Random House
Ireland, Morrison Chambers, 32 Nassau Street, Dublin D02 YH68.

Penguin Random House is committed to a sustainable future for our
business, our readers and our planet. This book is made from Forest
Stewardship Council® certified paper.

Contents

List of Illustrations

Gustave Caillebotte, *Paris Street, Rainy Day*, oil on canvas, 1877. (Charles H. and Mary F. S. Worcester Collection / Bridgeman Images)

Edouard Manet, *A Bar at the Folies-Bergère*, oil on canvas, 1881–2. (Bridgeman Images)

Edouard Manet, *Plum Brandy*, oil on canvas, c. 1877. (Bridgeman Images)

Second plate section

Shanghai at night. (Siyuan / Unsplash)

Skyscraper Souls, movie poster, 1932. (Warner Brothers)

Dead End, movie still, 1937. (World History Archive / Ann Ronan Collection / Agefotostock)

Queensbridge Housing Project in the shadow of the Queensboro Bridge, photograph, 1939. (*New York Daily News* Archive / Getty Images)

Visitors to General Motors 'Futurama' Exhibition, photograph, 1939. (Getty Images / Bettmann)

H. S. Wong, 'Bloody Saturday', photograph, 1937. (National Archives and Records Administration)

Henry N. Cobb, 'Warsaw, August 1947', photograph, 1947. (Henry N. Cobb)

Judge Harry Pregerson Interchange, Los Angeles, photograph, 2018. (Denys Nevozhai / Unsplash)

Cheonggyecheon, Seoul, photograph, 2008. (Michael Sotnikov/ Unsplash)

Rua Gonçalo de Carvalho, Porto Alegre, photograph, 2012. (Adalberto Cavalcanti Adreani / flickr www.flickr.com/photos/adalberto_ca/ 8248042595/)

Tokyo, photograph, 2017. (Erik Eastman / Unsplash)

Shinjuku, Tokyo, photograph, 2018. (Bantersnaps / Unsplash)

Comuna 13, Medellín, photograph, 2011. (imageBROKER / Alamy Stock Photo)

Lagos, photograph, 2018. (Alan van Gysen)

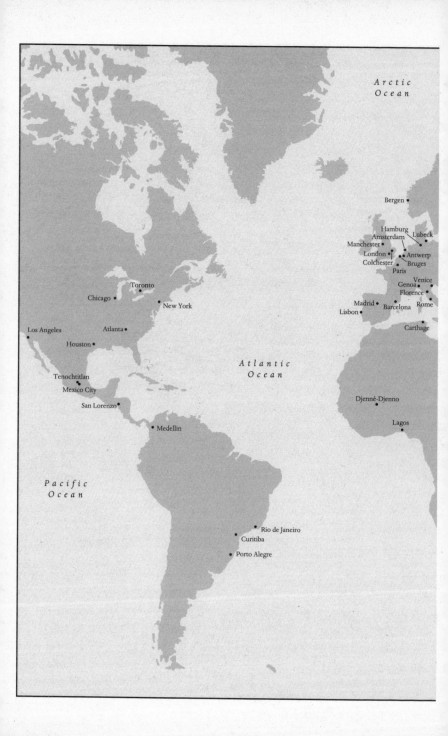

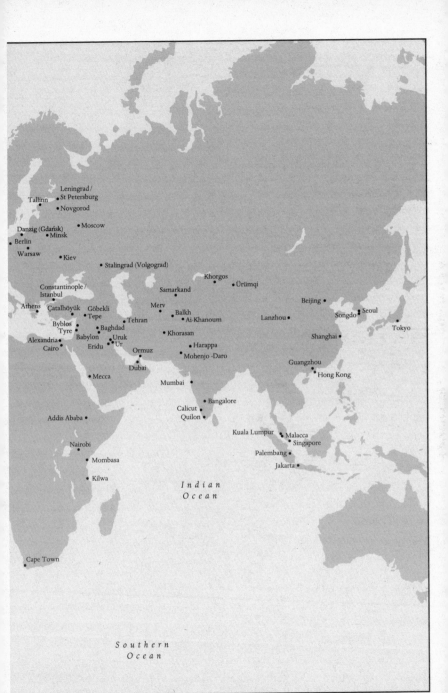

Introduction

The Metropolitan Century

Today the world's urban population grew by close to 200,000 people. It will do the same tomorrow, and the next day, and so on into the future. Two-thirds of humanity will live in cities by 2050. We are witnessing the greatest migration of history, the culmination of a 6,000-year process whereby we will have become an urbanised species by the end of the present century.[1]

How and where we live is one of the most important questions we can ask ourselves. Much of what we understand about history and about our own times flows from exploring that subject. Since the first urban settlements in Mesopotamia around 4000 BC, cities have acted as gigantic information exchanges; the dynamic interaction of people in the dense, cramped metropolis has generated the ideas and techniques, revolutions and innovations that have driven history. Until the year 1800 no more than 3–5% of the global population lived in sizeable urban areas; but this tiny minority had a disproportionate effect on global development. Cities have always been humankind's laboratories, the forcing houses of history. Drawn by the magnetic power of the city – like so many millions every single week – I began researching and writing *Metropolis* with this premise: that our past and our future are bound up, for good and ill, with the city.

I plunged into this vast, multifaceted, perplexing subject at a time of both spectacular urban renaissance and unprecedented challenges to the urban fabric. At the beginning of the twentieth century the traditional city was a place of pessimism not hope; the devouring industrial metropolis imprisoned its people, poisoning their bodies and minds; it was bringing about social breakdown. In the second half of the twentieth century the response to the horrors of industrialisation was in full swing: we seemed to be in a process of dispersal rather than concentration. Major global metropolises such as New York and London experienced population decline. Cars, telephones, cheap air travel, the frictionless flows of capital around the planet, and, latterly, the Internet allowed us to spread out, undoing the traditional cramped, intense city centre. Who needed urban social networks when you had limitless virtual social networks? Downtown – which was in any case suffering from crime waves and physical dilapidation– was being replaced by suburban business parks, campuses, home offices and out-of-town shopping centres. The closing years of the last century and the first decades of this millennium, however, upended those predictions.

Most notably in China, a series of ancient cities – and some brand-new ones – roared into life, fuelled by 440 million rural-to-urban migrants in three decades and crowned by an orgy of skyscraper construction. Across the world, cities reclaimed their central economic position. Rather than facilitating dispersal, the knowledge economy and superfast communications encourage large companies, small businesses, start-ups and freelance creative workers to swarm like bees in a hive. Technological, artistic and financial innovations occur when experts cluster: humans thrive when they share knowledge, collaborate and compete in face-to-face settings – and in particular in places that facilitate information flows. Where once cities tried to woo big manufacturing plants or capture a share of world trade, they now compete for brains.

The dependence on human capital and the economic benefits of urban density in post-industrial societies are remaking the modern metropolis. Successful cities transform entire economies – as the much-envied, urban-led growth of China shows. Every time an area doubles in population density it becomes 2–5% more productive: the energies contained in cities make us collectively more competitive and entrepreneurial. That force is magnified not just by density but by size as well.[2]

One of the major changes that has assailed the planet in the last three decades is the startling way in which major metropolises are pulling away from their countries. The global economy is skewed towards a few cities and city-regions: by 2025, 440 cities with a collective population of 600 million (7% of all people) will account for half of worldwide gross domestic product. Single cities in many emerging markets such as São Paulo, Lagos, Moscow and Johannesburg on their own produce between a third and half of their nation's wealth. Lagos, with 10% of Nigeria's population, accounts for 60% of the nation's industrial and commercial activities; if it declared independence and became a city state, it would be the fifth richest country in Africa. In China, 40% of the country's entire economic output is generated by just three megacity regions. This is not a new phenomenon. In fact, we are seeing a return to a situation common for most of history – the outsized role of the superstar city in human affairs. In ancient Mesopotamia or Mesoamerica before Columbus, during the rise of the Greek *polis* or the heyday of the medieval city state, a select group of metropolises monopolised trade and outcompeted mere nation states.

Throughout history, this divergence of major cities and countries has not just been economic. Their turbocharged success means they suck in talent and wealth from less favoured towns and regions; they dominate culture; and, like historical cities, they are more than ever characterised by a diversity not matched elsewhere. The proportion of foreign-born residents in some of today's most powerful metropolises is between 35% and 50%. Younger, better educated, richer and more multicultural than their national populations, global cities have more in common with each other. In many modern societies the deepest divide is not age, race, class or urban versus rural: it is between big metropolises and the villages, suburbs, towns and cities that have been left behind in the globalised knowledge economy. In some senses the word 'metropolitan' connotes glamour and opportunity; but it is also shorthand for a kind of elitism – political, cultural and social – that is increasingly resented. Hatred for the big city is not new, of course; we have spent a lot of our history worrying about the corrosive effect of the metropolis on our morals and mental health.

The astonishingly rapid spread of Covid-19 in 2019/20 across the planet was a dark kind of tribute to the triumph of the city in the twenty-first century; the virus spread through the complex social networks – both within cities and between them – that make them at once so successful and so dangerous for us. When urbanites began deserting cities such as Paris or New York for the apparent safety of the countryside they were often met with hostility, reviled not only for bringing disease with them, but for deserting their fellow citizens.

That backlash was a reminder of the antagonism between city and non-city that runs through history – metropolises as places of privilege and wellsprings of contamination; places that hold out the promise of wealth but from which one runs at the first sign of danger.

Plagues, pandemics and diseases have coursed along trade routes and mercilessly ravaged dense urban areas since the first cities. In 1854 6% of Chicago's population was killed by cholera. But it did not stop people herding to the miracle metropolis of the nineteenth century: its population surged from 30,000 at the beginning of the 1850s to 112,000 by the end. And so in our present age, the urban juggernaut shows no signs of slowing even in the face of pandemics; we have always paid a high price to share the benefits of the city even when its openness, diversity and density turn against us.

The scale of our recent urbanisation can be seen from space in the blobs of light that speckle the earth's surface at night. The renaissance is apparent at street level. From being dangerous and somewhat shabby in the mid to late twentieth century, many cities have become safer and highly desirable, hipper and more expensive, revived by a smorgasbord of high-end restaurants, street food, cafés, galleries and music venues. At the same time, the digital revolution promises us a slew of new technologies that will eradicate many of the downsides of city life, creating futuristic data-driven 'smart cities' with millions of embedded sensors that will allow AI to manage traffic flows, coordinate public transport, eradicate crime and reduce pollution. Cities have become, once again, places to rush towards, not escape from. Our contemporary urban renaissance can be readily glimpsed in the restless cityscape – in the gentrification of run-down areas, rising rents, repurposed buildings and the army of skyscrapers that are shooting upwards almost everywhere.

Shanghai transformed from a smoggy 'Third World backwater' (according to a local newspaper) in the early 1990s into the icon of the twenty-first-century post-industrial metropolitan revolution with its shimmering supersized towers. In imitation of Shanghai and other Chinese metropolises, global skyscraper construction has increased 402% since the turn of the millennium, bringing the total number of buildings over 150 metres and forty floors from little more than 600 to 3,251 within eighteen years; by the midpoint of this century there will be 41,000 such towers dominating the world's cities. The abrupt verticalisation of the urban landscape is evident the planet over, from traditionally low-rise metropolises such as London and Moscow to boom-time cities such as Addis Ababa and Lagos, all of which share a compulsive desire to advertise their virility on the skyline.[3]

And while cities are spiking upwards, they are also conquering territory. The old division between city centre and suburb has broken down. Far from being the monolithic, dull places of cliché, many suburbs have become steadily more urban since the 1980s with jobs, greater ethnic diversity, street life, crime epidemics and drug abuse – in other words, inheriting many of the virtues and vices of the inner city. The traditionally compact city surrounded by a hinterland of suburban housing has broken free and spread fast. The result is metropolises that occupy entire regions. The division, in economic terms, between London and much of south-east England is hard to see. Atlanta, Georgia, drapes itself over almost 2,000 square miles (Paris, by contrast, occupies forty square miles). The biggest megalopolis in the world, Tokyo, fits 40 million people into 5,240 square miles. Even that colossus will be overshadowed by China's planned urban mega-regions, such as Jing-Jin-Ji, a cluster of interlinked cities encompassing Beijing, Hebei and Tianjin, which will cover 84,000 square miles and contain 130 million people. When we talk about 'the metropolis' in the twenty-first century, we are not talking about the central business district of Manhattan or central Tokyo – the classic idea of where power and wealth resides – but of vast interconnected regions where cities melt into other cities.

It is easy to be intoxicated by the shimmering vision of newly assertive cities. The rage for vertical living has become the privilege of the very rich; it is symptomatic of a desire to escape the messy, congested, confusing city streets below and seek a haven in the clouds. According to the United Nations, slums and informal settlements lacking in basic amenities and infrastructure are becoming the 'dominant and distinctive type of settlement' of humanity. The future lifestyles of the majority of our species can be seen more readily in the super-dense, self-built and self-organised areas of Mumbai or Nairobi than in the gleaming central districts of Shanghai or Seoul or the lavish sprawl of Houston or Atlanta. Today, 1 billion people – one out every four city-dweller – lives in a slum, shanty town, *favela*, barrio, township, *kampung, campamento, gecekondu, villa miseria*, or whatever name is given to these kinds of unplanned, self-built urban areas. Some 61% of the global workforce – 2 billion people – make their living off the books, in the informal economy, many of them feeding, clothing and housing expanding urban populations. This kind of DIY urbanism fills the gaps left by city governments which are simply incapable of dealing with the torrent of incomers. We give a lot of attention to the knowledge-economy innovators who thrive in the centres of global cities. But there are other innovators – the ones working at the bottom who keep cities going through hard work and ingenuity.[4]

The rapid proliferation of skyscrapers and shanty towns alike heralds the present 'urban century'. Citizens of even the most strained megacity earn more, educate their children better and enjoy greater material comforts than their rural cousins. For the first generation of rural–urban migrants to Rio de Janeiro's *favelas* illiteracy rates were 79%; today 94% of their grandchildren are literate. In sub-Saharan cities with 1 million-plus residents, infant mortality is a third lower than in smaller settlements. Only 16% of rural Indian girls aged thirteen to eighteen whose family earns less than $2 a day go to school, compared to 48% in Hyderabad. Since China's breakneck urbanisation, average life expectancy has increased by eight years. If you live in Shanghai you can expect to live to eighty-three, ten years longer than in rural provinces in western China.[5]

Among the 200,000 people who migrated to a city today are people escaping rural poverty. Pushed off the land, the city becomes the only option to make a living. But cities also offer opportunities not available elsewhere, as they have always done. They also call upon resourcefulness and mental toughness. Squalid, insanitary slums in developing cities are some of the most entrepreneurial places on the planet. Yet they foster elaborate networks of mutual support that ease the shocks and strains of life in the megacity. One of the largest slums in Asia, Dharavi in Mumbai, squeezes close to 1 million people into just 0.8 square miles. Some 15,000 single-room workshops and thousands of micro-enterprises collectively make up an internal economy of $1 billion a year. Large numbers of people are involved in recycling the mountains of garbage discarded by over 20 million fellow Mumbaians. Despite its hyper-density and lack of policing (or other basic services), Dharavi, like other Indian megaslums, is markedly safe to walk around.

Starting in the late 1990s, a handful of self-taught computer geeks turned a street in Lagos into the biggest information and communications technology market in Africa: Otigba Computer Village, which has thousands of entrepreneurs and a daily turnover in excess of $5 million. The clustering effect does not just benefit bankers on Wall Street or Pudong New Area in Shanghai, advertising creatives in Soho, London, or software engineers in Silicon Valley and Bangalore; it transforms the lives and lifestyles of millions of people throughout the world as urbanisation spreads and intensifies. The DIY informal urban economy – be it on the streets of fast-growing Lagos or in a richer metropolis like Los Angeles – is testament to the human capacity to build cities from the ground up and organise functioning societies even in the midst of apparent chaos. It is the essence of the 6,000-year-old urban experience.

Cities are, for all their successes, harsh, merciless environments. If they offer the chance for higher incomes and education, they can also warp our souls, fray our minds and pollute our lungs. They are places to survive and negotiate as best we can – cauldrons of noise, pollution and nerve-shredding overcrowding. Somewhere like Dharavi – with its twisting maze of alleys, the sheer complexity of human activity and interaction, the constant struggle for survival, the overpowering concentration of people, its apparent mess and its spontaneous order – is reminiscent of urban life throughout history, be it in the labyrinth of a Mesopotamian city, the ugly anarchy of ancient Athens, the congested jumble of a European medieval town or a nineteenth-century slum in industrial Chicago. City life is overwhelming; its energies, ceaseless change and its millions of inconveniences, both big and small, push us to our limits. Throughout history, cities have been seen as fundamentally contrary to our natures and instincts, places that nurture vice, incubate diseases and induce social pathologies. The myth of Babylon echoes down the ages: as stunningly successful as they are, cities can crush the individual. For all that is compelling about the metropolis, there is a lot that is monstrous too.

The ways in which we take this hostile environment and shape it for our uses is fascinating. My approach in *Metropolis* is not simply to see cities as places of power and profit, but as human habitations that have had a profound effect on shaping the people who lived in them.

This is not a book just about grand buildings or urban planning; it is about the people who settled in cities and the ways they found to cope with and survive the pressure cooker of urban life. That is not to say that architecture is not important: it is the interaction between the built environment and humans that is at the heart of urban life, and of this book. I am more interested in the connective tissue that binds the organism together, not just its outward appearance or vital organs.

In the ways that cities are built on layers of human history, in the near-infinite and ceaseless intertwining of human lives and experiences, cities are as enthralling as they are unfathomable. In their beauty and ugliness, joy and misery, and in the inordinate, bewildering range of their complexity and contradictions, cities are a tableau of the human condition, things to love and hate in equal measure. They are volatile zones, in a ceaseless process of change and adaptation. They mask their instability with grand buildings and landmarks, to be sure; but around these symbols of permanence swirls remorseless change. The continual destruction and rebuilding worked by the force of the tide makes cities mesmerising, but frustratingly hard to grasp. I have sought, throughout *Metropolis*, to catch cities in movement, not in stasis.

In researching this book, I travelled to a range of cities in Europe, the Americas, Africa and Asia – to ones as contrasting as Mumbai and Singapore, Shanghai and Mexico City, Lagos and LA. Throughout the chronological narrative I have chosen a series of cities that tell us something not only about their own time, but about the urban condition in general. Some of these cities – such as Athens, London or New York – are obvious choices; others – like Uruk, Harappa, Lübeck and Malacca – might not be so familiar. In examining the history of cities, I looked for material in markets, souks and bazaars; in swimming pools, stadiums and parks; in street-food stalls, coffee houses and cafés; in shops, malls and department stores. I interrogated paintings, novels, films and songs as much as official records in search of the lived experience of cities and the intensity of their daily life. You have to experience a city through your senses – looking, smelling, touching, walking, reading and imagining – to understand its totality. For much of history, urban life has revolved around the sensual – eating and drinking, sex and shopping, gossip and play. All of those things that make up the theatre of city life are central to *Metropolis*.

Cities are successful in large part because they offer pleasure, excitement, glamour and intrigue as much as they do power, money and security. For over 6,000 years, as we will see, humankind has continually experimented with ways of living in the urban maelstrom. We are good at living in cities, and cities are resilient creations capable of standing up to wars and disasters. We are, at the same time, very bad at building cities; we have planned and constructed, in the name of progress, places which imprison rather than liberate, immiserate rather than elevate. Much needless tragedy has been caused by experts chasing the dream of the perfect, scientifically planned metropolis. Or, less drastically, planning often creates sanitised environments, drained of the energies that make city-living worthwhile.

In an age when there are not only more big cities but also large swathes of the inhabited world which are becoming urban, the question of how we should live in cities is never more pressing. Only by understanding the stupendous range of the urban experience through time and across cultures can we begin to grapple with one of the biggest challenges of the third millennium. Cities have never been perfect and can never be made so. Indeed, much of the pleasure and dynamism of cities comes from their spatial messiness. By that I mean the diversity of buildings, people and activities jumbled up together and forced into interaction. Orderliness is essentially *anti*-urban. What makes a city compelling is its incremental development – the process by which it has been built, and rebuilt, from the ground up over the generations producing a densely woven, rich urban fabric.

This messiness lies at the heart of what it is to be urban. Think of a city like Hong Kong or Tokyo, where skyscrapers tower above streets teeming with pedestrians, markets, small shops, street-food sellers, restaurants, laundries, bars, cafés, light industry and workshops. Or think of a settlement like Dharavi in a cacophonous megacity which is a scene of continual, frenetic street-level activity – one that provides all basic needs within a short distance. As the American–Canadian author Jane Jacobs argued in the 1960s, a city's density and its street life produces urbanity, the art of being a citizen. Walkable city neighbourhoods are one of the key ingredients of city-dwelling. Then think of the modern cities across the world, where retail, light industry, residential areas and offices are rigorously separated. In many cases, this sorting of functions into discrete districts has the effect of

sanitising cities, making them neat and tidy but drained of energy.
Planning can have this effect. So do cars. The advent of mass car-
ownership – first in the United States, then Europe and latterly Latin
America, Asia and Africa – has fundamentally reshaped cities.
Expressways not only facilitated suburbanisation and out-of-town
retail, but within city centres wide, busy roads and acres of car parking
helped to kill off what remained of street life.

When we talk of over 50% of the world's population being urbanised, we may well be falling into an error. A large proportion of
modern urbanites don't live urban or urbane lifestyles – if by that we
mean that they live in walkable neighbourhoods, have easy access to
culture, entertainment, recreation, employment, public spaces and
markets. Many of the 50+% live *sub*-urban lifestyles, be it in glitzy
single-family homes surrounded by lawns or in so-called 'arrival
cities' – squatter camps clinging onto the edge of fast-developing
metropolises.

The problem for the twenty-first century is not that we are becoming
urban too quickly, but that we are not becoming urban enough. Why
does this matter? It would not if we could be as lavish with our planet
as we liked. The fact that 200,000 people are streaming into cities
every day – or that we became a majority urban species around 2010
– is eye-catching. But it does not tell the full story. Much more alarming
is the knowledge that while the urban population is set to double
between 2000 and 2030, the area occupied by the concrete jungle will
triple. During those three decades alone, we will have extended our
urban footprint by an area equivalent to the size of South Africa.[6]

This global urban sprawl is pushing our cities into wetlands, wilder-
nesses, rainforests, estuaries, mangrove forests, floodplains and agricultural land – with devastating consequences for biodiversity and the
climate. Mountains are being moved to make way for this epic splurge
of urbanisation. This is literally true: from 2012 over 700 mountain
peaks were remorselessly razed in China's remote north-west and the
rubble tipped into valleys to create an artificial plateau on which a
shimmering new skyscraper city called Lanzhou New Area, a staging
post on the New Silk Roads, is being built.

Chinese cities – like American ones before them – are becoming
less dense in their cores as roads and office developments force people
out of tightly packed, mixed-use urban neighbourhoods to the suburbs.

It is part of a global trend of low-density, car-dependent urbanisation and sprawl. When people get richer, they demand more living space. If Chinese and Indian city-dwellers choose to live at the generous densities of Americans, their vehicle use and energy demands will increase global carbon emissions by 139%.[7] The coronavirus outbreak of 2020, and threats of future pandemics, could turn the tide against cities once again, encouraging people to flee metropolises, places where long periods of quarantine and lockdown are almost unbearable and where the risks of infection are greater. If that happens, the ecological damage will be grave.

In a hotter, wetter, harsher climate cities might offer a way out of the problem. As I show throughout the long history outlined in *Metropolis*, cities are resilient, adaptable entities capable of standing up to and responding to all kinds of disasters, and we are an adaptable, urban species long accustomed to the pressures and possibilities of city-living. And we had better carry on innovating. In the present century two-thirds of major metropolises with populations over 5 million, including Hong Kong, New York, Shanghai, Jakarta and Lagos, are under threat of rising sea levels; many more are baking as temperatures climb and suffering from destructive storms. Our cities are at the front line of looming environmental catastrophe; for that very reason they could be at the forefront of mitigating the effects of climate change. One of the most remarkable things about cities is their ability to metamorphose. Cities have adapted throughout history to climatic changes, shifting trade routes, changing technologies, wars, disease and political upheaval. The great pandemics of the nineteenth century, for instance, shaped modern cities because they forced developments in civil engineering, sanitation and urban planning. The pandemics of the twenty-first century will change cities in ways we cannot begin to imagine. By necessity they will adapt in an age of climate crisis.

What will that evolution look like? For as long as there have been cities, their size has been determined by the predominant mode of transport, external threats, the availability of resources and the price of adjacent agricultural land. For most of history, these factors restrained the growth of cities; only affluent and peaceful societies could spread their elbows. In this century, the threat to our security will not come from invading armies, but from an unstable climate.

Densely populated cities with public transport lines, walkable neighbourhoods and a range of shops and services produce much less
carbon dioxide and consume far fewer resources than sprawling settlements. Their compactness lessens, to an extent, the collision course
with nature because they avoid the sins of sprawl. I am not suggesting
we herd into city centres: clearly there is not enough room. What I
am talking about is the urbanisation of metropolitan neighbourhoods
– the suburbs and peripheral neighbourhoods – so that they take on
the forms and functions, the density, diverse uses and spatial messiness
associated with city centres.

During the lockdowns of 2020 urban density transformed from
benefit to threat. Sociability – one of the joys of city-living – became
something to be avoided at all costs as if one's fellow citizens were
deadly enemies. Rather than herd together, billions of people were
ordered to move apart; city life was inverted. But the vulnerability of
city populations to disease and the effects of lockdowns should not
blind us to the fact that densification is a vital way of achieving environmental sustainability. Economists and city planners rightly praise
the 'clustering effect' that has made modern metropolises so successful
in the knowledge economy. But it works in many different ways, not
just confined to tech start-ups. Compact urban areas spark all kinds
of innovations and creativity, including at the neighbourhood level
– the level not of high finance and technological wizardry, but of
everyday life. History shows that much. In other words, functional
and resourceful communities can help make cities more resilient
precisely at a time when we need resilient, adaptable cities ready to
face serious new challenges of climate change and pandemics. The
energy of Dharavi, Lagos's Otigba Computer Village and thousands
more informal communities demonstrates that urban ingenuity at
work every single day.

This kind of solution calls for an urbanisation of life on a truly
massive scale. Above all it requires widening our imaginations to
embrace the diversity of what cities can be. History is a vital way of
opening our eyes to the full range of the urban experience.

I

Dawn of the City

Uruk, 4000–1900 BC

Enkidu lives in harmony with nature. Strong as a 'rock from the sky' and possessing godlike beauty, his heart delights as he runs free with the wild animals. That is until he sees the naked figure of Shamat bathing at the waterhole. Entranced by his first sight of a woman, Enkidu makes love to Shamat for six days and seven nights.

Sated by their unbridled, rapturous sexual union, Enkidu attempts to return to the freedom of the wilderness. But his power over nature has faded. The beasts shun him; his strength is diminished; and he feels pangs of loneliness for the first time. Confused, he returns to Shamat. She tells her lover about her home, the fabled city of Uruk, a place of monumental buildings, shady palm groves and great throngs of humanity behind mighty walls. In the city men labour with their brains, not just their brawn. The people wear gorgeous clothing and every day there is a festival, when 'drums rap out the beat'. And there are the most beautiful women in the world, 'graced with charm and full of delights'. Shamat teaches Enkidu how to eat bread and drink ale. In the city, Shamat tells Enkidu, his godlike potential will be translated into real power. His hairy body shaved, his skin anointed with oils, and his nakedness concealed under costly garments, Enkidu sets off for Uruk. He has renounced the freedom and instincts of nature, drawn to the city by the lure of sex, food and luxury.

Cities from Uruk and Babylon to Rome, Teotihuacan and Byzantium, from Baghdad and Venice to Paris, New York and Shanghai, have bedazzled people as the idealised cities of the imagination made real, the pinnacles of human creativity. Enkidu represents mankind in a pristine state of nature, forced to choose between the freedom of the wild and the artificiality of the city. Shamat is the personification of sophisticated urban culture. Like her, such cities beguile and seduce; they promise the realisation of our powers and potential.[1]

The tale of Enkidu comes at the beginning of *The Epic of Gilgamesh*, humankind's oldest surviving work of literature, its written form dating back to at least 2100 BC. The epic was the product of the literate, highly urbanised Sumerian people, who lived in Mesopotamia, now known as Iraq. Someone approaching Uruk for the first time at its height in about 3000 BC, like the fictional Enkidu, would have had their senses assaulted. With a population of between 50,000 and 80,000 and occupying three square miles, Uruk was the most densely populated place on the planet. Like an anthill, the city sat atop a mound created by generations' worth of activity, layers of garbage and discarded building materials creating a man-made acropolis dominating the horizontal plains and visible for miles.

Long before reaching the city you would have become aware of its presence. Uruk had cultivated the surrounding area, harnessing the countryside to serve its needs. Hundreds of thousands of hectares of fields, artificially irrigated by ditches, produced the wheat, sheep and dates that fed the metropolis and the barley that provided beer for the masses.

Most stunning of all were the towering temples dedicated to the goddess of love and war, Eanna, and to Anu, god of the sky, constructed on gigantic platforms high above the city. Like the bell towers and domes of Florence or the forest of skyscrapers in twenty-first-century Shanghai, they were an unmistakable visual signature. Built with limestone and covered with gypsum plaster, Anu's great White Temple reflected the light of the sun as impressively as any modern skyscraper. A beacon in the plains, it radiated a message of civilisation and power.

For the ancient Mesopotamians, the city represented humankind's triumph over nature; the domineering artificial landscape made that strikingly clear. The city walls, studded with gates and projecting towers, were nine kilometres in circumference and seven metres tall. Enter through one of the gates and you would see immediately the way in which the city's inhabitants had won their own victory over nature. Surrounding the city proper were neat gardens producing fruit, herbs and vegetables. An extensive network of canals brought water from the Euphrates to the heart of the city. A subterranean system of clay pipes discharged the waste of tens of thousands of people outside the walls. The gardens and date palms gave way in due course to the inner city. The labyrinths of narrow, twisting streets and alleys crowded with small, windowless houses might have looked horrendously cramped and offered few open spaces, but this layout was designed to create an urban microclimate in which the shade and breeze offered by the narrowness of the streets and the density of the housing mitigated the intensity of the Mesopotamian sun.[2]

Noisy, cramped, busy, Uruk and its sister cities in Mesopotamia were unique on the face of the earth. In a work of literature from about the same time as *The Epic of Gilgamesh* the author imagines the goddess Inana ensuring that

> the warehouses would be provisioned; that dwellings would be founded in the city; that its people would eat splendid food; that its people would drink splendid beverages; that those bathed for holidays would rejoice in the courtyards; that the people would throng the places of celebration; that acquaintances would dine together; that foreigners would cruise together about like unusual birds in the sky ... that monkeys, mighty elephants, water buffalo, exotic animals, as well as thoroughbred dogs, lions, mountain ibexes, and *alum* sheep with long wool would jostle each other in the public squares.

The writer goes on to portray a city with huge granaries for wheat and silos of gold, silver, copper, tin and lapis lazuli. All the good things of the world flowed to the city for the enjoyment of the people in this highly idealised account. Meanwhile, 'inside the city *tigi* drums sounded; outside it, flutes and *zamzam* instruments. Its harbour where ships moored was full of joy.'[3]

'Uruk' means simply 'the city'. It was the world's first city and for over 1,000 years its most powerful urban centre. When people clustered into vast communities things changed with incredible velocity; the citizens of Uruk pioneered world-changing technologies and experienced radically new ways of living, dressing, eating and thinking. The invention of the city on the banks of the Euphrates and the Tigris unleashed a new, unstoppable force in history.

★

The end of the last Ice Age, approximately 11,700 years ago, profoundly altered human life on earth. Around the world, hunter-gatherer societies began to cultivate and domesticate wild crops that benefited from a warming planet. But it was in the Fertile Crescent – a semicircle that stretches from the Nile in the west through to the Persian Gulf in the east encompassing modern Egypt, Syria, Lebanon, Israel, Palestine, Jordan, Iraq, the south-east part of Turkey and the western edge of Iran – that provided the most favourable area for agriculture. This relatively small region contained a wide range of topographies, climates and altitudes, which in turn provided extraordinary biodiversity. Most importantly for human societal development, it contained the wild progenitors of much of modern agriculture – emmer wheat, einkorn wheat, barley, flax, chickpea, pea, lentil and bitter vetch – and large mammals suitable for domestication: cows, goats, sheep and pigs. Within a few millennia the cradle of agriculture became the cradle of urbanisation.

Archaeological work began in 1994 at Göbekli Tepe (Pot-Belly Hill) in Turkey under the direction of Klaus Schmidt. An extensive ceremonial complex, consisting of massive T-shaped stone pillars arranged in circles, was uncovered. This impressive site was not built by an advanced and settled agricultural community. The great twenty-ton stones were quarried and carried to the hill 12,000 years ago (construction of Stonehenge, in contrast, began 5,000 years ago). The discovery overturned conventional thinking. Here was evidence that hunter-gatherers congregated and cooperated on a truly massive scale. It is estimated that 500 people from different bands or tribes had to work together to quarry and carry the limestone megaliths to the hill. Their motivation was the worship of god or gods unknown to us and the fulfilment of sacred duty. There is no evidence that anyone ever lived at Göbekli Tepe: this was a place of pilgrimage and worship.

In the conventional interpretation, it was believed that such achievements came only after a surplus of grain freed up a portion of the community from the burden of daily subsistence and allowed them to do specialised, non-productive tasks. That is to say, after the invention of agriculture and villages. But Göbekli Tepe turns that thinking on its head. The earliest builders and worshippers on the hilltop were sustained by an amazing abundance of game and plants. That profusion of wild food, when it coexisted with a sophisticated system of religion, encouraged *Homo sapiens* to make radical changes to ways of life and tribal structures that had existed for over 150,000 years.

The temple came before the farm; it might even have made the farm necessary to feed a settled population devoted to worship. Genetic mapping shows the first ever domesticated einkorn wheat strains originated from a site twenty miles from Göbekli Tepe some 500 years after work began on the sanctuary. By that time, T-shaped pillars had been erected on hilltops in the wider area, and villages were established near them.

Göbekli Tepe lay preserved for modern archaeologists because it was deliberately buried for some unknown reason in about 8000 BC. No other such attempts at monument-building on this scale were attempted until the construction of the Sumerian temples in southern Mesopotamia 5,000 years later. In the intervening millennia the human population of the Fertile Crescent experimented with new ways of living.

The Neolithic revolution was fast. In around 9000 BC most people in the Fertile Crescent lived off wild foods; by 6000 BC agriculture had become established in the region. Hunter-gatherer tribes, with their varied diets and mobile lifestyles, gave way over the course of many generations to settled farming communities dedicated to cultivating a handful of staples and stock. Jericho began as a camp built by people who combined hunting with the cultivation of wild grains; within 700 years it was home to several hundred people who farmed emmer wheat, barley and pulses; they were defended by a stout wall and a tower. Çatalhöyük in modern-day Turkey, with a population in the seventh millennium BC of between 5,000 and 7,000, was a supersized community in prehistoric terms.

But neither Jericho nor Çatalhöyük made the jump to become cities. They remained overgrown villages, lacking many of the characteristics and purpose that we associate with urbanisation. Cities were not the product, it seems, of favoured locations, with lush and productive fields and access to building materials. Perhaps the living was *too* good. The land provided all that these communities needed, and trade made up any deficiencies.

Cities first appeared in southern Mesopotamia, on the edge of the Fertile Crescent. There was a long-standing theory explaining why. Here the soil and climate are not so favourable. Rainfall is low; the land is dry and flat. Only by harnessing the waters of the Euphrates and Tigris rivers could the potential of this wasteland be unlocked. People collaborated on irrigation projects to bring water from the rivers to create fields. Suddenly the land could produce huge surpluses of grain. Cities, therefore, weren't the product of temperate, bountiful environments, but of harsher zones that pushed ingenuity and co-operation to their limits. The world's first cities were therefore born in southern Mesopotamia out of the human triumph over adversity. At the centre stood the temple, and a priestly and bureaucratic elite that coordinated the transformation of the landscape and the management of a heavily concentrated population.

It is a compelling theory. But like so many of our notions of the early development of civilisation, it has also recently been revolutionised. The conditions that nurtured the roots of the city were altogether damper and more egalitarian.

The Sumerians, and the peoples who came to share their religion, believed that the first city emerged from the primordial swamp. Their stories talked of a watery world, where people moved about by boat; their tablets depicted frogs, waterfowl, fishes and reeds. Today their cities are buried under sand dunes in a bleak, inhospitable desert far from the sea and major rivers. Early archaeologists simply did not believe the myth of the swampy birth of these desert cities. But the fable of the amphibious origins of the city accords with recent discoveries about the changing ecology of southern Mesopotamia.

Climate change helped initiate urbanisation. In the fifth millennium BC the Persian Gulf rose about two metres above its current level, the result of the Holocene climatic optimum during which global temperatures shot upwards and sea levels rose. The head of the Gulf intruded 200 kilometres further north than it does at present, covering the arid regions of southern Iraq with great expanses of marsh. These deltaic wetlands where the Tigris and Euphrates entered the Gulf became a magnet for migrants as soon as they were transformed by this altered climate. They contained a rich variety of easily obtainable, nutritious foodstuffs. The salt waters teemed with fish and molluscs; the lush vegetation on the banks of the rivulets and streams in the delta provided cover for game. This was not a place of one ecosystem, but of several. The verdant alluvial floodplain supported the cultivation of grains, and the semi-desert the herding of livestock. This delta sustained peoples who came from the various cultures of the Fertile Crescent; these incomers brought with them knowledge from the north about such things as mud brick building, irrigation and ceramic production. Settlers built villages on sandy turtleback islands in the swamp, making the land stable by constructing foundations of reeds reinforced with bitumen.[4]

Many millennia before, at Göbekli Tepe, foraging communities had taken advantage of their hunting paradise to construct something bigger than themselves. Something similar happened before 5400 BC on a sandbank beside a lagoon where the desert met the Mesopotamian marshes. Perhaps at first people saw this place as sacred because the lagoon was a life-giving force. The earliest signs of human life here, in the sandy island that would be called Eridu, were the bones of fish and wild animals as well as mussel shells, suggesting this holy spot was a place of ritual feasting. In time, a small shrine was built to worship the god of fresh water.

Over the generations, this primitive shrine was rebuilt, getting bigger and more sophisticated each time; eventually the temple rose above the landscape on a brick platform. The mixed bounty of wild and cultivated foods provided by the delta supported these ever more ambitious building projects. Eridu became venerated as the exact location where the world was created.

In the Sumerian belief system, the world was a chaos of water until the god Enki built a reed frame and filled it with mud. The gods could now take up their abode on the dry land created from reed and mud – in the same manner as the original marsh-dwellers had built their villages. Enki chose to found his temple at Eridu, where water became land. In order 'to settle the gods in the dwelling of their hearts' delight' – in other words, their temples – Enki created mankind to serve them.

The marshes, sitting between the sea and the desert, represented the intersection of order and chaos, life and death. The amazing resources of the delta, an oasis amid hostile environments, fostered the belief that this was the most sacred place in the unfurling of divine creation. Yet for all the abundance it offered, this was a risky place to live. When the spring sun melted large volumes of snow in the faraway Armenian, Taurus and Zagros mountain ranges, rivers in the delta became unpredictable and dangerous. Villages of reed houses, and entire fields, could be swept away by violently shifting watercourses.

At other times rapidly encroaching dunes buried the landscape in sand. The temple, standing firm on its terrace safe from the flood, must have been a potent symbol of permanence amid the capricious swirl of nature. Not only was Eridu the location where the world became manifest, but the temple came to be seen as the actual dwelling place of Enki. Brickwork needs constant maintenance, and so the people who worshipped at Eridu were yoked into helping Enki keep chaos at bay.[5]

These divine workers needed to be provisioned and housed in their turn, and some kind of priestly authority was required to distribute the rations. Workshops grew up round the temple to create the decorations suitable for the god's house. Eridu never became a city. Sumerian myth explained why. Rather than share the gifts of civilisation and urbanisation, Enki selfishly kept them locked up in his temple. That was until Inanna, holy thief and goddess of love, sex, fertility and war, went by boat to Eridu and got Enki drunk. While Enki slept off his beer-drinking binge, Inanna stole the sacred knowledge and took it back across the brackish water to her own marshland island, Uruk. Back home, she unleashed the divine wisdom.

The tale mythologises what actually happened. Eridu inspired imitators; similar sacred sites appeared on island mounds in the swamp. At one man-made heap on the banks of the Euphrates a temple was built for Inanna. It was known as Eanna, the 'House of Heaven'. Hard by stood another temple on a mound called Kullaba, the household of Anu, god of the sky. The peoples of the marsh began worshipping and settling at this site in about 5000 BC.

Over the next few centuries these two temple districts of Eanna and Kullaba were built and rebuilt, each time with vaster ambitions and ever more architectural daring. The two mounds some 800 metres apart fused together to create one large settled area, known as Uruk. While Eridu's temple had been rebuilt successively along the same lines, the people of Uruk replaced it with something altogether bigger and more magnificent. This was a culture characterised by demolition and dynamism.

The driving force was a collective endeavour to create works of magnificence. The delta provided a natural surplus of food, liberating many bodies for the hard graft of construction, and brains to plan the public works. This watery environment also allowed for easy transport by boat. The wetlands provided the fuel for urbanisation; but propelling it forward was a powerful ideology. How else to explain the massive investment of physical labour and time? There was nothing utilitarian about the temple complexes of Eanna and Kullaba. The early temples resembled that at Eridu. But the builders of Uruk made spectacular leaps in architecture, developing entirely new techniques. They used rammed earth, waterproofed with bitumen, to make their platforms. They made foundations and walls with blocks of limestone (quarried over fifty miles from the city) and cast concrete. The adobe of the outer walls and columns was decorated with mosaics of geometric patterns made from millions of painted terracotta cones.

When work on a new temple commenced, the old one would be filled in with rubble. This would then form the core of the terrace upon which the next version would be built. These giant acropolises, true to the collective nature of their construction, were designed to be accessible, not remote from the populace. Huge processional staircases and ramps connected them to ground level; the main buildings were lined with rows of columns, opening their interiors to the world; they were surrounded by courtyards, walkways, terraces, workshops and irrigated gardens. These great edifices became the nucleus around which the city grew to an area of 400 hectares of packed narrow streets housing tens of thousands of citizens.[6]

But then in the second half of the fourth millennium BC southern Mesopotamia experienced another episode of rapid climate change. A quick increase in annual temperatures coupled with decreasing rainfall meant that the water levels of the two great rivers reduced. The shoreline of the Persian Gulf receded from its mid-Holocene peak. The marshes and rivulets that had given life to Uruk began to silt up and dry out.

The transformation of this landscape 5,000 years ago obscured for a long time the swampy origins of urbanisation. But looked at in a global context, and in light of some very recent discoveries, the Mesopotamian experience is far from unique. Where cities emerged in isolation, it was in the optimal conditions of the wetlands. The first urban centre in the Americas, San Lorenzo in modern-day Mexico, lay on raised ground overlooking a network of rivers that twisted through deltaic marshland to feed the Gulf of Mexico. Like the early builders of Eridu and Uruk, the Olmec people of San Lorenzo in the second millennium BC were fishermen and foragers, beneficiaries of their hot and humid aquatic environment; and like Eridu it was a cultic site, famous for its colossal stone heads of deities. The first cities that emerged in China during the Shang dynasty contemporaneously with the Olmecs (1700–1050 BC) did so in the marshy alluvial plain of the lower Yellow River. And in ancient Egypt, the great capital Memphis was founded at the point where the delta met the Nile. The story follows a similar trajectory in sub-Saharan Africa as well, where the earliest urbanisation occurred at Djenné-Djenno from around 250 BC in the swamplands of the inner Niger Delta in what is now Mali.[7]

The first cities did not emerge fully formed from the swamp, of course; nor did they occur without considerable interaction with other societies elsewhere. Rather, these enticing wetland niches sucked in people from different cultures; they brought with them building techniques, beliefs, tools, agriculture, crafts, trade and ideas. The changing climate made southern Mesopotamia the most densely populated place on earth.

In these wet and unpredictable environments, permanent cities were highly attractive propositions. They provided evidence of humankind's triumph over nature. Eridu was created by a collision of belief and topography. The superabundant, nutritious, self-replenishing resources of the wetlands not only caused cities to come into being in the first place but provided them with the energy to become larger and more complex than any other settlements.[8]

When the environment radically changed in southern Mesopotamia, the lifestyles associated with the wetlands disappeared. However, by this time the urban civilisation was, after a millennium of development, mature. The retreat of the marshes left Uruk high and dry. But the history of urbanisation is in large part the adaptation of humans to their changing environment, and the adaptation of the environment by humans to serve their needs.

Deprived of their former way of subsistence, wetland farmers sought refuge in the city, resulting in an urbanised population in lower Mesopotamia of 90%. This large collection of people, with a long tradition of architecture and engineering, was able to overcome the challenge of climate change and exploit the new potential of the alluvial plains by constructing large-scale irrigation systems capable of feeding substantial populations. Agriculture came before the city, to be sure; but an agricultural revolution of this intensity was the product of the urban revolution.

*

A city is never merely a collection of buildings: it is not so much its physicality that differentiates it from other settlements as the human activities it incubates. In the city, people can take up professions impossible in the village or the farm. Uruk was known as 'the smithy of the gods', a place famous for its highly skilled goldsmiths, copper smelters, metallurgists and jewellers. A significant proportion of the population were skilled craftsmen working in diverse materials, including stone, metals and gemstones. The luxury raw materials needed by the big city were unavailable in the vicinity. Climate change, however, had done more than provide bounteous harvests. The channels of rivulets that had once snaked through the brackish marsh were converted into a network of urban canals that connected the city to that mighty conduit of trade, the Euphrates.[9]

The islands now known as Bahrain provided mother of pearl and rare seashells. Gold, silver, lead and copper came from eastern Anatolia, Iran and Arabia. Urukian craftsmen hungered after obsidian, quartz, serpentine, soapstone, amethyst, jasper, gypsum alabaster, marble and other attractive materials. From the mountains of Afghanistan and northern Pakistan, over 1,500 miles away, came the highly desirable deep blue lapis lazuli; carnelian and agate came from further away, in India. The houses of the gods demanded such lavish materials to embellish them. But mere mortals could also enjoy sumptuously decorated jewellery, weapons, drinking cups and vessels. They could also savour wine and oil, which arrived by the boatload.[10]

Ancient Uruk was carved into ad hoc districts, each characterised by a particular specialist occupation. Individuals and families worked in their courtyard homes or in workshops. The density of the housing and the city's layout, with its cool, shaded streets, encouraged sociability and mingling – and with it an exchange of ideas, experimentation, collaboration and intense competition. Uruk's fierce dynamism and fast growth owed much to its role as the generator of trade.

The Epic of Gilgamesh poses questions about the city that seem surprisingly modern. How and why did people choose to make

Enkidu's bargain, and settle in cities in the first place? And what price did they pay for exchanging primitive liberty for the comforts of the city? The invention of the city is comparatively recent and our experience of it represents a minuscule portion of our time on earth. Why exchange a free-ranging lifestyle for stasis in a congested built environment? How can a species that evolved over countless millennia for one environment adapt to another that is almost entirely different? And at what psychological cost?

The authors of *The Epic of Gilgamesh* asked themselves variants of these questions. Like many others throughout history, the half-mortal, half-divine king of Uruk Gilgamesh finds city life burdensome. He lords it over the people of the city with the energies of a wild bull. The wild man Enkidu was created by the gods as a companion to help tame Gilgamesh. In a way Enkidu and Gilgamesh form a duality – our rural, natural instinct at war with our civilised, urban self. Complementing each other's strengths and energy, the urbane Gilgamesh and the savage Enkidu become firm friends. Enkidu encourages Gilgamesh to find an outlet for his passions by venturing hundreds of miles to the cedar forest on Mount Lebanon – the secret and forbidden seat of the gods – there to do battle with its monstrous giant guardian, Humbaba. A man can only truly be a man, we are told, when he pits himself against nature, far from the numbing luxuries of the city. The conquest of the forest will bring Gilgamesh the everlasting fame and honour that he craves.

It will also yield something else. Cities in southern Mesopotamia like Uruk lacked building materials, and the cedar of Mount Lebanon was a prized commodity for architects and builders. The roof of just one of Uruk's numerous temples, for instance, required between 3,000 and 6,000 metres of timber. Gilgamesh and Enkidu set out to wage war on nature on behalf of the city. The newly civilised Enkidu vows to fell the most magnificent cedar and raft it hundreds of miles down the Euphrates. Back in the urban world, he will fashion it into a mighty temple door.

The heroes succeed in defeating and slaying the giant, and in felling a marvellous crop of cedars for the city. Puffed up with pride, however, the heroic pair further offend the gods. Gilgamesh spurns the sexual advances of a goddess, who retaliates by sending the Bull of Heaven to destroy Uruk and kill Gilgamesh. But Gilgamesh and Enkidu slay the beast. That final act of hubris really enrages the gods; they strike Enkidu down with illness.

As he lies dying, Enkidu curses Shamat, the harlot who seduced him away from his free and happy life in nature. He curses the door he made from the sacred cedar tree. The decision he made to trade the natural life for the civilised one has sapped his strength and made him weak.[11]

Cities have been deadly killers. A city like Uruk, with tons of human and animal waste being discharged into open, stagnant water, might appear to be purpose-built specifically for the benefit of microbes. In industrial Manchester and Chicago in the nineteenth century, 60% of infants died before their fifth birthday and life expectancy was twenty-six, compared to figures of 32% and forty in the countryside. Throughout most of history, cities have been places to escape from. In the twentieth century in the United States and Europe there was headlong flight from the crime-ridden, cramped city to the promised land of leafy suburbia. In the 1990s, after decades of urban crisis, 60% of New Yorkers and 70% of Londoners reported that they would rather live elsewhere. Recent investigations using MRI scans to understand the neural processes associated with urban life showed that those brought up amid the social stresses of the frenetic city environment have reduced grey matter in the right dorsolateral prefrontal cortex and in the perigenual anterior cingulate cortex. These are key regions of the brain that regulate our ability to process emotions and stress. The city rewires our brain: urbanites therefore are much more likely to suffer from mood and anxiety disorders than those in the countryside. Crime, disease, death, depression, physical decay, poverty and overcrowding have oftentimes made the city a place to suffer and survive as you can.[12]

Until medicine and sanitation improved in the twentieth century, cities needed a constant stream of incomers to sustain the population and make up for those (mainly babies, infants and children) lost to diseases. Like so many others, Enkidu discovers the high price to be paid for entering the city. His death breaks the heart of his beloved comrade, Gilgamesh. The distraught hero now sees the city as representing not the pinnacle of human achievement, but death. He renounces Uruk and seeks solace in nature, roaming the wilderness dressed in the skins of wild animals in imitation of his dead friend.

Gilgamesh believes he can cheat death by seeking oneness with nature. His quest for eternal life takes him to the edge of the world, in search of Utnapishtim. Back in the mists of time, the god Enlil had become annoyed by the noise and din of humans in their cities; seeking peace and quiet, he sent a great flood to wipe them out. The plan was thwarted by another god, Enki, who ordered Utnapishtim to build a great ark and fill it with his family along with seeds and pairs of animals. When the flood abated, the survivors were allowed to repopulate the planet because the gods discovered that without people to serve them they went hungry. In return for preserving life, Utnapishtim and his wife were granted immortality; Gilgamesh wants to learn their secret. After many adventures, Gilgamesh arrives at Utnapishtim's dwelling. There the hero is eventually taught the painful lesson that death is an unavoidable condition of life.

The epic began with a hymn of praise to Uruk. By its end, Gilgamesh has come full circle. After the rigours of his quest and his rejection of civilisation he returns to his city and finally arrives at true understanding. Individuals may be fated to die, but the collective powers of humankind live on through the buildings they construct and the knowledge they engrave on tablets of clay. Gilgamesh builds great walls for Uruk and uses the written word (itself invented in Uruk) to tell posterity his story. Both the walls and the epic are eternal monuments that guarantee him the immortality he so desperately sought in the wilderness.

Even though he travelled to the ends of the earth, Uruk's magnetic power pulls him back: the city has become the controlling force of human destiny. As the epic closes Gilgamesh proudly invites the ferryman who has carried him back home from the end of the world to 'walk the walls of Uruk ... what human could ever equal them? Go up, go on; walk around – look at the foundations. Are they not magnificent? Didn't the Seven Sages themselves lay it all out?'[13]

Gilgamesh comes back from the edge of the world to remind the citizens of Uruk that their city was a gift from the gods and the finest thing created in the world: his quest ultimately serves to renew faith in urban life.

Sumerian deities did not reside in springs or woodland glades or in the clouds, but in the heart of real, physical cities like Uruk. The Sumerians were the people chosen to live with the gods in their hyper-advanced cities while the rest of humanity plodded on as fur-clad nomads or subsistence farmers. For all the strains of city-living, urbanites enjoyed the bounty of the gods – the written word, for example, as well as a host of privileges such as beer, exotic foods, technologies, luxury goods and sumptuous artworks.

For the Sumerians, the city and humanity were created at the same time, at the moment the world was born. There was no Garden of Eden; the city was paradise, not punishment, a bastion against the unpredictability of nature and the savagery of other humans. That belief in the divine origin of cities gave their urban civilisation a truly remarkable durability.[14]

In all of the locations where urbanisation first emerged, cities were planned as a way of aligning human activities with the underlying order and energies of the universe. Early Chinese cities, ordered as a square divided into nine smaller squares with a street plan orientated to the points of the compass, mirrored the geometry of heaven. In cities as in heaven, divine energy (*qi*) radiated from the centre to the periphery. This pattern endured in China from the second or first millennium BC to AD 1949, when the People's Republic was declared. Mayan cities aligned their street plans with the equinox, harnessing the sacred powers of the universe by replicating the pattern of the stars. These were not merely sacred sites: as with Mesopotamian metropolises, they were the place where mortals connected directly with the gods. That impulse to construct an ordered simulacrum of the heavens – an organised structure that tamed the primeval forces of chaos – partly accounts for why peoples, in different parts of the world, independently began to build settlements.

Cities are big, impersonal and alienating. They rely on cooperation between thousands (and later millions) of unknown individuals; their density and scale push our ability to tolerate strangers to the limit. They are vulnerable to famine, disease and war. They needed brutal forms of compulsion to build walls and temples, dig and maintain irrigation systems. They should not work.

But they do, emphatically so. The history of Uruk and the reasons for the birth of the first cities point a way to the answer as to why this is so. The Mesopotamian urban civilisation that Uruk kick-started lasted for close to 4,000 years, surviving wars, environmental disasters and economic collapses; it witnessed the rises and falls of numerous empires and kingdoms, long outliving these mighty creations. Such a civilisation depended less upon the resilience of its buildings than the robustness of its ideology. Living in a city is hard work and profoundly unnatural. The legend of Gilgamesh was one of the stories urbanites told themselves through the generations to remind themselves of the power and potency of their cities. City-living – a lifestyle denied to most of humanity – was a divine privilege, not a curse.

★

A city with so many needs and so few resources needed to pay its way. Throughout the so-called 'Uruk Period' during the span of the fourth millennium BC, artefacts from Uruk became commonplace throughout Mesopotamia, Anatolia, Iran, Syria and as far as Pakistan. The city traded costly luxury items produced by its skilled master craftsmen. But it also exported utilitarian items. Because of its large population and adoption of new technologies, Uruk was able to do this on a hitherto impossible scale using the first techniques of mass production.

A number of trenches and pits found in Uruk indicate a large-scale copper foundry that would have employed about forty people. Many of the city's female citizens wove wool into quality textiles using horizontal ground looms, a method that allowed them to maintain a high level of output. Uruk's community of potters deployed two crucial innovations: the Mesopotamian beehive kiln and the fast potters' wheel. The kiln provided much higher firing temperatures, while protecting pots from the flames. In earlier times, potters used a turntable, a stone disk fitted into a low pivot that was moved by hand. In the Uruk period, a flywheel was set in motion by a stick or by foot; the flywheel was connected by an axle to an upper working wheel, upon which the clay was thrown. This technology allowed Urukians to make pots faster and to a much higher grade. They produced fine-textured, lightweight dinnerware for the luxury market. But they were also able to pump out large amounts of coarser wares, such as standardised pots and the large storage jars that made bulk exports possible.

This rapid series of inventions and refinements was possible when humans clustered in a dense, competitive environment. Innovation begat innovation. The high temperature of the potters' kiln was used for experiments in metallurgy and chemical processes. Mesopotamian boatmen were the first to use a sail. It is a memorable and counter-intuitive fact that the invention of the city came long before the invention of the wheel. In fact, the city in all probability created the need and provided both the technology and collective brainpower to make the wheel/axle combination possible. Uruk had trained carpenters with the finesse and the latest cast-copper tools to fine-chisel perfectly round holes and axles. Urukians also had the need to make large quantities of pots in order to exchange for precious materials and convey their exports.

Information was being shared across huge distances: wheels from load-bearing carts have been found in Ukraine, Poland, the Caucasus and Slovenia as well as the urban heartland of south-west Asia. It is no surprise that the fourth millennium BC saw an upsurge in techno-logical development and the diffusion of ideas across landmasses. The far-flung networks of trade that radiated out across the wider region were vectors of ideas. Merchants from Uruk travelled along these routes, setting up trading stations in the areas in which they procured their materials and sold their wares. With them came not only the allure of wealth, but radical ideas about how to live.

The breakthrough at Uruk stimulated many imitators who leapt on the bandwagon of urbanisation. To the north-west of Uruk there were already towns of varying population densities: Jericho, Çatalhöyük and Tell Brak are the best examples of sizeable settlements. But Uruk was of an entirely different order. At numerous sites in modern Iraq, Iran, Turkey and Syria archaeologists find temples and public buildings built on the Urukian model and with the materials pioneered in Uruk. In the fertile plains in southern Mesopotamia dozens of new cities were started from scratch, some of which would, in time, rival and exceed Uruk – cities such as Ur, Kish, Nippur, Umma Lagash and Shuruppak. If Uruk was an experiment in how humans might live and thrive together, it proved highly attractive. People adopted Uruk's religious ideology, its dietary habits and social structures. Like a mighty seed head, Uruk broadcast its culture over a huge distance. It was the mother city, the world's original metropolis.[15]

This is not now a tale of one city, but of a network of intercon-nected cities, sharing a common culture and a system of trade.

A constellation of urbanised settlements multiplied the opportunities for interaction and the cross-fertilisation of ideas and technologies. And with this increasing complexity of human activity came developments every bit as significant as the wheel.

The evidence for Uruk's cultural influence comes in two main forms. The so-called bevel-rim bowl's crudeness indicates the speed with which it was mass-produced, not to say its disposability. Tossed aside after use, it is the prehistoric version of a cardboard coffee cup. Made in Uruk, the bevel-rim bowl is found in innumerable quantities at sites across south-west Asia.

The bowls were of a standard size and shape. Their use is hotly debated. It seems certain that their original function was religious. Filled with foodstuffs or beer, they were used as receptacles for daily offerings to the temple. In turn, the temple staff used them as units of measurement to distribute food for work carried out and services rendered. The temples stood at the centre of a complicated and heavily ritualised network of food distribution in which members of the community were compensated according to their contribution. The unprepossessing bevel-rimmed bowl had another function. The measure of one standardised bowl was called a *sila*. The *sila* became the universal measurement of value, a kind of barley-backed currency that established the price of, say, a day's labour, a sheep or a jar of oil. The *sila* system was pioneered in Uruk and spread across the region as a way of facilitating trade. Here is an example of another invention emerging from the creative ferment of the city: money.

But carting vast quantities of grain around as a form of payment is not efficient. This brings us to the second of the Urukian artefacts found in profusion in the sites of ancient cities: the cylinder seal.

Made from a variety of materials – limestone, marble, lapis lazuli, carnelian and agate among others – these inch-high cylinders were engraved with tiny and intricate motifs such as gods, scenes of daily life, boats, temples, and real and fantastical animals. When rolled onto wet clay they left a flat impression of the image. The resulting clay tablets were marks of identification and conveyers of information. In this new world of long-distance trade, such tablets served as brand logos for exports, receipts for purchases and seals that protected cargos and silos against tampering.

The seal impressions are also found on little clay envelopes called *bullae*. These containers stored clay tokens, which were shaped to represent a commodity – a bolt of cloth, for example, or a jar of oil or grain. *Bullae* were agreements specifying commodities to be delivered or labour performed in the future, the deals struck in wet clay by the seal impressions of the contracting parties. In Uruk, the storehouses of these 'contracts' and IOUs were the temples, bastions of financial trust every bit as powerful as the Bank of England in a later time. Faith in the gods and faith in the financial system went hand in hand. Indeed, people must have been attracted to live in the city to be physically near the place where financial transactions were made and stored. When the transaction was complete the *bullae* were cracked open and the accounting tokens removed to ensure the contract had been fulfilled, terminating the agreement.

If the bevel-rim bowls are the beginnings of money in human society, the *bullae* mark the origins of finance. But urban life became so complicated that tokens and seals were not enough to keep track of things. The seals and *bullae* began to encode more and more information. First came a way of ascertaining quantities of time and goods. The *bullae* and clay tablets began to record amounts in an abstract numerical code, the first number system in history. But numbers on their own were useless. Every commodity – grain, for example, or beer, textiles and metals – that was stored or traded had a pictogram and numerical value that indicated quantity, labour expended, rations paid, distances traded. In their early form, these symbols were simple pictures of the commodity in question – an ear of corn, a sheep, a jar, or a wavy line indicating a liquid – drawn onto the wet clay with a sharpened stylus and accompanied with a number.

But clay is not a good medium for producing accurate pictures and some 'things' cannot be simply drawn; over time the pictograms morphed into signs very different from the object they were supposed to represent. Using the Urukian triangular stylus, wedge-shaped marks were impressed into the clay, based on sounds used in spoken language. With this leap forward, the writer could convey much more information than he could with pictograms. These wedge-shaped marks – known as cuneiform – were the first steps towards writing.

Uruk was not just a storehouse of humanity: it became a data-processing centre. No society in history so far had had to manage such immense quantities of information. The marks in the clay were invented by accountants in Uruk to compensate for the deficiencies of human memory, which could not begin to hold such quantities of data. A millennium and a half later, the author of *The Epic of Gilgamesh* extolled the walls and monumental buildings of Uruk. Immediately after the hymn of praise to the physical city that opens the story comes this passage: 'Look for the copper tablet box, undo its bronze lock, open the door to its secret, lift out the lapis-lazuli tablet and read it, the story of that man Gilgamesh, who went through all kinds of suffering.'

Here, then, are Uruk's two gifts to the world: urbanisation and the written word. The first achievement led to the second. This was not a society afraid of radical innovation or assaults on established ways of thinking. Writing and mathematics emerged from the urban cauldron as an administrative technique of managing complexity. One of the earliest discovered tablets is a receipt written in clay. It reads: '29,086 measures barley. 37 months. Kushim.'[16]

It states the amount of the commodity, the length of time over which it was delivered or expected, and the accountant's sign-off. All very routine. But remember the name: Kushim is the very first person in history whose name we know. Kushim was not a king or a priest, warrior or poet. Nothing so exalted: our earliest known individual was a diligent Urukian bean counter who spent his life in the city totting up accounts and writing receipts.

Kushim and his ilk were the foot soldiers in a radical assault on the old ways of doing things. Much like the architects, metallurgists, brewers, weavers and potters in the expanding city, Kushim and his fellow accountants were on a quest to refine their practices. In Kushim's case, it meant experimenting with the earliest forms of written language and mathematics. He may have been able to keep meticulous records detailing the ownership and movement of goods; he could have drawn up legal contracts and made payments, forecast crop yields, calculated interest and managed debts; but Kushim could not inscribe his innermost thoughts. It took generations of Kushims, each adding to the store of knowledge and adapting their notation bit by bit, before the accountant's partial script evolved into a full text capable of conveying the emotional depth and poetic inventiveness of *Gilgamesh*.

In the hurly-burly of the expanding city, men such as Kushim were something entirely new in human affairs: professional administrators and bureaucrats. They managed the upsurge in trade, making and enforcing contracts, ensuring payment and fairness. Their seals are to be found far and wide along the trade routes. But they had a deeper impact on their society. Written records marked the transition away from a face-to-face society based on oral communication and memory to a more anonymous one, built on records and archives.

Generations of administrators like Kushim contributed to a well-run administrative system. Uruk in the fourth millennium BC was a hotbed of technological invention. There were the technologies of production and locomotion, of course, such as the loom and the wheel. But perhaps most significant were the technologies of control. Writing, mathematics and finance were closely guarded techniques, the preserve of an administrative and priestly elite. Those who possessed them had power.

And this power morphed as society became more sophisticated over the centuries. A professional bureaucrat such as Kushim possessed highly specialised skills, amassed over a lifetime of training. The same might be said for a goldsmith, an architect, an artist or a master potter and many more as the city grew and trade flourished. In a city rooted in the ritual distribution of food, it became apparent that some were more deserving than others. Uruk became a stratified society, graded according to wealth, skill and civic power.

This, then, is the darker side of urbanisation in human history. What perhaps began as a consensual, communal undertaking evolved into a highly centralised, highly unequal society. There was probably no sudden change or power grab: each generation built on the work of the last, and strides in efficiency were paid for with small sacrifices of freedom and equality. Rewarding labour with grants of food from the benevolent temple became, in time, a way of compelling hard work through the control of rations. Written records established ownership, created debt and enforced obligations. If you worked with your brawn not your brain you found yourself poorer and lower in status than the specialists and administrators.

Cities of Uruk's scale have always needed more bodies to do the dirty work than nature on its own can supply through procreation. An accountant's slab gives us three more names to add to Kushim's:

Gal Sal, En-pap X and Sukkalgir. And like Kushim, they tell us how fast human society was changing in the urban cauldron. En-pap X and Sukkalgir were slaves belonging to Gal Sal. Forced labour became a major commodity as the city demanded ever more muscle power to construct its temples, dig its irrigation canals, plough its fields and simply keep the complex urban machinery running. At the end of the fourth millennium BC the pictures on Urukian seals start to show a menacing aspect of city life: cowering prisoners, their hands bound, closely supervised by armed guards.

These miserable slaves were evidence of another by-product of the city: organised war. Uruk's walls were built in the early part of the third millennium BC. They were a sign of the new reality: by then Uruk's moment of unrivalled power had passed. Its system of trade and temple-based bureaucracy became impossible to sustain in a harsher world. Uruk's seeds had germinated, and the city was reaping a bitter harvest; newly minted rivals were flourishing in the Mesopotamian plain. Their birth marked a new era, one of competing military technologies, armies and warlords.

In the ruins of the Uruk temples archaeologists find maces, slingshots and arrow heads. The magnificent Eanna temple itself was destroyed, either in war or by a rebellious populace. Mesopotamia in the third millennium BC was marked by shifting leagues and alliances between a dozen or so highly organised city states. Peace broke down frequently as they battled over disputed land and water. War fuelled the growth of the city: more and more people flocked to its protective embrace. Big defensive walls were a feature of this age of city violence and non-urban nomadic raiders who attacked from the mountains and steppe. So too was kingship.

In ancient Sumerian 'lu' means man and 'gal' means big. The Lugal, or Big Man, emerged as the leader of a band of semi-professional warriors dedicated to protecting the city and its fields from predators, avenging wrongs committed by a rival city, and securing booty from raids. Power migrated from the temple to the palace, from priests and bureaucrats to warlords. Over time 'Lugal' came to mean hereditary king.[17]

Remarkable fragments of sculpture now in the Louvre reveal the goriness of the third millennium BC. The Stele of Vultures commemorates a battle fought between the cities of Umma and Lagash over a disputed tract of agricultural land that lay between their rival spheres of influence. The Stele is a slab of limestone two metres high; it has a round top and relief carvings on its sides. The carvings depict the king of Lagash riding a chariot, spear in hand, leading a phalanx of armed men into battle. The soldiers march over the prone bodies of their defeated enemies; vultures circle, the heads of the city's enemies in their beaks. Here we have the achievements of the city in the third millennium BC: the wheel deployed as a technology of war; armies and organised combat; writing and art used in the service of state propaganda.

*

Long before there were countries or empires or kings there were cities. The basic building block of political organisation, the city gave birth to the religion and bureaucracy that organised people into a corporate entity, and to the kings and armies needed to defend it and project its power. Love of city, pride in its achievements and fear of outsiders fostered the collective sense of identity that would in time expand across territories and empires. Over the passage of several centuries, writing evolved from a sign system recording transactions to a written language. The first works of literature come from third-millennium-BC Mesopotamia, epics that glorify kings, cities and their gods. *The Epic of Gilgamesh* repeatedly calls the hero's home city 'Uruk the sheepfold', a refuge of safety and a place of belonging in a hostile world, united under the ever-watchful eye of the shepherd. If the human tribal instinct still hankered after the protection and solidarity of the small kinship band, the city – threatened by war, but also shaped by it – replicated some of the features of the tribe. The city presented itself as the home and the family writ large, a place of protection and a new kind of kinship group. *Gilgamesh* is intended as a celebration of a city, the home of strong kings and powerful gods, and of a cohesive citizenry. Cities, like the countries that would emerge from them, needed these myths to bind their people into a super-tribe.

In the endless jockeying for pre-eminence, ultimate power did not last long; cities rebelled against their submission and another city state rose to claim the mantle. In 2296 BC Lugalzagesi, king of Umma, conquered Kish, Ur and Uruk as well as many of the other city states.

Given its sacredness and ancient pedigree, Lugalzagesi chose Uruk as his capital, restoring it once again to its lost metropolitan status. From there he ruled most of Mesopotamia as a single kingdom. But then Lugalzagesi faced a challenge from a brand-new city called Akkad and its charismatic, self-made ruler, Sargon. The challenger besieged Uruk, destroyed its walls and imprisoned Lugalzagesi. Sargon then went on to defeat Ur, Lagash and Umma.

Sargon's Akkadian Empire – the first in history – was born from the mature and ancient Sumerian urban civilisation; it was an extension of the power that had been incubated for almost two millennia behind the city wall. Centred on the dazzling city of Akkad – the first purpose-built capital – the empire's network of cities stretched from the Gulf to the Mediterranean. Akkad is portrayed like so many imperial metropolises throughout the ages: a city of monumental architecture, cosmopolitanism and incredible wealth. Throughout ancient Mesopotamian history Akkad was invoked in mythology as a kind of fabulous Camelot and the name of Sargon as the archetype of a mighty and just ruler. The Akkadian Empire prospered for almost two centuries under Sargon and his heirs.

Why this great empire crashed is much debated. It seems that another period of global climate change known as the 4.2 kiloyear event was at least partially responsible. Reduced rainfall in the mountains lessened the flows of the Euphrates and Tigris, spelling disaster for irrigated agriculture, the basis of city life. Tribal warriors known as the Gutians streamed down from the Zagros Mountains like ravenous wolves scenting weak but fattened prey.

'Who was king? Who was not king?' the records ask forlornly. The Gutians ushered in a period of chaos; trade petered out; the urban machinery came crashing down. 'For the first time since cities were built and founded, the vast fields did not produce grain, the inundation ponds produced no fish, the irrigated orchards yielded neither syrup nor wine.' Occupied and destroyed, all trace of mighty Akkad was wiped off the face of the earth.[18]

Cities are marvellously tenacious creations. The collapse of the Akkadian Empire was a disaster for some, but a glorious opportunity for others. The Gutians did not rule Mesopotamia as such. Rather they ravaged the countryside for decades. The remaining embers of civilisation were sustained behind the walls of a few cities which, though reduced, retained a semblance of independence. Eventually Ur emerged as the head of a regional kingdom. Wealthy thanks to its command of long-distance trade across the seas to India and elsewhere, Ur expressed its power with its vast ziggurat, a towering tiered temple that became the hallmark of Sumerian civilisation.

But just as Ur reached the heights of power and magnificence, it suffered the fate of Akkad. The people responsible this time were the Amorites. Nomadic tribal people from modern-day Syria, they began to migrate in large numbers in the last century of the third millennium BC as a result of the prolonged drought brought about by the changing climate. The encroachment of these people, 'a ravaging people, with the instinct of a beast' in Sumerian eyes 'who know no house nor town … who eat raw meat', began to nibble away at Ur's empire. Distracted by the incomers, Ur was powerless against another predatory people, the Elamites from modern-day Iran.[19]

The walls of the richest and largest city on earth were breached by the barbarians in 1940 BC. The temples were plundered and destroyed; the residential districts burnt to the ground. Survivors were herded into captivity or left to starve in the lunar landscape of the pummelled city. 'On the boulevards where festivities had been held, heads lay scattered. In all the streets where people had once promenaded, corpses were piled. In the places where the festivities of the Land had once taken place, people were stacked in heaps.' Even dogs abandoned the ruins.[20]

The reality of the rise, fall, annihilation and recovery of cities was deeply woven into the Mesopotamian psyche. For one thing, mud brick degrades very quickly, meaning that even great monumental structures did not last long. Then there was ecology. Very often the Euphrates or Tigris would abruptly change course, leaving a city abandoned. Years – or even centuries later – the river would return, the city would be resettled, and its carcass reanimated.[21]

In the year 1940 BC, Uruk and Ur were, after 2,000 years, ancient cities by any standard (as old as or older than London and Paris today). Against the torrid currents of history, the storms and strife of war, the rise and fall of mighty empires, barbarian invasions, mass migrations and climate changes, these cities had stood firm. And they still had life in them. Rather than being overrun and destroyed by nomadic tribesmen, they absorbed and civilised the 'barbarians'. The Amorites settled in the ancient cities and adopted the urbane lifestyles, religion, myths and learning of the people they had conquered. The supposedly savage victors rebuilt Ur with nine new temples and numerous monuments; other city states came under the rule of formerly nomadic tribal leaders. The urban civilisation begun by the Sumer in Uruk survived in Mesopotamia, transmitted to new peoples: Amorites, Assyrians and Hittites. Great new cities such as Nineveh and Babylon preserved the city-building techniques, mythology and religion pioneered in Uruk and Ur.

Uruk itself began a long decline, although it remained a functional and sacred city for a surprisingly long time. Close to the birth of Christ, it suffered environmental catastrophe when the Euphrates began to move away. By then the religion that had made Uruk and the other cities so precious was dead; there was no reason to keep the city going and in AD 300 little was left of it. The sun, wind, rain and sand combined to grind the great brick structures to dust; by 700 the mysterious ruins were completely abandoned, almost 5,000 years after Uruk had arisen from the marshes to greatness.

Deprived of irrigation, the great wheat fields were swallowed up by desert. When the city was rediscovered in 1849 it was a buried ruin among the dunes. Its discoverers found it hard to believe that a great urban civilisation could have flourished so long before biblical times and in such a hostile environment. Since then the lost Iraqi cities have – and still do – offered up more of their secrets, teaching us about a long-forgotten civilisation and the origins of our path to urbanisation, despite the violence and wars that have beset Iraq.

Uruk and the Mesopotamian cities speak powerfully to us. The ghosts of once mighty centres laid waste by climate change and economic decline, they are haunting reminders of the ultimate fate of all cities. Their long history is one of dazzling discoveries, human achievement, the lust for power and the resilience of complex societies. They were an overture of all that was to follow.

2

The Garden of Eden and Sin City

Harappa and Babylon, 2000–539 BC

'Woe to the city of blood,' screams the Book of Nahum in the Hebrew Bible, 'full of lies, full of plunder, never without victims! The crack of whips, the clatter of wheels, galloping horses and jolting chariots!' In the Bible paradise is a garden. According to the Hebrew Bible, the city was born in sin and rebellion. Evicted from his soil and cast into the wilderness after he murdered his brother, Cain was said to have built the first city and named it Enoch (after his son) as a refuge from God's curse on him. Rebellion and cities are firmly intertwined in the Hebrew Bible. Nimrod made himself a Bronze Age tyrant because he successfully seduced people away from God by providing them with cities. Nimrod was supposed to have built such ungodly things in Mesopotamia, including Erech (Uruk), Akkad and Babel.

In Genesis the city is humankind's ultimate symbol of hubris. God commanded people to go forth and populate the earth. But in direct contradiction of the commandment, people began herding into cities and filling them with symbols of their self-pride. 'Come, let us build ourselves a city, with a tower that reaches to the heavens,' say the people of Babel, 'so that we may make a name for ourselves and not be scattered over the face of the whole world.' Not for the last time, God destroyed a city. The rebellious people of Babel were separated, given different languages, and dispersed. The city stands for corruption, confusion and fragmentation.

The Hebrew Bible makes a good case, then: the cities of the second and first millennia BC were sources of violence and lust, the antipathy of the pastoral idyll and the good life. That thinking has coloured views of the city down to our own times. There is a deep strain of *anti*-urbanism in Western culture. Sounding almost like a prophet from the Old Testament looking at a city with disgust, Jean-Jacques Rousseau wrote that the bloated big city was 'full of scheming, idle people without religion or principle, whose imagination, depraved by sloth, inactivity, the love of pleasure, and great needs, engenders only monsters and inspires only crimes'.[1]

As cities have grown and become congested with layer upon layer of human activity, they have been seen as bloated, outdated and incoherent. A writer observing Paris in the 1830s saw 'a huge satanic dance, in the midst of which men and women are thrown together any which way, crowded like ants, feet in the mud, breathing a diseased air, trying to walk through encumbered streets and public places'. The squalor of the city produced squalid people, mentally and physically deformed.[2]

In the 1950s the American ethnologist and behavioural researcher John B. Calhoun built elaborate 'rat cities', in which rodents were forced to live at high density in urban-like conditions. Over time, 'rodent utopia' degenerated into 'hell'. Female rats abused and neglected their babies. Youngsters became vicious 'juvenile delinquents' or they withdrew as lacklustre 'social misfits' and 'drop-outs'. Taking advantage of social chaos, dominant creatures emerged as local 'king-pins'. The intensity of the city made many of these urban rats hypersexual, pansexual or homosexual.

Rats, like humans, do well in the city; but they are perverted by it because their evolutionary histories have not prepared them for the shocks and stresses of living in close proximity and chaotic built environments. Or that was what many architects and urban planners took from Calhoun's results. The modern city, for them, induced the same pathologies in humans as it did in rats. The experiments pointed to a coming age of complete societal meltdown in cities.

The rat is a symbol of city life. And the menacing, teeming masses inhabiting the dark recesses of the city have been frequently likened to rats: trapped in the overcrowded metropolis, separated from nature, they become subhuman and a threat to the entire social order. Yet every age has believed that the chaotic, unplanned, self-organising city can be perfected if it is torn down and rebuilt according to scientific or philosophical principles: plan the city properly and it can make us better people. Although literature and movies are full of nightmare visions of dystopian cities, visions of perfection are also cities, where technology or architecture have got rid of all the mess that holds us back. That dualism runs through history.[3]

The Bible – so hostile to real cities – imagines a perfected city, the New Jerusalem, purged of human vice and full of godly worship. If the Bible begins in the garden, it ends in the celestial city. Plato and Thomas More used philosophical reason to conjure up the perfect city. Leonardo da Vinci designed a functional, hygienic city in reaction to the devastating plagues that wracked fifteenth-century Milan. Canaletto's visions of Venice present the acme of urban civilisation in its pomp, a utopian rendering of what a city should be, architecturally awesome yet spectacularly alive, minus the grime and squalor.

Plan the city right, and you get better people. Sir Christopher Wren wanted to rip out the tangled lanes of medieval London and create a city of wide boulevards and straight lines that would facilitate movement and commercial activity and would express modern rationality. The Swiss architect Le Corbusier dreamed of razing the tangles of history that encrusted and strangled cities, replacing them with rationally planned, geometric modern urban environments. 'Our world, like a charnel house, is strewn with the detritus of dead epochs,' he said. The English social reformer Sir Ebenezer Howard wanted to break up the polluted, industrial, soul-crushing metropolis and create suburban garden cities limited to 30,000 people with planned industry, pleasant cottages and abundant green space. 'Town and country *must be married*,' he declared, 'and out of this joyous union will spring a new hope, a new life, a new civilisation.'[4]

History is littered with utopian schemes to rip up the messy city and replace it with a scientifically planned alternative. Le Corbusier never got his chance to demolish Paris or New York and start over. But experiments in modernist architecture – high-rise towers in the park – changed the face of cities throughout the world and the lives of people who lived in them after the Second World War.

The vision of perfecting the human character through utopian urbanism has been called 'salvation by bricks'. Although it takes different forms, top-down urban planning has enchanted every age. Rarely has it been entirely successful. In many cases, well-intentioned planning has wreaked havoc on urban life. History does not supply much hope. But what if there had been an urban civilisation that was

from the start free of the vices and abuses of other city-based societies? Archaeologists have been – and still are – recovering the remains
of just such a culture.

Over 1,500 settlements have been discovered spread over a million
square kilometres in modern-day Pakistan, Afghanistan and India.
Highly advanced towns and cities were located at strategic points on
the trade routes – on the coast and the river systems; they provided
homes for 5 million people and centred on five major metropolises,
known to us Harappa, Mohenjo-Daro, Rakhigarhi, Dholavira and
Ganweriwala, all with populations in the tens of thousands. (The
civilisation is known as Harappan, after the city.) Only in the 1920s
was the scale of some these cities discovered; since then, although we
have found out more, our knowledge of this society remains in its
infancy.[5]

The Harappans procured gold, silver, pearl, shells, tin, copper,
carnelian, ivory, lapis lazuli and many other desirable items from
around the Indian subcontinent and central Asia. They were famed
for their intricate and beautiful jewellery and metalwork made from
these imports with precision tools. Harrapan merchants travelled to
the heartland of urbanisation in Mesopotamia to set up shop. The
kings, courts, gods and elites of cities such as Akkad, Uruk, Ur and
Lagash craved the luxury items made in workshops in the Indus Valley,
as well as their exotic animals, textiles and fine ceramics. The flourishing of the Mesopotamian city states coincided with the rapid period
of city-building in the Indus Valley from 2600 BC. Merchants from the
Indus Valley would surely have carried back tales of the fantastic cities
that dotted the valleys of the Tigris and Euphrates. Urbanisation there
sparked a similar process elsewhere. Cities such as Harappa and
Mohenjo-Daro formed in response to the intense demand for luxury
crafts in Mesopotamia and the Gulf.[6]

But the wide-ranging merchant adventurers who travelled across
the ocean and walked the streets of Uruk or Ur brought back an idea,
not a blueprint. The Harappans lived in permanent settlements with
well-built houses and enjoyed a diverse source of wild and cultivated
foods. The Indus river system, like those of the Tigris, Euphrates,
Yellow River, Niger and Nile, produced large surpluses of grain. They
had advanced technologies, a writing system and highly specialised
craftsmen. Most importantly of all, this widespread society was bound

by a sophisticated set of beliefs that governed community relations. If they borrowed the rough notion of cities from tales brought from Mesopotamia, the cities they created were entirely the product of their own culture and ingenuity. In many ways they outdid their fellow urbanites in China, Mesopotamia and Egypt. Archaeologists are coming to believe that Mohenjo-Daro contained as many as 100,000 people, making it the largest city of the Bronze Age and perhaps the most technologically innovative place on earth at the time.[7]

But in striking contrast to the other major Bronze Age civilisations, these Harappan cities had no palaces or temples, no awe-inspiring ziggurats or pyramids; indeed, there is no evidence of priests or kings at all. The great public buildings were modest not monumental. They were civic in function and spirit: granaries, warehouses, assembly halls, bathhouses, marketplaces, gardens and docks. This people did not appear to have owned slaves or indeed have a sharply differentiated social hierarchy: the cities' houses do not show much variety in size or in possession of artefacts.

Whereas the city states of Mesopotamia degenerated very quickly into endless fratricidal conflict, wholesale destruction of cities and empire-building, those of the Indus Valley did not possess weapons, except those needed for hunting; no depictions of warfare have ever been found and the archaeological remains bear no trace of fighting. Likewise, there is no direct evidence of rulers or bureaucracy.

The Harappan urbanites were far ahead of their time in terms of infrastructure and civil engineering. The major cities were raised above the flood level of the Indus Valley on enormous brick platforms; the one at Mohenjo-Daro is estimated to have taken 4 million work hours to construct. Main thoroughfares running at right angles to each other formed a chequerboard pattern orientated to the compass points. These main streets divided the city into residential areas, with narrower streets and multistorey homes. Uniformity extended from the street layout to the size and appearance of houses to the dimensions of the bricks. There were even public rubbish bins. Most remarkable of all was the crowning glory of Indus urban planning, its citywide sewerage system.

Forget great public edifices soaring above the rooftops. The most important aspect of Mohenjo-Daro lay under street level. Few things symbolise collective civic endeavour more than the seriousness with which a city deals with its daily tonnage of human waste. The builders of the Indus cities put that consideration first. Every household had a flush toilet in the third millennium BC, which is more than could be said for the same region of Pakistan today, 4,000 years later. Indeed, it is more than could be said for the industrial city of nineteenth-century Europe: a slum-dweller in Manchester in the 1850s had to share a public toilet with a hundred others. Only in the mid-nineteenth century did the two most powerful cities in the world, London and Paris, begin to grapple with large-scale sanitation. In Mohenjo-Daro and Harappa the waste from the household latrine was discharged through terracotta pipes into drains in the smaller streets, which in turn flowed into a large system of underground sewers beneath the main thoroughfares. These large drains used gravity to flush the filth clear of the city walls. They also carried out dirty water from every household's bathroom.

Cleanliness wasn't next to godliness; it *was* godliness. The power of water in purifying the soul was central to the belief system. The folk of Mohenjo-Daro, and in other cities, enjoyed showers in their own homes in specially designed waterproof washrooms. The centre-piece of this metropolis was a large watertight basin, twelve metres by seven and 2.4 metres deep, the first of its kind in history, which served as a public bath. These cities did not have temples. But maybe the city itself – or at least its infrastructure of drains, wells, cisterns and baths – comprised a watery temple.

New evidence suggests that Harappan urbanisation was determined by a series of adaptations to climate change. While these cities were in their heyday around 2500–1900 BC, the environment became unpredictable, with shifting rivers and varying intensities in seasonal rainfall. Finding new ways to capture and store water, and to diversify crops, therefore became a key feature of Indus urbanisation. The cities were designed to be resilient in an environment that was getting hotter and dryer.[8]

The city of Dholavira, which lay in the hostile desert, engineered an advanced system of water conservation. A network of dams diverted the annual monsoon flood into sixteen vast rectangular stone-lined reservoirs. There it remained for the long dry months with aqueducts conveying it into the city or to irrigate the fields. Monsoon rainwater was also trapped in cisterns on top of a raised citadel, where gravity brought it down to the lower city as required. At Mohenjo-Daro at least 700 wells exploited the groundwater. So deep and well made were these wells that when they were excavated in recent years, they stood tall like watchtowers.[9]

The intricacies of water management had to be maintained at the cost of life and death. The cities were built physically on top of their pre-planned hydraulic systems; but in terms of ideology they rested on the foundations of a sacred reverence of water and an abhorrence of pollution. Mercantile successes, combined with advanced civil engineering, were no doubt instrumental in forging an equal, peaceful society.

The Mesopotamian cities – impressive as they were – did not possess urban planning of this sophistication, still less plumbing and a centralised sewage disposal system. Only with the Romans – 2,000 years after these cities flourished – was the hydraulic engineering and city planning of the Indus people exceeded. The earliest archaeologists believed these were cities of children because of the large number of toys and games they discovered. The Harrapans used a wide variety of foods and flavourings, including turmeric, ginger and garlic. Evidence taken from skeletons does not show that some people in society were better fed than others; indeed, life expectancy in the Harappan cities was high. The people were also well clothed: the oldest cotton threads ever found came from these cities.[10]

Mohenjo-Daro and Harappa offered a fantastically high standard of living not only in terms of the age in which they existed, but across history. Who could not be attracted by the orderliness and cleanliness of such a society? Perhaps this civilisation really is the forgotten utopia, a missed turning point in our urban journey. Maybe the Garden of Eden was actually a city, a place where our needs were satisfied and our safety ensured without having to pay a high toll.

The cities were abandoned from about 1900 BC. There are no signs of a cataclysmic event, a foreign invasion or widespread death. The populations voluntarily left their cities, making their de-urbanisation sound as peaceful and utopian as their urbanisation. The monsoon began to weaken as it shifted east. Huge metropolises, with their hunger for grain and thirst for clean water, were not viable in this new climate. Rather than slug it out for the dwindling resources, big-city populations dispersed into smaller farming communities and began to migrate towards the Gangetic plain. Deprived of the oxygen of city life, the Indus Valley written script fell out of use. The cities themselves disappeared into the sands of the encroaching desert taking their secrets with them.

The enigmatic Harappan civilisation continues to intrigue us. New discoveries in the ruins of the cities are widely reported across the world. Here is, it seems, an example of a technologically advanced, peaceful society. There is a good reason for this renewed interest in this apparent utopia. In our age there is a preoccupation with designing a New Jerusalem of our own – the ideal city that will be an answer to our problems. 'Science Fiction No More: The Perfect City Is Under Construction', reads one recent headline. Harappan urbanisation holds out this promise: if you can get the design right from the very beginning, your city becomes a place that draws out the best in humanity and lets its people flourish. The people of the Indus Valley seemingly cracked that conundrum – one that eluded Leonardo, Howard and Le Corbusier. But there is a belief that our modern technologies can recreate the spirit of Mohenjo-Daro. If the Harappans built their cities on a reverence for water, we are building ours on faith in the digital future.[11]

Imagine a city that has the breathtaking skyline and population density of Manhattan, but on the intimate, walkable scale of downtown Boston. Imagine it criss-crossed with Venetian canals and studded with green parks. The Parisian-style tree-lined boulevards contain no cars, but they have the street life and creative fizz of Soho. You do not need a car – you can walk or cycle everywhere in the city, to work or school. No need for garbage trucks or delivery vans either; rubbish is sucked into pneumatic tubes and sorted for recycling, while drones and boats bring everything you need. Human waste is turned into biomass energy to power the city.

Millions of sensors and surveillance cameras embedded throughout this leafy techno dreamscape – everywhere from private homes and offices to streets and water pipes – feed real-time data about the workings of the city back to a single-platform urban computer. Up in a skyscraper, a high-tech control room with massive data screens keeps restless watch on the city. Download a handy city app onto your smartphone, and you become a blinking dot on the computer screen as you move about the city, your wanderings measured and recorded to provide data on how the city should evolve. This is called the 'ubiquitous city'; the sensors are the nerve endings and the computer is the metro brain. The operating system monitors energy and water usage, automatically cutting waste by switching off lights, air conditioning and appliances. Any water that cannot be reused irrigates the prevalent greenery. Even a leaking tap reports back to the master computer. An accident, crime or fire is detected and the emergency services dispatched without human intervention. This city is not so much smart as sentient.

So far, so science fiction. But this utopian (or dystopian, according to taste) city already exists, or it does according to its publicity material and cheerleaders, and it exists in a country that is renowned both for its turbocharged economic growth and its profusion of soulless cities, with rows of identical tower blocks. Songdo in South Korea was built from scratch along these specifications on land reclaimed from the Yellow Sea at a cost of $35 billion. Labelled the twenty-first century's 'high-tech utopia', it is a living city, touted as the urgent answer to Asia's overcrowded metropolises. The population of Songdo is expected to reach 600,000 (at the time of writing it is a little over 100,000); citizens are won over with promises of a high standard of living. But more importantly it is both a laboratory and an urban showroom, exhibiting a clean, sustainable, safe, environmentally friendly future for sale to the rest of the world. Songdo was designed to be replicable anywhere. Many planners of new cities and rescuers of old ones head to Songdo to see the latest urban gizmos put to the test. You can buy the entire city operating system off the shelf for close to $10 billion.[12]

*

An urban utopia is surely a contradiction in terms. A clinical city such as Harappa or Songdo might satisfy some of our needs, but it leaves aside many more. Indeed, we don't always want cities to make us better people. The opposite is often the case; some might say that the whole point of cities is to provide anonymity and a labyrinthine mystique – that is, a unique kind of freedom. In the sixteenth century a visitor to Venice, a city of over 100,000 people, pointed out: 'No man there marketh another's doings or ... meddleth with another

man's living ... No man shall ask thee why thou comest not to church
... To live married or unmarried, no man shall ask thee why ... And
generally of all other things, so thou offend no man privately, no man
shall offend thee.'[13]

Cities also offer things that appeal to our baser human drives, such
as materialism, hedonism and sex. That is part of their appeal, and
their power over us. Greenwich Village in New York, Paris's
Montmartre, San Francisco's Tenderloin, the raffish Shanghais and
Berlins of the interwar years, contemporary Amsterdam, Bangkok
and Sin City itself – Las Vegas – have provided, or still do provide,
the walk on the wild side and the escape from conventional mores
that we want from cities.

The identification of anonymous city-living with illicit activities was
made real in early eighteenth-century London, a time when that city
was firmly coupled with the erotic. Commercialised masquerades and
carnivals became extremely popular. Social hierarchy, class distinctions,
customary morality and restraint broke down in a mass of thousands
of people disguised in fancy dress mingling together. Who was whom?
'I found nature turned topsy-turvy,' wrote one journalist, 'women
changed into men, and men into women, children in leading-strings
seven-foot high, courtiers transformed into clowns, ladies of the night
into saints, people of the first quality into beasts or birds, gods or
goddesses.'[14]

For those who worried that cities perverted human nature and
turned morality on its head, the masquerade was a vivid metaphor
and a nightmarish hallucination of the shifting identities and disguises
that define urban life. The city that most embodies confusion, materialism, excess and vice is Babylon, the glory of the ancient world and
the original Sin City. Babel (the Hebrew name for Babylon), the site
of the tower whose builders were punished by God with the confusion of tongues for their attempt to reach heaven, became an incom-
prehensibly vast city characterised by its cosmopolitanism, its dazzling
architecture that symbolised raw imperial power, and its sacrilegious
sensuousness. 'What city is like unto this great city!' marvelled the
Book of Revelation, which lists the merchandise on offer: gold, silver,
precious stones, pearls, fine linen, silks, ivory, marble, perfumes, wine,
oil, flour, livestock, chariots and slaves. Also for sale were the 'souls
of men'.

Babylon had 'sins piled up to heaven'. Chief among them was illicit sex and 'ungodly lusts', as it was in other abhorred fleshpots such as Nineveh, Sodom and Gomorrah. One of the deities of Babylon was Ishtar, the promiscuous goddess of love who hangs out with 'her people, the dancing and singing girls, the prostitutes of the temple, the courtesans'. Herodotus recounted salacious stories of temple prostitution. According to his account, young Babylonian women lost their virginity by selling themselves for sex in the street. A girl had to sit outside the Temple of Ishtar until a man threw a silver coin into her lap for the right to have sex with her. After the act was done, she was then free to return home. 'Tall, handsome women soon managed to get home again but the ugly ones stay a long time ... some of them as much as three or four years.' In the Book of Baruch, a scene outside a Babylonian temple is recorded. Full-time prostitutes (rather than the one-off sacrificial victims recorded by Herodotus) wait in the street wearing strings around their waist: 'when one of these has been picked up by a passer-by and been to bed with him, she then gloats over her neighbour for not having been thought as worthy as herself and for not having had her string broken'.

Babylon has never escaped its seedy reputation. The Book of Revelation personified the city as the Whore of Babylon: 'Babylon the Great, the Mother of Harlots and of the Abominations of the Earth.' If the Harappans have been seen as inhabiting the urban utopia, Babylon has stood for urban dystopia from its own time down to ours.

History's perception of the great cities of the first millennium BC was shaped by accounts in the Hebrew Bible, which chime with ancient Greek writings. The Babylonian Empire captured Jerusalem in 588 BC and destroyed the Temple of Solomon. The Judean elite were deported as prisoners to Babylon. This cataclysmic event decisively shaped the Jewish world view, not least the view of cities. A large part of the Hebrew Bible was the product of Babylonian influence. Living as hostages in the enemy's capital, a vast and varied metropolis of 250,000 people, Babylon epitomised all worldly evil and corruption. Jeremiah wrote that 'nations drank her wine, therefore they have now gone mad'. St John added a sexual dimension to those words: 'All the nations drink the maddening wine of her adulteries.'

Sex and the ancient city went hand in hand. Babylon's glory days stand almost exactly halfway through the chronological span of this

book. In other words, the foundation of Eridu was as distant from
the Babylonians as Babylon is from us. Nonetheless, the Babylonians
were well informed about their history and the urban traditions and
practices that linked them across the millennia to the first cities, Eridu
and Uruk. Remember, in *Gilgamesh* (a favourite Babylonian text) it is
the promise of unbridled sex that lures the wild man Enkidu away
from the innocence of nature to the delights of Uruk.

*

Perhaps there is more than a ring of truth in the story of Enkidu in
The Epic of Gilgamesh. The pleasures of sex are a powerful attraction
and they can be a compensation for the downsides of city life. Whatever
else they have done for us, cities have offered new ways of finding
pleasure. Pooling humans with diverse backgrounds in densely populated urban pockets is good for human invention; it is also good for
opening our eyes (and legs) to unheard-of sexual practices and like-
minded partners.

Cities shelter a diverse population for the compatible to find each
other; they also provide the privacy and anonymity for illicit encounters. To take one example from many, modern statisticians discovered
that in eighteenth-century Chester in Great Britain 8% of the population who were under thirty-five had some sort of sexually transmitted
disease in the 1770s, compared to 1% in the nearby countryside. Chester
was not a city of vice in that it had an usually high number of prostitutes. Men and women caught the pox in equal numbers, suggesting
that non-marital sex was commonplace. Similarly, a study in 2019
showed that while in the Belgian and Dutch countryside in the nineteenth century illegitimacy rates were 0.5%, they were 6% in the
industrial cities. It is doubtful whether city folk are more prone to sin
than their country cousins; they just have more opportunities (and
more hiding places) for illicit encounters.[15]

The ruling divinity of Uruk, and later a key figure in the Babylonian
pantheon, was Inanna. Sensuous, seductive, scintillating, Inanna was
a goddess like no other. She brought sexual freedom and lusty energy
to Uruk. No one could resist her charms, not even the other gods.
When the sun went down, she could be found wandering the streets
of the city in a skimpy outfit, prowling for a man to pluck from the

tavern. She frequented those taverns, places where young men and women, mere mortals, meet for casual sexual encounters. If the goddess did not literally stalk the night streets, Uruk was known for its sexual openness and its 'population of beautiful and voluptuous women with luxuriantly curly hair and available women in general'. Sex in the city streets was apparently a normal affair after dark.[16]

The nocturnal city as a sexual playground gets no better or more candid chronicler than James Boswell in the eighteenth century. 'At the bottom of the Haymarket,' he recorded in his diary on 10 May 1763, 'I picked up a strong jolly young damsel, and taking her under the arm I conducted her to Westminster Bridge, and then in armour compleat [i.e. wearing a condom] did I engage her upon this noble edifice. The whim of doing it there with the Thames rolling below us amused me much.' Most of Bowell's encounters were with poor women whom he paid small amounts or bought a drink. But that wasn't always the case. Walking along the Strand one evening he was tapped on the shoulder by a 'fine fresh lass', the daughter of an army officer. 'I could not resist indulging myself with the enjoyment of her,' wrote Boswell, recording how they went home together for a one-night stand.[17]

Casual hook-ups like Boswell's have been a feature of city life since Uruk. Boswell was just one of the first to write about them. Most urban areas have had a red-light district of one sort or another, places where the restraints and manners of the rest of the city do not apply. Centuries before Boswell's night-time prowls, London had Southwark, a borough on the south bank of the Thames, where the writ of the City did not run. People resorted there for its playhouses, bear-baiting, low taverns and brothels. The brothels, or 'stews', were leased from the Bishop of Winchester (who took a healthy slice from the wages of sin) and regulated by the 'Ordinances Touching the Government of the Stewholders in Southwark' issued by Henry II in 1161. Medieval Southwark had streets with names such as Sluts' Hole, Cuckold Court, Codpiece Lane and Whore's Nest. Elsewhere in London there were several streets named Gropecunt Lane, as there were in the centres of numerous other English cities and market towns.

Sodomites Walk, a dark narrow path in London's Moorfields, was so called because it was where men cruised for casual sex with men who worked in the 'rough trades' of the city. Cities have been places of both refuge and danger for gay people, most particularly when homosexuality had to be clandestine. In 1726 a gay club – or molly house, to use its contemporary name – was raided; three men were tried and executed for sodomy. The ensuing moral panic led to muck-raking journalists uncovering a profusion of molly houses spread through the city, along with other sexual venues, such as sadomaso-chistic and transvestite clubs. As one outraged journalist had it: 'In *Sodom* one vice was notorious; but *London* is a common receptacle for all manner of wickedness.'[18]

For moralists, evidence of a secret and widespread culture of homo-sexuality thriving throughout the city confirmed everything they already knew about urban life: it was the ferocious enemy of masculine authority and family values; it encouraged sexual excess and perver-sion. Gay people represented the urban condition, exploiting the confu-sion of the metropolis to seek their own pleasure in contravention of conventional morality. But the case also reveals an alternate city, an underground world of places where it was safe to be yourself and a network of people who offered protection. The gay city existed in parallel with the straight city. Negotiating it meant constructing an entirely different mental map of the city and code of behaviour to avoid the dangers of violence, blackmail and arrest. You had to know which pubs, coffee houses, bathhouses and clubs were safe; you had to learn a series of visual codes and cues and turns of phrase. There were known places where men could find men of similar inclination. In other words, a gay person would have to know the city better than almost anyone, exploiting a range of public and semi-public places as sites of pleasure, companionship and safety against homophobic violence that only a big city can provide.[19]

In gay literature before liberation in the 1960s, cities are represented as places charged with both erotic power and danger. But they are also depicted as places where sexual fulfilment is only ever fleeting and oftentimes has to take place hurriedly in sordid locations. In books, poems and memoirs published before the more permissive era, love in the city is lonely for homosexual men. In Constantine Cavafy's poems about Alexandria from the late nineteenth and early twentieth centuries, lovers meet in cafés, shops, in the street; their recourse for sex is in rooms rented by the hour. Pleasure is over too soon; strangers part; but for Cavafy the memory can last a lifetime.

The gay subculture of post-war Tokyo in Yukio Mishima's *Yellow Colours* is similarly a place where sex occurs opportunistically in bars, clubs, and night-time public parks: 'Homosexuals have on their faces a certain loneliness that will not come off.' In 'The Tunnel', a section of the American poet Hart Crane's 1930 poem *The Bridge*, love is described as 'A burnt match skating in a urinal' in a subway station – a reference to the transitory nature of casual sex in a public toilet in the subterranean city.

The often-sordid settings and anonymity of homosexual encounters made cities seem, for many, sexually threatening places, particularly at night. The AIDS epidemic that ravaged cities such as New York and San Francisco in the 1980s was used by the media and politicians to further stigmatise the gay city as promiscuous and dangerous. Once again, it was a deeply unfair stigmatisation: the transactional nature of love was also a feature of the heterosexual urban experience. For most of history, cities have been dominated by males. City streets were often seen as off limits for unescorted respectable women. By implication, solitary women on the streets were seen by men as sexually available; they were subject to predatory advances and assault. The after-hours city has always been permeated with sexual danger – or at least the all-pervading perception of danger. Cities, with their large populations of poor and migrants, have allowed the rich to rent the bodies of women and young men on a whim. This was particularly true of cities in sexually repressed societies, when men and women could not meet on equal terms, still less engage in casual flings without censure. The transitory nature of sex in the city, and its commercialisation, has made the metropolis seem like a place where love is a mere disposable commodity in contrast to the supposed innocence of the countryside.

Commercialised sex and hedonism are central to the economy of some cities – or of some parts of cities. In the nineteenth century, seedy, down-at-heel Soho, with its population of bohemians and immigrants and its theatres, pubs, cafés and restaurants, inherited the mantle of Southwark as a district of nocturnal adventure and surprise, where the rules of conventional domestic and business life are set aside for a while. Later it became the centre of the sex industry and a prime destination for city folk and tourists alike, a city within a city. Today people go further from home for their naughtiness, to the regulated red-light district of Amsterdam, for example, or to Vegas or Bangkok where sexual adventure has economic benefits. Los Angeles's San Fernando Valley – with its low rents, sunshine and proximity to Hollywood – became 'San Pornando Valley' or 'Silicone Valley', the suburban capital of a thriving multibillion-dollar adult entertainment industry.

The availability of sex in cities might well have been a motivating factor for people to move to them. When Uruk was described as a 'city of prostitutes, courtesans and call girls' it was meant not censoriously but as a compliment to its sexual freedoms. The prostitutes were attendants of fiery femme fatale Inanna, freed from the confines of marriage. Others who ministered to her included 'the party-boys and festival people who changed masculinity to femininity to make the people ... revere her'. The raucous entourage of courtesans, male and female prostitutes, homosexuals and transvestites make the armed guards 'do abominable acts' to please the heart of their goddess at festival time. Uruk's Inanna became Babylon's Ishtar and the Greeks' Aphrodite.[20]

None of this is to argue that Uruk and Babylon were free-love communes. Or that they had particularly enlightened attitudes towards sex or the rights of women. Rather, it is to show that an erotic charge was a key component of early urban life, particularly in public and religious contexts. The city and sensuality were inseparable: it was a place not only of bodily intimacy, but of spectacle, festivity and diversity, all of which heighten the emotions and provoke desire. How exactly that desire was satisfied, however, is hard to determine. Reconstructing the sex lives of ancient Urukians and Babylonians is next to impossible. But we do know that there was an openness about sex that lacked the squeamishness of later generations and a relatively high degree of permissiveness in certain contexts. Temples had clay models of male and female sexual organs, and depictions of intercourse between men and women and men and men. Anal sex was recommended as form of contraception. A list of the top hundred most important things in Mesopotamian life includes things such as the gods, religious practice, wisdom, arts and kingship. Sex comes in at number twenty-four and prostitution at twenty-five. Significantly, the first written law code in history – that of Hammurabi, king of Babylon 1792–1750 BC – does not mention homosexuality as a crime, even though we know it was common enough in Mesopotamian metropolises.[21]

What we do know from these law codes is that married women were punished with death not just for adultery but for any action that might shame their husbands in public. Virginity was a commodity that belonged to a girl's father; it was sold at marriage or, if it was illicitly stolen, the offender had to pay hefty compensation. Because of the secretive nature of the city, with its nooks and crannies for illicit encounters, harsh sanctions were necessary to protect daughters and wives. Cities create entirely new taboos and restrictions even as they liberate. And they enflame lust by thrusting people into close physical proximity, stoking a thirst that is hard to quench despite the apparently easy availability of its relief.

The high value placed on female purity in Mesopotamia, combined with a high value placed on libido, made prostitution a widespread practice. The same contradiction was the case in cities through the ages. Cities are nothing if not tantalising. Very commonly before the sexual revolution of the twentieth century they have been homes to large numbers of sexually frustrated young males and closely guarded females. In Uruk, Babylon and the other great cities the temple prostitutes, be they male or female, were the most expensive, desirable and skilful.

Quite what spiritual purpose sacred prostitution served is unclear, particularly for the sex worker, although it provided a healthy income for the temples. Likely it made sense in a society where the gods were sexual marauders and intercourse was celebrated as a central component of urban life. Most men resorted to cheaper means of sexual gratification – slave girls and boys, the poor and displaced who made up the lowest stratum of society and who plied the taverns and winehouses of the back streets. Babylon had a large population of migrants from the countryside or residents from distant places. Many of these young men and women, girls and boys, had to sell their bodies to survive. There is little indication that Mesopotamian men suffered any kind of censure for extramarital heterosexual or homosexual fornication.

*

No wonder cities are hated. The Bible takes special pleasure in their destruction in hails of brimstone: 'Even as Sodom and Gomorrah, and the cities about them in like manner, giving themselves over to fornication, and going after strange flesh, are set forth for an example, suffering the vengeance of eternal fire.'

The pursuit of 'strange flesh' includes homosexuality, but also the flesh of strangers of all sexualities and inclinations. There was a relish in wiping cities off the face of the earth. They were the enemies of the spiritual, rendering the godly, religious life impossible. And of course, Babylon was the epitome of Sin City. The Jewish captives deported there by Nebuchadnezzar entered the most powerful city the world had ever seen. They believed that their exile in Babylon was a just punishment meted out by God for their sins. No wonder then that they reacted so strongly against the city of their captivity, a place that contained hundreds of idolatrous temples, an immense and diverse crowd of humanity, and all the sights and sounds of a major metropolis. They had to resist Babylon's rich menu of worldly temptations with all their might.

With its massive grid pattern of streets, Babylon straddled the Euphrates, with an old city on the east bank and a newer one on the west. The vast walls that surrounded it, studded with towers every sixty-five feet, were so thick, Herodotus tells us, that a four-horse chariot could pull off a U-turn. Of the nine mighty fortified gateways, the breathtaking Ishtar Gate was by far the most magnificent. Today a reconstruction made from original bricks is in the Pergamon Museum in Berlin. Its magnificence is *the* emblem of Mesopotamian civilisation. It shone like a jewel of lapis lazuli, thanks to its stunning blue glaze and its gold bas-relief dragons, bulls and lions. Pass through this gate and you were on the Processional Way, a ceremonial street half a mile long lined with relief images of lions, the symbol of Ishtar/Inanna.

Visitors who went down the length of the grand Processional Way passed the great monuments of ancient urbanism, buildings which were the culmination of 3,000 years of city-building that began at Eridu. The stupendously vast royal palace was on your immediate right, separating you from the Euphrates. Next came Etemenanki, the vast ziggurat that towered high above the great city. Its name meant 'the House of the Foundation of Heaven and Earth'; it gave its name to the Tower of Babel, the ultimate symbol of urban hubris and confusion. The ancient skyscraper was made of 17 million bricks; it had a base that measured ninety-one metres by ninety-one, and was supposedly as tall as it was wide. Its summit was where the heavens met the city.

The centre of Babylon was called Eridu, as if the original marsh city, where the world began, had been transplanted to the new capital. It contained numerous large temples, the biggest and most sacred of which was Esagil ('House Whose Top Is High'), the Temple of Marduk, patron deity of Babylon and the head of the Mesopotamian pantheon. If earlier metropolises such as Uruk and Ur had been the home to one god, Babylon hosted a whole network of resident deities. With its astonishing palaces, mighty temples, imposing gates, supersized ziggurats and grand ceremonial boulevards, Babylon was designed as the embodiment of ultimate divine and secular power.

Maps put Babylon at the centre of the universe. A tablet from this time of triumph of the metropolis goes like this:

Babylon, city of abundance,
Babylon, city whose citizens are overwhelmed by wealth,
Babylon, city of festivities, joy, and dancing,
Babylon, the city whose citizens celebrate ceaselessly,
Babylon, privileged city that frees the captive,
Babylon, the pure city.[22]

The city's name is a byword for decadence. But that would be as true to the history of the city as if Amsterdam was judged for all time by a tourist who had only been to the De Wallen red-light district without visiting the Rijksmuseum. In its pomp Babylon was regarded as a sacred city, an intellectual and artistic capital without parallel. Hippocrates, the Greek Father of Medicine, relied on Babylonian sources, while the city's mathematicians and astronomers were highly advanced. The Babylonians had a passion for history: much like the archaeologists of the nineteenth century, experts scoured Mesopotamia to help understand their 3,000-year-old past and the result was a number of museums, libraries and archives. Another result was a flourishing of Mesopotamian literature based on the myths and legends that the experts had gleaned from their researches.

Babylon had the misfortune to be immortalised by one of its many captive populations, a people who viewed it as a scourge designed by God to punish them for their sins and whose books provided the basis for three of the world's major religions. The monstrous image of the city was passed down to Christianity. Babylon became shorthand for sin, depravity and tyranny, even though the city had lost its power by the time of Christ. Most powerfully of all, the Book of Revelation, with its vivid, hallucinatory language of apocalypse, sin and redemption, fixed Babylon for all time in the collective memory of Christianity and the cultures that emerged from it. The way that its enemies and victims portrayed it has, from that day until now, deeply affected how we see major cities.

*

Babylon's period of unrivalled greatness after the fall of Jerusalem lasted no more than a human lifetime. In 539 BC it was captured by Cyrus the Great of Persia, who let the Jews go. Seduced by the city, however, many remained in Babylon to benefit from its culture and wealth. Those who fulfilled their duty and returned to the godly city of Jerusalem spat venom at the site of their captivity and relished the thought of its complete destruction. Jeremiah imagined Babylon's impending fall with utter glee: 'Therefore marmots and jackals will skulk in it, desert owls will haunt it; never more will it be inhabited and age after age no one will dwell in it. It will be as when God overthrew Sodom and Gomorrah along with their neighbours, says the Lord; no one will live in it, no human being will make a home there.'

The fall of overweening Babylon as a punishment for its hubristic ambition became a literary and artistic trope. The reality is somewhat different. Babylon remained a great city even after the fall of its empire to the Persians. Cyrus did not loot or sack the metropolis. In 331 BC Alexander the Great defeated the Persians and planned to make Babylon his imperial capital and renew it with even bigger buildings and a gigantic new ziggurat. He died in the city before its rebirth could begin.

Babylon survived into the first millennium AD. Its demise was the result of changing economic circumstances. Seleucia, a new city on the Tigris, became the commercial hub of the region. Babylon remained a scholarly centre, however, the final custodian of the urban culture and traditions that went back to Eridu and the last place where a few experts could still decipher cuneiform. But the urban colossus was chipped away; brick by brick the former capital of the world disappeared, each one recycled for use in farms, villages and new towns. In the tenth century AD it had dwindled to village size, and within two further centuries it had vanished. Babylon's end was a 1,500-year long whimper, not a sudden bang.

But myth overtook reality. Suspicious of all things oriental, the Greeks were eager to make the Mesopotamian cities seem as despotic, luxurious and decadent as they could in order to magnify the glories of their own urban civilisation and obscure their debt to their eastern neighbours. Their propaganda had a massive impact on the Western artistic tradition in which Babylon was represented as a city of pornographic vice, ruled over by sadistic women and oversexed tyrants. Delacroix's *Death of Sardanapalus* (1827) and Edwin Long's *The Babylonian Marriage Market* (1875) are classic examples of how nineteenth-century painters feasted on Babylon for erotic purposes.

The Babylon of the Hebrew Bible became the archetype of a great metropolis in Western thinking. Above all it provided the most potent example of what inevitably went wrong with big cities. In Christian writing Babylon became conflated with imperial Rome and indeed with all big cities, a metaphor for all worldly sin and weakness. Babylon became the literal and symbolic antithesis of Jerusalem. Writing in the fifth century AD in response to the sack of Rome by the Visigoths, Augustine of Hippo imagined two cities. The first was the 'city of men who choose to live carnally', an earthly city where God is held in contempt. The 'cities of man' are Babylon and Rome, the New Babylon; later in history the mantle of Babylon has been passed from one great metropolis to another. Its opposite is the 'city of God' or heavenly city, where people renounce worldly things and live in harmony. Babylon is the archetypical 'city of man', characterised by materialism, lust and hubbub.

And of course, the image of Babel/Babylon, Sodom and Gomorrah, gave powerful ammunition to the enemies of the city. The divide between the big metropolis on one side and the small town or village on the other has been a feature of history. Virtue is said to reside in the latter, while the immoral cosmopolis, with its Babel of languages, collision of cultures, multi-ethnic groups, licentiousness and greed, is the corrupter of souls and of politics. The fast-growing London of the late seventeenth century was held by moralists to be a sink of vice and the breeding ground of religious disbelief; a visitor from the country was shocked to find 'much of atheism ... and great coldness in religion, among such a concourse of people as frequent this city'. His feelings have been expressed countless times both before and after him about any city you care to mention.[23]

Thomas Jefferson famously said of the United States that 'When we get piled upon one another in large cities, as in Europe, we shall become as corrupt as Europe.' Jefferson's belief that the health of the republic depended on the predominance of agriculture is a sentiment that courses through American history and culture, shaping a society that is profoundly *anti*-urban. Much later, Gandhi held up the self-sufficient village as the only true place that Indian spiritual and moral values could be realised. His idealisation of the rural village would have dire consequences in post-Independence India, when urban development was neglected. The soul of a country – its traditions, values, religion, morality, ethnicity and culture – belong, for many people, to the countryside, not a multicultural metropolis such as a Los Angeles or a London.

In numerous paintings from the Middle Ages and the Renaissance, Babylon is rendered as an architecturally perfect city, with incomparably beautiful buildings that look oddly Western. The splendour of the city, however, only seeks to magnify the depravity that teems within it. Very often the Babylon presented reflects the individual artist's current concerns. Pieter Bruegel the Elder's famous paintings of the ruined Tower of Babel depict an edifice that is classical in its architecture, but it lours over the Antwerp of the 1560s. In the Reformation, Babylon became the Rome of the papacy, a corrupt and spiritually bankrupt place.

The Tower of Babel is one of humankind's most powerful metaphors. When London passed the million-person mark at the end of the eighteenth century it was the first European metropolis since imperial Rome to do so. There had never been a city like it in terms of commercial power and extreme inequality. For many who experienced the booming global megalopolis of this time, London *was* Babylon reborn. Everything seemed out of proportion, bigger and more exaggerated than anywhere else. It possessed spectacular buildings, palatial homes, fashionable squares, luxurious shops and the produce of the world; it was dirty and squalid, dark and dangerous, the haunt of beggars and prostitutes, thieves and conmen. Sex was evident everywhere in Georgian London. Estimates from the 1790s put the number of professional and part-time prostitutes at 50,000 out of a population of a million. Like the Babylon of legend, everything was for sale, including the bodies and souls of men and women.

A runaway boy, the companion of street walkers and other marginalised people, addicted to opium, Thomas De Quincey roamed nocturnal London in 1803 and plunged into the heart of its immense darkness. Trying to return home after a night wafting through a trippy underworld on clouds of opium, De Quincey 'came suddenly upon such knotty problems of alleys, alleys without soundings, such enigmatical entries, and such sphinx's riddles of streets without obvious outlets or thoroughfares' to such an extent that he felt he had entered territory never before explored except by its inhabitants and which did not appear on any map. Later in life, when stupefied by opium, he would dream of the monstrous things he had seen and the faces of the people he encountered, as if the mad maze of the city had rewired his neural network. He called the whole thing 'Babylonian confusion'.

Thomas De Quincey brought this dark desolation to visceral life with the story of his friendship with a sweet-hearted, half-starved, homeless, underage prostitute named Ann. They had a brother/sister relationship, and lightened each other's harsh existence with small acts of kindness. Called away briefly from London, De Quincey and Ann arranged to go to a particular place at a set time every night after his return until they were reunited. But he never saw Ann again, despite waiting every night for her and searching frantically. This sudden loss tormented him for the rest of his life: 'doubtless we must have been sometimes in search of each other, at the very same moment, through the mighty labyrinths of London; perhaps even within a few feet of each other – a barrier no wider, in a London street, often amounting in the end to a separation for eternity!'

The symbol of the city becomes the lost boy and the teenage prostitute, poor souls lost in Babylon. Babylon crushes its citizens, flattening the individual amid a vast wilderness. As soon as you arrive in London, De Quincey wrote, 'you become aware that you are no longer noticed: nobody sees you; nobody hears you; nobody regards you; you do not even regard yourself'. The city-dweller is nothing more than 'a poor shivering unit in the aggregate of human life'. Everyone in the Babylon of the nineteenth century ('this colossal emporium of men') is a commodity: the city offered numerous temptations, including mind-altering narcotics; the poor families De Quincey encountered at night were reduced to insignificance, insecurity and abject dependence; Ann, like tens of thousands of others, had only her wasted teenage body to sell.[24]

*

Babylon – or at least the Judaeo-Christian view of Babylon – became the prism through which great cities have been seen. Augustine of Hippo wrote of the 'city of this world, a city which aims at dominion, but is itself dominated by that very lust of domination'. In other words, the city becomes a monstrous force beyond human control, devouring its children. The idea that Babylon was the great oppressor and city of sin has always been powerfully deployed from the pulpit. But it is the continued prevalence of Babylon in secular form that is most interesting. Not just De Quincey but Blake, Wordsworth and Dickens saw London in this biblical Babylonian sense – as a place of sin, guilt, oppression, injustice and corruption.

From the Romantics through to Hollywood – the precise period when Europe and the United States were undergoing rampant urbanisation – there has been a strong anti-urban bias in Western culture, seeing the city as a force that atomises human beings, destroys communities and distorts the 'natural' component of human nature. In the twentieth century sociologists followed suit, investigating the pathologies engendered by urban existence. Western Europeans and Americans have inherited an antipathy towards urban life that is absent in many other cultures, where urban living is more readily embraced. In Mesopotamian societies, in Mesoamerica, China and south-east Asia the city has been regarded as sacred, the gift of the gods to humanity. In the Judaeo-Christian world view, cities are oppositional to God, a necessary evil. This distinction runs through history.

And what happens to Babylon? In 1831, a few years after De Quincey published his *Confessions of an English Opium-Eater*, the most popular artist of his age, John Martin, produced a celebrated mezzotint called *The Fall of Babylon* based on his earlier painting of 1819. In it, the prostrate people of Babylon are dwarfed by the magnificent scale of the buildings and ziggurats, as they cower in the face of God's vengeance on their city. The public revelled in Martin's apocalyptic scenes; his melodramatic paintings of the destruction of cities such as Tyre, Sodom, Nineveh and Pompeii spoke powerfully to an anxious age experiencing hyper-rapid urbanisation. The city is inevitably fated to be destroyed by its all-consuming 'lust of domination', its heaps of sins and perversions, and for the chaos it has created.

The discovery of the ruins of Nineveh and Babylon itself in the nineteenth century brought added piquancy to these apocalyptic visions. Tales from Babylon – and the metaphor of Babylon – continued to grip publics around the world and shape how they understood their own cities. Here were the actual remains of once-mighty metropolises, every bit as splendid as the Bible and the Greeks said they were and as Bruegel and Martin had painted them. Nothing is forever. How long before London followed them and collapsed under the weight of its sins and the contradictions of its chaos?

The enduring power of the Bible influenced the great exponent of science fiction. H. G. Wells's 1908 novel *The War in the Air* is suffused with the language of biblical prophecy. This is particularly true of his attitude to the metropolis. In the novel, New York comes under devastating aerial attack. His description of the metropolis is inherited from the Hebrew Bible, via centuries of artistic embellishments. New York has, according to Wells, usurped London as 'the modern Babylon', becoming the centre of the world's trade, finance and pleasure. New York

> sat drinking up the wealth of a continent as Rome once drank the wealth of the Mediterranean and Babylon the wealth of the east. In her streets one found the extremes of magnificence and misery, of civilisation and disorder. In one quarter, palaces of marble, laced and crowned with light and flame and flowers; in another, a black and sinister polyglot population sweltered in indescribable congestion in warrens and excavations beyond the power and knowledge of government. Her vice, her crime, her law alike were inspired by a fierce and terrible energy.

What is interesting here is how Wells sees the modern city through a prism constructed by close to 3,000 years of biblical imagery; it is both attractive and repellent. But Babylon must fall. Wells describes with relish how prideful, lustful, multicultural New York is destroyed from the sky, just as Sodom and Gomorrah were obliterated in hails of brimstone. Like the babbling multi-ethnic Tower of Babel, the 'ethnic whirlpool' that is New York is condemned to violent dissolution.

It was fiction of course. But the New York that emerged in the 1920s was even more Babylonian. Its distinctive tiered skyscrapers were the Mesopotamian stepped ziggurats reborn. For its lifestyle and opulence as much as its skyscrapers, New York had the Babylonian title bestowed on it as liberally as London had a century before. Since Wells's fantasy New York has been wiped off the face of the earth in dozens of movies, including *When Worlds Collide* (1951), *Independence Day* (1996) and *The Avengers* (2012).

A few years after Wells's apocalyptic fantasy, another visitor shared the dream of razing New York. But he had a purpose. Le Corbusier did not see New York as the gleaming hyper-modern metropolis of the future. He saw so much clutter, confusion and senselessness. The city was too tangled; its skyscrapers were plonked willy-nilly without rational plan. The city might be 'overwhelming, amazing, exciting, violently alive' but it was chaotic and congested in every sense. For him, New Yorkers lived 'holed up like rats' amid 'sinister', 'pell-mell streets'. He wanted to clear away the dead old city that had been left 'to clutter up the pregnant present'. New York was not the future; but it pointed the way. Like a biblical prophet, Le Corbusier thought that Babylon had to be destroyed before the New Jerusalem could be built. Out of annihilation would come utopia.[25]

In the new New York 'glass skyscrapers would rise like crystals, clean and transparent in the midst of the foliage of trees'. For Le Corbusier it would be a 'fantastic, almost mystic city ... a vertical city, under the sign of new times'. Once the past was cleared away, a new rational metropolis would arise – the 'Radiant City' criss-crossed with raised freeways connecting high-rises set in verdant parkland. These new 'towers in the park' would truly be machines for living, working, shopping and playing; the high-rise Radiant City would give birth to a new urban utopia, liberating millions from Babylonian confusion.

The spontaneous New York was not levelled for the pre-planned radiant city. But Le Corbusier's ideas influenced generations of urban planners. After the Second World War the bulldozer was unleashed on cities all over the world, not just in war-damaged places but in metropolises unharmed by the bomber, such as in the United States. Very often it was the poorer districts of cities which were targeted for 'slum clearance' and 'urban renewal'. Settled, self-organising working-class communities were torn to pieces as Corbusian experiments in high-rise and highway living were tested out on them. These districts looked messy and ugly. The idea of the city as a wild and dangerous place courses through religion, politics and culture, from De Quincey's portrayal of the city as evil and Dickensian descriptions of urban depravity, to Hollywood film noir, which depicts the city as a place saturated with all-pervasive corruption and on to John B. Calhoun's experiments in his rat city. The urge to tear down Babylon and start again is infectious.

In China's recent mass urbanisation, the dense, congested cores of cities such as Beijing and Shanghai were bulldozed and their residents relocated to suburban high-rises. It was done in the name of creating glimmering, tidy cities that look and feel modern and ordered. In cities such as Mumbai and Lagos, informal settlements are targeted for demolition in an effort to give the cities the sheen of global metropolises. The idea that a scientifically engineered built environment can free us all from the jumble of the irrational overgrown urban chaos remains potent.

But what else gives cities their 'anarchic enterprise' and their 'fierce and terrible energy' (in H. G. Wells's words) but their chaos and confusion? Calhoun's urbanised rats may have descended into violence and viciousness under the pressures of high density, but humans are much more adaptable. Great metropolises are built on layers of history and myriad internal contradictions. No one knows how they really work, for all the theorising that has gone on over the millennia. They look so vulnerable and out of control, defying logic and on the brink of anarchy and collapse. They are powered by our lusts, vices and selfishness as much as they are by our rational brains and good intentions. They are scary and unfathomable, just as they are uplifting and inspiring. They are big, bad, ruthless places; but they are successful and powerful. They have sex shops and opera houses, cathedrals and casinos, peep shows and picture galleries. Sure, we want good sewers and fewer prostitutes; but a purified city is one that loses its electric spark. The coarseness, contrasts and conflicts of a city give it its intense excitement and pulsating energy. It needs the grime as much as it needs the sanitation. Places of low morals and even lower dives, of glamour and wealth, it is the discordant and disquieting character of big cities that gives them energy. The city is utopia and dystopia at the same time.

3

Cosmopolis

Athens and Alexandria, 507–30 BC

Singapore, New York, Los Angeles, Amsterdam, London, Toronto, Vancouver, Auckland and Sydney have this in common: between 35% and 51% of their residents are foreign-born. These global powerhouses are dwarfed by Brussels, with 62% born outside the country, and Dubai with 83%.

These figures alone don't tell the full story about diversity. They don't stipulate what proportion of the city's population are the children or grandchildren of immigrants, for example; nor do they give an indication of the range of nationalities or their status within the city. A minority of Dubai's foreign-born residents consist of small groups of highly skilled, wealthy people from all over the world; but the majority are overwhelmingly low-paid workers from Pakistan, India, Bangladesh, Sri Lanka and the Philippines. In contrast, Toronto's immigrant population – 51% of the total – originates from 230 nationalities, with no one group dominating. A further 29% of Toronto's residents have at least one parent who was born outside Canada.

The dynamism of cities is, to a large extent, the result of continual influxes of ideas, goods and people. Successful cities throughout history have been characterised by the legions of incomers knocking at the city gates. Not only do expatriate residents import new ideas and ways of doing things, but they bring with them connections to their homelands. Port cities have been innovative because, even if they did not have a large permanent expatriate population, they were places that connected to other places, the temporary resort for people and things that circulated across the globe. The stunning success of Athens in the fifth century BC was in large part ascribed to its openness to outside influences and that over a third of its free population were foreign-born. As was said of the Athenians' compulsive eclecticism: 'hearing every kind of dialect, they have taken something from each; other Greeks rather tend to use their own dialect, way of life, and type of dress, but the Athenians use a mixture from all the Greeks and barbarians'.[1]

When asked where he came from, the Greek philosopher Diogenes replied that he was *kosmopolites*, a citizen of the world. Uttered in the fourth century BC, it was a radical statement in an age of fiercely xenophobic city states. Plato's *Republic* opens in the home of a *metic* – a foreign-born resident of Athens – situated in Athens's port district, Piraeus, thus associating philosophical inquiry with immigration, trade, commerce and the wider world outside the city.[2]

This urbane setting in the most cosmopolitan district of Greece's most cosmopolitan metropolis points to what made Greek urban civilisation, and Athens in particular, so innovative. This was a new type of urbanisation – the urbanisation of the seafarer. The geography of the Mediterranean littoral – with its overlapping cultures, its criss-crossing trade routes and circulatory system of ideas – saw the creation of markedly different cities from those that had developed for millennia further inland. The Greeks were heirs of a process of city-building that originated in south-west Asia. In Greek mythology the princess Europa was abducted from the Levantine coast by Zeus and taken to Crete. The story mythologises the reality: south-west Asian and Egyptian urbanisation was transmitted to Crete not by lusty Zeus, but by seafarers from the Levantine port of Byblos.

Standing at the crossroads connecting Egypt, Mesopotamia and the Mediterranean, the port of Byblos in modern-day Lebanon was one of the great gateway cities of the ancient world. Famous for its exports of papyrus, the city's name gave the Greeks the word for book – *biblios* – from which we get the Bible. The mercantile Canaanite people of Byblos supplied the two great civilisations of Mesopotamia and Egypt with other commodities, including the coveted cedar of Mount Lebanon. They were a restless, seafaring people. Sailors from Byblos pushed out west into the Mediterranean in the early second millennium BC, reaching Crete. A new urban civilisation, the first in the continent that would later take its name from Europa, took root there around 2700 BC, its people known to us as the Minoans. In turn, the

Minoans exported the concept of the city to mainland Europe, to the Mycenaeans of Greece.

The sea circulated goods and ideas. But the waves also brought danger. From about 1200 BC the mysterious Sea Peoples devastated the Mediterranean civilisations. The Mycenaean civilisation was swept away by this confederation of rootless pirates, leaving the ruins of palaces. Later generations of Greeks venerated their ancestors as the heroes of the Trojan wars. Greece entered what is called its 'Dark Age', a period of fragmentation and smaller-scale communities.

This disruption and the collapse of cities unleashed a new wave of urbanisation. The port cities of the Levant occupied a narrow strip of land between the Mediterranean and the mountains in today's Turkey, Syria, Lebanon and Israel. The people were known as the Phoenicians, although Phoenicia was not a kingdom or single entity, but rather a confederation of Semitic city states united by language, culture, religion and a ruthless sense of business. Byblos, Tyre and Sidon were the three main centres. The prophet Isaiah wrote that Tyre was 'the crowning city, whose merchants are princes and whose traders are the honoured ones of the earth'. Cities like Tyre were small in size of area and population (about 40,000). But they packed a bigger punch than states many times their size.

Excellent navigators, sailors and entrepreneurs, the Phoenicians pushed further into the western Mediterranean than anyone else. In their voyages they carried with them the seeds of future cities from south-west Asia. The urban world exploded onto the European and African coast with the proliferation of Phoenician trading stations and colonies. The most famous of them was called 'New Town', built in what is now Tunisia as a replica of Tyre and populated with its expatriate citizens. New Town is better known as Carthage, a Phoenician franchise that, centuries later, grew to contest with Rome for control of the Mediterranean. The Phoenicians set up trading stations in Italy, Sicily and Iberia; they passed through the Pillars of Hercules into the Atlantic, trading along the coast of Morocco. The future cities of Cadiz and Lisbon originated as Phoenician emporia. They exchanged olive oil, perfumes, scented oils, textiles and jewellery for other precious items to sell in the far distant markets of Nineveh and Babylon: silver, gold, tin, copper, lead, ivory, salted fish, whale products – and the murex snail.

The snail was the great treasure that lured the merchant adventurers into the unknown immensity of the Atlantic. The snail's mucus produces a dye known as 'Tyrian purple', the priceless colour of royalty lusted after by the rulers and high priests of Babylon and other great cities. In order to dye just the trim of a garment you would need to painstakingly extract the secretions of 12,000 snails; no wonder that an ounce of the stuff was worth at least twenty times more than an ounce of gold. The purchasing power of the Mesopotamian metropolises pushed the Phoenicians into the Atlantic, leaving a string of urban settlements in their 2,000-mile wake, on the hunt for the snail.

The Greeks did not like the Phoenicians very much. Homer tells of how Odysseus was almost cheated out of his fortune and his life by an unscrupulous Phoenician merchant. The Greeks saw the far-roving seafaring citizens of Tyre, Byblos and Sidon as rivals to be outcompeted at all costs. But the Phoenicians gave the Greeks two incomparable gifts.

Rather than using clumsy and time-consuming hieroglyphs and cuneiform, the hard-nosed Phoenician businessmen developed letters. The Phoenician alphabet – the first of its kind – was the pared-down, efficient script of merchants on the move; it became the basis of Greek, Latin and pretty much all alphabetic scripts in the world since. It spread as the tentacles of their trading empire reached along the North African coast towards the Atlantic and grasped up into the Aegean. There, interactions between merchants bequeathed it to the Greeks sometime between 800 BC and 750 BC.

The adoption by the Greeks of their own script had profound implications for urbanisation. Settlers from mainland Greece pushed out to the Aegean islands and the coast of Asia Minor, founding new cities such as Phocaea, Miletus and Ephesus. They brought with them their myths, histories, songs, plays, sports and rituals – the things that would bind them across great distances so that they retained their Greek identity. They also took with them a fiercely competitive spirit – particularly in regard to their trading rivals, the Phoenicians. Like the Phoenicians, the Greek cities set about planting hundreds of replica cities from the Crimea to Cadiz, imbued with the same ethos and self-governance as their mother city – their metropolis – and integrated into the urban network.[3]

A story illustrates this process. Greeks from the city of Phocaea, a large metropolis on the coast of modern-day Turkey, looking to found a trading emporium chanced upon a cove fed by a freshwater stream in what is now the south of France. They arrived just as the chief of the local Ligurian tribe was holding a banquet to find a husband for his daughter. No doubt impressed by the exotic visitors, the girl presented the ceremonial drinking cup to the leader of the Greek colonists, signalling her choice of husband. The fruit of their union was the city that is now called Marseilles.[4]

In seventh-century BC southern Italy, Etruscan traders came into contact with Greek colonists. As a result the Etruscan tribes began to build their own city states in the Po Valley and in the region that became Tuscany. A little further south, on the river Tiber, the Latin speakers who lived on a settlement of huts on the Palatine Hill drained the swampy valley below them and began to fill it with tons of earth. The Latins were influenced by their Etruscan neighbours and by Greek traders, who may have established a small colony below the Palatine Hill. Their city, which they called Rome, was not the result of slow evolution from village to town to city: it was the result of ideas that arrived by ship from across the Mediterranean.

Greek civilisation evolved within a constellation of 1,000 Greek cities that perched on coasts and islands throughout the Mediterranean, as Plato memorably put it, like frogs round a pond. The intermingling of Greeks and a host of diverse peoples – as the cases of Marseilles and Rome illustrate – opened the Greek mind to cultures the length and breadth of the Mediterranean. In Anatolia they drew upon Asian ideas and techniques; they were open to Phoenician, Mesopotamian, Persian and Egyptian influences, and the traditions of the many peoples among whom they settled. It was no accident that the intellectual heat of the Greek cosmos was generated in the Ionian cities of western Anatolia, porous metropolises with links to Asia. The works of Hecataeus and Herodotus evince intense curiosity about other cultures, the product of a civilisation that lived alongside so many other different peoples in the jagged Mediterranean littoral, borrowing and improving their theories of navigation, astronomy, medicine and philosophy. Democritus, famous for formulating the atomic theory of the universe, was born in Thrace and spent his life on the move, travelling between the Greek cities and into Asia and Egypt before settling in Athens.

At the heart of Greek society was the *polis*. It is the root of words connoting things urban – 'metropolis', 'metropolitan' and 'cosmopolitan' – as well as those to do with the organisation of human society itself – 'polity', 'politics' and 'political'. Political philosophy has its roots in the search for the rational city. *Polis* could simply be understood as 'city' or 'city state'; but its full definition as the Greeks understood the word cannot be translated so neatly. Put simply, the *polis* was a political, religious, military and economic community of free (male) citizens organised within an urban environment.[5]

The *polis* in its political sense does not exist in the epics of Homer, composed in the eighth/seventh centuries BC, but it was widely understood by the sixth. In other words, it came into use during the period of Greek expansion. It is possible that Greek colonists far from home developed the notion of autonomous communities of citizens as they worked together to set up cities in hostile lands, and it was re-exported back to Greece. Or it may have been the result of rapid urbanisation at home and abroad, an answer to a problem. The creation of a *polis* was called *synoecism* – 'the bringing together of households'.[6]

When he wrote that 'a human being is by nature a political animal', Aristotle did not necessarily mean we love the nitty-gritty of political drama. A better translation might be that we are by nature 'a city animal': we tend to coalesce together to satisfy our needs and form culture. For the Greeks, the city was the natural state of humankind and a sacred thing in itself. In fact, it was infinitely superior to nature because it alone provided the conditions for the good life and justice. In Greek thought the *polis* was not primarily a physical place; it was a community. Greeks referred to 'the Athenians' when they talked of the city rather than saying 'Athens'. It is a telling distinction.

Deeply embedded in Greek self-identity was not only a relish for city life, but also the notion of personal independence and a hatred of living in thrall to authority. Most Greek city states overthrew their kings in the ninth and eighth centuries BC. Participation in the *polis*'s institutions made Greeks see themselves as freer and more fully human than barbarians. Greeks shared not only language and culture, they told themselves, but a unique way of inhabiting cities that united them whether they lived on the coast of the Black Sea or Spain; 'there is only one Hellas,' said the poet Poseidippos, 'but there are many *poleis*'.[7]

The Greek world was not an empire controlled from the centre; it was a civilisation made up of hundreds of self-governing *poleis* – with citizen populations ranging from 1,000 to 50,000. They were sites within which theories about how one was to live in cities were put to the test. They took the forms of oligarchies, monarchies, dictator-ships, aristocracies and democracies; they changed in response to new needs and threats. This period of intense experimentation in numerous urban laboratories laid the foundation for political thought. It also had a durable impact on the physical city.

*

The murder of a fifteen-year-old boy, Alexandros Grigoropoulos, by police brought thousands of people into the streets of Athens in protest. In December 2008 the city experienced violent rioting and looting in response. In the aftermath of the riots, and at the onset of the Greek financial crisis, a group of activists peacefully occupied a former car park at the heart of the Exarcheia district in central Athens, near the spot where Alexandros was gunned down.

The plot had been set aside to be converted into a public space in 1990. But the city government had failed to purchase it by 2009, and it was slated for development. The occupiers immediately ripped up the car park's asphalt and planted trees and flowers; they organised a celebratory public event and some remained to guard Navarinou Park against the authorities. In the months and years that followed, the neighbourhood convened to decide what the park should be. It has become a green jewel in the heart of Athens, a place for play, recrea-tion and relaxation, public discussions and host to numerous public events.[8]

The story of Navarinou Park was part of a wider global movement in which protestors reclaimed and repurposed public spaces and build-ings in cities throughout the world. In 2011 protestors occupied Tahrir Square in Cairo and the Puerto del Sol plaza in Madrid. The Occupy Wall Street Movement set up camp in Zuccotti Park in New York and similar Occupy protests broke out in cities across the world. In 2013 demonstrators camped out for months in Gezi Park, Istanbul.

All these examples of anger at authority had numerous and different causes. But they also had much in common. They tell us a lot about how cities have changed over recent decades. In many ways, societies have become more introverted, with private space taking priority over shared, civic space. The post-9/11 era has made security and surveillance a key feature of city centres, places where movement and activities are monitored. Across the planet, public areas have in many cases been privatised, sanitised and regulated. Malls, shopping centres, financial districts and shopping streets are neither fully public nor private, but something in between. The occupation and transformation of Navarinou Park – and other car parks and buildings in Athens – came after a long period when public space in the city had been eroded. The Turkish protests of 2013 were sparked because President Recep Tayyip Erdoğan's government wanted to bulldoze one of the last remaining green parks in Istanbul and replace it with a shopping mall. Tahrir Square – which means 'Liberation Square' – has been the focal point for numerous protests over the years. But under the regime of President Hosni Mubarak 'public space' equated with 'government space': places that were under strict discipline and where anything smacking of politics was banned.

People of divergent religious and political opinions and different backgrounds and income came together in Tahrir Square. 'The square was gradually transformed into a city within a city. In three days, camping areas, media rooms, medical facilities, gateways, stages, restrooms, food and beverage carts, newspaper booths, and art exhibitions were established.' Every day, the protestors were diverted with 'concerts, competitions, discussions, speeches from major media figures'. Occupations in squares and parks across the globe were self-consciously a critique of the contemporary metropolis, and an attempt to recreate a kind of ideal, utopian city within the existing city – places where political dissent and discussion rub shoulders with performance, satire, food, recreation, markets and social interaction – at a time when urban public life appeared to have subordinated to the needs of security, cars and commerce.[9]

Temporarily occupying places close to the epicentre of financial power (as at Zuccotti Park) or political power (Tahrir Square) and transforming them into sites of democratic protest served ideological ends. In Gezi Park people highlighted the wider ways that Istanbul was being changed contrary to the will of its citizens. But in many places urban areas have been transformed by their residents because they want to reinject public life into the heart of the metropolis. In Madrid, residents of the La Latina neighbourhood took over a building site and decided on how it should be used. During the summer, El Campo de Cebada (the Barley Field), as it was renamed, is filled with inflatable pools; there are neighbourhood meetings, twice-weekly debates, citizens' breakfast clubs, plays and open-air cinema screenings; residents set up a basketball court and established gardens. For decades in Hong Kong, thousands of Filipina migrant domestic workers have filled the streets every Sunday around the city's banks, designer shops and five-star hotels to picnic, dance, socialise and protest. A different sort of city emerges for a few hours as the city's poorest, least secure people take temporary possession of the lustrous financial centre and adapt it for their own ends.

Public space is contested space. In autocratic regimes – from Mesopotamian metropolises to medieval monarchies to communist states – open areas in city centres have been used primarily or exclusively for displays of state power and military might, arenas of spectacle rather than participation. In cities influenced by Confucianism, public space was sacred, governed by rituals of obligation, leaving little room for everyday social interaction. Irritated at having to bow continually to nobles riding horses on Jong-ro, Seoul's main road, ordinary folk retreated to the narrow alleys parallel to the main thoroughfares during the Joseon dynasty (1392–1897). Known as Pimagol – 'Avoid-Horse-Street' – these cramped passages, with their restaurants and shops, became places to gather, talk and mingle – an unofficial public space away from the rules that governed the official part of the metropolis.[10]

Street activity is integral to the public nature of cities. Yet there has always been a tension between the different uses of the street. Is it a place of community socialising, business, sitting, strolling and play? Or is it for circulation of traffic and social control? That tension exists throughout the history of cities. For Jane Jacobs, the mixed-use, pedestrian-dominated neighbourhood street lay at the very heart of urbanity. As she powerfully articulated, the spontaneous order produced in cities was built up from the myriad daily activities and interactions at street level. She was writing in the 1950s and 60s, when the vibrancy of Manhattan's sidewalk life was under threat from urban expressways. Nothing was more deadening to the vitality of the sociable street than the advent of the motor car. The fightback against this encroachment on urban public space is, however, part of the wider battle for the soul of the city in the twenty-first century.

Public space is common ground, accessible to all, where civic society takes form. Cities have been laboratories of political experimentation and occasionally places of radical change; that is why the right to access the city has been so passionately contested. What distinguished the ancient Greek *poleis* from cities that had come before them – and which makes them so vital in the history of urbanisation – is the way the political development of the *polis* sculpted the physical layout of the city. The Greek word for 'I shop' – *agorázō* – and 'I speak in public' – *agoreúzō* – come from the word 'agora'. The beating heart of the *polis*, the agora was the place where the collective energy of the *polis* – its commerce, entertainment, gossip, legal proceedings and politics – fused together in a babble of conversation. You would see and hear dancing and singing in one part of the agora; in another a sword swallower, vying for attention with a juggler. On rows of tables set out in the sun, the city's bankers transacted their daily business, straining to be heard over the cries of fishmongers and fruit sellers. Shops and tented market stores provided all a civilised person could want. In China, Mesoamerica, Babylonia, Egypt and Mesopotamia, by contrast, the heart of the city was a place for the enactment of sacred authority, not for people.

The poet Eubulos captured the gloriously jumbled nature of the Athenian agora's public and private, political and commercial life: 'You will find everything sold together in the same place at Athens: figs, witnesses to summonses, bunches of grapes, turnips, pears, apples, givers of evidence, roses, medlars, porridge, honeycombs, chickpeas, lawsuits, first milk, puddings, myrtle, allotment machines, irises, lambs, waterclocks, laws, indictments.' In *The Clouds*, Aristophanes jokes that Athenians went to the agora to make 'rude jokes about other people's sex lives'. They also discussed the news and the political affairs of the city. Talk and the sharing of information in public – from adulteries to administration – were integral to urban life.[11]

The site of the thirty-seven-acre Athenian agora had been cleared by the populist tyrant Peisistratus and his son Hippias, who ruled for much of the time between 561 and 510 BC, intended for the kind of self-glorifying buildings that adorn dictatorships. Under Cleisthenes, the radical aristocrat who seized power in 507 BC, the agora got a more democratic, if chaotic appearance. Under the sway of democracy, market stalls and shops were invited into the hallowed precinct. Colonnades known as *stoa* offered respite from the summer sun and the winds of winter. New civic buildings appeared, including the council house and the courts. Civic government mingled and merged with the grubby, workaday hubbub of the community.[12]

Most Greek *poleis* were small face-to-face societies where everyone knew each other. Athens – with 40,000–50,000 adult male citizens out of a total population of 250,000 – was of a different magnitude. Under Cleisthenes' radical reforms, the ancient tribal society of Attica had been violently pulled apart; in its place came ten artificial civic tribes – purged of clan and local loyalties. This democratic *polis* was a city of strangers who were being asked to cooperate in the running of the state. A system of such complexity was made to work by changing the very fabric of the city.

The 500 members of the council, chosen every year by lot from the entire citizen body, sat in their own building in the agora. From here the city was administered behind the building's high walls. The courts, however, were entirely different. The courthouse was roofless and had a low wall. Every citizen was entitled to sit as a juror, and they were chosen by lot for the daily round of cases. A jury consisted of at least 201 citizens for a normal trial, but for a state trial the minimum was 501 and it could go as high as the capacity of the building, 1,500. The court was deliberately open to the swirl and drama of the agora; lawsuits certainly provided topics for the endless discussions in the square as people milled in and out of the building. Conversation, courtroom and commerce all collided and coexisted in the city, the casual shading seamlessly into the official; the result was to weave the citizen's public and private lives together so they were almost indistinguishable. The man who had no public business, the saying went, had no business being in the city.

In most *poleis* the citizens' assembly took place in the agora. The sheer scale of the Athenian democratic experiment entailed an innovation in the city's political topography. Ten minutes' walk from the agora, at the foot of a bowl-shaped hill, workmen had cut steps into a rock, creating a platform. The hill became an auditorium capable of (just about) holding 6,000 citizens; everyone had the right to stand on the speakers' platform and address his fellow citizens. This, the meeting place of the Athenian assembly, was called the Pnyx. Its creation in 507 BC, at the onset of Cleisthenes' reforms, established in physical form the reality of popular sovereignty and mass participation.[13]

At the meetings the citizens had the final say on legislation; elected and held to account the city's magistrates and generals; and voted on foreign policy, military matters and the internal business of the city. A quorum of 6,000 was required for the assembly's regular business, so the hillside would have been filled to capacity once a week to debate and ratify public business. The name of this arena, Pnyx, means 'tightly packed together'. In such a large *polis*, where public responsibilities were shared between strangers, the importance of personal and public visibility and transparency could not be overstated. The Pynx allowed people to see how their fellow citizens were reacting to a speech, how they voted, how they conducted themselves.

The Athenian general and statesman Pericles, in his famous oration made in 431 BC, urged his fellow citizens to love their city. But he was not using 'love' in a casually general sense or even as a kind of patriotic fervour. The precise meaning of his 'love' was *erastai*, the erotic passion felt between lovers.[14]

All Greeks had a passionate attachment to their city. Male citizens were expected to fight and die for their *polis*. Competitors at the Olympic Games represented their *polis*; attachment to your city was the bedrock of personal identity and, as Pericles hints at, deeply emotional. How else could a *polis* work? In a world long dominated by tyrants, priests and warrior aristocrats, self-government was a new idea in human affairs; Athenian democracy was even more radical. The creation of public space helped foster the collective energy needed to make the city work. There were the institutions of municipal republicanism; there were also gymnasia, theatres and stadiums, places where people could meet and mingle. But the kind of passion Pericles talked about was generated by other means. A critic of democracy complained that Athens's public business frequently ground to a halt because 'they have to hold more festivals than any other Greek city'. One day out of every three of the Athenian calendar saw a street party, procession, sporting event or religious rite.

The Panathenaea, 'the festival of all the Athenians', was the most lavish and sacred occasion in the calendar and the event that brought the city into euphoric unity. Just as exciting – if not more so – was the 'Dionysia' held in the spring. All sections of Athenian society took part, many carrying food, oversized loaves and enormous wine skins for the feasting that would come later. The male citizens carried phalluses made of wood, gold and bronze on poles, or enormous erect penises pulled by cart. After the procession there were fiercely competitive choral contests between large groups of citizen singers. These were wild and ecstatic songs and dances in honour of Dionysus that included 500 participants at a time. There followed feasting and a night-time procession known as the *komos*, a disorderly masked and costumed revel through the torchlit streets until the early hours.

Just as the hangover was kicking in, the main event of the Dionysia took place. From 440 BC it happened at the *odeon* or song hall built by Pericles. There, the senior magistrate introduced the three playwrights who had been selected to compete over the coming days. Each playwright had to put on three serious tragedies and a bawdy, taboo-breaking, prank-filled satire. In the days that followed, the plays were performed back to back in the Theatre of Dionysus. Over the decades, audiences witnessed the premieres of seminal plays by the likes of Aeschylus, Euripides, Aristophanes and Sophocles.

'The road to Athens is a pleasant one,' wrote the philosopher Dicaearchus of his approach to the fabled city of philosophers, poets and statesmen, 'running between cultivated fields the whole way.' But the city itself had a poor water supply. The streets were 'miserable old lanes' and the houses were predominantly mean and shabby, even those of the rich. Any first-time visitor, remarked an appalled Dicaearchus, 'would hardly believe that this is the Athens of which he has heard so much'. Archaeology backs him up: houses were roughly constructed, small and dingy. They were crammed together, slum-like, with very narrow streets and blind alleys. There was no drainage system, so rainwater ran down the potholed streets.

Athens was very cramped and very intimate. Private life was subordinated far below public life. The jumble of the streets and the bedlam of the agora thrust all kinds of people together. The organic growth of Athens, irrational and higgledy-piggledy as it was, might have been one of its greatest strengths. Athenians, Herodotus tells us, had 'shirked and slacked' under tyranny. But after Cleisthenes and the advent of democracy, he continued, they became a great power: 'Not just in one field, but in everything they set their minds to, they gave vivid proof of what equality and freedom of speech might achieve.' In order to make it work, democracy and its workings had to be fetishised. Free expression and limitless inquiry into the meaning of life are supremely challenging for human societies because they are dangerous and destabilising. But it was accepted because it *worked*. Athens was riding high in the fifth century BC, an economic, military and imperial powerhouse. In a city on the make, humming with ideas and unafraid to make daring experiments, philosophy had tangible benefits.

Writing much later, Cicero observed that Socrates applied philosophy to 'ordinary life' by 'directing his inquiries to virtues and vices'. General truths about the human condition could be discovered in the messy, tangled lives of 'ordinary' people. The street and the market provided exactly that sort of insight – particularly the warren of Athens with its culture of open-air association. Socrates frequented the Kerameikos neighbourhood of Athens – the down-at-heel district of potters and prostitutes. Because young men were not allowed into the agora, he hung around the workshops on its fringes, where artisans went about their business and shoemakers banged nails into leather sandals. He exercised at the inferior Cynosarges gymnasium outside the city walls, in which 'bastard citizens', boys and men who had one foreign-born parent, were allowed to exercise. Socrates moved about the city, asking questions and getting into discussions with the people he encountered, the high and the low, freemen, women and slaves; when he was old enough, he talked in front of crowds in the agora.

The young Socrates encountered the philosopher Parmenides, and his companion Zeno, in the seedy Kerameikos district, where they were staying. These thinkers had travelled from southern Italy. Athens had not been renowned for its literary endeavours, philosophers or scientists: much of the intellectual and artistic energy of Greece came from Asia Minor and other colonies. Upstart Athens – with its experimental democracy, military successes and burgeoning wealth – attracted people from all over the Hellenic world. The fathers of history and medicine – Herodotus and Hippocrates – were resident aliens drawn to Athens, as were the scientist Anaxagoras, the political theorist Protagoras, the mathematician Theodorus, the rhetorician

Gorgias, the poet Simonides and the philosopher Aristotle. Many more foreign-born people contributed skills as sculptors, artists, craftsmen, engineers and merchants. 'Our city is thrown open to the world,' boasted Pericles. 'Because of the greatness of our city the fruits of the whole earth flow in upon us; so that we enjoy the goods of other countries as freely as our own.'

The dynamism of Athens in the first half of the fifth century BC was in large part a result of a citizen population that rocketed from around 30,000 in 480 BC to 50,000 by 450 BC, the result of immigration and the sudden injection of fresh thinking. The cosmopolitan atmosphere that Socrates encountered on his peregrinations through the city had come about because Athens allowed access, through its public spaces and open institutions, to an array of newly minted citizens. The congested, intimate urban environment facilitated the circulation and exchange of ideas; its cocktail of politics, philosophy, art, retail and business at street level gave it its remarkable effervescence.

Things changed in the middle of the century. In 451–450 BC Pericles' Citizen Laws created a new category, the free resident alien, or *metic*. In response to immigration, the rights of citizenship were restricted to those born to two Athenian citizens. Immigrants were still welcome – they were needed to power the city – but newcomers and their descendants could no longer participate in the political process or enjoy property rights; they could not now intermarry with the 'indigenous' population. The citizens of Athens accounted for just 15% of the total population. And even among this hallowed elite there would have been a significant number who were poor and marginalised. (There is much in common between the Athens of the fifth century BC and the Dubai of today. In the Gulf city, just 15% of the population is native-born. It has its own version of *metics* – privileged expatriates who enjoy the right of making money and spending it. And then there is a vast pool of poor and insecure migrants who build the city and service the manifold needs of its wealthy inhabitants. In Athens, as in Dubai, there were two cities: the city of the citizen and the city of the marginalised.[15])

Women in Athens were uneducated, and if they were wealthy and respectable they were kept secluded from the rest of society. Women would have been part of the hubbub in the agora, but they would have been slaves, *metics* and from the lower orders, buying, selling and running errands. The festivities and private symposia included women, but they were dancing girls and prostitutes who were at the beck and call of men. This was a male city, and a city in which men actively suppressed women.

Athens's golden years did not last long. Increasingly high-handed in its attitude to foreigners at home and abroad, it made enemies. In 430 BC plague swept through the city. The epidemic entered Athens, the crossroads of the ancient Mediterranean, through its busy port of Piraeus and ravaged the city, its progress hastened by abysmal sanitation, overcrowding and the habit of incessant mingling. Between a third and two-thirds of the population succumbed. Decades of war followed. In 404 BC – barely a century after Cleisthenes' reforms had propelled it to greatness – Athens's power was gone and its constitution abolished.

*

'Every city', wrote Plato, 'is in a natural war with every other, not indeed proclaimed by heralds, but everlasting.' The long-standing competitiveness between city states had sharpened them into some of the greatest cities known to history. But a jarring, sparring collection of dispersed city states brings great weakness. War between *polis* and *polis* was endemic. As a unit of government, the independent city state offered its citizens plenty of benefits. But ultimately it could not defend them from big, heavily populated territorial powers.

Philip of Macedon swept through Greece, crushing the last independent city states by 338 BC. Under his son, Greek ideas and cities continued their advance – this time deep into Asia. Alexander the Great subdued the Persian Empire. He took Babylon. He marched to India. Along the way, from the Balkans to the Punjab, dozens of new cities were founded by Greek colonists and army veterans that bore the ideological and physical stamps of the ancient *polis*. The amphibious city state was crawling inland.

Greeks absorbed ancient learning in such places as Babylon and the Persian city of Susa. Perhaps the most intriguing example of Hellenic hybridisation occurred in the Graeco-Bactrian kingdom that emerged long after Alexander's death. Stretching from the Caspian Sea through

The winds that gusted in Alexandria's diverse population also brought the greatest scholars of the age, most notably Euclid and Archimedes. Their fellow scholars in Alexandria included two other great thinkers, the mathematician and astronomer Conon of Samos and Eratosthenes of Cyrene. Herophilus of Chalcedon altered how humans understood their bodies. Before him, the heart was considered to be the controlling organ of the body, as Aristotle had argued; but Herophilus identified it as the brain, tracing its connection to the spinal cord and the nervous system. In a similar way, work on astronomy and geography over the centuries culminated in the break-throughs made by Claudius Ptolemy in Alexandria in the first century AD. As with Euclid in the field of mathematics and geometry, Ptolemy's teaching would dominate human understanding of the universe for over a millennium and a half.

They came to Alexandria because it was the only depository of *all* written works. Ptolemy I and his successors consciously set out to make Alexandria the greatest city the world had ever seen. Key to that ambition was to make it an unparalleled intellectual and research centre. Armed with limitless reserves of cash, agents of the Ptolemies scoured the known world for any and every scroll they could lay their hands on. Under the direction of Demetrius of Phalerum – an exiled Athenian statesman and a former pupil of Aristotle – the Alexandrian Library began to systematically organise the world's knowledge for the first time. The grammarian Zenodotus came from Ephesus to edit the extant texts of Homer. Callimachus, prolific poet and writer, was summoned from Cyrene to organise and catalogue Greek literature. The great works of poetry, science and philosophy that might other-wise have been lost were archived for posterity within the palatial precincts of the museum.

Athens and Alexandria provide the supreme examples of two very different cities. The irregular outline of the Athenian cityscape and its open culture encouraged street-level discussion and debate. According to Plato, Socrates did not write anything down because he saw philosophy as something that was conducted in dialogue with fellow citizens, in the public places of the city. Alexandria, in contrast, with its rational, rectilinear street plan, is portrayed as regimented, where ideas were imprisoned in institutions away from the life of the city. If Athens was spontaneous and experimental, Alexandria had an encyclopaedic and conformist mindset. Athens triumphed in philosophy, politics and theatre; Alexandria in science, mathematics, geometry, mechanics and medicine.

But if Alexandria was expressly designed to control its populace and to advertise ultimate power, it could not do so indefinitely. The Alexandrian crowd became less biddable as time went on, rowdier and more vocal. The Egyptian metropolis was not imprisoned by its gridiron structure; it took on a life of its own as a place of serious learning as well as of notoriously hedonistic excess and urban tumult. The cosmopolitanism of this imperial megacity gave it a distinct intellectual character. Athens was bonded together because it turned itself into a super-tribe, united by love of city, militant patriotism, democratic participation and racial exclusivity. Alexandria was in its vastness and diversity more like a microcosm of the world. The tolerance of innovative thinking – as long as it did not stray into dangerous philosophical or political speculation – brought minds from all over the known world into contact with other minds. The compilers, collators and editor of the Library were not hidebound by nativist ideas of what did and did not constitute culture and knowledge. They feasted on Babylonian, Phoenician, Egyptian and Hebrew texts (among others), as well as Greek.

Alexandria teemed with human life; it was a true cosmopolis, a city of 500,000 people and a hybrid of different races and traditions held together by autocracy. It permitted and encouraged the collision of cultures and civilisations in a way that was unknown on such a scale anywhere else and which would have been impossible in a participatory democracy suspicious of outsiders. Its intoxicating exoticism became an irresistible lure for the rising world superpower.

As Roman power advanced inexorably through the Mediterranean, the Ptolemies went into decline. In turn, Alexandria would play a crucial role in the political crisis that gripped Rome. The heady influences of the city acted like a narcotic on the minds of a succession of Roman statesmen. When Julius Caesar intervened in the Ptolemaic civil war, he not only encountered a mysterious culture and the wealthiest city in the world, but fell in love. Not a great beauty perhaps; but Cleopatra was the true daughter of the city of Alexandria. Witty, supremely well educated and fluent in Greek, Latin, Hebrew, Ethiopic, Aramaic and Egyptian, her tongue was, as Plutarch wrote, 'like an instrument of many strings'.

Looking back on their history, Romans later believed that Cleopatra and Alexandria had bewitched their greatest men and spurred on the death of their republic. Caesar not only fell in love with Cleopatra, but became intrigued by the hybrid Hellenistic and Egyptian culture he found there. Not least was the concept of divine monarchy. After the assassination of Caesar in 44 BC and the ensuing civil wars, Cleopatra sided with Mark Antony, one of the three allies of Caesar who ruled Rome. Cleopatra and Antony became lovers in Alexandria in the winter of 41–40 BC, a season of non-stop parties, banquets and orgies. 'It would be tedious to chronicle Antony's many follies in Alexandria,' sighed an appalled Plutarch. Like Caesar before him, Antony succumbed to the fabulous luxury of the great city. He ruled the eastern part of the Roman Empire from Alexandria; the western part of the empire meanwhile was under the control of Caesar's adopted son, Octavian. Rome watched with horror and repugnance as Antony immersed himself in the political world of Alexandria and set about creating a new Asian empire. Fully Alexandrianised, Antony was hailed as the living god Dionysus; Cleopatra was worshipped as the reincarnation of Aphrodite and the Egyptian goddess Isis. The final straw came with the Donations of Alexandria, proclamations which divided portions of the Eastern Empire between Cleopatra and her children: her son with Julius Caesar, and the three children she had had with Antony.

The Roman senate refused to ratify these outrageous plans. Octavian, for his part, would not countenance the legitimisation of Caesar's and Cleopatra's son because it would make the Alexandrian boy pharaoh heir to the Roman world. Look at Antony, his enemies said, with his pretensions to oriental divinity and his love for Alexandria over Rome. Rome fell into civil war and Alexandria played a pivotal part in it. When Octavian defeated Antony at the battle of Actium in 31 BC, Antony and Cleopatra fled to their last refuge, the great Ptolemaic metropolis. It was there, in 30 BC, with Octavian's army taking control of the city, that they committed suicide. Egypt lost its independence and became part of the Roman Empire; Alexandria was reduced from imperial capital to one of several large cities in the orbit of Rome.

At this moment of triumph in Alexandria, with his rivals dead, Octavian became supreme ruler of Rome. In time he would metamorphose into Caesar Augustus, emperor in all but name. Like other Romans before him, Octavian/Augustus marvelled at the size, beauty and grandeur of Alexandria. He famously transformed Rome from a city of brick to one of marble, no doubt inspired by what he saw in Egypt.

Alexandria remained for a long time an intellectual fountainhead. But bit by bit the Library fragmented, its papyrus trove of learning nibbled away by fires, wars, rapacious emperors, book-burning bishops and humidity. In AD 365 what remained of the glories of the Ptolemaic cosmopolis was flattened by a tsunami set off by an underwater earthquake.

Rome became, as Alexandria had been, the world's universal city. Recent studies of the DNA of bodies uncovered in the city by archaeologists show that during its period of growth down to 27 BC its population was made up of a mix of Italians and people from the eastern Mediterranean and North Africa. During its imperial heyday its was 'a genetic crossroads of Europe and the Mediterranean', with peoples from north Europe through to central Asia. It was, according to the Greek orator Aelius Aristides, 'a citadel which has all the peoples of the earth as its villagers'.

4

Imperial Megacity

Rome, 30 BC–AD 537

Bigger was always better for the Romans: bigger cities; bigger public buildings; bigger ambitions; more territory, more luxuries, more power, more *stuff*. Getting a sense of the scale of the great megacity and its enormous urban empire overwhelms the mind.

If you wanted to experience the glory of Rome at its fullest extent there is one building that encompasses its gargantuan appetites. 'Toil and care, depart!' eulogised the poet Statius. 'I sing of the baths that sparkle with bright marbles!'[1]

By the third century, Romans had eleven vast imperial public bath-houses (*thermae*) to choose from and about 900 smaller and often private *balneae*. The most awe-inspiring of all were the *thermae* built by the psychopathic and fratricidal emperor Caracalla in AD 212–16. Their structure was clad with 6,300 cubic metres of marble weighing 17,000 tons. The complex sat within parkland; at the centre of the palace was an enormous dome – almost as large as that of the Pantheon.

A Roman bather followed a set routine when he or she bathed. After undressing the bather might choose to exercise before taking to the water. First came the *frigidarium*, a cold plunge bath. Things got warmer when you wallowed in the *tepidarium* and decidedly hot in the *calidarium*. Having followed this sequence of baths from cold to hot, the bather was then massaged in oils and perfumed unguents. 'I'm oiled, I take my exercise, I have my bath', as Pliny the Younger neatly summarised proceedings. That was the basic pattern of all Roman bathing, whether it took place in the imperial capital, in Asia Minor, North Africa or in the freezing wilds of northern England.

In the Baths of Caracalla, however, the experience was taken to its ultimate extent. When you entered the cool waters of the *frigidarium* you did so at the centre of the building under monumental forty-metre-high barrel- and triple-groin-vaulted ceilings. The great ceiling was supported by gigantic fifty-ton, eleven-metre-high grey Doric columns made from Egyptian granite and topped with intricately decorated white marble capitals. This colossal vaulted ceiling was stuccoed and painted in vivid colours and decorated with frescoes and glittering glass mosaics. The polished marble walls reflected the sunlight that streamed through large arched windows. Looking down from niches between the towering columns were statues of gods and emperors. The *frigidarium* also contained, at ground level, a display of mighty statues, including the three-metre-high Farnese Hercules. Mosaics, frescoes and statues depicted, in startling detail, gods, emperors, heroes of myths, superstar athletes, wrestlers and gladiators.

The Baths of Caracalla, and later those of Diocletian, inspired future grandiose building projects, including the great Gothic medieval cathedrals. Designed as a gateway to the greatest city on earth, New York's Pennsylvania Station was opened in 1910 and, until its senseless demolition in 1963, it was one of the architectural triumphs of the twentieth century, a temple not only to its city's glory but to the very idea of modern transportation. Its facade was modelled on Rome's Colosseum, but its cavernous main hall was a replica of Caracalla's baths. Lit by huge arched windows, the hall was New York's largest and grandest indoor space. 'In catching or meeting a train at Penn Station,' recalled architectural historian Richard Guy Wilson, 'one became part of a pageant – actions and movements gained significance while processing through such grand spaces.'[2]

Romans enjoying the splendours of the baths took part in just such a pageant. The Baths of Caracalla were one of several palatial complexes. Every day of the year its glories were open to all Romans – patricians and plebs, rich and poor, foreign-born and native, citizen and freedman. By the fourth century AD it was estimated that over 60,000 Romans could enjoy a bath at any one time. Agrippa (in 25 BC) and the emperors Nero (AD 62), Titus (81), Trajan (109) and Commodus (183) had already bequeathed the city vast public *thermae*; bigger and more opulent baths would follow in succeeding centuries built by

Severus Alexander, Decius, Diocletian and Constantine. Ornate bath-houses were, above all, expressions of power – the power of the emperor, the power of Rome over the world, and the power of the city over nature. High and low could share in the glories of Roman magnificence and munificence in one place – the bath. All that was refined about urban civilisation became manifest here among the marble and mosaics.

Water was just part of what was on offer. The bathhouses had saunas and rooms for massages, perfuming, grooming and cosmetic procedures (Seneca recounts the disturbing sound of yelps from customers having their armpit hair plucked). Serious workout – weight-lifting, wrestling, boxing and fencing – took place within two large gymnasia in the shadow of yet more masterpieces of ancient sculpture; the sole survivor is a colossal group scene, known as the Farnese Bull, carved from a single block of marble. Out in the gardens those in search of exercise took part in athletics and games. If they were in a more reflective frame of mind bathers could attend lectures in special halls or take a Latin or Greek text from one of the two libraries to a reading room. There were snack bars and shops selling perfumes and other pampering accessories. Below them a network of tunnels provided drainage and access to the furnaces that consumed ten tons of wood every day to heat the pools and saunas.

Merely describing the Baths of Caracalla makes it sound like a genteel spa or sanatorium. It was anything but. 'I'm in the midst of a roaring babel. My lodgings are over the baths!' moaned Seneca. Important individuals imperiously entered the baths with entourages of naked followers in their wake to remind the people of their status and wealth. People went to conduct business, argue about politics, gossip and solicit dinner invitations. They went to see and be seen. They ate, drank, argued, flirted and, occasionally, had sex in alcoves; they scrawled graffiti on the marble. People who would later dine together congregated for a pre-meal soak. Wine was readily available. The commodious imperial bathhouses reverberated with din, from the cacophony of thousands of conversations and sometimes argu-ments, to the calls of salespersons hawking cakes, sweets, drinks and savoury snacks. Weightlifters grunted and panted; the current score in a ball game was shouted out; the noise of the masseurs' hands slapping on flesh filled the vaulted halls. Some annoying folk liked to sing as they bathed. Crowds gathered around performers such as jugglers, jesters, conjurers, magicians and gymnasts.

Ovid writes that baths were a prime location for young lovers to meet in Augustan Rome: 'the numerous baths hide furtive sport'. Similarly Martial saw the bathhouses as a place where men and women could easily initiate sexual encounters. An unnamed man is described by Martial as using bathing as an excuse for unabashedly gazing at the penises of young men, while a chaste wife named Laevina was so corrupted by the enflaming experience of mixed bathing that she ran off with a toy boy. A charming piece of graffiti in a bathhouse reads: 'Apelles ... and Dexter had lunch here most pleasantly and fucked at the same time.' On a return visit the pair scrawled: 'We, Apelles the Mouse and his brother Dexter, lovingly fucked two women twice.'[3]

The baths offered a unique and all-encompassing urban and urbane experience. Above all it was a communal activity. Rich and poor came into close contact; friendships were made and affirmed; business deals were brokered; conversations bubbled and frothed. That chance for socialisation in the city, in whatever form it took, was probably its main pleasure and well worth the time Romans lavished on bathing. 'I must go and have a bath,' wrote an excited Roman schoolboy after his lessons were done. 'Yes, it's time. I leave; I get myself some towels and follow my servant. I run and catch up with the others who are going to the baths and I say to them one and all, "How are you? Have a good bath! Have a good supper!"'[4]

*

A question has always nagged at the Roman penchant for bathing. Was it a fatal vice? The more time passed, the more intense the rage for bathing – and its associated activities – became. Bathing soaked up increasing amounts of time. Surely all that pampering, wallowing and titivating could not be more at odds with the austere and stoical spirit that made Rome the master of the Mediterranean and western Europe?

The capacious bath-palaces contrasted uneasily with many of the other public buildings of the imperial capital. The public spaces of Rome told a story of the city state's progress from a rude collection of huts perched on the Palatine Hill to a world-bestriding superpower. Like all major global metropolises, Rome drew energy from its myths and history. The gargantuan Temple of Jupiter Optimus Maximus on the Capitoline Hill, the largest temple in the world, was started by the last king of Rome, Lucius Tarquinius Superbus; but, as legend had it, was completed and dedicated the year that Romans overthrew the monarchy and established the republic, 509 BC. In the battles against the deposed king, the gods Castor and Pollux were seen to be fighting in the ranks of the republicans. The temple dedicated to them remained one of the most iconic buildings in the Forum Romanum, a monument to the Romans' struggle for *libertas* – freedom – and to the city's divinely sanctioned constitution.

History suffused the city. Walking through its centre was a reminder of Rome's achievements, particularly those that occurred in quick succession between the fourth and first centuries BC. The Romans had a habit of looking back and comparing themselves unfavourably with their supposedly rugged and stern ancestors, fearing that they were becoming softer and more effete. The acquisition of an enormous empire brought these anxieties to the fore. Luxuries of all kinds streamed back to Rome as it swelled from a modest but ambitious rural town into a fully fledged imperial metropolis. Foreign imports included exotic foods, theatres, slaves, artworks, immigrants, precious metals, jewels and everything the varied lands of the new conquests could provide. They also included baths.

Bathing came to Rome at the same time as the city itself was becoming grander. During its period of ascendancy, Rome lagged behind the great cities of the age in terms of the splendour of its cityscape. Antioch, Alexandria, Carthage and Corinth were decidedly more impressive cities. Indeed, Rome was disparaged by sophisticated Macedonians as backward, an opinion confirmed when an ambassador fell into an open sewer. All that changed in the second half of the second century BC, during which Rome was given an extensive make-over befitting the metropolis of a colossal empire. The great magnates of the first century BC – Sulla, Crassus, Pompey and Caesar – expressed their munificence in temples, forums, basilicas, triumphal arches, altars, theatres, gardens and other civic and religious edifices. But baths were below their dignity. If you wanted a bath, you did so at your own expense.

In the wake of decades of civil wars, and after the deaths of Antony and Cleopatra, Octavian emerged as the sole ruler of Rome, the only strongman who could keep it all together. In 27 BC he was given the titles of Augustus and *princeps*; the republic existed in name only. At Augustus' right hand stood the statesman and general Marcus Vipsanius Agrippa. Like the great men of the earlier part of the century, Augustus and Agrippa expressed their power in monumental buildings. Agrippa commissioned the Pantheon and the Basilica of Neptune, among other noble marble edifices. But he also began work on a bathhouse in 25 BC, which was supplied with 100,000 cubic metres of fresh water every day from Agrippa's private purpose-built aqueduct (the Aqua Virgo, which still feeds the Trevi Fountain). It marked a sudden shift in the late republican period from modest private *balneae* to sumptuous public *thermae*.

When Agrippa died in 12 BC his bath complex was bequeathed to the people of Rome. The bequest elevated bathhouses to legitimate public edifices befitting the architectural ambitions of the great. The next great public establishment was that built by Nero in the 60s. Rome's unique political dynamic had always worked in large part because of the ways in which elites and masses competed to enjoy the benefits accrued by their city state. As the republic gave way to the imperial age, large, high-tech recreational spaces provided by the state became central to the public life of Romans.[5]

In the early first century AD Seneca visited the house of Scipio Africanus, the hero who had defeated Hannibal in 202 BC. The great general's bath was small and dark. In those days, wrote Seneca, Romans bathed only occasionally and then out of necessity, 'not merely for delight'.

What a change a couple of centuries made to the frugal and manly Roman character:

> we think ourselves poor and mean if our walls are not resplendent with large and costly mirrors; if our marbles from Alexandria are not set off by mosaics of Numidian stone ... if our vaulted ceilings are not buried in glass [mosaics]; if our swimming pools are not lined with Thasian marble, once a rare and costly sight in any temple ... and, finally, if water is not poured from silver spigots ... What a vast number of statues, of columns that support nothing are built for decoration, merely in order

to spend money! And what masses of water fall crashing from level to level! We have become so luxurious that we have nothing but precious stones to walk upon.

A contemporary of Seneca might say of their republican ancestors: 'Yes; pretty dirty fellows they evidently were! How they must have smelled!' But Seneca had this retort for his fastidious countrymen: 'they smelled of the camp, the farm and heroism'. Their workaday grubbiness, in short, spoke of unaffected republicanism and valour. Seneca drew a deeper moral lesson about cleanliness. 'Now that spick-and-span bathing establishments have been devised,' he concluded, 'men are really fouler than of yore.'[6]

The disapproval of bathing as encouraging depravity and decadence has influenced generations of historians who have seen in it the seeds of Rome's decline and fall. Emperors, it is said, tranquillised the Romans into numb submissive obedience with lavish gifts of bread and circuses, and grand public baths belong in exactly the same category. But we could instead look at public bathing in the way the Romans did, as marking the summit of urban civilisation. Cleanliness differentiated a Roman from a coarse unwashed barbarian. More than anything else, bathing defined what it was to a Roman: urbane, refined and modern.[7]

But there is yet another way of looking at the Roman bathing phenomenon. The Rome of Seneca's age was very different from that of Scipio Africanus. It was a city of over a million people, the first of its size and scale in history. Rather than seeing bathing as evidence of decadence or even of extreme urbanity, it makes more sense to see it as a basic human need for urbanites. In order to tell that side of the story, we must step out of the world of Rome to tell a universal tale of water and the city.

*

Bathing is a primal encounter with nature, a delicious experience of bodily liberation from the physical contortions and standards of decorum that we experience daily as we are funnelled through tight spaces as part of a marching crowd and forced into intimate proximity with the odours and bodies of complete strangers. Nakedness, or near-nakedness, when the costumes and clothing that indicate social status are temporarily shed, is also a rare levelling experience. Writing in 1936, when open-air swimming pools were enjoying a boom on a global scale in the developed world, the economist and banker Sir Josiah Stamp declared that 'Bathing reduces rich and poor, high and low, to a common standard of enjoyment and health. When we get down to swimming, we get down to democracy.'[8]

Copacabana Beach provides just such a glorious outlet for the 7.5 million residents of Rio de Janeiro. This stretch of sand and the other Rio beaches offer not only water and respite from the grim realities of city life, but an entire urban culture in themselves – a cornucopia of football and volleyball tournaments, casual encounters and family occasions, parties and festivals. The beach is not so much convenient public space as non-stop spectacle. Locals say *'Tenha uma boa praia'* – have a good beach – rather than 'Have a good day'. In a profoundly unequal city, the beach strips away the outward signs of hierarchy. The beach has a deep resonance in Los Angeles, a metropolis that is poor in inclusive public spaces. The right to access and enjoy the forty-mile coastline that stretches from Malibu to Palos Verdes is fiercely defended from the encroachment of luxury housing.[9]

Other metropolises also have beaches close at hand – such as New York's Coney Island – but it is rare for them to be in the city itself, easily accessible to all its citizens. But why not bring the beach to the city? Since 2003 Paris has instituted urban beaches so that people trapped in the summer cauldron could cool off and relax. A stretch of the Georges Pompidou expressway beside the Seine is closed to traffic in the summer months, and it is covered with sand, palm trees, hammocks and sun loungers. Paris Plages was conceived by the city's socialist mayor as a way of allowing Parisians 'to take possession of public space and to experience city life differently', particularly Parisians confined in bleak *banlieues* who cannot afford a holiday. Its institution was a political act. According to the mayor at the time: 'Paris Plages will be a nice hangout at which people, with their differences, will mingle. It is a philosophy of the city, a poetic time for sharing and brotherhood.'[10]

Here was an attempt to recreate something that was once an intrinsic – and long-forgotten – aspect of city life. Throughout London's history the Thames and semi-rural streams in suburbs such as Islington, Peckham and Camberwell were used by legions of male bathers on Sundays. A poem from the seventeenth century celebrated the sight of thousands of Londoners enjoying the refreshing coolness of the Thames in 'the summer sweeter evenings'. Jonathan Swift recorded his naked dips around Chelsea: 'I am cruelly thirsty this hot weather, I am just this minute going to swim,' he wrote in a letter. Fifteen years later, Benjamin Franklin swam from Chelsea to Blackfriars Bridge (a distance of three and a half miles) demonstrating overarm, breaststroke and backstroke. A century on and a Victorian writer was disparaging 'that miserable substitute of a degenerate civilisation called a bath'. A real swim, according to him, had to be done naked and 'in living or running water ... or it is no bathe at all'.[11]

But in the mid-nineteenth century, urban swimming and senses of propriety were no longer compatible. Houses and naked bathers evidently did not go together any more. A writer to the newspapers primly complained that he had been forced to keep his wife and daughter away from windows with a view over the Thames because of 'disgusting exhibitions' of swimmers who 'perform all manner of evolutions without the slightest control' (they were merely swimming to a steamboat and back). Another man complained about the 'yells and discordant noise' made by 'hundreds of naked men and boys' swimming in the Serpentine in Hyde Park. In vain did urban bathers retort that their leisure had been permitted since time immemorial.[12]

Prudery intervened before the Industrial Revolution made naked wild swimming in city rivers a hazardous undertaking. By the 1850s the Thames was a stinking pool of sewage as lavatories discharged the faeces of 3 million humans straight into it. Until the intense urbanisation of the nineteenth century many city-dwellers had easy access to the countryside and its streams and ponds. The introduction of public swimming pools coincided with the time that this access to nature from the city centre became impossible. Anxieties about exposed flesh and inappropriate contact between men and women (particularly men and women of different social classes) forced urban swimming into controlled and segregated environments. The first modern municipal baths opened in Liverpool in 1829, designed to be as grand and monumental as a museum or town hall. They symbolised the city's commitment to public health and recreation, and sparked a competition among British cities to build bigger, more beautiful and better baths, handsome edifices that rose tall amid the urban sprawl. Germany followed suit in the 1860s, and the United States in the 1890s.

The situation in New York's slums in the late nineteenth and early twentieth centuries reveals the high price people pay to sate their desire for immersion. One slum-dweller recalled that in the absence of parks 'the only recreation was to go down to the East River where the barges were. The people would swim in it, but they also moved their bowels there.' In the 1870s and 80s twenty-three floating baths were installed in the Hudson and East rivers for the city's poorest and dirtiest residents. Breaststroke was compulsory in order to 'push the garbage away'. Nonetheless, swimming remained wildly popular, particularly for the urban poor in cities around the world. Municipalities that tried to ban public swimming met furious resistance from working-class men determined to defend one of the very few opportunities for exercise and play available to them.[13]

That was the spirit too of the 1935 hit Broadway play *Dead End*, which opened with half-naked adolescent street boys from the tenements of the Lower East Side playing at the end of a wharf on the East River. The street toughs may not have much of a future in the Great Depression, but they have their lithe, athletic bodies and the chance to escape the urban sweatbox in the cool water. The one leisure activity available to these boys would have conveyed a powerful meaning to the theatregoers who flocked to *Dead End*. A year before it opened 450 people drowned in the river (almost exactly the same number as those who died swimming every year in the Thames in late Victorian London). And if you didn't drown the germs would get you: swimmers bathed in raw sewage, oil slicks and industrial effluence; polio and typhoid fever thrived in this environment. In any case, the opportunity to swim was being curtailed by what we call 'gentrification'. In *Dead End*, the boys' rough waterfront play area is threatened by new luxury apartments which were colonising the riverside in search of good views and jetties for private boats.[14]

A year after *Dead End* premiered on Broadway, during the record-breaking heat of the summer of 1936 eleven enormous outdoor pool complexes opened in New York City's most densely packed and impoverished districts at a cost of $1 million each as part of the New Deal. During that sweltering summer more than 1.79 million people made use of the swimming, diving and wading pools. At the same time in Britain, the leader of London County Council, Herbert Morrison, wanted London to be a 'city of lidos', in which every citizen would be in walking distance of an outdoor pool.[15]

Working-class American families who lived in cramped and stifling tenements could gather in the sunshine beside clean water and picnic alongside others from the neighbourhood. Thomas Jefferson Park pool in East Harlem could accommodate 1,450 people at a time; Colonial Park pool in central Harlem had room for 4,500 and Betsy Head Recreation Center in Brooklyn 5,500. They were places of play, where boys and girls mingled and forged friendships and romances. The new pools were the centrepieces of public parks, which had been revamped with play equipment, baseball diamonds, running tracks, bandstands and gymnasia.[16]

The monumental European baths of the nineteenth century were also sites of sociability and mingling, not simply of cleanliness; they were purposefully elegant and uplifting, *the* pre-eminent symbols of civic pride. New York's New Deal open-air swimming pools and parks – along with the glorious art deco lidos opened at about the same time in European cities – announced something else. They put play at the heart of the city. Most radically, for the first time they gave teenagers a space that was theirs, a respite from the concrete jungle of the inner city. When Mayor Fiorello La Guardia opened the Thomas Jefferson Park pool in East Harlem he shouted to the swarms of eager children, 'Okay, kids, it's all yours!' In a city short of spaces for many of its poorest people, pools quickly became the beating heart of community life, particularly the centre of nascent youth culture in the 1930s and 40s. In socially conservative migrant districts like East Harlem, open-air pools broke down gender boundaries, allowing boys and girls not only to mix equally but to do so without many clothes on and away from the prying eyes of parents.[17]

The pools were not officially segregated. But they were at the front and centre of urban race problems. When it opened, Thomas Jefferson Park pool was the preserve of the white working class, particularly Italian Americans. Harlem's African American families frequented Colonial Park pool. Bathing had long been divided according to gender. But with the advent of mixed bathing in the 1930s and radically revealing swimwear (popularised by the movies), anxieties about

African American men mixing with white women at the pool became acute. That was not the case in all pools, notably Betsy Head in Brooklyn, where a predominantly Jewish working-class population was being joined by African Americans in the 1930s.

In the 1950s fights broke out between black and white adolescents over access to pools. In East Harlem, male Italian American teenagers resented newly arrived Puerto Rican immigrants trying to get into *their* Thomas Jefferson Park pool to flirt with *their* girls. In Edwin Torres's 1975 novel *Carlito's Way* the Puerto Rican protagonist and denizen of Spanish Harlem recalled the territorial battles over the pool:

> Lemme tell you about them rumbles. The wops said no spics could go east of Park Avenue. But there was only one swimming pool and that was Jefferson on 112th Street and the East River. Like, man, you had to wade through Park, Lexington, Third, Second, First, Pleasant. Wall-to-wall guineas. The older guys be standing around in front of the stoops and stores, evil-eyeing us, everybody in his undershirt; the kids would be on the roof with the garbage cans and in the basements with bats and bicycle chains ... We took a beating – their turf, too many guys ... We was tryin' to melt into the pot but they wouldn't even let us in the swimming pool. *Hijos de puta.*[18]

Swimming pools became key sites in the working-class city, places to be defended (by in-groups) and besieged (by newcomers). Much later, Puerto Ricans recalled the symbolic importance of the pool and their determination not to be browbeaten. More to the point, they wanted to enjoy the pool and be part of its social life like everyone else. Many of them succeeded despite intimidation at street level; in time the pool became as much Latino as it had been Italian. Their story is testament to the timeless importance for city-dwellers of immersion. The swimming pool (or river or beach) is not an add-on or appendage to a city: it is one of the most cherished of all urban public spaces and an invaluable liquid asset.

*

Lavari est vivere reads a piece of Roman graffiti: 'To bathe – that is to live!' The experience of cleansing warm water, clouds of steam, marbled elegance, the perfumed atmosphere and luxurious pampering added up to a pitch of mental and physical bliss the Romans termed *voluptas*. 'Baths, wine and sex ruin our bodies,' goes a Roman epitaph, 'but baths, wine and sex are the essence of life.'[19]

It is perhaps no coincidence that the imperial *thermae* appeared during the period when Rome became the city of a million souls. The tangled rabbit warren of streets in the city was noisy and congested with people and vehicles day and night. Smoke from stoves, fast-food shops, bakeries, foundries and from the fires that heated the baths filled the air. The Tiber was polluted with sewage, industrial effluence and discharged bathwater. Many of the poor lived near the river, in damp conditions favoured by mosquitoes; epidemics of malaria broke out every few years. The scale of urbanisation meant that there were no longer streams or rivers available for the city's poor.

How could a person write poems in the city, asked Horace in the first century. The mind was assaulted by careening carts, huge cranes hoisting beams into the sky, dogs scampering about and muddy pigs getting in the way. The forums and the street corners were always full of knots of people engaged in 'feverish quarrels' about this and that, and endless conversations. Writing in about AD 110, Juvenal depicted the streets of Rome, with 'carts thundering through the narrow twisting streets and the swearing of drivers caught in a traffic jam'. The human traffic was worse: 'I am blocked by a wave of people in front of me and the people in a huge rank jab my back. One man digs an elbow into me; another strikes me with a hard pole. One man bangs my head with a wood beam, another with a wine jug. My legs are plastered with mud. Then huge feet kick me on all sides, and a soldier plants his boot's nail right on my toe.'[20]

Most of the population of Rome crammed into tenement blocks known as *insulae*, the Latin word for islands. In the fourth century AD, when Rome's population was past its peak, there were estimated to be 46,000 *insulae*, compared to just 1,790 single-family homes. Like many a resident of today's global financial hubs, they paid exorbitant rent for tiny spaces. Rome's *insulae*, which sometimes rose to eight, nine or even ten storeys, were notoriously badly built, poorly maintained and prone to fire. No wonder, according to Juvenal, the tenements 'shook with every gust of wind that blew'. If a fire broke out 'the last man to burn will be he who has nothing to shelter him from the rain but the tiles, where the gentle doves lay their eggs'.[21]

Regulations stipulated that the walkway around *insulae* need only be seventy centimetres wide, so they were tightly packed into city blocks. Shops and *tabernae* occupied street level, with apartments on the higher floors; the first floor had the most spacious and expensive accommodation, but rooms got smaller and cheaper (and more dangerous) the higher up in the building they were. The rented rooms did not provide much in the way of kitchens or toilets. Residents used chamber pots to relieve themselves, the contents of which were dumped into barrels situated in the ground-floor stairwell; they were only periodically emptied. Meals were taken in the numerous bars and fast-food joints that littered the city streets.[22]

With close to a million sweaty people living in more or less slum conditions, it is little wonder that life took place out of the home, in the shopping arcades, markets, street corners and public parks. The Roman day started at first light, when men left their tenements to visit their patrons, a routine of deference to the powerful that took two hours. The third, fourth and fifth hours were taken up with *negotia* – business – before lunch and siesta in the sixth hour. Then came pleasure, *voluptas*.

Martial stated that the best time to bathe was in the eighth hour, when the water had reached its Goldilocks temperature, not too hot and not too cold. At that time, about two o'clock in the afternoon, the great bathhouses would begin to fill up with the surging mass of Roman humanity.

The opulent baths contrasted with the reality of daily life. In a metropolis that teemed with a million people, the bonds and opportunities for participation that united a simpler and smaller city were no longer possible. At the bathhouse, the citizen could feel distinctively Roman, part of the communal whole and not lost in the crowd. Private squalor was compensated with public magnificence.

The Roman phrase *teatrum mundi* was translated by William Shakespeare as 'all the world's a stage'. The baths provided the key setting for the theatre of urban life, part of a culture that put pleasure and entertainment centre stage. In the first century AD, ninety-three days a year were given over to lavish public games; by the fourth century it had risen to 175 days a year. The whole city could be entertained simultaneously in numerous arenas on one of these frequent holidays. The Circus Maximus, as reconstructed by Trajan (a builder of baths himself), had a capacity of 150,000–200,000; the Colosseum's audience was over 50,000. The city's three leading theatres could hold 50,000 between them.

The Baths of Caracalla were central to a new concept of displaying Rome. They were set on a new and beautiful street that deliberately took a first-time visitor to the city past Rome's most imposing and astonishing buildings: the baths themselves, the Circus Maximus, the Palatine and the Colosseum. Note the purpose of these buildings: leisure. Horse-racing, charioteering, gladiatorial contests, re-enactments of naval battles, wild animal massacres, theatrical extravaganzas, military triumphs: this was a place of continual spectacle and entertainment, much of it bloodthirsty and sadistic.

The Romans knew that leisure and extravaganza are not luxuries or frivolities; they are the key ingredients of any large successful city, as indispensable perhaps as law courts and public monuments. Being part of an exuberant, roaring crowd – whether in the Colosseum in the second century or in the Stade de France in the twenty-first – is an intoxicating experience. You can subsume yourself into the crowd and feel part of the city. In the modern world, football has given members of communities numbering in the millions a tribal identity. The ability of a city to stage an Olympic Games, big pop concerts or marathons, and to supply near-constant entertainment in the form of sports, theatre, museums, parks and nightclubs is central to its purpose and claim to greatness. The Big City offers wealth and opportunity; it also gives you the chance to be part of something bigger than yourself. For that you can put up with living in squalor amid splendour or paying exorbitant rent for your minuscule living space. Cities that can offer this have always reaped the rewards in the form of legions of talented incomers and high-spending tourists.

*

Bathhouses became the defining feature of Roman urban expansion into parts of the world that had never before known, seen or experienced cities. Bathing was, in essence, the way by which a German, a

Gaul or a Briton was cleansed of barbarism and became not just Roman, but urban.

Inhabited by humans for 10,000 years before the Roman occupation, the British Isles were all the same devoid of anything resembling a city. The closest Britain came to one was the *oppidum*, or fortified town. From the early first century BC Britons started moving down from hill forts to the lowlands to build *oppida*, settlements protected by earthworks. Often they stood near river crossings and estuaries or on inland trade routes; some began minting their own coins. They are best described as 'proto-urban' rather than urban. The most extensive of these British *oppida* was on the banks of the river Colne in modern-day Essex. Known as Camulodunon, 'The Stronghold of Camulus', the British god of war, the Colne defended it and gave access to maritime trading routes.

In AD 43 this thriving settlement was faced with the most ruthlessly organised fighting force in the world, which included war elephants, artillery and the Roman emperor in person. Caratacus, king of the Catuvellauni tribe, fled in the face of this almighty army; the emperor Claudius accepted the surrender of several other British kings at Caratacus' former capital, Camulodunon.

As soon as Claudius left, work on Britain's first city, now known as Colchester, began. It started life as a Roman military fortress built over the existing *oppidum* with a defensive wall and a grid system of streets. Most of the building consisted of long rectangular barrack buildings laid out with military precision to accommodate the 20th Legion, a Thracian cavalry regiment and the 1st Cohort of the Vangiones.

Within six years the fortress was demolished and a new grid was put in place. It doubled in size as a civilian city, the capital of the brand-new Roman province of Britannia, peopled for the most part by a population of urbanised military veterans, their hangers-on, as well as local elites undergoing Romanisation. At the centre of the city stood a Roman temple clad in Mediterranean marble. There was a forum, civic buildings, a theatre and a monumental double-arched gate. The remains of public baths have not yet been found. They must lie buried under the modern city. It is inconceivable that in the first and second centuries a Roman town or city anywhere in the empire did not have an elaborate bathhouse, ranging from small private establishments set up by entrepreneurs to vast municipal *thermae* such as the Hadrianic Baths in Lepcis Magna in Tunisia, those in Conimbriga in Portugal, and the Thermes de Cluny in Paris, none of which would be out of place in Rome itself.

Roman soldiers expected, as a minimal condition of their service, to be bathed and entertained as if they were in Rome, or at least their home cities in Italy, southern France or elsewhere in the empire. In the cold, soggy north, baths provided troops deprived of the Mediterranean sunshine with much-needed warmth. Consequently, the first stone buildings constructed in a Roman military camp, such as Exeter or York, were the bathhouse and an amphitheatre for games and performances. Like Colchester, these military fortresses soon became *coloniae*, or towns for veterans. With 10% of the vast Roman army stationed in Britain in the second century, there was no shortage of recruits for the city-building programme.[23]

The experience of Britain in the first decades of Roman occupation was a repeat of what had happened elsewhere in the non-urbanised world, in Iberia, Gaul, Germania, Pannonia (modern-day Hungary and Austria) and Dacia (Romania and Moldova). First came the shocking tsunami of violent invasion and occupation that left people and ways of life dead in its wake. Then came a process of urbanisation.

The Roman Empire was a networked urban empire, thousands of towns built along the Mediterranean model connected by roads and bridges. As the case of Britain demonstrates, urbanisation provided not only military-administrative centres in newly conquered lands but homes for retired soldiers who were retained as auxiliaries in case of local trouble. They also served another function. Towns offered conquered peoples, particularly the elites, powerful incentives to accept Roman rule and embrace Roman lifestyles. The word 'civilisation' derives from the Latin *civis*, town, while 'urbane' comes from *urbanitas*, one of the meanings of which is the art of turning your tongue to wittily allusive and polished speech, an accomplishment that can come only from living hugger-mugger with a diversity of other people in the city. The Latin word *cultus*, from which we get culture, means refinement and sophistication, the opposite of *rusticitas*, rural oafishness.

Boom-town Londinium was a gateway for the foreign influences surging in Britannia, an emporium of exotic goods and peoples from every corner of the Roman world. It came into existence at the high tide of the empire. We know from shipwrecks discovered in the Mediterranean and the study of pollution in the Greenland icecap that levels of trade and metal production in the first and second centuries were at their highest level in Europe before the Industrial Revolution in the late eighteenth and nineteenth centuries.

Bathhouses were physically imposing symbols of 'civilisation' and would have dominated the earliest urban forms seen in the wild west of Europe. A bathhouse in Londinium dating from the last few decades of the first century AD when the city was taking shape, known now as the Huggin Hill Baths (a few yards south-east of the site of St Paul's Cathedral), was a massive complex in a relatively small urban area, serving a mixed clientele of Roman merchants and British aristocrats immersing themselves in Roman-ness.[24]

*

One thing baths did not do was make people clean. The emperor Marcus Aurelius commented, 'What is bathing when you think of it – oil, sweat, filth, greasy water, everything revolting ...' Quite how often the water was changed in the imperial *thermae* is unknown. Thousands of daily bathers would have left the water even worse than Marcus Aurelius described; they wallowed in a warm invisible stew of bacteria, germs and the eggs of parasites. Finds of combs, clothing and even faeces from around the empire show that the Romans, for all their advanced hydraulics and lavatories, were as infested with intestinal parasites, fleas and lice as non-bathing societies, perhaps more so. Piped water introduced lead poisoning, which weakens the immune system, and shared water helped spread dysentery and other diseases. A city of hundreds of gleaming baths, maybe, but it did not stop Rome being wracked with plague on a regular basis. All those hours spent luxuriating in warm water may even have reduced sperm counts, driving down the birth rate. If that is true, then it adds a completely different dimension to the connection between bathing and the decline and fall of the Roman Empire.[25]

But then hundreds of theories for the fall of the empire have been proposed over the years. In the third century, the empire came under severe crisis with enemy invasions across the Rhine, Danube and Euphrates, recurrent civil wars, vicious pandemics and irreparable disruption to trade networks. Although Rome recovered, the intimations of long-term decline were evident on the broadest canvas the Roman world had – its cityscapes. After the crisis of the third century the very idea of the Roman city was undermined in the West. In Paris the mighty amphitheatre was demolished and its stones recycled as a wall to protect the city from barbarian bands. Such pillaging of monumental buildings happened in city after city in Gaul and elsewhere. Where they survived, forums, amphitheatres and grand main thoroughfares were gradually overrun with small makeshift shops. In Britain, a layer of 'black earth' within cities suggests that market gardening began to invade the urban sphere from the fourth century.

The trade that had summoned cities into life never recovered. Picts, Goths, Saxons, Huns, Visigoths stalked the frontier. Shorn of their splendid amenities and relegated to overcrowded citadels, cities no longer offered anything like the full panoply of civilisation. The investment required for bathhouses was no longer available. Two of the most magnificent bathhouses in western Europe – in Paris and Trier – fell into ruin in the third century. The elites in the provinces of western Europe sought their Roman fix elsewhere – in sumptuous private villas, with their fountains, statues, columns, mosaics and heated baths. In an age when cities were being literally and figuratively dismantled, the villa became the last bastion of Roman-ness, a kind of private fantasy land that recalled the good old days for a lucky few.[26]

Cities are fragile things. Without constant investment, renewal and civic-mindedness their fragmentation is extraordinarily swift. In his *On the Ruin of Britain*, the cleric Gildas recorded the destruction of all twenty-eight Roman cities immediately after the last Roman troops departed in 407. But by then, these 'cities', after two centuries of gradual de-urbanisation, were mere shells. Londinium was completely abandoned by the end of the century. Much later, a Saxon village called Lundenwic was established a mile away from this ghostly metropolitan ruin in an area that is now Covent Garden. In Gaul and Germania, Roman cities shrank to the size of overgrown villages. Trier, once a provincial capital of 100,000, fractured into several villages grouped round a cathedral; even by 1300 its population had only recovered to 8,000. Autun, founded by Augustus in Gaul, went from a city of tens of thousands of people spread over 2,500 acres to a village of twenty-five acres. In Nîmes and Arles people took refuge within the huge protective walls of the amphitheatres, where they created towns. Cities were now magnets for pillagers and raiders; roads were no longer vectors of trade but highways of invasion. In Greece, the Balkans and Italy, people abandoned their lowland, roadside cities in favour of defensive hilltop villages which resembled those their ancestors had inhabited before the coming of Rome. Likewise, in northern Europe something like the *oppidum*, with earthworks and log cabins, reappeared.

Construction in stone ceased. Literacy rates plummeted. According to measurements of pollution in the Greenland icecaps, metalworking declined to prehistoric levels. With no long-distance trade to sustain them, large cities became economically unviable. Power and wealth decamped from the city and settled in monasteries, manors and castles. Europe would not recover the extent of Roman urbanisation – its infrastructure, technology, sanitation, water-supply systems, population, civic culture, standards of living and refinement – for at least another 1,300 years. No city exceeded a million people again until 1800. Once they were gone, the bathhouses – the emblem of urban sophistication – did not reappear for mass use until the Pier Head baths opened in Liverpool in 1829.

'He who has once bathed in Christ has no need of a second bath.' So said St Jerome. Not only were the skills and technology lacking for bathhouses, but so too was the culture of public bathing. Christians disapproved of nudity; they abhorred the vanity and wasted time of all that Roman pampering and titivation; they saw the frivolous bathhouse as a hotbed of licentiousness and sin. All that remained was a religious tradition of washing pilgrims; the social and communal culture of urban bathing, not to say its pleasures, was dead.[27]

In Rome, however, the great viaducts continued to fill the heated pools of the palatial bathhouses. In 408 Roman citizens still trooped off to the baths of Agrippa, or of Caracalla or of Diocletian, as generations had done before them. At the beginning of the fifth century, when the urban fabric of Europe was being torn to shreds, Rome remained a beacon of what a great metropolis could and should be. Grain from Sicily and North Africa, olive oil, Chinese silk, Indonesian spices and much more besides continued to arrive. With the empire divided into two, and the emperors of what was left of the western half absent for years on end, the city of Rome had a pale shadow of its former power. Its senate, once the arbiter of the mightiest empire ever seen, dwindled to little more than a municipal council; its forum, formerly the scene of world-shattering political drama, had become a piazza; its pagan temples were locked up by the Christian authorities. But it remained the greatest city on earth, with most of its magnificence and amenities still functioning. The population, which had dipped to 800,000, was an ethnically diverse, well-fed and well-entertained multitude. An inventory of the city listed two main markets, two amphitheatres, two circuses, three theatres, four gladiator schools, five lakes for mock sea battles, six obelisks, seven churches, eight bridges, ten basilicas, eleven forums, eleven imperial *thermae*, nineteen aqueducts, twenty-eight libraries, twenty-nine avenues, thirty-six marble arches, thirty-seven gates, forty-six brothels, 144 public latrines, 254 bakeries, 290 warehouses, 423 neighbourhoods, 500 fountains, 856 private bathhouses, 1,790 houses, 10,000 statues and 46,602 blocks of flats.[28]

The year 408 was also the year that Rome was besieged by a vast Visigoth army led by Alaric. Two years later, and eight centuries since the last time the city's defences had been breached by a barbarian army, Alaric sacked Rome. The Visigoths stayed in Rome for just three days, so the harm inflicted on the city and its people was relatively mild. The psychological damage, however, was irreparable. 'The City which had taken the whole world was itself taken,' marvelled St Jerome. Things got worse when the Vandals invaded and set up kingdoms in Sicily, Sardinia and the province of Africa (Libya). These were Rome's granaries. Deprived of its grain convoys, Rome could not feed its huge population. The Vandals sacked Rome in 455, during which they plundered many of its treasures over fourteen days of looting. As its population drained away, falling from 650,000 in the middle of the century to 100,000 by the end, Rome had little to live on but its legacy. And it was a pretty fat legacy. The city began to eat itself.

Those who remained among the deserted crumbling tenement blocks and decaying monuments to long-lost greatness began to strip stone, marble, bronze and lead from the noble imperial edifices. In the Augustan Forum they set up lime kilns in which they burnt marble statues, plinths and columns to make plaster. The city's cannibalised fabric was either sold or used to make churches. For centuries hence,

Romans made a living selling its antiquities and art. Where it was not desperately patched up with stolen stone, the city fell into decay, with vast broken porticoes, stumps of columns, chunks of statues and piles of paving stones dumped unceremoniously; grass grew everywhere, including in the Circus Maximus. Yet despite its ongoing decay, as Cassiodorus wrote, 'the whole of Rome is a marvel'. It was 'a wonderful forest of buildings' that included 'the huge Colosseum whose top is almost beyond human vision; the Pantheon with its lofty and beautiful dome as large as a whole region of the city'. Also still in use were 'the baths built as large as provinces'.[29]

Romans continued to enjoy their precious baths. That was until the fateful day in 537 when the last drop of water dripped into the Baths of Caracalla and the other *thermae*. The Ostrogoth army that was besieging Rome had severed the aqueducts. The water would never run again; but the people's palaces remained substantially intact for several centuries, their structure and immense vaulted ceilings providing striking visual evidence of the extinct Roman civilisation. Enough of them remained to be recorded by artists into the sixteenth and seventeenth centuries. The Baths of Caracalla, because they lay outside the city, degenerated into imposing ruins. Those of Diocletian were incorporated into new buildings. Michelangelo converted its *frigidarium*, with its colossal cross-vaulted hall and surviving red granite columns, into the nave of the basilica church Santa Maria degli Angeli e dei Martiri. Later, other parts of its mighty structure were used as a grain silo, and later still they became part of the Museo Nazionale Romano. The shape of its vast semicircular exedra was preserved as the outline of the Piazza della Repubblica.

Rome had long since ceased to be a power in the world. The closure of the baths in 537 is a key date in its history. The wellspring of ancient Roman urban culture had run dry. Without its aqueducts, Rome could support a population of only about 30,000. If you wanted to wash in Rome you had the Tiber. The home of the papacy, the centre of Christian pilgrimage, and a site of fabulous ruins to stir the imagination (or ransack for profit), Rome survived to beguile future generations. Western Europe lost its last great metropolis. In cities in the eastern Roman Empire – in North Africa and south-west Asia – the municipalities kept the waters running; bathing remained central to the urban experience. The tradition and amenities of public bathing in hot water were inherited and adapted in hundreds of Islamic cities. Public baths – called *hammams* – were essential for the ablutions required before praying. They also served as the key sites for socialising for men and women. In Islamic cities, the *hammam*, the mosque and the souk were the troika of institutions forming the bedrock of urban life. *Hammams* proliferated in cities in south-west Asia, North Africa and Iberia; Damascus, for instance, had 85 within the city walls and 127 in the suburbs. Similarly, in Japan bathing began in temples as ritual purification in water. By the thirteenth century, mixed-sex commercial public baths – *sentos* – with both large pools and steam rooms had become a feature of cities and a ritual of daily life. They served as places of communal interaction, a form of socialising and neighbourhood bonding known as *hadaka no tsukiai*, or 'naked association' that lay at the heart of Japanese society. In the twentieth century this form of physical intimacy was renamed *sukinshippu* ('skinship'). In the eighteenth century Edo (Tokyo), with a population close to a million, had around 600 public *sentos*; in 1968 the number in the city peaked at 2,687. Tokyo's skyline was characterised by chimney stacks poking upwards from its numerous bathhouses, striking visual evidence of the centrality of bathing to the social life of the city.

Bathing is a measure of urban vitality. In much of Europe the ruins of bathhouses and aqueducts denoted the collapse of urbanity. Their survival in Muslim metropolises and cities throughout Asia symbolised the thriving of city life. While the western tip of Eurasia dwindled back into insignificance, most of the rest of the world was swept by a period of ferocious energy and urbanisation.

5

Gastropolis

Baghdad, 537–1258

They were diving for sea cucumber. Instead they pulled out a block of coral embedded with ancient ceramics. In 1998, Indonesian fishermen stumbled upon one of the most sensational shipwreck discoveries of all time. For over 1,100 years the ship and its cargo lay under sediment in the Java Sea that had preserved it from the ravages of marine worms; 60,000 items were recovered from the wreck. Some of these were exquisite, and very expensive, bronze, gold, silver and ceramic ornaments made for the super-rich. There were eighteen silver ingots.

Most of the cargo was not treasure at the time it was made, in about AD 826, however – 98% of it consisted of inexpensive, everyday items made in China and destined for non-elite customers. But for archaeologists and historians, it is priceless because of the light it sheds on everyday life in the Middle Ages. Some of these ceramics are displayed in the Museum of Asian Civilisations in Singapore. The mass-produced Changsha bowls from Hunan with their attractive bright glazes and abstract designs look so new that it is like entering the museum gift shop. They are a small sample of 55,000 such bowls taken from the wreck. Today, placed centre stage in the museum, the effect is overwhelming; they are testament to a medieval trading system and an urban civilisation that flourished for centuries.

The dhow would in all likelihood have been carrying spices, textiles, silks and jungle produce, things which do not survive a millennium underwater (although considerable quantities of star anise have been detected). There were other mass-produced items: 763 identical inkpots, 915 spice jars and 1,635 ewers. Fired in kilns throughout China, they were designed with the global market firmly in mind, and sent to port via a network of rivers and canals. There were lotus symbols for Buddhist customers in south-east Asia and motifs appropriate for homes in Persia and central Asia. Most of the bowls catered for the huge Islamic market with their geometric and lozenge designs, inscriptions from the Koran and Arabic words. The 10,000 or so foreign merchants living in Guangzhou commissioned such pieces based on their knowledge of what was in fashion in, say, Baghdad or Samarkand or Cordoba. White ceramic ware and green-splashed bowls were popular in Persia, while the ravishing blue and white Chinese porcelain, so familiar to us, was entirely dictated by the tastes of people in Baghdad.

The Belitung ship (as it is known, after the island near which it was found) contained a treasure trove of cargo which had been bound for the sumptuous bazaars of the greatest city on earth, Baghdad. It had picked the merchandise up from another vast global trading metropolis, Guangzhou, in (or shortly after) 828, probably in return for pearls from the Gulf, Middle Eastern glassware and perfumes, as well as cargos of spices and rare woods picked up along the way. Trading between Baghdad and Guangzhou involved a 12,600-mile round trip that started in the Persian Gulf and navigated the Arabian Sea, the Indian Ocean, the Bay of Bengal, the Andaman Sea, the Strait of Malacca and the South China Sea.[1]

One unspectacular cargo ship travelling in a single season illustrates in startling colours an intermeshed world. The diverse merchandise shows how widely tastes in household ware and food were spreading and hybridising. The dhow would have hopped from port city to port city, trading and exchanging goods appropriate for the local market as it made its way home to the Gulf. Its sinking in the Java Sea represented the loss of money and, without doubt, life; but its recent discovery has revolutionised how we see the Middle Ages. The vessel itself embodied the interconnectedness of the world it sailed across. It had been built in the specialist shipbuilding city of Siraf, in modern-day Iran, with timbers made of African mahogany, a keelson of *Afzelia bipindensis* imported from distant Zaire, and beams of Indian teak. The twine holding it together was probably made from Malayan sea hibiscus, no doubt a replacement for the original hemp derived from the Caucasus or India. The storage jars were made in Vietnam and, as revealed by their personal items found on board, the crew and passengers were Arabs, south-east Asians and Chinese. Some of the cooking utensils were made in Thailand and other items came from Sumatra.[2]

But in this world of long-distance trade and multiplying connections, there was one place rich and powerful enough to generate the heat of global trade. The preserved cargo of the Belitung shipwreck represents just a sliver of the exotic wonders that streamed to Baghdad not just from China and south-east Asia but from central Asia, the steppes, the Levant, Africa and the Mediterranean.

The great glittering instant skyscraper cities of the late twentieth and early twenty-first centuries, such as Dubai or Shenzhen, have their ancestor in Baghdad. Only sixty-seven years before the Belitung ship set sail to bring back a rich haul of exotic and utilitarian goods, the Abbasid caliph al-Mansur had traced out in cinders on bare earth the outline of what he ordained to be the intellectual, spiritual and commercial capital of the world. Purpose-built with the most sophisticated and dazzling urban design by an army of 100,000 architects, surveyors, engineers, carpenters, blacksmiths and labourers, the city was complete a mere four years after al-Mansur had founded it in 762. Within a few decades its population breached the million-person mark and at its zenith perhaps had as many as 2 million. 'Was Baghdad not the loveliest of cities,' asked the poet Ali ibn Abi Talib, 'A spectacle that held the eye spellbound?'[3]

Baghdad, standing at the hub of a vast urban empire that straddled three continents, was designed to demonstrate the triumph of a new global civilisation. Islam was carried to the corners of the world by the nomadic Bedouin tribes of the Arabian desert; but it was rooted in urban culture. Rich on the profits of trading valuable goods to the cities of the Levant and Persia, Mecca was a wealthy city of merchants in the sixth century. One of those engaged in commerce between the Indian Ocean and the Mediterranean was a young man named Muhammad. A desert city, with little agriculture to support it, Mecca relied almost entirely on international trade. The good times came to a halt, however, when the markets in the Levant and Persia dried up as a result of the titanic wars between the Romans of Constantinople and the Persian Empire.

Not only in Arabia, but across what was left of the Roman Empire trade withered away in the face of war and pestilence. The situation resembled the fall of the empire in the west a couple of centuries before. Corinth and Athens were all but abandoned. The city of Antioch, one of the four great metropolises of the world, was sacked and destroyed by the Persians in 538; 300,000 of its citizens were deported. Roman cities in Asia Minor, such as Ephesus and Sardis, contracted to fortified garrisons with a few mean houses camped out amid the decaying grandeur of better times. Three years after the sack of Antioch, in 541, bubonic plague broke out in Alexandria; its streets were blocked by thousands of rotting corpses. Trading ships spread the lethal disease to cities throughout the Mediterranean, wiping out a third of the population. Constantinople, the glittering capital of the Roman Empire, fell into a steep demographic decline in the seventh century.

It was against this apocalyptic backdrop – devastated cities, tottering empires and social upheaval – that Muhammad began receiving revelations from God dictated through the angel Jibril. Commencing in 610, the revelations not only explained what was going on in this war-ravaged, pestilence-filled world, they offered a fast track to worldly success and spiritual salvation for those who chose to serve Allah. Above all it was a message of unity for the divided, quarrelsome and fiercely independent desert tribes of Arabia. But it was born amid struggle. The polytheistic elites of Mecca reacted with hostility to Muhammad's radical monotheistic message. The preacher and his followers were forced to flee to the agricultural city of Yathrib (now Medina) in 622.

It was here that Islam took shape, converts flocked to the faith and the first conquests were made. Mecca fell in 630, and before the Prophet's death in 632 most of Arabia was under Muslim control. With astonishing speed, it absorbed much of what remained of two exhausted world empires – those of the Romans and the Persians. Over the following decades and centuries Islam's march of conquest and conversion took it west along the North African coast, across the Strait of Gibraltar to Spain, and east along the Silk Roads to the borders of China and India.

In striking contrast to the barbarians who dismembered Rome's Western Empire, the Arabian invaders, many of them non-urbanised, adapted to city life. Urban centres had after all been crucial to the success of Islam from its very beginning. A place where people of different backgrounds could worship together helped break down tribal and ethnic identities and solidify the notion of the *ummah* – the wider Muslim community drawn from people spread from the Indus to the Atlantic, from the Sahara to the Caucasus – that was united by faith alone.

A Roman city was instantly recognisable as Roman. That uniformity was not evident in the Islamic city. The *dar al-Islam* (literally 'house of Islam'), for one thing, was a global empire, encompassing territories that contained some of the world's oldest cities and urban cultures, from the central Asian city states to the metropolises of Iran and Iraq to the classical *poleis* of the Mediterranean basin. Muslims inherited cities with long-standing urban foundations and settled populations of Christians, Jews, Buddhists and Zoroastrians. But the physical fabric of the classical city was undergoing metamorphosis long before the period of Islamic expansion.

In the eastern cities of the former Roman Empire, wide streets, open public spaces, monumental buildings and grid layouts were being swallowed up by people greedy for space. In a long process of infilling and densification that occurred in the centuries before the Islamic conquest, colonnaded boulevards became narrower as shops and houses ate into them, creating a jumble of snaking lanes; forums, agoras and public areas were built upon; buildings were subdivided. In addition, Islamic authorities, in contrast to earlier Roman municipal governments, were often more laissez-faire in their attitude to town planning, giving property owners and neighbourhoods a lot of latitude to build as they liked and the city to develop organically as needs changed.[4]

Cities tend to form around their primary mode of transport – be it human legs, horses, trains, trams, subways or cars. By the time that Islam rose to pre-eminence, the wheeled cart (which requires a lot of street room) was being replaced by a more cost-efficient bulk carrier – the camel. Rules stated that a street only had to be wide enough to allow two camels to pass each other. Householders were also allowed to build extensions that bridged the upper storeys of buildings separated by a street. Streets therefore often became enclosed corridors burrowing through the dense cityscape. It is telling that the Arabic word for market – *sūq* – derives from the Akkadian word for 'street' – *suqu* – which in turn comes from the word *saqu*, narrow. The open agora became the linear street market of the souk radiating through the city along a convoluted pattern of slender alleys.[5]

The apparent chaos and congestion did not stifle the city; rather, hyper-density released a new kind of dynamism. Its higgledy-piggledy nature was not a sign of urban failure, but of success – people flocked to the city for religious and business reasons, filling all available space. The commercial souk, with its specialised districts where traders clustered, exceeded in complexity and sophistication the agora and forum. Islamic city centres were dominated by two institutions new to urban history – the souk and the mosque. The latter served many urban functions – the site of communal worship, law courts and education.

Worshipping at the mosque gave access to the immense material wealth of the souk, which was drawn from the global trading system. The Islamic city was open to the entire *ummah* regardless of a resident's ethnicity, city of birth or whether or not they were a convert. The Arab Empire encompassed the most productive parts of the globe and its urbanised heartland: the Mediterranean, Syria, Egypt and Mesopotamia. Its trading routes delved deep into the Sahara, along the Silk Roads to central Asia and China, and across the seas to East Africa, India and south-east Asia. Taking control of the economic centre of the world, and enjoying all its fruits, was regarded by Muslims as the just result of obeying Allah.

Throughout the Middle Ages, nineteen of the world's twenty largest cities were Muslim or in the Chinese Empire. (The only non-Muslim, non-Chinese city on the list was Constantinople.) The wealth and energy of the human world were concentrated on a network of cities strung like a pearl necklace over land and sea from Cordoba in Spain and Ghana City in West Africa to Guangzhou in China, with Baghdad as its radial point. For Europe it was the Dark Ages; most of the rest of the world, however, enjoyed a golden age.

*

'I have seen the great cities, including those noted for their durable construction,' wrote the essayist al-Jahiz in the ninth century. 'I have seen such cities in the districts of Syria, in Byzantine territory, and in other provinces, but I have never seen a city of greater height, more perfect circularity, more endowed with superior merits or possessing more spacious gates or more perfect defences than [Baghdad].' An admirer of Euclid, the Abbasid caliph al-Mansur decreed that his city be perfectly round. The circumference of the massive wall was pierced by four equidistant gates. Four perfectly straight roads led from these gigantic gates to the centre, a circular city within the circular city. The people of Baghdad could see the enormous green dome of the imperial palace and the Great Mosque within this round precinct. But they could not venture into this private zone, which was reserved for the caliph's court, his family, guards and imperial bureaucracy. It resembled Beijing's Forbidden City, a space of sacred sovereignty at the core of the city. By intention and design, Baghdad expressed geometric and urban perfection. 'It is as though it is poured into a mould and cast,' marvelled al-Jahiz.[6]

The Abbasid caliphs regarded their city as 'the navel of the universe', and its perfect roundness was an embodiment of that metaphor. Mesopotamia was considered to be the centre of the world, and Baghdad the centre of Mesopotamia. The city was a series of concentric circles, representing the layout of the cosmos, with the palace at its heart, equidistant from all countries and peoples. All roads, by land, river and sea, led to Baghdad. The four gates with their four straight roads leading to the centre of the dial made Baghdad a literal as much as figurative crossroads of the world. The Damascus or Sham Gate pathed the way to Syria and the Mediterranean, and the Kufa Gate to the Arabian Peninsula and Mecca. In the north-east, the Khorasan Gate connected the city to Iran, central Asia and ultimately China; in the south-east quadrant the Basra Gate pointed the way to the maritime world of the Indian Ocean and east Asia. The ninth-century geographer Ahmad al-Yaqubi put words into al-Mansur's mouth as he looked at the river beside which Baghdad stood: 'This is the Tigris; there is no obstacle between us and China; everything on the sea can come to us on it.'[7]

Geography did not, of course, make Baghdad the centre of the universe. Power and money did. The wealth of the world, in the form of taxes raised from the wealthiest commercial empire on the planet, flowed to the new imperial capital. Baghdad became an important military arsenal and the residence of the elite imperial officials. Their immense spending power and thirst for luxuries made the city highly attractive for migrants, who came in the hundreds of thousands from Arabia and Persia.

In time they would be joined by Muslims from all over the empire, as well as smaller groups of Europeans, Africans and Asians, including a number of Chinese goldsmiths, painters and silk weavers. All were lured in by the superabundance of wealth concentrated in the imperial metropolis. The slave population was perhaps even more cosmopolitan, made up of – among others – Slavic, Nubian, Ethiopian, Sudanese, Senegalese, Frankish, Greek, Turkish, Azerbaijani and Berber men, women and children. There was a Christian quarter, complete with churches and monasteries. The city was also home to about 45,000 Jews. Only a few of the city's multicultural inhabitants lived in the so-called Round City. They were the officials and administrators of the empire who resided close to the caliph's palace within a doughnut ring of residential areas squeezed between the outer wall and the palace wall. The real city, the city where people lived and worked, sprawled outside the walls of the circular metropolis. Baghdad was a city of many cities.

Al-Mansur's master urban planners placed four large districts outside the Round City, densely populated quarters with avenues, streets, apartment blocks, shops, mosques, gardens, hippodromes, bathhouses and souks. Baghdad expanded across the Tigris, with an eastern city growing in parallel to the original western one, connected to each other by the famous bridge of boats. Succeeding caliphs and nobles migrated out of the cocoon of the Round City, building palaces and mosques for themselves and their extended families in various city locations.

'Everything produced from the earth is available there,' wrote Du Huan, a Chinese prisoner. 'Carts carrying countless goods to markets, where everything is available and cheap. Brocade, embroidered silks, pearls and other gems are displayed all over markets and street shops.' A writer describing the city in its prime recorded that 'Here every merchant, and each merchandise, had an appointed street: and there were rows of shops, and of booths, and of courts, in each of those streets.'[8]

The markets contained the wealth of the world: earthenware and porcelain from China; silks, carpets and fabrics from central Asia; plums from Shiraz; quinces from Jerusalem; Syrian figs; Egyptian pastries; Indian pepper and cardamom; east Asian spices. There were streets and souks reserved for livestock, horses, slaves, precious metals and stones, jewellery, carpets, carpentry, hardware, fish, bread, puddings, cheeses, sweetmeats, soaps and detergents, herbs and spices, and just about everything, in its allotted space, that the heart could desire. Watermelons for instance, packed in snow to keep them fresh, were express-couriered from Bukhara.

In the story from the *Arabian Nights* 'The Porter and the Three Ladies of Baghdad', a porter is hired to accompany a woman on a shopping spree around the city. The first stop is for a jar of the finest wine. Next it is the fruiterer for 'Shami apples and Osmani quinces and Omani peaches, and cucumbers of Nile growth, and Egyptian limes and Sultani oranges and citrons, beside Aleppine jasmine, scented myrtle berries, Damascene nenuphars, flowers of privet and camomile, blood-red anemones, violets and pomegranate bloom, eglantine, and narcissi'. Then on to the butcher for mutton. Next stop is the grocer for dry fruits, pistachios, Tihamah raisins, shelled almonds; then to the confectioners to buy 'open-worked tarts and fritters scented with musk, and "soap cakes", and lemon loaves, and melon preserves, and "Zaynab's combs", and "ladies' fingers", and "Kazi's titbits" and goodies of every description'. By now the porter is tired, but the woman is far from finished: the perfumer supplies 'ten sorts of waters, rose scented with musk, orange-flower, water-lily, willow-flower, violet and five others ... two loaves of sugar, a bottle for perfume-spraying, a lump of male incense, aloe wood, ambergris, and musk, and candles of Alexandria wax'. The last stop is the greengrocer for 'pickled sallower and olives, in brine and oil, with tarragon and cream cheese and hard Syrian cheese'. It is an orgiastic fantasy of foodie treats which turns into a sexual orgy when the porter returns to the lady's sumptuous Baghdad home.

Donning the disguise of a common labourer, the ninth-century caliph al-Ma'mun was wont to slip out of the palace to sample the famous street food of his capital. To the horror of his courtiers, his favourite hangouts were the market cookshops that sold *judhaba*, a chicken, duck or fatty cut of lamb roasted in an outdoor *tannur* clay oven over a pan of sweet bread-pudding seasoned with honey, rose-water, sugar, dry fruit, spices and saffron. The fats and juices of the slowly-roasting meat would drip into the sweet-bread, producing an irresistibly delicious sweet and salty dish that was popular as a takeaway in markets and roadsides for the masses of the city, and the occasional incognito caliph.[9]

Al-Ma'mun's nephew, al-Mutawakkil, the tenth Abbasid caliph, once smelt a *sikbaja* being cooked by a sailor on board a ship. Unable to resist, he ordered the pot to be brought to him. A Baghdad speciality, *sikbaja* was a sweet and sour meat or fish stew cooked in vinegar, honey, dried fruit and spices, and garnished with spicy sausages; it was a dish relished by the very richest as well the most humble. Al-Mutawakkil ate the man's dinner and returned the pot stuffed with money; he pronounced it the most delicious *sikbaja* he had ever tasted.[10]

From the culinary extravaganzas of the caliphs and the super-rich down to the poorest, Baghdadis took food very, very seriously, using rare and costly ingredients. This was a city where caliphs personally supervised the cooking of favourite dishes, where poets composed elegies to recipes, and where chefs became celebrities. You could munch on a succulent and spiced mutton *shawarma*, the ancestor of the doner kebab, or a *bazmaward*, which was a kind of ninth-century chicken burrito with chopped nuts and herbs. Another street-food favourite was *badhinjan mahshi*, cooked and chopped aubergine mixed with ground walnuts and almonds, caramelised onions, fresh herbs, vinegar, cinnamon and caraway seeds.

*

As the caliph al-Ma'mun would tell you, street food can be among the best you can get. In a megacity such as Rome in the second century or New York in the nineteenth, urban living did not leave much room for domestic kitchens with their space-occupying stoves. Street food therefore became a necessity and, in any city that prized its culinary delights, it was of a high standard. More than that, the function of street food and takeaway food is fundamental to the economy of megacities, particularly the informal economy that keeps incomers and marginalised groups alive. Preparing food has been the way into the city for many immigrants without much else to sell. Both Mexico City and Mumbai have close to 250,000 street vendors each, a high proportion of the working population. London in the mid-nineteenth century had tens of thousands of mobile food sellers including 500 who sold nothing other than pea soup and hot eels, and 300 specialising in fried fish.[11]

The sprawling city of present-day Lagos resembles a massive market and open-air kitchen set in a traffic jam. One of the most common sights are the sellers of the soft Agege bread. It is baked in hundreds of small-scale bakeries in the Lagosian district after which it is named, and distributed to thousands of hawkers to supply the morning commuters. The hawkers carry the bread on their heads, covered in cellophane and piled in a pyramid with tubs of butter and mayonnaise, touring the city with their distinctive cry: *Agege bread ti de o!* Often they are accompanied by someone selling a bean stew known as *ewa ayogin*. Even more ubiquitous are the corn cobs roasting on tripod stands along the roads. Corn vendors reckon the start-up costs are under $30 for a grill, stand, charcoal, pots and corn; you can make a profit of around $4 a day – slightly above the average daily pay – selling it to passing motorists, along with its traditional accompaniments: coconut, pears and kernels. Corn is a staple in Lagos. As one vendor put it: 'The business ... puts me on the road, has placed food on my table, pays my rent and enabled me to fund my children's education as a widow. Nigerians cannot do without eating corn and we can never stop making money from their taste.'[12]

Grab-and-go food makes sense in a big, jostling city, where everyone is on the move. The majority of meals in developing countries are consumed in the streets. If it wasn't for the informal sector and its army of entrepreneurs, many people would not eat at all. Flexible and mobile, street traders are able to carve out new markets in parts of a city that are poorly supplied by the formal economy. It is a precarious life for these Lagosian vendors – the majority female – threatened by rivals or the police. In Victorian London, as in Lagos, street-food hawkers consisted of the unemployed, the illiterate, the outcasts, the casual poor and newcomers; they were seen as subversives and threats to the order of the streets, classed with beggars, prostitutes, hustlers and thieves.

Londoners were fed by an army of street-food sellers, mostly women, who traversed the streets with barrows or baskets on their heads. Hot pies, nuts, strawberries, cherries, fish, oysters, cakes, milk – all these and more were available. Street-side sausage fryers and apple roasters competed with a bevy of other street traders: boot polishers, knife grinders, clothes menders, ballad sellers and second-hand-clothes dealers.

The reformer, author and co-founder of *Punch* Henry Mayhew listed the most popular street foods and beverages of the 1850s: fried fish, hot eels, pickled whelks, sheep's trotters, ham sandwiches, pea soup, hot green peas, penny pies, plum duff, meat puddings, baked potatoes, spice cakes, muffins, crumpets, Chelsea buns, sweetmeats, brandy balls, tea, coffee, ginger beer, lemonade, hot wine, fresh milk, ass's milk, curds and whey, and sherbet drinks. For the working poor, breakfast on the street consisted of coffee and warm food from a stall or a cart; shellfish 'of many kinds' made up lunch; dinner was a choice of hot eel, a pint of pea soup, baked potato, cakes, tarts, pastries, nuts and oranges. Late at night theatregoers, pleasure seekers and party animals could revive themselves with coffee, sandwiches, meat puddings or a trotter.[13]

In a city packed with food sellers, their distinctive, lyrical cries and songs burnished themselves into the collective memory. They were part of the poetry of the street, a hubbub that mingled with the smells of cooking food. 'Cherries ripe-ripe-ripe!', 'Hot pudding-pies hot!', 'Brandy balls – balls – balls! Here you are! Brandy balls, four a penny! Hot spiced gingerbread – the raal sort – hot as fire!', went some of the sing-song patter.[14]

The history of street food is a history of the city itself. It is the history of the migrations that have fuelled urban growth. Londoners in Mayhew's day, like their forebears going back to Roman times, consumed oysters from street sellers by the hundreds of millions each year. 'It is a wery remarkable circumstance, sir,' notes Sam in Charles Dickens's *The Pickwick Papers* (1836), 'that poverty and oysters always seem to go together.' That was until the second half of the nineteenth century when the oyster beds that had sustained generations of Londoners became exhausted by the demands of the megacity's 3 million population; the mollusc became a luxury thereafter, and people switched allegiance to the most British of street foods, fish and chips. The practice of deep-frying fish was brought to London and popularised by Sephardic Jewish refugees fleeing persecution in Spain and Portugal from the sixteenth century; its double act with chips dates to the 1860s, when Joseph Malin, a teenage Ashkenazi Jew from eastern Europe, abandoned his family rug-weaving business after a flash of inspiration made him pair the two. He sold them on the street from a tray hung round his neck; success on the street led to a permanent shop in the East End.

By the 1920s it was the ubiquitous takeout food of the working class, with 35,000 fish and chip shops in Britain. Tastes have diversified again over the years. In the later part of the twentieth century fried chicken became the ubiquitous street food of many inner cities around Britain, reflecting the tastes and cuisines of Africans, Afro-Caribbeans, Asians and east Europeans, not to say the culture of late-night drinking. In multicultural cities, fried chicken cuts across ethnic, religious and class divisions.

Brought to London by Jewish refugees, fish and chips were later cooked and sold by successions of newly arrived immigrant groups to the city: Italians, Chinese, Cypriots, Indians, Poles and Romanians. Likewise, in the Lower East Side of New York many fast-food staples were first sold from pushcarts to garment-factory workers by entre-preneurial immigrants desperate to make a living: Jewish salt beef, bagels, cream cheese, smoked salmon, falafel, pickles and pastrami; hamburgers, hotdogs, pretzels from Germany, Austria and Switzerland; Italian pizzas and ice cream; Greek souvlaki. From the early twen-tieth century, official efforts to sanitise the city and reclaim the sidewalk pushed the carts off the streets of the Lower East Side. A tradition of outdoor socialising around street food that bound immi-grant communities came to an end. The subsequent waves of street-food fashions attest to the social changes that have swept through modern cities. Jewish and east European pushcarts have been succeeded by Chinese, Vietnamese, Tex-Mex, Japanese and Korean foods, and latterly by Afghans, Egyptians and Bangladeshis selling halal dishes.

A way to a city's heart is through its stomach. And food changes how a city is lived in and experienced. Los Angeles has had a long love affair with street food, beginning with Mexican tamale wagons (*tamaleros*) and Chinese street vendors in the late nineteenth century. Starting in the 1960s, *loncheros* trucks that had been converted from ice-cream vans sold tacos, tostadas, burritos, gorditas, ceviche and tortas to the growing Latino population of the city's Eastside. The rapid growth and dispersal of LA's Latino community from the 1980s changed the culinary face of the city. The popularity of *loncheros* spread from immigrant districts to university campuses, nightlife hotspots and then to the wider metropolis.

The combination of the financial crisis of 2008 and the advent of social media saw an explosion of food trucks in LA. Chefs who could not afford restaurants, customers with shrunken incomes and technologies that publicised gourmet ventures meant that the number of street-food trucks grew to over 3,000, selling street food from all over the globe. This revolution was conducted in the face of strict laws and official disapproval, an attitude which condemned street food as messy, intrusive and unhygienic. The spread of Latino food-vending – and others who joined the trend – created pockets of street life in a metropolis that had been long dominated by the car. People travelled to places they might never have thought of visiting, tempted by the latest gourmet fad broadcast on foodie blogs and social media. The lure of food sparked a car-park and sidewalk culture of eating, drinking, music and socialising where it had not existed before.

The hawkers of Lagos, like the costermongers of Victorian London, the pushcart vendors of New York and the truck chefs of LA, are among the most entrepreneurial people in the city. Markets, cheap cafés, fast-food carts, loncheros and the like are the beating heart of the urban community and economy. In the twenty-first century a city is judged by the quality and diversity of its food; tourists are lured as much by markets, restaurants and street food as they are by museums and cityscapes. Often we eat our way through the city, learning its geography by its distribution of ethnic cuisine and markets.

As the story of the porter from the *Arabian Nights* illustrated, a meal is assembled by traversing the city, from one specialised market district to another. For most cities, for most of history, the city has been a massive market and al fresco kitchen, a sequence of outdoor and indoor spaces devoted to retail of one sort or another. Working through the night when the city slept, big wholesale food markets such as the Tsukiji fish market in Tokyo, Les Halles in Paris and Covent Garden in London spawned a supporting ecosystem of all-night bars, cafés, street food and restaurants. The nocturnal activities of food-selling kick-started urban nightlife. Most meals have, through the ages, been cooked on the street and eaten on the hoof. The life and bustle of cities have been generated as part of filling one's belly and tantalising one's taste buds. For the citizens of Mumbai or Lagos, sociability, civility and conviviality are bound up with the timeless activity of procuring staples and luxuries alike throughout the day and night on virtually every street. Cities that have been sanitised of street markets and vendors have lost one of the most important ingredients in creating urban sociability.

In his 2015 novel about present-day Lagos, *Every Day Is for the Thief*, Teju Cole describes the centrality of the city market to urban life: 'One goes to the market to participate in the world. As with all things that concern the world, being in the market requires caution. The market – as the essence of the city – is always alive with possibility and danger. Strangers encounter one another in the world's infinite variety; vigilance is needed. Everyone is there not merely to buy or sell, but because it is a duty. If you sit in your house, if you refuse to go to the market, how would you know of the existence of others? How would you know of your own existence?'[15]

*

Baghdadis did not want just to eat delicious recipes; they wanted to read about them too. The Sūq al-Warrakin contained over a hundred booksellers. Many of the volumes on sale were dedicated to all aspects of food culture. The rage for cookery was instrumental in boosting a new and revolutionary technology: paper-making.

The foundation of Baghdad coincided with the introduction of paper-making from China, allowing the diffusion of written materials on an unprecedented scale. The first paper mill was established in Baghdad by the Barmakids, a central Asian clan who had risen to a peak of wealth and power under the Abbasid dynasty (paper would not be made in Europe for almost half a millennium, until the thirteenth century). A new profession of copyists came into existence to satisfy the rage for literature.[16]

As the 'crossroads of the universe', Baghdad attracted the wealth of the world and, with it, the knowledge of the world. In this city – 'the region of men of refinement, the fountainhead of scholars' – successful poets could become wealthy celebrities if they attracted the patronage of the super-elite, or the caliph himself. Among the recoveries from the Belitung shipwreck were hundreds of inkpots, striking evidence of the explosion in literacy.[17]

The impetus, however, came from the very top. By the middle of the ninth century Baghdad was by far the biggest storehouse of knowledge in the world. The Bait al-Hikma – the House of Wisdom – was a massive royal archive of manuscripts and books. The concept of Baghdad as the 'crossroads of the universe' did not just apply to trade. The geographical position of the Abbasid capital had significant consequences. Not only did scholars come from the West, bringing the immense corpus of Greek and Latin knowledge rooted in the teachings of Athens, Alexandria and Rome, but also from Persia, India, central Asia and China. Thanks to the introduction of paper and the omnivorous curiosity of Baghdadis, much of the knowledge of past centuries, which would otherwise have been lost, was preserved and enlarged. Open to all points of the compass, Baghdad was the meeting point not just of cuisines and people, but of ideas.

The influx of knowledge from east and west, and its resulting collision, is well illustrated in the towering achievements of Muhammad ibn Musa al-Khwarizmi (c.780–c.850). A Persian Zoroastrian by origins, al-Khwarizmi was born in an oasis city in Khorasan, modern-day Uzbekistan, and, like so many of the most powerful intellects of the time, was inexorably drawn to Baghdad's House of Wisdom. There he imbibed the massive collections of Greek, Babylonian, Persian, Indian and Chinese works on mathematics, geometry, science and astrology, a range of knowledge brought together for the first time in Baghdad.[18]

The Compendious Book on Calculation by Completion and Balancing was the revolutionary result. In it al-Khwarizmi advanced human understanding of mathematics with one giant stride. His *magnum opus* took ancient-Greek geometry, Chinese mathematics and Indian number theory and used them to lay the foundations for modern algebra, and with it a method of solving linear and quadratic equations. His second great work on arithmetic, *The Book of Addition and Subtraction According to the Hindu Calculation*, had as great a consequence: it introduced the Hindu numeral system to the Arab world and later to Europe. The Latinised version of his name, Algoritmi, hints at his contribution to computation; today algorithms rule our lives. In the Middle Ages, however, an 'Algorist' was someone who adopted al-Khwarizmi's system of encoding numbers with nine numerals and a zero. Within a short time, Algorists (or followers of al-Khwarizmi) started using decimal fractions.

To write that al-Khwarizmi came from an oasis city in Uzbekistan makes it sound like he was plucked from obscurity and sent to the Big City to make his name. That is not the case. So long sidelined or simply ignored by modern histories, with attention focused on Roman, Greek or Arab cities, central Asia had one of the most sophisticated urban cultures and some of the most advanced cities on the planet.[19]

Trade coming to and from China made commercial centres such as Balkh, Samarkand and Merv extremely prosperous; the major sites of the vast region were shaped and reshaped by travellers and migrants over the centuries, each group – from Greeks, Jews and Chinese to Indians, Iranians, Turks, Syrians and Arabs – bringing their cultures, techniques, technologies and religions with them. These cities also acted as magnets for nomadic tribes from the steppes, who brought honey, wax, falcons and animal skins, pelts and furs to market. The cities boomed. Merv, for instance, was described by the Arab historian al-Muqaddasi in the late tenth century as a 'delightful, fine, elegant, brilliant, extensive and pleasant city'. Like many other cities on the Silk Roads, it possessed monumental architecture and cutting-edge infrastructure.[20]

Buddhist converts to Islam from the city of Balkh in the Oxus Valley (in present-day northern Afghanistan), the Barmakids were, after the caliphs, the richest and most powerful dynasty in Baghdad. They brought not only paper to the new metropolis, but also the intellectual energy and open-mindedness of their homeland. Now a heap of ruins, Balkh was one of the great cities of late antiquity, known to the Romans as indescribably rich and to the Arabs as incomparably beautiful.[21]

These great diverse and cosmopolitan cities flourished as intellectual centres, with particularly skilled scientists, astronomers, doctors and mathematicians, and a passion for books. In aiming to become the metropolitan colossus of the globe, it was natural that Baghdad tapped into the intellectual energy so long nurtured in the central Asian cities. Al-Khwarizmi was just one of many drawn to the capital of the cali-phate from the metropolises of central Asia. The rise of the Barmakids made central Asia's intellectual energy the foundation of Baghdad's phenomenal growth.

In the centuries before and just after the beginning of the Common Era, Alexandria provided the setting for gigantic strides in knowledge. From the 1660s, London hummed and frothed with scientific excitement after the foundation of the Royal Society of London for Improving Natural Knowledge provided the meeting point for Isaac Newton, Robert Boyle, John Locke, Christopher Wren and Robert Hooke among other luminaries. Sitting chronologically midway between these scientific revolutions, Baghdad joins Alexandria and London as one of the three sites of major scientific explosions before the modern period. Why did such episodes of acceleration in human knowledge occur in these cities at these times? There is no easy answer, of course, but at the very least these three cities shared a series of factors that coincided to ignite the fuse. They were powerful both politically and commercially. They had ambitious elites prepared to reach deep into their pockets to sponsor scientific experimentation. They also had lively and curious publics, which helped to create a culture of enquiry. Above all else, they opened their doors to new ideas and people.

The outstanding wealth of Baghdad, and its passion for knowledge, brought together a dazzling array of polymaths who worked, thought and (it being Baghdad) ate together. At the heart of Baghdad's intellectual life was the House of Wisdom and Baghdad's astronomical observatory. The city's scholars did, among other things, groundbreaking work on optics, medicine, chemistry, engineering, metallurgy, physics, music theory and architecture. The great polymath Abu Musa Jabir ibn Hayyan (known in the West by his Latinised name Geber), is considered to be the 'father of chemistry' and the pioneer of laboratory-based experimentation; he has been put on a par with Robert Boyle and Antoine Lavoisier in the history of science. His contribution is often ignored. An alchemist who wrote in mystical language and sometimes code, his Latinised name is the origin of the word 'gibberish'.[22]

One of the hallmarks of the Islamic renaissance was the way in which masses of knowledge – both ancient and modern – were brought together, synthesised, and simplified for everyday use. In other words, it was utilitarian. Mathematics, astronomy and geography were the key to world mastery because they produced, among other things, maps and navigational aids. In researching his book *The Best Divisions*

for Knowledge of the World (985), the geographer al-Maqdisi travelled
to the ports of the Persian Gulf and Red Sea and interviewed numerous
'shipmasters, cargo masters, coastguards, commercial agents, and
merchants, and I considered them among the most discerning of
people'. These were the expert practitioners of complicated instruments and mathematical and astronomical calculations.[23]

★

The maritime Silk Road that connected the Persian Gulf and the Pearl
River was made up of routes that had been plied for centuries by
Buddhist missionaries and traders. These were roads not only of trade
but also of learning. The Korean Buddhist monk Hye-ch'o travelled
from his homeland to Guangzhou to study at a monastery. From there
he boarded a ship, perhaps owned and crewed by Persians, and travelled from city to city through south-east Asia in the 720s. He went
through India and back to China via the overland roads. Monks such
as Hye-ch'o were part of an information exchange that spread knowledge through the network of Asian cities. Religion, ideas and trade
were transmitted by the new enabling technology – paper.[24]

One of the great cities of the medieval world, Quilon is hardly a
household name today. Its curious story, however, illuminates the
urban boom of the turn of the millennium and the strange, diverse,
exotic world of Asian urbanisation in its heyday. Quilon (now called
Kollam) is on the Malabar Coast of Kerala in southern India. Even
before the ninth century it had had a long and illustrious history as a
port. But in the early ninth century, its fortunes were ailing. Udaya
Marthanda Varma, the Tamil king, called in two Christian monks
from Syria, Mar Sabor and Mar Proth, to rebuild the port and manage
its trade.[25]

The Christian contractors did a good job: opened in 825 Quilon
became not just the busiest port in India, but one of the four giant
entrepots of the early medieval world, ranking alongside Alexandria,
Cairo and Guangzhou. Quilon had a significant Chinese expatriate
community; it was home to Nestorian Christians, Arab and Persian
Muslims, Jews, Jains, Hindus, Buddhists and peoples from all over the
Indian Ocean. The Persian merchant Sulaiman al-Tajir described
Quilon in the ninth century as full of large Chinese merchant junks

A modern reconstruction of Uruk, the world's first city, made in 2012 and showing the city in 2100 BC.

The now demolished Pennsylvania Station, New York City, displaying the same grandeur and vastness as the Baths of Caracalla in Rome (216 AD) on which it was modelled.

Swimming has been one of the primary forms of recreation in the city. Here, in 1938, children from the poorest immigrant district of New York City dive out of an abandoned industrial building into the polluted East River. Within in a year, this area had been converted by Robert Moses into the 57-acre East River Park.

Buying and eating food in the street is at the heart of urban sociability, as this timeless photograph of Hester Street, NYC, in 1903 shows.

The Islamic city: Bukhara.

Tashkent: the Silk Roads transmitted not only commodities but knowledge. Baghdad may have been the biggest storehouse of knowledge in the world in the ninth century AD, but much of its intellectual energy and scholars came from the great cosmopolitan cities of central Asia.

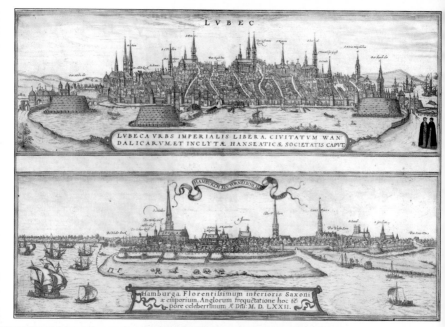

The rapid rise of Lübeck (top) was made vivid by its soaring steeples. Along with Hamburg (below), Lübeck was one of the pre-eminent trading metropolises of northern Europe in the Middle Ages. These compact cities were at the cutting-edge of military technology.

The great metropolis of Mesoamerica: Tenochtitlan.

The home as a bastion of orderliness and virtue amid the urban inferno. In Pieter de Hooch's *Interior Beside a Linen Cupboard* (1663) the private home is elevated to an almost sacred space, with the outside world of the city framed in the doorway.

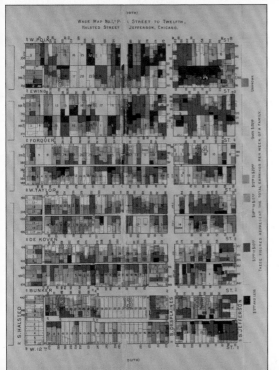

The secrets of the city revealed: a poverty map of a few blocks of Chicago, produced by Hull House in 1895. Founded in 1889 by Jane Addams and Ellen Gates Starr as an institution devoted to education and social reform, Hull House led the way in cleaning up the mess of the industrial megacity.

The slum, the factory and the street: children in Newcastle, c. 1900.

The actress Violet Carson – in character as Ena Sharples from the soap opera *Coronation Street* – surveys Manchester's industrial cityscape from the balcony of a newly constructed high-rise in 1968. 'When I was a little lass, the world was half a dozen streets, an' a bit o' waste land, an' the rest was all talk,' she recalled.

Vincent van Gogh's *On the Outskirt of Paris* (1887) depicts the poor of Paris displaced to the unloved 'bastard countryside' on the edgelands of the metropolis.

In *Paris Street, A Rainy Day* (1877), Gustave Caillebotte captures not only the sanitised city of the nineteenth century, but the social alienation fostered by the modern metropolis.

Edouard Manet's unsettling *A Bar at the Folies-Bergère* (1881–2) is one of the great artistic commentaries on modern urban life. His city is one of spectacle and movement, in which human relationships have become blurred and uncertain. The defiant face of the barmaid is that of all modern urbanites, forced into continuous interaction with strangers who may or may not be predators.

Manet's *The Plum* (1878) captures the unease of liberated women in male-dominated urban public spaces.

using the port as their transhipment hub on the route between Guangzhou and Baghdad. The wealth of this city rested on its key global function: it was for centuries the centre of the trade in one of humankind's most desirable commodities, black pepper.[26]

Food and our shifting taste for it changes the world. According to the monk Yijing, Chinese food had for generations been bland and uninspiring. The discovery of Indian cuisine and ingredients had revolutionised Chinese cooking and in so doing kick-started a trade bonanza. In turn this network of interlocking trade conducted over 12,000 miles brought into life major global metropolises such as Quilon.[27]

Cities across the monsoon seas, from Mombasa to Guangzhou, reflected a strikingly similar urbanity and cosmopolitanism. Quilon was not unusual in its diversity; it was the norm for the cities of the monsoon seas. Living alongside the native population of Saymur, a city sixty kilometres south of present-day Mumbai, were 10,000 first-generation immigrants from Oman, Siraf, Basra and Baghdad and their Indian-born offspring. Saymur was one of many cities on the Gujarati and Konkan coasts that contained such a hubbub of religions and tongues.

Mogadishu in modern-day Somalia became a wealthy and powerful commercial metropolis, famous for its fabrics, frankincense and gold exports and its wealthy mercantile community. The archaeological record shows the extent of its connections: coins have been found there from Sri Lanka, Vietnam and China. In time, Mogadishu was eclipsed by Kilwa, a city state founded by Persian colonists in the tenth century on a tiny island off present-day Tanzania. The citizens of Kilwa were middlemen: merchants, financiers and shippers, importing goods from India, China and Arabia and selling them in mainland markets in exchange for African gold, ivory, rhino horn, big-cat skins, tortoiseshell, mangrove wood and iron, which they exported across Asia and especially to China. The presence of a dominant commercial city off the coast sparked the emergence of satellite towns on the mainland that processed the merchandise from the interior of Africa and provisioned the offshore city with foodstuffs.

The wealth of the monsoon trading system was funnelled, as it is today, through the straits of Malacca and Sunda. The Malay Peninsula, Sumatra and Java saw numerous independent city states that emerged to compete for a slice of the profits from the merchant fleets. Second only to Baghdad, and later Cairo, this region was the wealthiest in the medieval world. In the summer the monsoon brought traders from the Spice Islands (Maluku) of Indonesia with their cargos of cloves, nutmeg and mace. But there were no customers for them to trade with directly because merchants from India, Arabia and China arrived by the winter monsoon. As a result, the spices and other commodities had to be warehoused during the interval before being transhipped to world markets.

For hundreds of years the dominant power in this crucial global crossroads was the all-but forgotten confederation of city states called Sri Vijaya. Its dominant metropolis was Palembang on Sumatra, which, from the eighth century, rose to control a league of cities spread across Sumatra, the Malay Peninsula, Java and parts of Burma and Thailand. Arab dhows, Indian ships and Chinese junks came to this rich Buddhist entrepot to trade and refit their vessels. Palembang was where the traders of the two greatest empires on earth, those of the Abbasid caliphate and the Tang dynasty, encountered one another.

For centuries a booming, busy, cosmopolitan place, Palembang ranks as one of the great vanished world metropolises of history. Unfortunately, not much remains of the city; the Sri Vijayan Empire was wiped off the face of the earth in the thirteenth century and Palembang's estuarine site thoroughly looted and then buried under sediment. In its prime it was a place of magnificent wealth and an intellectual centre of international repute; but in truth we know more about Uruk in the fourth millennium BC than we do about Palembang in the eleventh century AD. Indeed, much of the medieval Indian Ocean urban world is like that: it was an ever-shifting, free-flowing, outward-looking culture, that left scant remains in its wake.

It is likely that Palembang, even in its zenith, consisted mainly of wooden floating houses: this was a nimble urban civilisation, ready to up sticks and move if nature or shifting trade patterns dictated. Yet, for all that is lost to history, we can imagine a place of haggling merchants from all over Asia and East Africa standing around sacks of spices, bales of textiles and crates of porcelain. The scene was familiar throughout the chain of interlinked monsoon cities. The clockwork-like seasonal winds blew in armadas of foreign traders to these ports; the merchants stayed there for months, conducting business, deepening contacts, socialising and exchanging ideas before the monsoon winds took them homeward. Some stayed in a foreign city for years and many intermarried with the local populations.

A Persian merchant recalled an immense population and 'more markets than can be counted' at Palembang; he saw 800 money changers in one bazaar alone. In the sixth-century Tamil epic *Manimekalai*, the city of Kanchipuram (near present-day Chennai) is described. There were shops housing fishmongers, potters, goldsmiths, brass workers, carpenters, masons, painters, leather workers, tailors, musicians, jewellers, conch cutters and garland makers, as well as the butchers and sellers of sweets, street food, betel leaves and aromatics in the main broad street. Off it lay streets for the grain merchants, streets for minstrels and entertainers, the street 'where courtesans who gave sexual pleasure lived', a street for elephant tamers and another for horse trainers, a street where the security guards of shops lived. In addition, there were 'streets with the beautiful houses of assayers of gold; streets where many gem sellers lived; where the Brahmins lived; the main royal street; the street where ministers and important state officials lived; the public area of the city assemblies, and squares and street corners'.[28]

Palembang was also thick with warehouses. The 500,000 pieces of cargo recovered from the wreck of a Malayo-Indonesian ship discovered in 2003 off Java, dating to the late tenth century, hint at the splendour contained in the warehouses and markets of Palembang: Chinese green-glazed ceramics, mirrors and money; expensive perfume bottles from western Asia and Egypt; rock crystal from Africa and Kashmir; Afghani lapis lazuli; gems from Sri Lanka; drugs from Arabia; fine ceramics from Thailand. Most likely there would have been foodstuffs, spices and textiles as well.[29]

The Belitung ship also foundered close to Palembang. Perhaps it was about to put in there to exchange some of its cargo; or maybe it was leaving having struck some good deals and picked up spices. The wreck yielded a Sri Vijayan coin and hanging scales from there too. Most likely the dhow would have traded in other emerging port cities in Angkorian Cambodia, Burma, Java, Thailand, Malaya and Vietnam.

The decision to house the finds of the Belitung wreck in the Museum of Asian Civilisations is telling. Singapore sees itself as the modern-day standard-bearer of an urban civilisation that has thrived in the Straits for millennia and the natural heir of powerful city states such as Palembang. For Singaporeans the Belitung shipwreck and others that have emerged in the twenty-first century reveal a timeless Asian urban tradition. Singapore, like Palembang before it, dominates the vast volume of shipping that funnels through the Straits and provides it with sophisticated port facilities. Like its forebear it hosts a massive and fluctuating expat population drawn from all over the globe to finance the trade, provide entertainment, mix cocktails and cook gourmet meals. Like the monsoon metropolises of the past it has an array of religions living cheek by jowl: Taoist, Hindu and Jain temples next to mosques; Buddhist temples and synagogues; most Christian denominations, along with Zoroastrians, Sikhs and atheists.

Above all, in identifying so readily with its historic legacy, Singapore claims to be a beacon of a distinctive form of urbanism, one that owes less to the West and to British colonialism, and more to ancient pan-Asian notions of city-building. Singapore has always been seen as a British creation, dating back no further than 1819. The discovery of the Belitung shipwreck changed that, allowing Singapore to claim the mantle of the city states that flourished from the ninth century until the sixteenth.

This urban tradition adds a deeper dimension to Singapore's urban ambitions and claims to moral leadership in terms of managing our urban future in the present millennium. By pioneering smart-city technologies and green policies and trumpeting its architecture, cleanliness, safety and quality of life, it offers an Asian alternative to the West. Placed deliberately at the centre of the Asian Civilisations Museum, the Belitung shipwreck, and the world it represents, foregrounds a time when Asia was the world's urban powerhouse and Europe was an unsophisticated, marginal backwater.

The rich history of the medieval land and sea routes is also used to legitimise China's modern rejuvenation of the Silk Roads – its Belt and Road Initiative. Both the long-distance high-speed trains and the sea lanes that connect China to western Europe are, like their predecessors, forces of urbanisation. Places deep inland like Lanzhou, Ürümqi and Khorgos are being turned into cities of trade, touted as the Dubais of the twenty-first century. On the sea routes too Gwadar in Pakistan, Hambantota in Sri Lanka, Kyauk Phyu in Myanmar and

Bagamoyo in Tanzania are being developed by the Chinese into what are promised to be glittering skyscraper port cities.

Whether these cities will replicate the cosmopolitanism, intellectual effervescence and excitement of their predecessors is too early to tell. The trillions of dollars being poured into high-speed railways, port facilities, power plants, pipelines, bridges and airports are nonetheless spurring city-building in an effort to shift the world's economic centre of gravity back to Asia. Back, that is to say, to where it was before Columbus.

*

In the early years of the thirteenth century, Genghis Khan consolidated his power on the Mongolian plains, bringing numerous tribes under his control by force of arms or negotiation. Lacking siege equipment, cities would be taken by breathtaking acts of terror and savagery. The imperial capital Zhongdu (modern-day Beijing) came under siege by the Mongols in 1213. Zhongdu was considered impregnable. After a year, the Jin emperor abandoned Zhongdu, leaving its inhabitants to starve to death. In June the gates of the city were finally opened. In poured the Mongols to this vast, hitherto invincible city. Thousands were massacred; parts of the city burnt for months after. Genghis was in control of most of northern China. No city could be safe now that the Mongols had learnt the pitiless arts of siege warfare. Added to that, the nomads had gleaned something vital from Chinese cities: an armoury of advanced siege technologies.

The Mongol army burst into the urban heartland of central Asia, 4,000 miles from Zhongdu. First of the major cities to fall was Bukhara, one of the largest metropolises in the world with 300,000 people, and a centre of wealth and learning. Most of the outer city was burnt. The inner citadel was reduced to surrender by a battery from the most advanced siege engines available. Among the survivors, the young men were pressed into military service, women and children sold into slavery, and the artisans deported to Mongolia. The Mongols moved onto Samarkand, which received the same treatment. Likewise, Nishapur came under a pummelling from 3,000 giant crossbows, 3,000 stone-throwing machines and 700 flamethrowers; after its population was massacred the city was razed and ploughed over. Balkh, the great intellectual fountainhead and home town of the Barmakids, was razed in 1220.

Moscow was destroyed in 1238, Kiev in 1240. With a population of over 100,000, Kiev was one of the largest cities in the world, and a key node in trade routes which connected the Silk Roads, the steppes and Scandinavia. The Mongols pushed further into Europe, sacking Lublin, Krakow, Buda and Pest and destroying towns as far as the Balkans. In 1258 Mongol invaders burst into Baghdad and 'like hungry falcons attacking a flight of doves, or like raging wolves attacking sheep' rampaged through the streets killing the city's people. The Abbasid caliph was rolled in a carpet and trampled to death under the hooves of horses. The exquisite city of learning and luxury lay in ruins.

The destruction, in the thirteenth century, of several global cities – Palembang, Merv, Kiev, Baghdad and Constantinople – disrupted ancient patterns of world trade. But this titanic disruption sparked the emergence of new cities and urban cultures. The thirteenth century was to be pivotal in the history of urbanisation.

6

Cities of War

Lübeck, 1226–1491

The waters of the Trave and Wakenitz rivers reflected the full moon on the clear frosty night of 28/29 March 1942. Their silvery outline gave navigators on 234 Royal Air Force bombers a clear run to their target. The medieval heart of the port city of Lübeck was gutted by the 25,000 incendiary bombs dropped on it by the RAF that night.

Lübeck was the first German city to taste Britain's firebombing campaign in the Second World War, a deliberately soft target that had little strategic value. The Nazis retaliated with the so-called 'Baedeker Blitz', aerial attacks on cities chosen for their historical rather than military value: Exeter, Bath, York, Canterbury, Norwich, Ipswich and Colchester among others. In May 1942 Cologne became the first city to face a 1,000-bomber raid. The medieval urban heritage of northern Europe was in flames.[1]

It's unlikely Hitler shed a tear on the morning of 29 March. Back in 1932, during the presidential elections, Lübeck's senate had banned Nazi speakers, the only city in Germany to do so. Forced to give his stump speech on the outskirts, in a village called Bad Schwartau, Hitler could never speak Lübeck's name again; he referred to it only as that 'small city close to Bad Schwartau'.

That humiliation was neither forgiven nor forgotten by Hitler. When he came to power he stripped 'the small city close to Bad Schwartau' of its independent status, which had survived wars, conquests and political upheavals for 711 years, and had its civic leaders executed.

Its centre restored after the war, today Lübeck is one of the most beautiful of all northern European cities, a rabbit warren of medieval streets punctuated with glorious Gothic architecture. Tourists flock to its famous wine shops, seafood restaurants and confectioners. The latter specialise in marzipan, which the city claims to have invented.

Wine, herring and marzipan: unlikely as it may seem, these items help explain not only why Lübeck rose to become one of Europe's richest metropolises, but why Europe emerged from backwardness in an explosion of urbanisation from the twelfth century.

*

Lübeck offers the prime example of a 'free city': a small, efficient, prosperous and militarised self-governing entity that provided the bedrock for Europe's rise to global dominance. Like many European cities, it was hardened and shaped on the anvil of war.

The original settlement of Lübeck was called Liubice, which means 'lovely'. A fortified West Slavic settlement, it lay on the frontier of numerous warring pagan and Christian tribes. Lübeck itself began life four kilometres away from Liubice in 1143, founded by Adolf II of Holstein on a defensible river island as part of campaign to replace the Slavs with German and Danish colonisers. The Slavic lands were rich in resources and lay on important trade routes established over previous centuries by the Vikings. They offered enticing prospects for booming populations in the German kingdoms as well as for Flemings, Frisians and Hollanders hungry for plundered land. Four years after the establishment of Lübeck the campaign for Slavic land became a formal Crusade, with the infant town firmly in the front line of hostilities. According to the papal bull issued by Pope Eugene III, the Crusaders were given indulgences forgiving their sins; they were also enjoined to fight without mercy for the subjugation or forced conversion of the pagans.

Lübeck consisted of a wood and earth castle; the 'town', probably a collection of huts, burnt down in 1157. Its rise to greatness began when it was refounded and rebuilt two years later by Henry the Lion, Duke of Saxony and Bavaria, and granted *iura civitatis honestissima*, 'the most honourable charter of town rights'. A dominant force in the crusades against the Slavs, Henry the Lion was an eager builder, founding and developing not only Lübeck but also Munich, Augsburg and Brunswick, among other cities. It was said of him that on all his various crusades 'there was never a mention of Christianity, but only of money'. New cities gave him – and other lords – exactly what they thirsted for: quick financial return.[2]

Holy war and city-building went together. These were places used by migrants from the west as platforms for further conquest, conversion and colonisation. As a result, Henry the Lion was prepared to give the pioneers moving to Lübeck wide-ranging autonomy. The *iura civitatis honestissima* gave the leading citizens the right to make their own laws and govern themselves. Henry sent envoys to Denmark, Sweden, Norway, Gotland and Russia offering merchants free right of access to Lübeck without paying tolls. He established a mint and a market. Most important of all, Lübeck merchants were given the important right of trading in the Baltic. 'From that time onwards,' noted a German chronicler, 'there was ever-increasing activity in the town and the number of its inhabitants rose considerably.'[3]

In its early stage as a frontier town, Lübeck prospered serving the needs of further conquest. It supplied new waves of crusaders with arms, food and transport. It was the jumping-off point for warriors, traders and migrants taking part in *Drang nach Osten* – the drive to the East. Decades and centuries of onslaught and ethnic cleansing conducted by the Teutonic knights and the Livonian Brethren of the Sword against the Slavic and Baltic peoples resulted in the creation of a string of powerful German cities across the region from modern Germany through Poland, Lithuania, Latvia and Estonia.

There was an intimate connection between holy war and Europe's urban take-off, beginning in the twelfth century and gathering momentum in the thirteenth. In the second half of the thirteenth century some 300 new towns were being created in central Europe every decade. In their hunger for land, relentless pace and energetic city-building, the settlers of Europe's new lands resembled the pioneers who surged west across the United States in the nineteenth century.[4]

A great disruptive event, the Crusades, sparked these developments. The campaign to wrest the Holy Lands in the eastern Mediterranean from Islam and return them to Christendom, beginning at the close of the eleventh century, brought belligerent western Europeans, from places such as Normandy, France, Flanders, Germany and England, into contact with the Islamic urban archipelago, exposing them to the sophistication of its cities, its intellectual richness, and the staggering wealth of its markets.

The fates of Italian republics such as Genoa, Venice and Pisa were transformed by the Crusades, during which they made fortunes as shipping contractors and naval forces. The port cities won not only a warm glow of piety, but invaluable commercial privileges in the form of direct trading links with the eastern Mediterranean. The capture of Antioch (in 1098), Edessa (1099), Jaffa (1099), Jerusalem (1099), Acre (1104) Tripoli (1109) and Tyre (1124) gave Italian merchants bases from which to trade directly with Muslim and Jewish middlemen whose interests delved down through the Red Sea and onward to the vast and mature monsoon trading system. Luxury goods – spices and textiles – began to be imported back to the Italian city states and from there to the far reaches of Europe, to the German markets, the Low Countries and England.

The Italian city states were locked into intense and violent rivalry as they fought to monopolise the trade. In 1099, for instance, the Venetians sank twenty-eight Pisan ships in a battle off Rhodes. Pisa sacked its rival Amalfi on two occasions in the 1130s. These hungry, grasping Italian cities still lay in the shadow of the greatest city of Christendom and the dominant empire of the Mediterranean. Jealous of each other and determined to secure monopolies for their home cities, Pisans, Genoese and Venetians fought each other in the streets of Constantinople.

The relationship between the great metropolis and the aggressive Italians was fraught. In the 1170s the Byzantines fell out with Venice and imprisoned its resident merchants. For two decades trade between Venice and the Byzantine Empire ceased. Revenge came soon enough. En route to the Holy Land in 1203 for the Fourth Crusade, the Venetians managed to divert the Christian army to besiege Constantinople on the pretext of intervening in a dynastic dispute.

The rough and rude Crusaders 'looked on Constantinople for a long time because they could scarcely believe there could be such an enormous city in all the world'. At this time, no western European city exceeded 20,000 people; a settlement of even 10,000 was a rarity. Constantinople was home to about half a million people. The Crusaders stared with wonder at the cityscape: its massive walls and towers, the huge churches, the palaces, the marble streets and ancient columns, and of course the vast ethereal dome of Hagia Sophia.[5]

'O City, City, eye of all cities, universal boast, supramundane wonder ... the abode of every good thing! O City hast thou drunk at the hand of the Lord the cup of his fury?' wailed the Phrygian historian Niketas Choniates, who was in Constantinople when it was sacked. Some of the great treasures of the city were carted off to adorn the upstart Italian cities; many more were burnt and destroyed by intoxicated, marauding soldiers. Women, including nuns, were raped, and children left to die on the streets. When the work of pillage, massacre and rape was done, a third of Constantinople's 400,000 residents were homeless; the metropolis suffered rapid depopulation from which it was never to recover. From the carcass of the Byzantine Empire, the great Italian city secured strategically vital territory – islands and bases from which to dominate the seas.[6]

Although only a relatively small player in the global economy, the magic of Asian luxuries cast a spell over Europe. Urbanisation, so long a dormant force in that underpopulated, underdeveloped corner of the world, surged again in Italy with the influx of intercontinental trade. Were it not for luxury imports such as spices and textiles, cities like Venice and Genoa would have remained small fishing villages. As it was, in the thirteenth century, these cities took on the aspect of grandeur. Genoa's population leapt to 60,000; Florence grew from 30,000 in the middle of the century to 120,000 by the beginning of the fourteenth. By 1300 every bit of available land in Venice was built upon and bridges connected the islets. Its population reached 100,000 by the fourteenth century.

The facade of St Mark's Basilica was adorned with columns, capitals and friezes looted from Constantinople. Byzantine influences permeated Venice; but much of its urban design and architecture was borrowed from Islamic cities. The new palazzos, with their inner courtyards, winding staircases, underground cisterns and versions of *mashrabiyyah* windows, not to say their external design, imitated Levantine houses. The city itself, with its narrow streets, resembled a souk. The Doge's Palace, built from 1340, borrowed liberally from the Ibn Tulun Mosque in Cairo. The famous Venice Arsenal, the state-owned complex of shipyards and armouries, got its name from the Arabic *dar al-sin'ah* (house of industry). In Andalusia the Reconquista conducted by Christian warriors against Islam yielded western

Europeans other treasures. Knowledge that had been amassed in Baghdad in the ninth century and studied and preserved in Toledo, Cordoba and Granada diffused into Europe, along with paper-making.

In 1252 bankers from Genoa and Florence began minting gold coins. Bullion coin had not been issued on the continent for well over five centuries. Gold, credit and global trade heralded the rejuvenation of the European economy and the rebirth of cities.

*

The word 'bourgeois' derives from the Germanic word *burg*, which means fortress. In tenth-century England, Alfred the Great set up fortified settlements called *burhs* to defend against Viking raids; it was the origin of 'borough', the term for municipal administrative divisions in the United Kingdom, Australia, the United States and elsewhere. In the British Isles place names that end with '-burgh', '-bury', '-borough' and '-brough' (such as Edinburgh, Canterbury, Middlesbrough) recall this. The French *'bourg'* has the same origin (Strasbourg, Luxembourg), as does the Scandinavian *borg*, the Italian *borgo* and the Iberian *burgo*. It is possible that the word 'ghetto' derives from *borghetto*, Italian for 'little town'. Place names and the word 'bourgeois' recall the beginnings of urbanisation in Europe against a background of periodic nomadic raids, conquest and warfare. They are all rooted in the idea of defensiveness.

If you were 'bourgeois' in the Middle Ages it meant that you lived in a borough, a burgh, a bourg or a burg: you were defined as an urban-dweller, the denizen of a self-governing community, as opposed to being a peasant beholden to a feudal lord. The division between urban and rural, in terms of lifestyle, quality of life, occupation, opportunity and personal freedom, was a sharp one in the Middle Ages.

Lübeck is the exemplar of this new form of urbanisation. *Stadtluft macht frei*: 'city air makes you free'. So went the saying in Germany in the Middle Ages. The phrase had a particular legal meaning: any serf that resided in a city for a year and a day was automatically freed. But it also had a more general meaning. No longer under the control of margraves, counts, hereditary dukes, bishops or kings, Lübeck prospered from 1226, the year when it became a Free Imperial City. It owed nominal obedience to the distant Holy Roman Empire; power, according to its constitution, was in the hands of the *Rat*, its council made up of twenty *Ratsherren* (councillors) each appointed from the city's merchant guilds. Clergymen and knights were not only banned from sitting on the council, but also from buying urban land. The *Rat* invested executive power in up to four *Bürgermeister* (mayors). The mayors of Lübeck were, for a few centuries, among the leading political figures of Europe, more influential than many kings whose names are better known to history.

The corporate civic ideal was written in brick. The newly independent citizens of Lübeck built their own parish church, the Marienkirche, in the heart of the merchants' quarter, close to their market and their warehouses. This was no ordinary parish church: it was the biggest brick church ever built. A soaring masterpiece of Brick Gothic, its basic design was taken from France and Flanders and given a Baltic makeover. The twin-tower facade thrusts 125 metres into the sky above the flatlands of northern Europe; it remained one of the tallest structures in the world for centuries.

It made the nearby Romanesque cathedral, the seat of the Bishop of Lübeck, look mean and puny. The Marienkirche was a two-fingered Gothic salute to the bishop, with whom the citizens were constantly in dispute. It said: this is where power now resides in this city. The cathedral was on the edge of the city; the citizens' Marienkirche stood at its centre. It connected to the *Rathaus* (the town hall), the cockpit of mercantile power, the focus of communal civic life, and another showy experiment in Brick Gothic that stood in the northern part of the market. The church itself served a secular, mercantile purpose as well; it stored grain and served as a bourse on non-holy days. The numerous green spires that spiked above the city broadcast that Lübeck, an obscure city that had only just emerged on the periphery of Christendom, was the centre of all that was new and daring.

Lübeck, like so many other cities in Europe, began life as a frontier fortress. And like American cities in the nineteenth century, it was built by pioneers and migrants seeking fortune and fame. The councillors and merchants who built up the city in the early thirteenth century were men who had travelled, traded and negotiated in France,

Flanders and Italy. They brought with them the latest ideas of urban planning and civic architecture. Their *Rathaus* was based on municipal halls elsewhere; but, as with their Gothic church, it was to be bigger and more beautiful.

It is one of the finest examples of a medieval town hall, an imposing building studded with round spires begun in bourgeois Brick Gothic and improved with Renaissance add-ons. The people and things celebrated here are not warriors, aristocrats and kings, but merchants, civic dignitaries and guilds, whose statues and coats of arms adorn the complex. Commodities, including cloth, were traded here. The council met in its barrel-vaulted chamber to make laws and steer the city's course; the municipal court sat in the Long House in a chamber above an open vaulted arcade where traders and artisans, including the goldsmiths, did business.

Most impressive are a sequence of vast vaulted cellars in which were stored cloth and other commodities. The most important and oldest subterranean vault was the *Ratsweinkeller*, the municipal wine cellar. Down there, under the supervision of two town councillors who served as *Weinmeister*, the wine traded in Lübeck was tasted, evaluated and awarded prizes. But more than that, it was the site of communal celebrations, banquets and wine-drinking. The guilds, corporations and seafarers' societies met in the *Ratskeller*, as did the Zirkelgesellschaft, the 'Circle Society' otherwise known as the Brotherhood of Foreign Trade Merchants, an elite club made up of the urban patrician class who intermarried, socialised, did business together, and ran the city.

Four times a year the mayor or chamberlain strode out onto the hall's senate balcony for a ceremony known as *Burspraken*. This word is the German equivalent of the Latin '*civiloquium*', or civic speech. But *Burspraken* goes further; its origins in Middle Low German and peasant society implies dialogue with the very lowest townsfolk, in language they could understand. At the *Burspraken* ceremony Lübeck's statutes were read out to an assembly of the people gathered in the market, along with matters concerning the everyday life of the city: recent by-laws, prohibitions, legal decisions, council resolutions, taxes, shipping and trade regulations, and other newsworthy items. *Burspraken* did not mean participatory democracy. Rather, it was the glue that held the urban community – the bourgeoisie – together, a set of constantly updated rules that dealt with everything from foreign trade to how to dispose of refuse.[7]

That binding process was essential for the success of cities such as Lübeck. A prime example is the Holy Spirit Hospital, one of the oldest and most significant social welfare institutions in Europe, which was begun in 1286. It was a gift to Lübeck's citizens from its richest merchants. Memorialised in this building is one of its co-founders, Bertram Morneweg, merchant and town councillor. An orphan, he was adopted by a Lübeck citizen. Bertram set out into the world and constructed a business empire that stretched from Novgorod to King's Lynn in England via Riga. Long absent from his home city, he nonetheless participated in the civic life of Lübeck and bequeathed the hospital from his enormous wealth. His widow, Gertrud, augmented the family fortune by lending money to the city and to the people of Lübeck at an unbeatable 6.5%. Their son Hermann, like so many young merchants, learnt the ropes of international trade the hard way, as an expatriate in a foreign trading station. Hermann worked in King's Lynn before returning home to serve as councillor and then mayor. International businessmen, civic dignitaries, diplomats and urban patrons, the Morneweg dynasty continued to adorn Lübeck and serve on its council over the generations.

The wealth and civic spirit that made Lübeck one of the richest cities in the world can still be seen in the elegant multi-tiered step-gabled town houses with their steep A-framed roofs and decorative windows built by the burghers after the great fire of 1276. It can be seen in the *Salzspeicher*, Lübeck's stately, ornate salt warehouses. This style of architecture is beautiful. But it is a northern European type of beauty: its apparent modesty belies its underlying statement of power and wealth. Lübeck's pretty gabled houses were living quarters, offices and warehouses rolled into one. Much later Amsterdam, in many ways Lübeck's heir, would adopt near-identical architecture. Behind the imposing mercantile town houses were courtyards and alleys, accessible through narrow passageways. These were where the employees of the business lived in small apartments.

A succession of Germanic cities were planted, exactly like Lübeck, on the sites of Slavic settlements or Crusader fortresses, and settled with colonisers from the Rhineland, Westphalia and Saxony. A hundred towns and cities adopted Lübeck law, among them Riga (1201), Rostock

(1218), Danzig (1224), Wismar (1229), Stralsund (1234), Ebling (1237), Stettin (1243), Greifswald (1250) and Königsberg (1255), and also took on the distinctive appearance of their mother city: Brick Gothic and soaring green spires that served as landmarks for sailors. These cities, like their parent, built big – bigger than anyone had done before (or would do so again until the age of the skyscraper), announcing their new power and their arrival on the international stage. The church spire of the Marienkirche in Stralsund reached 151 metres; bigger than the Great Pyramid of Giza, it was only a few metres short of Lincoln Cathedral, the tallest man-made structure in the world.

*

For long-distance travellers, these cities, with their near-identical cityscapes, Gothic elegance, decorative gables and enormous spires, would have been a reassuring sight. An urban civilisation, based on a common language – Middle Low German – as well as shared laws, architecture and mercantile values emerged on the northern trade routes.

German merchants organised themselves into guilds through which they coordinated their activities to exploit the less developed and more dangerous eastern Baltic, and to provide mutual defence on the high seas. In hostile lands they banded together into enclosed Germanic communities, defended by walls and weapons. The German word for this kind of guild was *Hanse*, a term which originally meant armed convoy. Trade and the sword went hand in hand in a world where no state was able to offer security for long-distance exchange. Hansa merchants, spread across northern Europe and united by ties of kinship, drove down the costs of long-distance trade by pooling risks and rewards.

The Indian Ocean and the Mediterranean carried spices and silks, low-volume but highly lucrative luxuries. Merchants from Lübeck and other trading city states were after different kinds of commodities. Russia supplied beeswax, much in demand for candles used in churches and cathedrals, and furs in vast quantities. The Hansa merchants deployed the largest cargo ships seen in Europe, called 'cogs': large, cheap, clinker-built ships that could withstand long voyages. They were vessels for bulk trade: wax, fur, timber, resins, flax, wheat and rye from the eastern Baltic; wool, cloth, wine, salt, butter, spices, copper and iron from Scandinavia and western Europe. Unglamorous products, maybe; but vital for daily life. The Hansa cogs carried Crusaders and colonists, as well as supplies of food and arms to sustain their campaigns in the East.

Lübeck emerged as the leading player in this rapid takeover and exploitation of the Baltic. The first German city on the Baltic coast, its internal strength and legal rights gave it a hegemonic position over the newer cities. If another one emerged as a rival it was subdued, a fate which befell ambitious Stralsund in 1249 when Lübeck burnt it to the ground. Individual merchants pioneered the Hansa system; very quickly their home cities followed suit. Lübeck entered into an alliance with Hamburg in 1241, coordinating their trading and military activities.

Lübeck controlled the Baltic trades and connected the flow of goods to and from the interior of Germany; Hamburg had direct access to the North Sea (or German Sea as it was known). The two great cities sat close to the salt mines of Lüneburg. Access to sea and salt turned these two cities into great metropolises because they supplied much of the rest of Europe with the jet fuel of urbanisation.

Cities simply cannot exist without year-round sustenance. The humble but protein-rich herring, pickled and preserved, provided medieval cities in the cold north of Europe with the means to exist and grow. Salt procured from Lüneburg was taken to Lübeck, which exported it to Skåne, in southern Sweden, where the herring came to spawn. In 1360, 250 herring ships put into Lübeck alone, carrying tons of the silver delicacy. From there the fish was re-exported to the urban heartland of northern Europe, booming textile manufacturing towns such as Ghent, Ypres, Arras and Bruges that were dependent on preserved foodstuffs.

Imports of herring were supplemented with cod fished extensively off the coasts of Norway, Iceland and Greenland and brought back to Lübeck. Preserved cod found markets not only in northern Europe but in Iberia and the Mediterranean. Medieval Lübeck was like a modern-day oil-rich sheikhdom, only the fuel then was fish and salt.

Traders from Lübeck specialised in big, bulky cargos; they dealt in the necessities of life, the things that fed cities. Herrings were one part of that. Rye bread, still a staple in north-eastern Europe today, is a reminder of the large cargos of rye and wheat imported from the newly conquered lands of the eastern Baltic. Timber, much sought after for building, came from that region too. Beer, the delicacy of northern Europe, was carried on German ships to sustain growing urban populations. Rhineland wine was exchanged for various commodities. English wool and Russian furs provided warmth and elegance on the streets of Europe's towns and cities, a sure sign of rising living standards.

Lübeck almost certainly did not invent marzipan (as it often claimed), which consists of honey and ground almonds, but it still produces the highest-regarded confection. Munching on marzipan at the Café Niederegger, opposite the *Rathaus*, is a gastronomic history lesson. It speaks of the prosperity of medieval Lübeck. Almonds came to the city via Bruges on ships that had travelled from the distant Mediterranean. Genoese, Venetian and Florentine galleys, and vessels from Catalonia, the Basque Country and Portugal came to Bruges from the end of the thirteenth century carrying peppers, ginger, nutmeg, cloves and almonds. Honey came along the trading routes that emanated from the Gulf of Finland.

In 1356 the representatives of several German cities met in Lübeck's *Rathaus*. This marked the emergence of one of Europe's most potent political forces, the Hanseatic League, and the heyday of its de facto capital, Lübeck.

The origins of the Hanseatic League, or Hansa, went back to the alliance formed between Hamburg and Lübeck in 1241, which showed the force that united cities could have. The Lübeck city councillor, Hermann Hoyer, and the Hamburg city notary negotiated commercial privileges in Bruges in 1252. In 1266 Henry III of England granted Lübeck and Hamburg a charter to trade in his realm free of tolls. Eager to join an emerging network of cities that enjoyed such privileges, other cities such as Wismar, Rostock, Cologne, Bremen, Stettin (Szczecin), Riga, Reval (Tallinn) and Stralsund soon joined the alliance; in time it became a network of 200 towns, cities and city states.

The collective power of these cities enforced trade embargoes against Flanders in 1280 and Norway in 1284 until they won trading privileges in both. They also shut their key competitors, the English, Frisians and Flemish, out of the Baltic. Fluid in structure, the Hanseatic League was a flexible confederation of like-minded cities that did not have a formal identity until 1356, the date of the first Hansetag (Hanseatic Diet or assembly) in Lübeck.

Keeping open the trade routes required near-constant diplomacy and bargaining. That was the preferred method; if it failed force became necessary. In the second half of the twentieth century after the fall of the Western empires, a few lean, agile cities such as Hong Kong, Singapore and Macau were able to outperform for a few decades the much larger countries in their region, becoming financial and shipping giants. The Hansa was able to access markets and gain vital trading privileges in some of northern Europe's richest areas – Flanders, Russia and England – by virtue of its stranglehold on international trade. Mighty kingdoms capitulated to the cartel of small German cities.

The League fought a war against Denmark in the 1360s, destroying Copenhagen and gaining a complete monopoly over the herring fisheries. The military machine of the Hanseatic League was deployed against pirates operating in the Baltic, North Sea and English Channel. It waged intermittent war at sea against the kingdom of England in the fifteenth century.

The Hansa brought England to the negotiating table at Utrecht in 1474. Hinrich Castorp, mayor of Lübeck, along with Johannes Osthusen, syndic of Lübeck, and Hinrich Murmester, mayor of Hamburg, dictated terms to the king of England. The English were forced to pay £10,000 in compensation; they were banned from trading in the Baltic; and they conceded the Hansa merchants numerous trading privileges and trading posts. The Hansa was not an organisation to be trifled with.

The Hansa was hated because it had held England in economic subservience for close to two centuries. Its power was growing in the second half of the fifteenth century. One of the richest fruits of the League's immense collective bargaining power was its ability to establish *kontors* – offices and trading posts, the name of which means 'counter' – in foreign towns and cities. That makes them sound bland; in fact, *kontors* were walled cities-within-cities, self-governing communities with their own residences, churches, counting houses, weighing houses, port facilities, cloth halls, guildhalls, guards and wine cellars. German merchants resident in a Hanseatic *kontor* enjoyed both the protection of the League and the privileges it negotiated for them, usually in the form of free access to markets and favourable duties and tax rates.

After England's capitulation in the Anglo-Hanseatic War, the London *kontor* was rebuilt on the site of what is today Cannon Street Station. Known as the Stalhof or Steelyard, the *kontor* was one of the biggest trading complexes in Europe, a large walled free-trade zone in the heart of the City of London from which goods could be loaded directly onto German ships. The staggering wealth of Hanseatic merchants operating from the Steelyard was made clear in a series of portraits they commissioned from Hans Holbein in the 1530s. The merchants look like princes: grave and commanding, dressed in the richest red satin and surrounded by artefacts of affluence such as bronze clocks, Venetian glass vases and Turkish carpets.

From London and the North Sea ports, the Hansa controlled the trade in England's primary source of wealth, its white gold – wool. Cogs from Lübeck and elsewhere exported this vital commodity, selling it to the industrial cities of Flanders to be turned into cloth. The self-governing Steelyard, close to London Bridge, with its collections of art, its cranes, its visible wealth and tall tower topped with a blue cupola, was a daily reproach to ambitious English merchants who would dearly have loved to trade directly with Scandinavia, Prussia and Russia on their own account.

Wool represented one of Europe's most valuable resources. The Hansa *kontor* in Bergen on the Norwegian coast allowed Lübeck to control the highly valuable cod trade. That in Novgorod provided the gateway to Russia and to the Silk Roads. The fourth major *kontor*, in Bruges, was perhaps the most significant of all. Bruges gave Hanseatic traders access to northern Europe's biggest concentration of cities and its cloth-making industrial heartland.

The Hansa jealously guarded its enclave in Bruges, the main spice and textile market of Europe, the bridge between the Mediterranean and northern Europe. But it offered more than luxuries. The port city gave access to the enormous markets offered by the industrial cities of Flanders, hungry for herrings, beer, rye and wool. It offered other, brand-new forms of trade. The pioneering capitalist city of northern Europe, Bruges was the first major money market north of the Alps, the home of expatriate Italian bankers who brought with them new ideas about currency exchange and traded debt.

The changes that assailed Europe from the twelfth century were generated in the urban realm, specifically those small, walled cities like Lübeck that enjoyed political autonomy and were designed around trade and war, providing a bastion against disorder. In terms of their material comforts and civic rights, city-dwellers were far ahead of the rural peasants, villagers and townsfolk who comprised more than 90% of the population.

*

The bombs that eviscerated Lübeck in 1942 also destroyed one of the greatest works of art of the late Middle Ages, a thirty-metre-long painting depicting the Dance of Death. Painted in 1463 by Bernt Notke it showed in exquisite detail the outline of Lübeck, its forest of spires, its gabled houses, the walls that defended it and the ships that ensured its wealth. In the foreground death, personified by grinning, capering skeletons, leads every section of society in a merry dance towards the grave. Here is the Pope, the emperor, cardinals and bishops, kings and counts, the mayor and the councillors, usurers and merchants, physicians and priests, clerks and craftsmen, peasants, nuns, maidens and children.

As they are led to the final reckoning, they all plead for one last chance for redemption. 'It's far from me to be unprepared,' wheedles the Lübeck merchant, 'I have had great pains [to obtain] goods, by land and water, through wind, rain and snow. No travel has been too hard for me. [But] my reckoning is not ready. Had I done my reckoning then I would gladly go with thee.' Good at reckoning his accounts, perhaps; less so at showing the debits and credits of his immortal soul. Here's the message: however grand and wealthy you are, you share the same fate as the poorest and weakest when the time comes.

The Black Death emanated from central Asia and followed the Silk Roads first into China and India before it coursed west. It reached Caffa (Feodosiya, in the Crimea), then travelled on a Genoese galley that departed Caffa in 1347. Its subsequent progress followed the map of Europe's intercity trade networks. From Genoa and Venice it travelled to Marseilles and thence to the Atlantic cities in Iberian and France; from there to Calais and England. Then it jumped ship to the Hanseatic network, reaching Bruges and Lübeck. From Lübeck it spread on to Bergen, Copenhagen and all along the Baltic to Novgorod. It followed the German trading roads inland as well, to Cologne and the interior of Europe.

Worst hit were prosperous, crowded trading cities. Florence's population crashed from 120,000 to 50,000 and Venice's declined by 60%; half of Paris's 100,000 inhabitants succumbed. Lübeck's population halved as well. In all, 25 million people – over a third of Europe's population – perished.

Death mocks human folly in Lübeck's *danse macabre*, and the citizens were invited to laugh along when they saw it displayed in the Marienkirche. Here is a corrupt mayor given his due; so too is the idle nobleman who abused his peasants. No amount of wealth will save you. Death, disease and wealth lived side by side. Here is art for an uncertain age, an age of recurrent war and pestilence. It is also art for the merchant: life is risky and great fortunes can be blown away like dust. The first recorded *danse macabre* was painted in Paris in 1424–5. Lübeck's masterpiece from 1463 was one of the most famous; it was reproduced in numerous printed books where the cast of characters was expanded to include, among others, students, apprentices and journeymen.

It reveals the fragility of city life. Until 1800, life expectancy in Europe was 50% higher in the countryside compared to the city. No such price for city-dwelling existed in China; there urbanites on average lived *longer* than their rural cousins. European cities were death traps because they were dirty; Chinese cities were beacons of cleanliness. Europeans liked meat and lived close to their pigs and chickens; Asians had a predominately vegetarian diet and did not pack their urban areas with noisome animals. Because Europeans lived permanently on the cusp of war, their cities were fortified and therefore were physically restrained from growing, increasing their density for the benefit of the microbes. War sent armies marching across the continent, diffusing germs. In China strong central authority reduced conflict, allowing cities to sprawl outside their walls, distributing both people and markets over a wider area. East Asians had better standards of personal hygiene; waste was removed to fertilise nearby fields. European town-dwellers lived with their filth.

But the spread of the Black Death had a galvanising effect on city-building in Europe. The collapse of the urban population, particularly among artisans, encouraged peasants, eager to escape rural feudalism, to migrate into cities in search of high-paying jobs. The reduced population forced rents down and wages up. In Lübeck the upper artisanal class – brewers, butchers, amber workers, smiths, glovers and weavers – were far removed from the mercantile dynastic elite and they were excluded from power. But they enjoyed a high degree of wealth. Elert Stange, an armourer who served as mayor during a time of turmoil when artisans were briefly allowed to sit on the council, had a property portfolio that included a city mansion, a warehouse, five town houses and two apartments. Artisans such as Stange prospered thanks to the upsurge in trade after the ravages of the Black Death.[8]

With a declining rural population, cities needed more food such as herring and cod, rye and wheat, beer and wine. By the fifteenth century over 1,000 grain ships left Danzig every year to feed the cities of the Netherlands. The urban survivors of the plague and the generation that followed ate better, dressed more finely, built stronger houses and had superior standards of living than their forebears. Profits were poured into the palatial buildings – much of the Venice and Lübeck we know was a result of this boom – and sumptuous works of art. One of the major bulk traders of commodities, Lübeck stood to benefit from this demand for resources such as beer, wax, grain, herring, cloth and furs.

The Dance of Death reflects these grim realities and ambiguities. Come to the city to get rich, it says; but the crowded, unsanitary city is the frolicking place of death. Yet don't despair: dance while you can, for death is dancing with you. It was also art for a relatively new class in Europe: a knowing, worldly-wise urban audience. The vast painting reflected the lived experience of the city: the citizens of Lübeck did dance. The city was noted for its carnivals, a time when the social hierarchy was subverted by lords of misrule and public performances that satirised the greed of the wealthy merchant families. Carnival time provided the occasion for an outflowing of plays and poems. There were performances to suit differing tastes: moral allegories or bawdy humour, take your pick. Carnival season was rounded off with nocturnal dancing and heavy drinking. The mayor and councillors led the citizens on a torchlit dance through the streets, past lines of drummers beating out a raucous rhythm.

Death may come at any minute; all human wealth is transient; dance and make money while you can. These uncertainties nibbled at the urban mind. The acknowledged fragility of the city perhaps acted as its most potent binding force. After all, Lübeck started as a business venture and it owed its very survival to being an efficient corporate entity. Its civic ethos, expressed in municipal architecture, *Burspraken* ceremonies and carnivals, tied people to its communal undertaking. This was a small city of 20,000 citizens dominated by its corporate guilds, representing the main trades and professions: shippers, cobblers, herring dealers, drapers, long-distance merchants, bakers, brewers, tailors, smiths and so on. There were fraternities that brought together merchants who travelled to Bergen, Riga, Novgorod and Stockholm. Based in their own guildhalls, organised as brotherhoods, the companies dominated the economic, social and political life of the city.

Plague and pestilence did not, as Bernt Notke's masterpiece made clear, spare the powerful and prosperous. Consequently, the governing council never became the preserve of a hereditary elite, but voted in new members, many of them born elsewhere. The archives show that at no time between 1360 and 1408 were a majority of council members related by blood to previous councillors. These were the men addressed as 'lords' by no less than Charles IV, Holy Roman Emperor, when he visited the city in 1375.[9]

Fortune favoured the daring; death winnowed out entrenched privilege. Enterprising merchants who grew rich on risky long-distance adventures could become burghers, responsible for running the city and determining the direction of the Hanseatic League, 'lords' of trade and finance. Serving as a councillor gave a man status, and many of them came from families that had never grasped power in the city before. Many merchants from Lübeck, hardened on perilous trading ventures to Russia and the eastern Baltic, took leading roles as diplomats, envoys and negotiators on the chequerboard of northern-European power politics; some commanded Hanseatic fleets in war. Business always came first. The Hansa fought for gold and profit, not God and country; they were led not by kings, earls and knights, but by merchants, town councillors and mayors.

★

Tranquil and modestly beautiful as it looks, Lübeck maintained its prosperity because it could inflict famine on Norway and economic ruin on Flanders and England. Its craftsmen were rich because Lübeck and its fellow cities were powerful enough to monopolise trade and corner the market in major commodities, beating any competition by economic dominance, political muscle and sometimes force of arms.

Urbanisation in Europe possessed a distinctive flavour, very different from other, more developed parts of the world. The Indian Ocean had for centuries been a gigantic free-trade zone. Although far from peaceful – it was beset with pirates and intense rivalry for a share of the immense profits – these were seas open to all traders who braved their dangers, be they Arab or Chinese, Muslim or Buddhist, Jew or Hindu. As a consequence, the cities smacked of the same freedom and cosmopolitanism as the sea lanes; religious, ethnic and political divisions were subordinated to the serious business of making money. The mixed-race metropolises of south-east Asia were not walled like European city states; they sprawled luxuriously.[10]

'In the name of God and Profit.' So read the motto on the hundreds of account ledgers belonging to the great Italian merchant Francesco Datini. God played a role: reurbanisation in Europe was intimately related to war, particularly religious wars in the Levant, the Baltic and Iberia. And profit was linked to the tendency of Europeans to secure monopolies by suppressing, by whatever means, competition; the free-trading ethos of the Indian Ocean urban network was alien in that part of the world. Venice and Genoa fought a series of exceptionally bloody battles with each other to secure trading privileges in the Black Sea. Both believed they had a right to control absolutely the Adriatic (in Venice's case) and the Ligurian Sea (in Genoa's), just as the Hansa ruled the Baltic, permitting no intruders. Together they comprised the most sophisticated military machines in Europe.

Trade or no trade, the inherent fragility of cities forced them to become militarised. Medieval Europe, fractured as it was into thousands of antagonistic cities, city states, autonomous towns, republics, marquisates, bishoprics, counties, duchies, principalities, kingdoms and empires, became extremely good at fighting. Venice, Florence, Paris and Milan were highly unusual in having populations at or above 100,000; no other European cities reached that size (unexceptional in China, south-east Asia and Mesoamerica) until the seventeenth century.

In this vicious, dog-eat-dog world, cities had to harness and perfect the science of war. 'The city must, first of all, have sufficient forces to defend itself and to be free of the constant fear of external aggression,' wrote the historian and statesman Francesco Guicciardini. 'Internal good order and the rule of law would be of little use if the city were subject to being overcome by force.' Civic liberty, municipal wealth and military force went hand in hand in war-torn Europe. The fragile city, howsoever rich, always had rivals ready to strike."

Guicciardini's home city, the Republic of Florence, constantly at war with rival cities such as Siena, Lucca, Pisa and Milan and with emperors and popes, reached deep into its capacious pockets to hire the cream of European mercenaries, professional officers, archers, lancers, crossbowmen, cavalrymen and infantry. Florence mercilessly gobbled up many of its neighbouring city states before they grew as rivals. In the development of modern battle tactics, military architecture and engineering, firearms and artillery, the wealthy Italian city states were at the cutting edge.

But where medieval cities excelled was in the development of humankind's most technologically complex machine before the spacecraft: the ship. The evolution of the Venetian great galley, the Hanseatic cog and the Portuguese caravel and carrack as vessels, interchangeably, of war and commerce was the work primarily of the competing European maritime cities. The Mediterranean city states were the first to place artillery on their galley fleets, a game-changing development in naval warfare. The greatest military-industrial complex in the world before the Industrial Revolution was owned by a city, Venice. The Arsenale Nuovo (1320), with its workforce of 16,000, was capable of getting a ship to sea every single day, an incredible feat at a time when even seafaring kingdoms such as England lacked permanent naval dockyard facilities because they did not have anything like the wealth, organising capabilities or cohesion of a city state. No other place makes manifest so clearly the medieval city as a bastion of war.

*

Of all the crimes committed in Paris in the 1410s, a mere 7% involved theft; the most prevalent form of crime – over 76% – was spontaneous, impulsive acts of violence between citizens. The coroners' records of medieval London reveal simmering violence in public places, particularly congested markets where young, armed men jostled in the hurly-burly of the commercial city. Using the urinal at the top of Foster Lane, William Roe accidentally pissed on another young man's shoes. When the man complained, Roe struck him. Then Philip of Ashendon got involved, berating Roe. Philip's skull was smashed in by Roe's poleaxe. At another time, a fight broke out between Walter le Clerk de Edelmeton and Alexander de Staunford on Gracechurch Street on the doorstep of the Florentine Bardi banking house; Walter died from a vicious blow to his head from Alexander's quarterstaff. Robert Paunchard had his throat cut by a cook during a brawl after closing time at a tavern. Riding dangerously through the streets and endangering women and children, a young squire killed a potter who begged him to ride more carefully. A priest stealing apples stabbed the gardener who remonstrated with him. Young men fought and killed each other over women and over 'honour'. Gangs started fights in taverns, which spilt out into the streets. The litany of trifling quarrels that flared into homicide goes on, a catalogue of casual murder.[12]

Of the murders in medieval London between 1320 and 1340, 56% were knife crimes; 87% happened between the hours of 5 p.m. and 2 a.m.; and 68% occurred outdoors in a public space. The metropolis was an arena of daily hot-headed violence. A smith at work with his anvil on the Porta di San Piero in Florence was merrily singing as he worked. Suddenly a man burst in and started throwing his tools – his hammer, his scales and so on – into the street.

'What are the devil are you doing?' shouted the smith. 'Are you mad?'

'What are *you* doing?' the madman asked.

'I am trying to do my job. But you are spoiling my tools and throwing them into the street.'

'Well,' said the stranger, Dante Alighieri, 'if you don't like me spoiling your things, don't spoil mine.'

The hapless smith had been singing one of Dante's poems, and mangling them, forgetting some words, adding others. Another example of urban street violence in a city where, as Dante himself wrote, 'avarice, envy, pride, those fatal sparks set the heart of all on fire'.[13]

Intense competition in a city like Florence shortened lives, to be sure, but it was also the divine spark of creativity. Dante and Boccaccio

wrote against a background of deadly factionalism. The urban cauldron, with its storms of controversy, political machinations and wars,
forced people to dissect human nature and political motivation. What
is the best way to tame a tiger like Florence, with its murderous feuds,
its inordinately wealthy bosses, its politically conscious lower classes
and its republican attachment to liberty? How can you balance all
those competing elements within the city? With the authors of antiquity, such as Aristotle and Livy, on one hand and recent, bitter
Florentine history on the other, writers such as Niccolò Machiavelli,
the heirs of a long republican tradition, laid the foundations not just
of modern Western political thought but of the study of history. The
rivalry between cities in Italy, and the competitiveness within them,
provided the kindling for an artistic and architectural golden age.

Having reached the zenith of their magnificence in the fifteenth
century, small, efficient cities like Lübeck – many of them republics
– found themselves increasingly at a disadvantage against centralised
states, with their vast reserves of manpower. Once-impregnable walls
were no match against modern artillery. Francis I, king of France,
gobbled up Milan in 1515. The Holy Roman Emperor Charles V took
Milan from France in 1525, sacked Rome two years later and besieged
Florence in 1530, destroying the republic. Genoa fell to the French,
then became a satellite of the Spanish Empire. Caught between the
might of France and Spain in Italy and threatened by the Ottoman
Empire at sea, Venice began a long decline. The Hanseatic League,
by the sixteenth century, faced stronger, better-organised kingdoms
such as England, Sweden and Denmark. Many of its member cities
lost their autonomy as they were drawn into countries undergoing
internal consolidation such as Poland and Prussia. By the time the last
Hanseatic Diet was held in 1669 (attended by nine remaining member
cities), the League had ceased to mean anything.

Yet cities remained on the front line of European war. During the
sixteenth and seventeenth centuries warfare on the continent became
a science of siege and counter-siege, an arms race between gunners
and engineers on either side of the city walls. Huge star-shaped fortifications were built around cities such as Lübeck to make them invincible against artillery bombardment. These long, gruelling wars made
European military engineers experts in the art of sieges; campaigns
of attrition gave the continent's armies technology far in advance of

peoples elsewhere in the world. Urbanisation in Europe surged as a result of the entrepreneurialism of its people, to be sure; but its dynamism also came from less positive sources: the Black Death, Crusades, endemic warfare and deadly intra-city rivalries.

The emerging European metropolis was substantially different from cities elsewhere. They were not democratic in our sense; but they allowed more political participation and social mobility relative to kingdoms and bureaucratically managed Chinese and Japanese cities. Literacy was not universal; but more people could read in European cities than elsewhere. Small and vulnerable, they nevertheless fashioned a military and commercial revolution that would be unleashed on the entire planet.

The decline of Lübeck, like that of Venice, was due in the main to the dramatic shift in global trading patterns at the close of the fifteenth century. With the discovery of the Americas and of direct routes to eastern Asia, vast new markets opened up for Europe. Closer to home, Lübeck's dominance of trade was undone by a new kid on the block, the rising city of Amsterdam. The Hanseatic League might have declined rapidly; but its legacy of sharp business practices, monopoly trading and strong-arm tactics spread around the world.

7

Cities of the World

Lisbon, Malacca, Tenochtitlan, Amsterdam, 1492–1666

'Illustrious and glorious' Lisbon stunned the physician and geographer Hieronymus Münzer of Nuremberg when he visited in 1494. Transformed from a European backwater to the continent's most exciting city, Lisbon stood on a new frontier.

At the docks Münzer saw not only vast quantities of hazelnuts, walnuts, lemons, almonds, figs, apples and sugar, but a near 'infinity of articles' brought from Africa: gorgeously coloured fabrics, carpets, copper cauldrons, cardamom, innumerable branches of peppercorns, elephant tusks and gold. He saw an enormous crocodile suspended above the choir in the monastery of Santa Trinidad, marvelled at a pelican's beak and encountered caged lions at St George's Castle; he was besotted by the dragon trees, brought from the Gulf of Guinea, which he saw growing all around Lisbon. He inspected gigantic sugar canes, African weapons and huge saws made from the bones of big fish.

A museum of a world that was being discovered in the closing years of the fifteenth century, Lisbon was a city unlike any other in Europe. By the turn of the century, some 15% of the population was made up of African slaves. There was a sizeable Muslim community. Münzer noted the large numbers of 'immensely rich' Jewish merchants. Many of them would have moved to Lisbon after they were expelled en masse from Spain in 1492. Even richer were the Dutch and German traders who lived on the Rua Nova dos Mercadores, 'built in the German style'.[1]

Lisbon presented a sensuality and exoticism unobtainable in other European cities. Soon after Münzer's visit, a daring kind of architecture transformed the city further. The ornate style known as Manueline, still to be seen at the Belém Tower and the Jerónimos Monastery, is emblematic of Lisbon's eclectic borrowings from the globe. The style is a bombastic synthesis of late Gothic, Moorish, African, Italian and Flemish urban designs, and Indian temple decorations laced with nautical themes and icons of discovery: armillary spheres, twisted rope patterns, decorative knots, anchors, carved images of rhinoceroses, elephants and other exotic beasts.

The goods, people and buildings to be seen in late fifteenth-century Lisbon were remarkable because no other European city enjoyed direct trade with Africa and Asia; only a handful of Venetians had travelled outside the continent. In 1500 seven of the world's twelve largest metropolises – Vijayanagara, Gauda, Guangzhou, Beijing, Nanjing, Hangzhou and Tabriz – were in Asia. Benin City in modern-day Nigeria, the largest city in sub-Saharan Africa, and Tenochtitlan in Mesoamerica were both bigger than Paris, which with 185,000 people was the only Christian European city in the top twelve. The urban heartland of the world remained in Asia.

And if Europe was isolated, Portugal had been for centuries a marginal place on the edge of the continent, wedged up against the unknowable vastness of the Atlantic. Its warrior aristocracy was dedicated to crusading in North Africa. Lisbon, by contrast, was virtually a city state within a deeply conservative, poor country. Its merchants, many of whom were Jewish or descendants of Muslims, had strong trading links with Islamic North Africa, Italy and northern Europe. Mutually hostile as the rural and urban populations were, their apparently opposed world views – the yearning for religious war and the lust for worldly wealth – would fuse together.

In 1415 the nobility got what they wanted: a Crusade in Morocco. Tiny Portugal shocked Europe and the Islamic world with the capture of Ceuta on the African coast of the Mediterranean. The holy warriors of Portugal came face to face with a jaw-dropping city. The 'flower of all other cities of Africa', it made Lisbon look shabby. Merchants lived in palaces and dealt in African gold, ivory and slaves and Asian spices. According to a Portuguese chronicler, merchants came from 'Ethiopia, Alexandria, Syria, Barbary, Assyria [Turkey], as well as from the Orient who lived on the other side of the Euphrates River and from the Indies … and from many other lands that are beyond the axis and that lie beyond our eyes'.[2]

This was truly a glimpse at another world, an unknowable world sealed off from Europe. Prince Henry, son of João I of Portugal, fought at Ceuta. The riches of that city, combined with his crusading lust, gave him the desire to destroy Islam and make Portugal great by finding a route to what lay beyond the Sahara: not just gold and spice, but – it was believed – a mysterious lost Christian realm. Prester John, the mythical Christian emperor of Ethiopia, lay 'beyond the axis'; so too, apparently, were Christian kingdoms dotting the Indian Ocean. Find a way to those lands, and instead of Europe being strangled by Islam, Islam would be encircled by united Christendom.

Under the aegis of the infante Dom Henry (later called Henry the Navigator), caravels left Lisbon to explore the Atlantic coast of Africa. By the 1470s traders, slavers and explorers from Lisbon had pushed as far as the Gulf of Guinea; in the following decade they reached the Congo. Then, in 1487, an expedition led by Bartolomeu Dias swung out *west* from the coast of Namibia into the Atlantic. The daring decision solved at last the riddle of how to reach the Indian Ocean. Out in the ocean westerlies blew Dias's little ships eastwards, rounding what he was to call the Cape of Good Hope. Dias had disproved the Ptolemaic theory that the Indian Ocean was an enclosed sea. It was accessible from Europe.

Or, more precisely, it was accessible from Lisbon.

The city became a magnet for those who wished to profit from the age of exploration and those who wished to understand the world as it shifted beneath their feet. Christopher Columbus of Genoa came to the court of João II, attracted by the rage for discovery and the teams of experts who pored over every new map and every scrap of information that came back with the explorers. Martin Behaim, merchant of Nuremberg and gifted cartographer and cosmographer, was naturally attracted to Lisbon in the 1480s where he made improvements to the astrolabe and worked on navigational tables. The astrolabe was taken to the Gulf of Guinea by the Jewish scientist José Vizinho in 1483 to measure the altitude of the sun. Out of these voyages came detailed maps of the hitherto unknown eastern Atlantic. Behaim constructed a terrestrial globe between 1491 and 1493 called the *Erdapfel* (the earth apple), a summary of Western understanding of the world on the eve of the discovery of the Americas.[3]

Scientists such as Behaim and Vizinho sat at the feet of the great Abraham Zacuto, rabbi and royal astronomer. Spanish by birth, Zacuto was given refuge in Lisbon after the expulsion of the Jews from his home country. Zacuto's astronomical tables, collated as the *Almanach Perpetuum*, revolutionised oceanic exploration by allowing seafarers to determine their position at sea. João's committee of experts, headed by Vizinho and Behaim, rejected Columbus's proposal to sail west across the Atlantic to the Indies, judging rightly that he had gravely underestimated the size of the world.

Hieronymus Münzer marvelled at Lisbon's military infrastructure with its factories, headed by German and Flemish founders and gunners, turning out an array of advanced weaponry. Portuguese ships carried state-of-the-art onboard gunnery, large bombards that were fired from caravels, and light, rapid-fire breech-loaded swivel guns called *berços* that were mounted on ship's boats. Fuelled by the dreams of a visionary king, the desire for wealth beyond the horizon, and by religious zeal, Lisbon had been propelled from relative obscurity into the very first rank of European metropolises.

After João's death in 1495, his successor Manuel I remained committed to the task. Within two years another expedition departed, lavishly equipped with the best ships and arms Lisbon's dockyards could produce and the latest navigational aids. Its leader, Vasco da Gama, was instructed to reach the great spice city of Calicut, where he was to search out Christian kings and establish a trade in spices. According to the papal bull *Inter caetera*, the world outside Europe was divided by a north–south line in the Atlantic. All land to the west belonged to Spain; Portuguese had the east. The imaginary line was later amended by the Treaty of Tordesillas; what it meant was that the Portuguese were sailing into what they thought was *their* private territory, as granted by the Pope.

Following the course of Bartolomeu Dias, da Gama headed west into the Atlantic in order to swing east under the tip of Africa. He worked his way up the coast of East Africa. When the flotilla stopped at the port-town of Mozambique the Portuguese got their first whiff of the new world they had entered. Here were elaborately dressed Arab merchants, their ships laden with gold, silver, cloves, pepper, ginger, pearls, rubies and other precious stones. On they pressed to other cities: to Mombasa and then to Malindi. Everywhere they saw wealthy cities and buoyant trade. Nowhere was there any evidence of the Christian cities they had expected to find.

The scurvy-ridden European sailors, with their measly cargo of trinkets, did not have much to offer this sophisticated, polyethnic urban world where the wealth of Asia and Africa was traded from city to city. What they did have was the default aggression and hatred of all things Islamic which they had learnt in gruelling Crusades in Morocco and Tunisia. They had ships bristling with the most advanced military technology in the world. And they used these weapons from the moment they arrived in the Indian Ocean to get what they wanted. Suspicious of this strange ocean, with its great cities and complicated networks of trade, the Portuguese opened fire on African villages and the town of Mozambique. The mistrust and belligerence of the intruders was a taste of what was to come.[4]

★

One of the great cities of the age, the centre of the spice trade, Calicut rose up from the beach to the foothills of the Ghat mountain range. Whitewashed merchants' houses and wooden palaces of the nobility, with views out to sea, peeked out from behind palm trees. Minarets spiked towards the sky from mosques that lay near large Hindu temples. When da Gama's exhausted and nervous men arrived in this vast, densely packed city – unworldly Europeans as they were – it must have seemed like entering some strange exotic, unexplored land. In one of those ironies of history, the first people they encountered were two merchants from Tunisia, a short journey from Portugal. 'The Devil take you!' one of them accosted the weary travellers in Castilian. 'What brought you here?'

The answer was simple: they came, they said, in search of Christians and spices. It did not seem to occur to the interlopers, when they were hailed in European languages, that the world was a lot more interconnected and economically integrated than they could imagine. Da Gama's men had come the hard way, via the Cape of Good Hope. The Tunisians had simply followed the well-trodden Islamic roads direct from home.

There were no Christian kings. And spices needed to be paid for. What did the Portuguese have to exchange? Da Gama unpacked his gifts to impress the king, the Hindu Samoothiri, 'the Lord of the Sea': twelve pieces of striped cloth, four scarlet hoods, six hats, four strings of coral, six basins, a case of sugar, two casks of honey and two of oil.

When he saw them, the Samoothiri's official laughed; the poorest merchant of Mecca brought better presents than the king of Portugal. He refused to even set them before his master.

This was a commercial city, and its sovereign was a commercial king. Calicut, with its vast temples and palaces, its innumerable crowds and its mix of Jews, Muslims, Hindus and Buddhists, made Lisbon seem provincial. Traders came from all over the monsoon seas, as they had for a millennium, bringing merchandise of value. The Samoothiri profited from free trade, collecting duties from the hundreds of ships that used Calicut as the major transhipment metropolis of the Indian Ocean. He had no interest in engaging in diplomatic politeness with the representative of a king of a faraway country who brought nothing in the way of business.

And it wasn't just the Samoothiri. When they saw the Portuguese goods, the Muslim merchants of Calicut just spat, and hissed 'Portugal! Portugal!' In a city where the wealth of the world, from China to Venice, was piled up in the markets, no one wanted to buy what the Europeans had brought; little wonder that a fine shirt worth 300 *reis* in Lisbon fetched thirty *reis* in Calicut. A sack of spices, by contrast, cost two *cruzados* in Calicut and thirty in Lisbon.

Unable to comprehend economic reality, da Gama, with the suspicion and rancour he had imported from Europe, assumed that the Muslim merchants were conspiring against him, preventing the sale of Portuguese bracelets, cloths and shirts. Worse was to come when the king demanded payment of the port duties required of all visiting traders. Da Gama could not pay in gold, and his paltry merchandise was not worth enough to cover the costs. He decided to leave without paying. Before he did so he kidnapped six high-caste Hindu traders. As the Portuguese flotilla sailed, they were pursued by a swarm of the Samoothiri's warships. No match for Portuguese gunnery, they were crippled by cannon fire.[5]

Da Gama brought back a small amount of spices and the information that Portuguese ships were by far the most powerful vessels in Asian waters. Venice and Genoa anticipated ruin when news of da

Gama's success spread through Europe. Manuel, now styling himself 'Lord of the Conquest, Navigation, and Commerce of Ethiopia, Arabia, Persia and of India', dispatched another expedition under Pedro Álvares Cabral in 1500.

Sailing out into the Atlantic to catch the westerlies, Cabral discovered the land that would be called Brazil. In Indian waters he set about attacking Muslim shipping. Relations with the new Samoothiri of Calicut broke down. A Muslim crowd attacked the Portuguese trading station in the city. During the fighting the Portuguese claimed they 'killed a mountain of people' in the streets of Calicut with their crossbows. Cabral slaughtered 600 Arab merchants and sailors who were moored in the City of Spices. He looted their goods, burnt their ships and captured three war elephants (which the Portuguese ate). Then he turned his powerful cannon on the city itself and bombarded Calicut. Once again the Portuguese reported with glee that 'we slew an endless number of people and did [the city] much damage'.[6]

Now the Indian Ocean saw wave after wave of ships dispatched from Lisbon. Vasco da Gama returned. At Kilwa, the main trading port in East Africa, he warned the sultan that 'if I chose, in one single hour your city would be reduced to embers'. He told other cities that Manuel was 'lord of the sea' and sovereign of their coast. He sent shock waves through the entire Indian Ocean when he looted and destroyed a dhow carrying 380 passengers, including some of the business elite of the monsoon seas. All but the children were massacred.[7]

Back again at beleaguered Calicut, he ordered the Samoothiri to expel all Muslim merchants and ban trade with them. The Hindu king retorted that the Portuguese were more or less pirates and that his 'port had always been open'. Da Gama's answer was 'a continuous storm and rain of iron balls and stones' on the city. During this terrific bombardment, da Gama hanged thirty-four Muslim traders and Hindu fishermen from the yards of his ship. Within a few years, Calicut, one of the world's great cities, was ruined. People were leaving as fast as they could.[8]

Faced with this brutal and persistent intimidation, and without the means to defend themselves, the cities of the Malabar coast began to come to terms with the violent incomers. The Portuguese established a protection racket over the whole ocean, obliging ships to purchase certificates or face annihilation. One Muslim ruler said with horror: 'It is unheard of that anyone should be forbidden to sail the seas.' It wasn't now, with the coming of the Portuguese. Muslim trading communities, aware that the game was up, were returning home. Most of the Swahili and Malabar coasts were under Portuguese control. Forts were built and local rulers were forbidden from trading with anyone except the Portuguese, and then only at prices set by the invaders.[9]

The Indian Ocean urban archipelago that had grown peacefully over centuries was facing violent destruction. Alarmed by Portuguese inroads, the Mamluk sultan in Cairo organised (with covert Venetian help) a fleet to take on the trespassers. Kilwa, a small but very rich city that had mosques that rivalled Cordoba's, was sacked in 1505; Mombasa, a big, beautiful trading city, was looted and burnt to the ground shortly after. Ormuz, a great maritime city, was captured and occupied. The Indian city of Cochin, dominated by a Portuguese fortress, became the main spice port.

From that city base the military genius Afonso de Albuquerque masterminded a fresh onslaught in 1510. The city of Goa was comprehensively sacked and 'cleansed' (Albuquerque's word) of its Muslim population and Islamic buildings. Then another city came into his sights, the greatest city state of them all, the prize of the Indian Ocean – the Eye of the Sun, as it was nicknamed.

The Portuguese writer Tomé Pires reckoned that there were eighty-four different languages spoken in Malacca, this giant city of 120,000 people. Stretching ribbon-like for about ten miles, hemmed in by jungle on one side and sea on the other, it was a city to behold from an incoming ship, with thousands of palm-thatched houses, warehouses, temples and mosques. Its port, it was said, had room for 2,000 ships, from gigantic Chinese cargo junks to oared sampans. Barely a century old, there was no doubt, according to Pires, 'that Malacca is of such importance and profit that it seems to me to have no equal in the world'.[10]

The Eye of the Sun was an apt nickname. Like Palembang before it and Singapore after, this city was the radial point of a trade network that flowed from China and Japan, the Spice Islands and Java, Thailand and Burma, India and Ceylon, Africa, Europe and the Persian Gulf. It stood at the end of one monsoon system and the beginning of another, so all trade was concentrated here. Spices, cloth, lacquerware, slaves, drugs, perfumes, precious stones, porcelain, ivory and gold came here from Asia and Africa; so too did the best of European merchandise, which arrived via Venice and Cairo. Malacca lay at the middle of the world.

Pires reeled off an exhaustive list of foreign merchants: they came from Cairo, Mecca, Ormuz and Aden; from Abyssinia and Kilwa; there were Turks and Christian Armenians rubbing shoulders with Chinese, Burmese, Javanese, Siamese, Cambodians, Gujaratis, Bengalis, Bugis and Malays; there were Hindus from Calicut and Tamils from Ceylon; traders from Brunei, the Moluccas, Timor, Sunda, Pegu, the Maldives … and so the list went on. The various merchants formed into large trading corporations and guilds, spreading risk and negotiating prices and customs dues much like the German Hansa.

In a metropolis where every street and house was part of the never-ending souk, you could buy anything you liked or gamble on the most advanced money market on the face of the earth. Ruled by a sultan, it had become a fabulously wealthy city from the duties charged on international trade. Malacca outshone even the glistening cities the Portuguese had destroyed or captured in India. 'Men cannot estimate the worth of Malacca, on account of its greatness and profit. Malacca is a city made for merchandise, fitter than any other in the world.' The Portuguese intruders like Tomé Pires were beginning to understand the interconnectedness of the world: 'Whoever is lord of Malacca has his hands on the throat of Venice.'[11]

So it was no surprise when a Portuguese fleet arrived off Malacca on 1 July 1511, having left a trail of destroyed cargo-carrying junks in its wake. For three weeks Albuquerque's warships stood menacingly off the city, making stringent demands on the sultan and bombarding the city to keep up the pressure. On the 24th Albuquerque attacked. The key to Malacca was the bridge that crossed the river that bisected the megacity, a kind of tropical Rialto where business was conducted. In the battle for the bridge, under an intense sun, the heavily armoured Portuguese soldiers encountered a barrage of artillery, a deluge of arrows, deadly poisoned darts fired from blowpipes and twenty maddened, trampling war elephants. They briefly captured the bridge, but, sapped by the heat and humidity, had to withdraw.

Street fighting hardly came more intense than this. Most of Albuquerque's commanders, spooked by the poison darts and the beating sun, wanted to give up. But Albuquerque held out the prospect of capturing the richest city on earth. On 10 August they attacked again. This time there would be no sudden descent on the bridge; the onslaught would be governed by Albuquerque's iron discipline. Under the cover of cannon positioned to sweep the streets, the Portuguese pikemen formed into squares, six men on each side, and advanced inch by inch through the web of streets and lanes. No Muslim, man, woman or child, was spared. For nine days these formations systematically cleared their opponents from the city. Then the Portuguese were permitted to loot, and only then under the same system of rigid discipline. Arson was banned and flags demarcated houses to be spared from the plunder. In small groups, the sailors first, the Portuguese were given a set time to pillage; when the trumpet sounded, their brutal supermarket sweep had to end so the next group could have its turn ransacking the greatest souk in the world.

By the time they had finished Malacca's bloodstained streets were littered with the leftovers, things the victors could not be bothered with because they were laden down with even richer things. Discarded jewels glittered in the dust; fine Chinese porcelain lay broken and neglected; damask, silk and taffeta were trodden under foot; jars of musk lay abandoned. These things alone would have commanded a king's ransom in Venice. Then it was back to work. Decimated by malaria, Albuquerque's men toiled in the broiling heat to construct a fort made from the ruined stones of the mosques. Malacca belonged to Portugal. Some 900 Europeans had defeated an army of 20,000 defenders. As well as its position as the fulcrum of global trade, it served as a springboard for Portugal's push towards the Spice Islands, China and Japan.

*

'Whoever is lord of Malacca has his hands on the throat of Venice.' Not only Venice: he also had his hands on the throats of Cairo, Alexandria and Mecca. The city's capture marked a turning point in world history. With strategic ports such as Malacca, Goa, Cochin and

Ormuz under its control, Portugal could oust its Muslim enemies and control the trade of the Indian Ocean.

The wealth of the world rained down on Lisbon, the newly minted capital of global trade: the luxuries of Brazil, Africa and Asia. Charles V famously said, 'If I were king of Lisbon, I would soon rule over the whole world.' Note that he said 'Lisbon', not 'Portugal'.

In 1498 Manuel cleared space on the banks of the Tagus for an enormous palace called the Paço da Ribeira, the Riverside Palace. A supreme example of the exuberant Manueline style, it was one of the highlights of the Renaissance not only for its exotic hybrid architecture but also for its role as a meeting place for poets, playwrights, artists, philosophers, scholars and scientists from all over Europe. The palace complex also housed the major administrative departments regulating Portugal's extensive global trade monopolies: the Casa da Índia (House of India), the Casa dos Escravos (House of Slaves), the Casa da Flandres (House of Flanders), the Casa da Guiné (House of Guinea) and the Customs House. The palace was linked to the mighty arsenal, the royal mint, warehouses such as the Armazéns de Índia, and the dock-yards. Part royal residence, part commercial headquarters, the new palace allowed Manuel to watch the vast wealth of the world being unloaded on his doorstep and smell the spices that perfumed the air of Lisbon. His palatial warehouses contained sacks of sugar, cloves and pepper. Disparagingly, Francis I of France nicknamed him *le roi épicier*, 'the grocer king'.

But that was envy speaking. By 1510 Dom Manuel the Grocer was netting a cool 10 million *cruzados* a year from the spice trade alone. Anyone arriving by ship at Lisbon was greeted by sumptuous riverside buildings such as the Belém Tower and the gigantic Jerónimos Monastery, a wonder of the age, built as it is said by pepper, or at least by a 5% levy on spices and a gift from the Florentine banker and slaver Bartolomeu Marchione. Agricultural land was cleared to make way for the vast Hospital Real de Todos-os-Santos.[12]

The new palace dragged Lisbon down from the hills to the water's edge, reclaiming land from the Tagus as if it yearned to edge closer to its new worlds. Merchants constructed waterfront palaces of their own. As Lisbon's population grew with its wealth, land was cleared for suburban development under the direction of a royal urban masterplan. A good example is Barrio Alto – today the tourist and nightlife hub of

Lisbon – which was built on a geometrical pattern to house the swelling number of specialised maritime craftsmen – the caulkers, rope makers, sailcloth sewers and metal forgers required by a commercial metropolis. Lisbon is famous for its mosaic pavements; their history goes back to 1500 when Rua Nova dos Mercadores and other major thoroughfares were cobbled with expensive granite from the Oporto region.[13]

The Rua Nova's 'infinity of shops' and arcades sat beneath multi-storey buildings, in which people lived like 'sardines'. The Rua Nova became the commercial heart of Lisbon; you could buy, among other things, monkeys, turkeys and parrots, Japanese lacquerware and Ming porcelain, gems and ginger, ivory and ebony from West Africa, pepper and pearls, Persian carpets and American chillis, silks from Asia, tapestries from Flanders and velvet from Italy. It contained banking and exchange offices; every day notaries took their stations at open-air stalls to record transactions. Europe did not contain a more exotic or energetic street.[14]

On a visit in 1514 the Flemish nobleman Jan Taccoen was wide-eyed at the whirl of life. 'You can see many animals and strange people in Lisbon,' he wrote. There were the elephants he saw every day in the streets. There were Manuel's frequent processions, in which he was led through the city by a rhinoceros followed by five elephants covered in gold brocade, an Arabian horse and a jaguar. In the year of Taccoen's visit, Manuel showed off his wealth and power by sending the Pope a present: a white elephant called Hanno, along with parrots, leopards and a panther. A year later he dispatched a white rhino.

Taccoen marvelled at the thousands of African and Brazilian slaves; he witnessed a ship disgorge a cargo of spices and 300 naked captives. Taccoen came across free Africans, who had come on diplomatic business, and Indians festooned with gems. A few travelled from as far away as Japan and China; they flocked in greater numbers from Germany, Flanders, England, France, Italy and elsewhere to set up businesses exchanging goods across Europe. Taccoen lodged with Gilles de Backere, a man who had given up the trade of barrel-making in Bruges, attracted by the legendary wealth of Lisbon. Gilles had become a merchant and made his fortune in the city of dreams. 'Every day he uses silver platters, salvers and plates and many gold goblets.'

For Taccoen, Lisbon was a wild, boisterous city undergoing rapid growth. But they could not build it fast enough; families shared cramped houses that, according to Taccoen, often did not have toilets or chimneys. Unbelievable wealth lived alongside poverty. Slaves and migrant workers did the dirty work of the city as cleaners, cooks, boatmen, fast-food sellers, labourers, cobblers and blacksmiths; every morning the streets down to the Tagus were filled with slaves carrying chamber pots that were emptied into the river.[15]

If one place on earth symbolised the shock of the new during the Renaissance and the collision of cultures, it was surely this city. Lisbon's triumph meant the decline of Venice and a string of Asian metropolises, most notably Malacca. Here is the tale of one global city engrossing its rivals and growing fat on their carcasses. And like other global cities, Lisbon became the hub of a network of satellite cities stretched across the planet: Antwerp, Macau, Goa, Cochin, Malacca and others. It was the first of a new type of city, the imperial metropolis able to exploit markets on a global scale. Such leviathans rendered obsolete city states such as Lübeck and Venice. More importantly, they displaced the great cities of Asia and the Americas, places that had carried the banner of urban civilisation for so long.

*

The preference for monopoly over free trade; the honing of instruments of war; and the intolerance of other faiths. All these things had been nurtured in European cities during the re-urbanisation that had taken place since the twelfth century. In an age when the big global cities increasingly resemble each other, it is worth recalling that the world once contained a diversity of cities. Lisbon exported European practices and attitudes and, in doing so, fatally disrupted another urban civilisation, one based on free trade and cosmopolitanism. But it was in Mexico that Europeans came face to face with an urban civilisation that had developed independently of the influences of Mesopotamia, China, Athens or Rome.

For the Spanish soldier Bernal Díaz del Castillo, the first sight of Tenochtitlan in 1519 was like 'an enchanted vision'. Years later he confessed: 'It was all so wonderful that I do not know how to describe this first glimpse of things never heard of, seen or dreamed of before.' Here was a city of the imagination, a metropolis numbering 200,000 people at a date when the largest city in Europe, Paris, housed 185,000.

Great crowds gathered to watch the Spanish conquistadors enter the city. Entranced, the Spanish rode along the main causeway, trying to take in the sight of the towers, temples and great buildings that seemed to rise out of the waters of the lake upon which the city stood. The stuccoed houses, which were burnished until they gleamed like silver, seemed to be like jewels reflecting the sun. At the end of the causeway, the 450 Spanish, led by Hernán Cortés, were welcomed by Moctezuma II, ninth *tiatoani* of Tenochtitlan and ruler of the Aztec Empire.[16]

The Spanish had entered one of the most spectacular cities on the planet. 'Venice the rich' they called it in their wonder. The Mexica people, for their part, took in things they had never before encountered: horses and armour, arquebusiers and steel swords, the wheel and the cannon.

The city state was built on a rocky island on Lake Texcoco, one of five interconnected lakes in a mountain plateau; drained in the seventeenth century, the clay bed now provides the foundations for Mexico City. Long bridges and causeways linked Tenochtitlan to the mainland, alongside which were *chinampas*, hydroponic floating gardens. Highly productive, they grew the vegetables that fed the city.

The metropolis itself was criss-crossed with canals, cut into quarters by the grand avenues, and subdivided into twenty administrative districts called *calpulli*. The houses of the nobility were made of stone masonry; those of the wealthy of adobe brick. The mass of the people lived in thatched-roof houses made of reeds and plastered with mud. These dwellings were whitewashed or painted in bright colours. The Spanish marvelled at the flower-strewn houses, their ornamentation and their household goods. Such domestic standards could not, they said, be bettered anywhere.[17]

At the centre of the city stood its public buildings, temples, courts and palaces in a walled plaza called the Templo Mayor. Overshadowing all them was the Great Temple, sixty metres high. Here, thousands of people were sacrificed to the gods every year. Tenochtitlan's huge main market was said to be twice the size of the Spanish city of Salamanca. Bernal Díaz noted his astonishment at the sheer numbers of people shopping there 'and the regularity which prevailed, as well as the vast quantities of merchandise'. Even Granada's markets could not supply such a range of textiles. There were many things the Europeans had never experienced before: chillis and chocolate, tomatoes and turkeys. Like Lisbon, Tenochtitlan was an imperial capital, and its markets displayed the foods, wares and people from all over Central America and as far as the Inca Empire.

The order that reigned in Tenochtitlan was presided over by its chief urban planner called the *calmimilocatl*. This official's job was to enforce building standards and maintain the gridiron pattern of streets as the city expanded out of its original rocky island and onto islets and reclaimed land. More than a mere civic functionary, the job of the *calmimilocatl* was sacred. Aztec cities were gifts from the gods; Tenochtitlan was the 'foundation of heaven', the centre of the universe. The site was chosen by the god Huitzilopochtli, who signalled his choice by having a golden eagle perch on a prickly pear and devour a rattlesnake; the legend is depicted on the present-day flag of Mexico. The city's orthogonal layout and the orientation of its main streets and buildings were designed as a cosmological map reflecting the movements of the stars and planets. The island city floating in the lake was a microcosm of the world – 'the root, the navel, and the heart of all world order'. Designed as a perfect city, Tenochtitlan served as the spiritual and political centre of a vast empire, the place from which power radiated from the centre to the periphery.

Urban planners were required to maintain the holy symmetry of the city, at least in its centre. Tenochtitlan was like a machine, well fed from its engineered agriculture and watered from long terracotta aqueducts that brought fresh water from the mountains. The four grand avenues were kept pristine by an army of labourers; the citizens were provided with public toilets which were regularly emptied and the contents used for tanning leather and to fertilise the *chinampas*. Compared to the fetid cities of Europe, Tenochtitlan was hyper-advanced in terms of technology and sanitation. Not that any European was interested in learning any lessons.

Built by nomadic immigrants on a rock in a lake, faced with neigh-bouring hostile city states in the Basin of Mexico, Tenochtitlan's early survival was not guaranteed; it was only in the fifteenth century that, after a series of wars, Tenochtitlan broke free of vassalage and emerged as a major metropolis and the head of a league of city states known as the Triple Alliance, or Aztec Empire. When Cortés marched in, its history as a vast, imperial metropolis had been short. It was a modern city, to be sure, but it was the legatee and final flowering of an ancient urban tradition.

Mesoamerica had seen numerous sophisticated urban civilisations rise and fall long before Europe had its first cities. The Olmec people were the first city-builders in Mesoamerica from 1200 BC. Much like the pioneers of Mesopotamia, the complexities created by urban life resulted in the development of information technologies which evolved into writing. The Mayans built magnificent ceremonial cities, of which 230 have been found; the largest, Tikal, which reached its zenith between AD 200 and 900, could have had a population of up to 90,000 people. Further to the north, Teotihuacan reached a population of between 150,000 and 200,000 in around AD 450. After the collapse of the Teotihuacan Empire, central Mexico broke up in numerous city states. But Teotihuacan remained the archetype of Mesoamerican urbanisation, influencing those city states that emerged in the subsequent centuries: the Tollecs, based in their capital Tula, the Tepanecs in Tlacopan, and finally the Mexicas and their glorious city of Tenochtitlan.

The sophistication of the Mesoamerican urban system barely survived its first encounter with Europeans. The population of Tenochtitlan was reduced by a third after an outbreak of smallpox following the Spanish arrival. In 1521 Cortés returned with an army, advanced siege weapons and boat-builders. Tenochtitlan held out for seventy-five days. As in Malacca a decade earlier, there was exceptionally brutal street fighting. Tenochtitlan was secured only when Cortés razed it house by house, building by building. Over the ruins of the last great Mesoamerican city he had the urban planner Alonso Garcia Bravo construct a European city; it became known as Mexico City.

The opening decades of the sixteenth century saw across the world the eradication or subversion of urban cultures. The predominance of the European city type, on a global scale, thus had its beginnings in the ruins of Tenochtitlan, Calicut, Mombasa, Malacca and others. Cities such as Rio de Janeiro, Mexico City, Cape Town, Bombay, Calcutta, Singapore, Batavia (Jakarta), Shanghai, Hong Kong, Melbourne and New York represented, over the succeeding centuries, a new type of global city modelled on European imperial metropolises.

*

Beneath the veneer of Lisbon's apparent freewheeling cosmopolitanism lurked something very dark. The city welcomed thousands of Jewish refugees from Spain in 1492. But the condition was that, along with the Muslim community, they had to leave or convert by 1497. Unwilling to lose the wealth, talent and international connections of his Jewish subjects, Manuel forced thousands of them to convert. The so-called New Christians, vital to the economy, faced continual hostility. At Easter 1506 the seething animosity exploded into violence on the streets of Lisbon. Jewish men, women and children were rounded up and killed by mobs; many were burnt in pyres on Rossio Square. Then in 1536 the Inquisition arrived in Lisbon. Within two years New Christians suspected of remaining Jewish in secret were being burnt at the stake outside the Paço da Ribeira.

Lisbon remained, by virtue of Portugal's empire, a major European port. What it lost was more valuable than all the spices in the world: its human capital. Many of the New Christian descendants of Sephardic Jews in Spain and Portugal, particularly the wealthy and well-connected merchants, emigrated to other cities. They went to Hamburg and to Venice, to Constantinople and Thessaloniki, to Marseilles and Bordeaux. But there was one city, rising to global supremacy, that was particularly attractive to Portuguese Jewish refugees in the closing decades of the sixteenth century: Amsterdam.

An overgrown village sitting in a shifting muddy bog with a population of 4,000 in 1450, Amsterdam had become a major global metropolis by the end of the sixteenth century, a city of migrants. Much of the mercantile and banking elite of Antwerp – Europe's financial capital – had fled there in the 1580s during the Dutch Revolt from the Spanish Empire. They were joined by Sephardic Jews from Lisbon and by people from all over Europe escaping persecution and war. In 1570 the population was 30,000; by 1620 it had leapt to 88,000 and twenty years later it was 139,000. At the point of its take-off, Amsterdam was the same size as it had been back in 1450; the city became overcrowded. A ramshackle slum formed outside the walls, the dwelling place of labourers 'who are there in great numbers and who are not in a position to pay the high rents for houses within the city'. The English ambassador noted in 1616 that 'the numbers of all nations, of all professions and all religions there assembled, but for one business only, of merchandise. Their new town goeth up a pace.'[18]

This unpromising marshy town became rich because it attracted human capital from more successful cities. Amsterdam, wrote a foreign diplomat, 'triumphs in the spoils of *Lisbon* and *Antwerp*'. Its rapid rise came as a result of geopolitics in part, but it was built on the foundations of northern European urbanism – the municipal republicanism of the Hanseatic League that had influenced cities in the Netherlands and which they in turn had developed in their own distinctive way. With its dense cluster of modest-sized cities the Netherlands was the most urbanised part of Europe, with close to a third of its population living in cities in the early sixteenth century, compared to the continent's average of just 9%. During the course of the century, while the proportion of urbanised Europeans remained more or less stagnant, it skyrocketed in the Netherlands; in Holland by 1675 the urbanisation rate was 61%.[19]

The Dutch phrase *schuitpraatje* means 'barge talk'. Canal barges were ubiquitous in cities; they were slow and carried all kinds of passengers – perfect therefore for lengthy discussions about politics, philosophy and religion. The phrase is brilliantly expressive: the Dutch were avid in their discussion of new ideas. The unusual prevalence of city-living helped fashion an urbane society, making the Netherlands exceptional in Europe. In other states, the landed aristocracy – with their domination of agriculture – retained their political power. Not so in the Dutch Republic, where domestic food production had ceded its central role in the economy to urban activities such as shipping, trade, commerce and industry. The elites of the towns regarded themselves as the heirs of the ancient Greek *poleis* and the free cities of the Hanseatic League. Cities and citizens, merchants and traders, enjoyed considerable autonomy and political power within the republic. The striking individualism and liberties evident in Dutch urban society were not merely the result of republicanism and the peculiarities of national politics. In striking contrast to other countries, the Netherlands was a patchwork of different faiths, with no one religion predominating, making toleration a necessity. Dutch cities were open to immigrants. Literacy rates were exceptionally high in the cities; bookshops were widespread; and Amsterdam established itself as the epicentre of northern European publishing.

Freedom of citizenship, of conscience and of commerce made the Netherlands – and the city of Amsterdam in particular – supremely attractive for freethinkers, dissenters and entrepreneurs. Amsterdam became a cauldron of radical ideas. The city's publishers reeled off the most controversial books of the age, such as those by the philosopher Thomas Hobbes, which were censored in England, and by Galileo, Spinoza and Descartes. An exile in Amsterdam from political turmoil in England, John Locke's thinking on political and religious toleration, civil government and empirical philosophy was shaped among the circles of freethinking Protestant dissenters who had associated with Spinoza. Extolling the virtues of Amsterdam as a place for philosophy, Descartes wrote of his pleasure watching ships arrive laden with the produce of the entire planet: 'Where else on earth could you find, as easily as you do here, all the conveniences of life and all the curiosities you could hope to see? In what other country could you find such complete freedom, or sleep with less anxiety, or find armies at the ready to protect you, or find fewer poisonings, or acts of treason or slander?'[20]

Innovative thinking helped push the Netherlands from relative obscurity to the most powerful state in Europe, perhaps the world. The people who came to Amsterdam seeking a haven from war and persecution brought with them their skills and their international connections. In 1595 a consortium of Amsterdam merchants – many of them recent migrants to the city with trading connections with the Baltic, Portugal, Spain, Venice and the Levant – invested in a highly risky voyage to Indonesia. Rather than act as middlemen for the Portuguese, selling spices and other Asian goods on their behalf, they went straight for the goodies themselves. The success of the venture propelled Amsterdam to the forefront of global trade. Twelve new companies were created in the next seven years; Amsterdam sent fifty ships to Asia while another thirty left other ports in the Dutch Republic.

Rather than liquidate themselves after the voyages, these companies ploughed their profits back into new expeditions and merged with one another to maximise their profitability. The merger of all mergers occurred in Amsterdam in 1602 with the formation of the world's first formally listed company. The Vereenigde Oostindische Compagnie (VOC), or Dutch East India Company, was funded by shares offered for sale to the general public of the Dutch Republic. Almost 60% of the capital invested came from Amsterdam, where the megacorporation was based. The VOC was granted a monopoly over the spice trade by the Dutch government and given the right to maintain an army, build forts, fight wars and make treaties with foreign powers. Above all, it was to supplant the Portuguese as the main player in Asia. In 1641 Malacca was captured by the VOC from the Portuguese.

The VOC became a government-backed for-profit corporate imperial power run from its headquarters in Amsterdam. It set up colonies and bases on the Coromandel and Malabar coasts of India; in Ceylon and Bengal; in Vietnam, Thailand, Indonesia, Malaysia, Taiwan and Japan; in Mauritius and the Cape of Good Hope. In 1619 the VOC founded Batavia in Indonesia, a European city on Java. Batavia was one of the first Dutch cities planted around the globe. New Amsterdam on the southern tip of Manhattan was founded in 1624; Cape Town began life in 1652 as a waystation on the route to the Indies.

Throughout history the riches of Asia had acted as the most powerful city-building force in the world. Now, at the beginning of the seventeenth century, the flow of goods transformed Amsterdam into a leviathan. Exiles from Antwerp brought with them large amounts of capital, but also sophisticated financial techniques that had been pioneered in that city. The Amsterdamsche Wisselbank (Amsterdam Exchange Bank), founded in 1609, invented many of the things we take for granted in modern banking – the system of cheques, direct debits and transfers between accounts. Based in the city's town hall, it was a public, municipal institution, its confidence generated by the prosperity, stability and wealth-generating potential of Amsterdam itself.

The corporation and the bank represent two of the pillars of the modern economy. The trinity was completed with the Amsterdam stock exchange. The flotation of the world's first major public corporation – the VOC – created, overnight, the world's first securities market. The Amsterdam bourse saw the rapid development of securities trading, forwards and futures, puts and calls, hedge betting, options, margin-buying and short-selling. Amsterdamers called this kind of futures trading *windhandel* – trading in the wind. You weren't dealing in herring or grain or spices or anything tangible; you didn't even own the thing you were selling; you might as well be trading the wind that blows or the air that you breathed. Nothing perplexed uninitiated contemporaries more than this liquid form of capitalism being pioneered in Amsterdam, where fortunes were made and lost on paper and the future itself was bought and sold in the imagination. José Penso de la Vega, a Spanish Jewish merchant and stockbroker who had emigrated to Amsterdam, wrote a book about the activities at the bourse. It was entitled *Confusion of Confusions*.

The big fish in the market were the stockbrokers who represented the richest speculators and financiers. These powerful brokers swaggered in, dressed to impress and projecting confidence. Just down a peg or two from them were the brokers who bought and sold for the big merchants and traders of the city. Such professional players worked quickly, buying and selling their clients' shares, watching prices, watching each other, getting hold of information first, detecting tremors in the market. Deals were struck by a seller opening his hand for the buyer to shake it; the bid was made and when it was accepted the price was confirmed by a second handshake. But the market moved too quickly for a long handshake: the ritual became a wild performance of fast hand-slapping in all directions as deals were made, bets hedged and prices set in mere seconds. De la Vega wrote that 'hands redden from the blows ... The handshakes are followed by shouting, the shouting by insults, the insults by impudence and more insults, shouting, pushes and handshakes until the business is finished.' This was not a place for the hesitant or shy.[21]

Following in the wake of the big players amid the bedlam of the exchange were many smaller fry, people who gambled feverishly on micro-fluctuations in the market, with shares they did actually not own. Such a small-scale speculator could be seen amid the hubbub, according to de la Vega, as he 'chews his nails, pulls his fingers, closes his eyes, takes four paces and four times talks to himself, raises his hand to his cheek as if he has toothache, puts on a thoughtful countenance, sticks out a finger, rubs his brow' before he rushes 'with violent gestures into the crowd, snaps with the fingers of one hand while with the other he makes a contemptuous gesture, and begins to deal in shares as though they were custard'.[22]

Outside the exchange, everyone, including women and children, was at it, speculating on duction shares – shares that had been subdivided up into tiny parts so that they were affordable for even schoolchildren. Trading cheap duction shares in taverns, in coffee houses or on the street corner was as addictive as participating in the hurly-burly of the stock exchange. According to de la Vega: 'If one were to lead a stranger through the streets of Amsterdam and ask him where he was, he would answer, "Among speculators", for there is no corner where one does not talk shares.'[23]

In an age when wealth was reckoned in land owned and gold locked away and other physical commodities, the revolution occurring in Amsterdam was truly mind-blowing. Contemporary visitors puzzled why a small waterlogged city could become so rich and powerful so quickly. The answer had a lot to do with the city itself. The ethos of the city was moneymaking and the removal of obstacles to its fulfilment. Religious persecution was bad for business; free discussion and political liberties were good for it. The creation of modern banking and finance, the VOC, and a globe-spanning trade system, were innovative and unorthodox, the result of a city culture focused on profit and unafraid of free thought. The spirit of the place, with its ambitious incomers and ruthless businesspeople, was dynamic and speculative. The city represented a giant social network, a place where ideas and practices spread through the system in the most efficient way, igniting change.

Amsterdam functioned as a complex information exchange. From the professional brokers in the stock exchange to speculating artisans, the city feasted on knowledge of global events. Hear the news first and you could make a killing on the bourse. Information came along diplomatic channels; it came with foreign businessmen and through correspondence sent between business houses all over the world. In 1618 Amsterdam got the world's first recognisably modern broadsheet newspaper, the *Courante uyt Italien, Duytslandt, &c*, which digested political and economic news gleaned from the city's information exchange.

Amsterdam was not so much a collection of buildings and people as a circulatory system. It circulated abstract things – ideas, news, futures and money – through the social network; but it was designed to circulate physical things as well. *Schuitpraatje* – barge talk – eloquently unites the tangible and the intangible, the city of information exchange and the city of hard business. In 1610 the city government developed a plan to transform Amsterdam. The city carpenter Hendrick Jacobszoon Staets designed a functional city based around the *grachengordel*, a belt of concentric canals radiating out from the centre. Markets and warehouses throughout the expanding city were connected to the port by the liquid network. Startlingly modern in the seventeenth century, the fan-shaped city mirrored the commercial mindset that had propelled Amsterdam to greatness. But it was designed not just around efficiency, but also according to ideas of liveability.

Amsterdam was an imperial metropolis, built on the wealth streaming in from Asia, Africa and the Americas. But it hardly looked like one. There are few great squares, bombastic statues, grand boulevards, palaces or imposing buildings on the scale of, say, a Rome or a Lisbon. Amsterdamers preferred a liveable and planned city – one of regular, neat streets, elegant bridges, advanced street lighting and convenient canals. The rage in Europe was for cities with grand boulevards and imposing monumentality – stage sets for the theatricality of absolute monarchy. But in the republican Dutch city there was no power capable of bulldozing through private property rights and the desires of its citizens. As in Tenochtitlan the city's municipal building inspectors held great sway, decreeing everything from the appearance of new buildings to the maximum size of a house's front steps. When new houses were built their facades had to be 'in conformity with the plan of the city architect'. Canal-fronting houses were particularly closely regulated by official planning, in order to maintain the outward appearance of Amsterdam.[24]

In an age of dirty, reeking streets, well might an English traveller write with near disbelief: 'The beauty and cleanliness of the streets are so extraordinary, that persons of all ranks do not scruple, but even seem to take pleasure in walking them.' Householders scrubbed not only their front steps but the pavement in front of their houses. Spitting was banned. People washed frequently. Polluting the canals was taboo. Elms and limes lined the streets and canals and were treasured as the 'jewel' of the city. A decree from 1612 prohibited damaging the trees because they were essential for the 'sweet air, the adornment and agreeableness' of Amsterdam. This was a city conceived around the needs of its citizens, not around monumentality or expressions of power. This is what makes Amsterdam so radical in the historical development of the metropolis: a citizen-sized city.[25]

The agreeable tranquillity of Amsterdam, its industrious, soberly dressed citizens, and its conformity of architecture masked the frenetic energy of the place. If Amsterdam did not have monuments and boulevards, its true glory was in the homes of its citizens. Visiting Amsterdam in 1640 the English traveller Peter Mundy was impressed by the 'neat and clean' dwellings of even the ordinary citizens, which 'were full of pleasure and home contentment'. There were the 'costly and curious' furniture and ornaments, such as rich cupboards and cabinets, paintings and prints, porcelain and 'costly fine cages with birds'. Ordinary Dutch families were avid consumers of art; Mundy said that not only was every middling home replete with imagery, but every butcher's and blacksmith's stall had an oil painting. We are talking about millions of paintings produced in the seventeenth century.[26]

In this overflowing of artistic talent, we witness the life of a city and the chaos of its streets for the first time. Drunkards in the tavern become characters every bit as much as grand merchants at the bourse. The paintings depict the gritty reality of city life – or the artist's impression of it – rather than the idealised cityscape of the past. Urban life – with its comic accidents, mysteries, contrast of types, bustle and energy – is the staple of modern art, literature, music and movies. It had its origin in Dutch genre painting in the seventeenth century, particularly in depictions of Amsterdam's racy taverns: people drink, smoke, flirt, kiss, fight, play music, gamble, stuff their faces, fall asleep. The split second of chaos, confusion and movement is caught by the artist.

These Dutch paintings celebrate a new way of living in the city. The taverns might provide opportunities for humour and moralising; but the fine, tidy middle-class home is fetishised. We are brought into what seems like intimate proximity to the urban abode, invited to marvel at the neatness and domestic harmony. Housewives and maids sweep and scrub; linen is folded; pots and pans are scoured; chores are assiduously accomplished; children play quietly; there is not a speck of dust. Amsterdamers were famously fastidious in matters of hygiene and cleanliness. Many of the paintings extol idealised virtues of orderliness and domestic perfection as a bastion against the corrupting effects of a wealthy, materialistic global city. The sanctified household was like a dyke holding back a tidal wave of urban vice, the antidote to the dog-eat-dog world of capitalism and the corrupting effects of the tavern. This is also a new urban world where respectable, well-to-do women are kept away from the messy, jostling, immoral life of the city. The mean streets appear to be a man's world, not suited to a lady, whose job was to create the ideal home.[27]

This, then, is art for the urban middling sort, showing off their good habits, frugality and contentedness even in the face of temptations and inordinate wealth. They, after all, had become the arbiters of artistic judgement through the power of their money in the artistic marketplace; their tastes reflected the kind of city they wanted to create. Idealised these images may have been, but they broadcast a powerful message: the city-dweller's home was the foundation of civic values. Since the birth of cities urban life had been public life. Socialising and business took place in communal settings, in agoras, markets and forums, in amphitheatres, bathhouses and town squares, in temples and churches. Now the private was beginning to take over from the public.

Portrayals of Amsterdam homes delighted in *stuff*. Turkish carpets, Chinese porcelain, Delft tiles, beaver hats from Canada, Indian calico, Japanese lacquerware, Venetian glass: all these and more catch the eye in Dutch genre paintings from the middle of the seventeenth century. Such items – luxurious and exotic – embellished the home with their beauty, further securing its central place in urban society. From the mansions of the rich merchants – stuffed with costly items from around the world – to the artisans and craftsmen, with their few cherished luxuries, visual art made the household the stage set for the greatness and global power of Amsterdam. The ability to afford such material possessions was a gift enjoyed by Dutch city-dwellers, and they enjoyed it to the full.

Amsterdam heralded a new kind of city, one based on consumerism and individualism, as much as financial capitalism. Populous cities have always created markets; but a city like Amsterdam was successful in large part because it involved a large proportion of its citizens in the getting and keeping of wealth, turning them into consumers of luxuries and art. The city of the future was one that satisfied and gave an outlet to popular culture, that entertained and enlightened. Here was a new urban public – urbane, sophisticated, literate, informed and demanding leisure activities and novel amusements. The consumer society was arriving, and Amsterdam was the first to cater to it. Its successor – London – would take things to new heights.

8

The Sociable Metropolis

London, 1666–1820

Caffeine flows through the veins of the modern city. You only have to look at your town or city to see the influence of the black stuff.

Coffee fuels a particular kind of social alchemy in cities. The revival of coffee houses from the 1990s filled a gap in urban life – a gap of sociability that had become acute in cities particularly in Britain, the United States and Australia where city centres had become impoverished. Starbucks claimed that coffee houses were a 'third place' in the city – 'a comfortable, sociable gathering spot away from home and work, like an extension of the front porch'.[1]

In South Korea, coffee had been drunk on the go, purchased cheaply from vending machines until Starbucks burst upon the scene in 1999. It created new urban tribes: *k'ap'emam* (cafémum), *k'op'isǔjok* (coffice tribe) and *k'ap'ebǔrŏrijok* (cafébrary tribe, or those who use the café as a library). In a culture that did not have many urban public spaces and still fewer for women, Starbucks provided a comfortable, modish environment where young women could linger and socialise outside the restrictions and gender expectations of the family home. Not just in South Korea, but everywhere, coffee houses are places where you can go to be alone in the city; where you can people-watch; or where you can throw yourself into the torrents of city life.[2]

Cafés are the most powerful symbol of private-public urban space. Open to all comers, they nonetheless retain an individual character that helps build a community. In Tehran, as in other cities, there are cafés that cater for distinct urban tribes: intellectuals, readers, jazz aficionados, classical-music lovers, film buffs, political dissidents, students and so on. You choose the café, and it provides the ambience and sense of community. Cafés in Tehran are often anonymous-looking from the outside, promising security and a refuge with like-minded companions; inside they have a 'social table' set aside for those who want to meet and talk. They are central to metropolitan youth self-identity in the city, havens from the constraints and restraints of the official city.[3]

As such they are subject to raids by the morality police; in 2012 eighty-seven coffee shops were shut down for 'not following Islamic values'. A year later Café Prague – popular with students, intellectuals and dissidents – closed rather than comply with the law requiring coffee houses to install surveillance cameras for 'civic monitoring'.

The central position of the café in modern urban culture is deeply embedded in history and romance. Paris became the cultural capital of the nineteenth century, wrote Ralph Waldo Emerson, because its 'supreme merit is that it is a city of conversation and cafés'. From the 1860s city-centre cafés spilt out onto the boulevards. An American tourist in 1869 was amazed to see people of all classes on the pavement 'smoking, drinking, chatting, reading the papers'. 'Here is true democracy,' he concluded. And here was the modern sociable city in action: a place for chance encounters, people-watching, mingling and the constantly unfolding theatre of the streets. By the 1880s there were 40,000 cafés, offering a massive range of choices about where to socialise and whom to socialise with. There were ornate fashionable cafés on the boulevards and dingy, rough, working-class versions, and plenty in between. You could go to an establishment that recalled a bucolic village café or another where you could pick up a girl. Most importantly, they operated at the heart of neighbourhoods, smoky places smelling of coffee and wine, resounding with the sounds of dominoes, backgammon, the folding of newspapers, 'good humour, and emulation, and curiosity and labyrinthine chatter'. The working-class phrase 'café friend' meant a regular you associated with in your neighbourhood café but would never meet outside that milieu. Intensive city-living would have been impossible without the social networking effect of the café.[4]

Edgar Degas and James McNeill Whistler went to the Café Molière. Café Gerbois attracted Claude Monet, Alfred Sisley, Camille Pissarro, Paul Cézanne, Pierre-Auguste Rodin, Émile Zola, Louis Edmond Duranty and Stéphane Mallarmé. Impressionism emerged from café society, as did cubism and literary modernism. Monet cherished the 'perpetual clash of opinions' at Café Gerbois, which 'kept our wits sharpened'. Café culture was the spark of conversation; and conversations were the fuel of art. 'From them', Monet wrote, 'we emerged tempered more highly, with a firmer will, with our thoughts clearer and more distinct.'[5]

The urbane ambience of the coffee shops, with its associations of artistic brilliance and bohemianism, makes it central to the backdrop of fashionable city life. Today the arrival of hipster coffee shops in inner-city areas is a sure harbinger of gentrification and rising property prices; the ideal moment for property investors is held to be when the number of coffee outlets matches fried-chicken shops in a hitherto neglected area. In Harlem in the 2010s real-estate brokers secretly invested in coffee shops in order to artificially accelerate gentrification and initiate a property boom. They were the Potemkin villages of gentrification.[6]

Things like factories, railways, cars, electricity and reinforced concrete have very obviously shaped cities. Coffee should be in that list. Not least is its transformative effect on one of the most vital building blocks of cities – sociability.

*

Coffee's journey to ubiquity began in Ethiopia, where it was first cultivated. From the fifteenth century Yemeni traders exported it to Sufi monasteries in order to help worshippers remain wakeful during their all-night devotions. Coffee then spread to Mecca and Medina, and on to Cairo, Aleppo and Damascus. In the 1550s coffee houses began to appear in Constantinople; by the end of the century they were everywhere in the city.

The Englishman George Sandys, visiting Constantinople in 1610, was dismayed not to find any taverns in which to network with merchants and make contacts. Instead he found a place called a 'Coffahouse': 'There sit they chatting most of the day; and sip of a drink called Coffa (of the berry that it is made of) in little china dishes, as hot as they can suffer it: black as soot, and tasting not much unlike it.'[7]

Coffee houses transformed Constantinople because they provided a new space in the city for meeting and talking outside the traditional confines of the mosque and home. English traders in cities such as Aleppo, Smyrna and Constantinople began to drink the beverage and, like billions more in years to come, got addicted to the stuff. Returning from Smyrna in 1651, the merchant Daniel Edwards brought with him coffee-making apparatus and coffee beans. At the house of his wealthy father-in-law in the heart of the City of London, Edwards provided coffee for fellow merchants. So popular was the brew that the constant calls of caffeine-addicted City men looking for their fix became a nuisance. Edwards therefore decided to open up a stall in a churchyard in St Michael's Alley, run by Edwards's Greek servant Pasqua Rosée. In 1654 Rosée moved into a house on the other side of the alley, the first coffee house in western Europe.[8]

The exotic drink attracted the curious, including the polymath Samuel Hartlib who reported: 'It is a Turkish kind of drink made of water and some berry or Turkish bean ... It is somewhat hot and unpleasant but a good after-relish and caused breaking of wind in abundance.'[9]

A novelty, no doubt, in a city attracted to diversions and spectacles. But few would have wagered on coffee's success. By the 1660s there were over eighty coffee houses in the City of London, and more in Westminster and Covent Garden. At the close of the century the number was pushing 1,000. Coffee houses had spread to towns and cities across England, Scotland and Ireland as well, across the Atlantic to Boston, New York and Philadelphia, and over the Channel to Paris, Amsterdam, Vienna and Venice. Within a few years of their introduction in London 'all the neighbourhood swarm [to coffee houses] like bees, and buzz like them too'.[10]

'What's the news? ... Bring a dish of coffy,' a parrot shrilly demanded of every new customer entering a particular London coffee house. It was copying the constant refrain of hundreds of daily visitors seeking a cup of the brand-new beverage. 'What's the news?' was the opening gambit of the coffee-house habitué. For a penny you could sip your coffee at a huge table littered with newspapers, satires, lampoons and tobacco pipes.[11]

News, in late seventeenth-century London, was becoming a valuable commodity, and the coffee house became the primary hub of news. Engulfed by a civil war in the 1640s that led to the execution of the king, England and Scotland were in ferment when Pasqua

Rosée set up shop. In 1659/60 the country was again in crisis as factions vied for control. The coffee house came into its own as a forum for discussion and the exchange of news during these heady days. The young Samuel Pepys, eager for news, gossip and connections with the powerful, began to frequent coffee houses to hear the debates. At the Turk's Head coffee house in Westminster he rubbed shoulders with noblemen, political philosophers, merchants, soldiers and scholars arguing over the future direction of the country.

Pepys and others were amazed at the erudition of these coffee-house discussions and the politeness of the debate. A tavern or inn could not create this atmosphere; there was something about the hot dark brew that fostered calmness and reason. You behaved in a distinctively *metropolitan* way, as you sipped your distinctively metropolitan beverage.

Coffee-house clientele consumed news; but they made it as well. Journalists harvested much of their news from the talk of the town in cacophonous coffee houses. Government spies trawled them for up-to-date information. Discussing the state of the world had gone public, and in a very particular setting at that.

In a coffee house you had to take your seat as it came and sit next to whoever was there; no special places were reserved for men of rank. A coffee house, said Samuel Butler, is where 'people of all qualities and conditions meet, to trade in foreign drinks and news, ale, smoke, and controversy'. The owner 'admits of no distinction of persons, but gentleman, mechanic, lord and scoundrel mix, and are all of a piece, as if they were resolved into their first principles'.[12]

The government feared the impact of this radical new public space, believing coffee houses were hotbeds of sedition and republicanism. The fad was attacked over and over again in print. Often the criticism was aimed below the belt. According to the author of *The Womens Petition Against Coffee* 'the excessive use of that newfangled, abominable, heathenish liquor called coffee ... has so eunuched our husbands and crippled our more kind gallants, that they have become as impotent as age, and as unfruitful as those deserts whence that unhappy berry is said to be brought'.[13]

Yet even these allegations did coffee no harm: it had more of a stimulating effect than an enfeebling one. Just as coffee houses helped kick-start the news business, they also had an important economic effect. Stockbrokers were considered too rowdy for the Royal Exchange, so London's first securities exchange took place in the more congenial setting of Jonathan's Coffee-House on Change Alley. Coffee houses provided news of all kinds: up-to-date lists showing the prices of commodities, stocks and currencies were posted regularly in Jonathan's. Coffee houses mushroomed on Change Alley, providing environments of sociability in which stock-market trading could operate and all kinds of people could access the market. Garraway's coffee house, also on Change Alley, conducted auctions in which wholesalers disposed of newly arrived long-distance cargos fresh from the wharves.

Borrowing ideas pioneered in Amsterdam, London in the early years of the eighteenth century was remaking capitalism. The Bank of England was established in 1694 in order to raise vast loans for the British state. The creation of a publicly financed national debt propelled Britain to global-superpower status. It also turned the coffee houses of Change Alley into markets for government and bank stock, as well as shares in the enormous companies. This emergence of modern financial capitalism required eye-to-eye deal-making; the coffee house was its natural birthplace. Stockbrokers and stockjobbers (dealers) worked the coffee houses that filled the alley, feasting on the news, rumour and gossip that flowed through them.

Underpinning this world of speculation was a new industry that would help propel London further ahead as a commercial giant. Edward Lloyd's coffee house specialised in obtaining the most reliable shipping news before anywhere else, attracting sailors, shippers and long-distance traders to meet, talk and trade. From high on a pulpit a waiter read out the latest shipping news. It was then pinned to a wall before being sold more widely in the city. Amid the bustle of this coffee house, merchants and shippers came together to hedge the risks of global trading ventures. Lloyd's coffee house became not only London's but the world's main insurance market; all day brokers negotiated with the underwriters, seeking out the best deals for their clients.

The financial revolution took place outside institutions; it was organic, face-to-face and sociable. The coffee house was not like the agora, the forum, the market square or even the Roman bath; it was poised between the public and the private, an extension of the proprietor's home, but open to all. Coffee houses specialising in various trades and activities brought together people who would otherwise not have met, allowing them to exchange information and forge networks. Functioning as stock, credit and insurance markets, trading floors, commodity exchanges, wholesale dealers and news sites, they were also the business office and meeting room of formative capitalism. In other words, the galaxy of coffee houses in London provided a dynamic, free-flowing, informal public space that had not existed before.

Late seventeenth-century London was a centre of science as much as it was of business. The foundation of the Royal Society of London for Improving Natural Knowledge made science a matter of public debate. The moving force of the Royal Society was a coffee-house addict. Robert Hooke's diaries reveal that he visited sixty-four different London coffee houses between 1672 and 1680, going to at least one a day, sometimes three and on one occasion five. The public nature of late seventeenth-century science was made real at the coffee house. These places became stages for the performance of virtuoso science. Hooke's formal lectures at Gresham College were poorly attended, sometimes not at all. In the more relaxed and sociable environs of a coffee house he could count on an eager audience.[14]

James Hodgson gave free lectures on Newtonian mathematics and astronomy at the Marine Coffee-House and demonstrated an array of air pumps, microscopes, telescopes, prisms and other apparatus that had never been seen before outside the Royal Society. The City men were interested in mathematics and science because they promised to improve navigation, a matter dear to the heart of traders as much as insurers at Lloyd's coffee house. Coffee-house culture brought theorists into contact with sailors who possessed a wealth of practical knowledge. The Financial Revolution and the Scientific Revolution met over a cup of coffee.[15]

Just as each branch of trade had its favoured rendezvous, coffee houses catered for a wealth of activities and desires. One might offer lessons in fencing, another in French. Go to Will's in Covent Garden and later Button's and you'd meet the city's great poets and writers. Go to Duke's and you were among actors and playwrights; at Old Slaughter's you would encounter a coterie of artists. Men of fashion and courtiers gathered at White's in St James's Street. Booksellers and publishers congregated at Child's, adjacent to St Paul's Cathedral.

'Coffee-houses make all sorts of people sociable, the rich and the poor meet together, as do the learned,' commented John Houghton, a fellow of the Royal Society.[16]

Pepys did not like coffee much. Small quantities of ground beans were boiled in a cauldron; it was a weaker and less tasty version of that which we make now. But then the beverage was never the main attraction. 'I find much pleasure [in coffee houses]', said Pepys, 'through the diversity of company – and discourse.' They provided a vital function for cities, supplying the motive and location for spontaneous encounters and the emergence of informal networks. In the spillover of knowledge between finance, science and the arts in late seventeenth-century London we can see very clearly how cities maximise the opportunities for accidental meetings, chance encounters and information exchange. The profusion of places for socialising and leisure made cities more dynamic than they had ever been.

Coffee cast magic in another way. The coffee house, with its rituals of sociability and informal exchanges of information, embodied a newly forming urban civility.

*

Long an insignificant and marginal city, London prospered in the late seventeenth century and would be the dominant global metropolis of the eighteenth, stealing Amsterdam's mantle as it became more assertive as an international trading centre and imperial metropolis. Its population was doubling every century: over 250,000 at the beginning of the seventeenth and 500,000 when it ended; by the close of the eighteenth it was the first European city to exceed a million inhabitants since Rome in the second century AD.

And it was not just the population which was surging. Income per capita rose by at least a third between 1650 and 1700, the period when coffee houses burst onto the scene. People had money to spend. They did not just spend it in newfangled coffee houses, but on a whole range of consumer items, fashions and literature. Most importantly they lavished it on leisure activities.[17]

And with this rapid growth in wealth came gnawing anxiety. London's giddy expansion, its newly enriched middling classes, its showy consumer culture and its cycles of boom and bust were a dire threat to the conventional social system. For some the coffee house may have been a bastion of polite discourse and urbane sociability; for others it represented the horrors of the modern city itself – a discordant babel of unrestrained conversation, a hodgepodge of classes indiscriminately mixed together, and a commercialised place that defied the traditional authorities of church and state.

Destroyed by fire in 1666, the City of London that rose from the ashes was unlike any city that had been before. Densely populated and inordinately wealthy, it was Babylon reborn, a bewildering monster of a place beset by swarms of people and incessant traffic. 'The Town of London is a kind of large Forest of *Wild Beasts*,' warned a moralist, 'where most of us range about at a venture, and are equally savage, and mutually destructive of one another.'[18]

The 'strange hurries and impertinences', the 'busy scramblings and underminings', were bad enough. Much more alarming was the way in which a vast metropolis anonymised people, allowing them to disguise their true identities so that 'villainies, cheats and impostures' abounded in the city.[19]

Nonsense, came the reply. Far from degenerating morals, the city was an engine of improvement. In the city 'we polish one another and rub off our corners and rough sides by a sort of amicable collision', wrote the Earl of Shaftesbury in 1711. Later in the century the Scottish philosopher David Hume held that men and women who 'flock to the cities' experienced 'an increase of humanity, from the habit of conversing together, and contributing to each other's pleasure and entertainment'.[20]

Conversation, pleasure and entertainment: leisure was chief among the things that helped to refine society in the modern metropolis. British urban culture, from the late seventeenth century, became increasingly dominated by 'politeness' and 'civility'. Hundreds of conduct books hit the market offering advice on how to behave in public and private. Traditional ideas of good manners and courteous behaviour had emanated from royal courts and the great rural houses of the aristocracy, guiding expectations of deportment and conversation. By the time of the coffee-house boom, civility was coming to be associated with something entirely different. Manners engendered by urban living were taking over from the stuffy and rule-bound courtly culture of bygone days. Just as scholarly discussion, political debate and business had broken out of the closed worlds of the university, Parliament and the guilds into open forums like the coffee house, so culture and artistic activity were becoming commodified and finding expression in the public sphere.[21]

Politeness and civility were urban and distinctively modern. London offered myriad opportunities for the sociability that made people more refined. In turn, civility made city-living easier because it provided the lubrication for interactions between strangers in the congested urban environment. 'Conversation creates those agreeable ties which bind us one to another,' enjoined a treatise called *The Polite Gentleman*. Another writer declared that the true aim of civility was 'to render company and conversation easy and agreeable'.[22]

A city is one of the miracles of human existence. What prevents the human ant heap from degenerating into violence is civility, the spoken and unspoken codes that govern day-to-day interactions between people. Every moment on any city's streets is witness to complicated, unorchestrated ballet dances of behaviours, as people negotiate shops, streets, offices and mass-transit systems.

Acceptable behaviour shifts over time. How people of different races, ethnicities, sexualities, genders and identities interact in public has been deeply contested. In bars in Los Angeles (for example), minimum civic behaviour is spelt out for all clients: 'There will be absolutely: No Sexism; No Racism; No Ableism; No Homophobia; No Transphobia; or Hatefulness within this establishment or you will be asked to leave.' The Shanghai government issued a publication called *How to Be a Lovely Shanghainese* as it geared up for the World's Fair in 2010. It covered everything from how to dress to stern advice on table manners. The city's list of 'Seven Don'ts' setting out 'civilisation standards and civic moral norms' was published and displayed everywhere in 1995 as Shanghai was undergoing rapid transformation and receiving millions of immigrants, many of them rural: don't spit, don't litter, don't damage public property, don't damage greenery, don't jaywalk, don't smoke in public areas, don't utter obscene words. Its 2017 update shows evidence of how the city had changed over twenty-two years: out went injunctions on spitting, swearing and vandalism (they were thought to be sufficiently internalised); in came orders to not to park your car in an inconsiderate way, not to let your

pets disturb the neighbours, not to cut in line, not to create a distur-
bance when speaking.

For men on the make in boom-time London, finding a way to
ingratiate yourself with your social or business superiors was essential.
If you didn't behave properly, you wouldn't get on. Politeness was in
part a reaction against the anxieties generated by London's vertiginous
take-off, an antidote to the fears of a commercialised city and free-
market economy in which the glue that bound society was weakening.
If good manners no longer emanated from the court or the church,
said writers like Addison and Steele, then they came from modern
commercial society itself. And likewise, royal London no longer served
as the epicentre of art, literature, theatre and music; cultural production and consumption shifted to the urban realm. The market became
the arbiter of taste.

And the market responded in surprising ways. It left a physical
imprint on London which is very much evident to this day. The layout
of London's growing fashionable West End by speculative builders,
with its terraces of handsome houses and verdant garden squares, was
politeness made manifest. Ornate display in domestic architecture was
out; classical refinement was in. The uniformity and restraint of the
dominant neoclassical Palladian style reflected the self-mastery and
simplicity of individual politeness. One contemporary architect called
Georgian town planning 'the theatre of the polite world', a series of
interconnecting squares, streets, gardens, parks, coffee houses, assembly
rooms, theatres, museums, churches and promenades that collectively
added up to a 'polite' public sphere that encouraged sociability and
mingling.[23]

Here we are in the modern city, governed not by ancient authorities
but by market forces and shaped around the leisure activities, fashions
and tastes of its citizens. A new kind of city, instantly recognisable
today: one with restaurants, cafés, bars, museums, art galleries, nightclubs, theatres, shopping malls, department stores, arenas and a smorgasbord of diversions that exist to entertain us and give the city its
raison d'être. But such an urban experience, its public realm designed
around the changing tastes and disposable incomes of its citizens, is
very recent in historical terms. It burst onto the scene as London
emerged from backwater to global metropolis.

★

The radical coffee-house culture of the 1660s and beyond heralded this change. But the coffee house was only one of many new commercial ventures catering to prevailing notions of civility and sociability. Vauxhall Pleasure Gardens, on the south bank of the Thames, opened in the 1660s as well. In 1729 it came under the management of Jonathan Tyers, a property developer and impresario. Tyers remodelled the gardens to capture the tastes of the time, designed as an elaborate stage set for polite living and informal public interaction.

Tyers turned what had been a wood with a tavern in the middle into an eighteenth-century urban theme park. Visitors arriving by boat entered Vauxhall and promenaded through the gravel walks illuminated by hundreds of lamps hanging from the trees. The grid system of avenues encouraged chance meetings. As they walked, they could admire the series of paintings displayed in glass cases and listen to music played by an orchestra in an octagonal bandstand in the grove. Wealthier visitors would take their seat in one of the partially open supper boxes placed near the orchestra or in semicircular colonnades along the promenades. Here sat the aristocracy and beau monde, eating in public and semi-privacy at the same time, seeing and being seen by the throngs of Londoners while maintaining their exclusivity. The idea of eating in public was, it should be remembered, a very new and shocking thing. The nobility, conversing and eating as the music played, were as much part of the show as anything put on by Tyers. Here was an aspect of eighteenth-century London in microcosm: people of different classes sharing the same experience, yet separated by invisible barriers of class and status.

Those not smart enough for the boxes ate al fresco on picnic tables under the trees. If the weather was bad, the orchestra played in the large rotunda, illuminated by one of the largest chandeliers in the country, and visitors ate in the exotic Turkish Tent. Elsewhere in the gardens there were pavilions, statues, follies and triumphal arches. The edge of the park was screened with scenic trompe l'oeil paintings that gave the illusion of rustic beauty disappearing into the distance. Every season Tyers would have had to add to the enchanted gardens in order to provide novelty and spectacle. Mozart made his English debut at Vauxhall, one of many of the finest musicians of the day who played there. Similarly, the venue was a showcase of modern art, a public gallery before public galleries existed. The lights, music, paintings, buildings, fireworks, elegant landscaping and crowds of people had a powerful impact. As Henry Fielding put it: 'I must avow, I found my whole soul, as it were, dissolved in pleasure ... discourse, while there, was a rhapsody of joy and wonder ... I scarce believe the bewitching scene was real.'[24]

Vauxhall Pleasure Gardens marked the beginning of modern mass entertainment. It was London's nightclub which, according to a German tourist, was 'an entertainment, which has no equal, that I have heard, in Europe'. A normal night would see 2,000 visitors, often many more, perhaps some 7,000 people all clamouring for food. On the night of the first performance of Handel's *Music for the Royal Fireworks* in 1749, 12,000 people crammed into the gardens. Towards the end of the century on a weekend evening at Vauxhall 16,000 people might pass through the gates, paying the affordable entrance price of just one shilling.[25]

Pleasure gardens and coffee houses were among the attractions that drew people to the intoxicating metropolis. Those with landed wealth wanted to spend their money in the capital – in these newly emerging public places of consumption and pleasure. At the start of the century there were just two theatres in London, the Theatre Royal in Drury Lane and the Lincoln's Inn Theatre, both operating under royal patents. From the 1720s more and more playhouses popped up, catering to the rage for entertainment, including the massive Covent Garden Theatre. Stage sets became ever more elaborate and technologically advanced to wow and attract the crowds. The new playhouses were built in the fashion that we know today, with private boxes, orchestra pits and galleries, and footlights and sidelights illuminating the stage.

By the end of the century over 3,000 went nightly to the Covent Garden Theatre out of a total capacity of 29,500 seats available in London's wider theatreland. Theatres just down in size from Covent Garden – such as Sadler's Wells, the Adelphi or the Royalty in Tower Hamlets – averaged 1,800 a night. A French tourist described how the lower sort of Londoner – sailors, servants, 'low tradesmen' and their wives and girlfriends – 'enjoy themselves as they please' in the upper galleries of Covent Garden. Sitting high in the 'gods' of the auditorium, they acted like gods 'hurling down their thunder on both actors and spectators in the shape of apples and orange peel'. Watching the aristocracy in the boxes, particularly the ladies and higher-class courtesans, was considered a show in itself; the highest were exposed to catcalls and ribald jokes as much as the actors on stage. This was where aristocratic feuds, snubs and intrigues were played out; it was the hub of town gossip.[26]

Londoners relished the theatre because it was a place where people of all classes mingled, from servants and journeymen to City traders and barristers to plutocrats and aristocrats. The middling and economically insecure paid a shilling to go to the playhouses and the pleasure gardens partly 'for the purposes of forgetting their [social] separation' by sharing the same entertainments as the highest. The theatre was a place where it *felt* like the city of a million people came together. That gave it its power. And God save anyone who got in its way. London footmen rioted in 1737 when attempts were made to ban servants from the gallery at Drury Lane. The Covent Garden Theatre saw sixty-seven nights of consecutive protest in 1809 when it raised ticket prices. No one wanted to be excluded from the beating heart of the city.

A book of 1728 purportedly written by A. Primcock called *The Touchstone* catalogued the 'reigning diversions of the town'. Primcock's tour of London's 'new commercial diversions' includes the premier entertainments of the city, its music and dancing venues, its theatres, operas, assembly rooms and masquerades. But mixed up with 'high' culture, he included a whole range of other diversions on offer to Londoners: puppet shows, tumblers, rope dancers, jugglers, open-air farces, strolling players, prizefighting, cockfighting and bear-gardens. There were waxwork museums, freak shows, acrobats, contortionists, menageries, fairgrounds, exhibitions of curiosities, Punch and Judy shows, street singers. The streets were enlivened by numerous ballad sellers, who sold and sang popular songs, many of them bawdy. From the 1730s cricket matches began drawing crowds of 10,000 paying customers to the Artillery Ground, marking the arrival of commercialised mass sporting events. Astley's Amphitheatre in Lambeth was a highly lucrative circus that specialised in horse-riding displays and tricks. In *The Female Spectator* Eliza Haywood castigated 'our modern diversion-mongers', the entrepreneurs who were reshaping the city around pleasure.[27]

★

Raucous behaviour in the theatre, bear- and bull-baiting, cockfighting: this was not a polite city, despite what people told themselves. As London became the biggest metropolis in the world it drew in thousands of workers to construct the graceful new squares, to service the growing leisured classes, to man the docks and to do all the other hard and dirty work of a commercial leviathan. The rabbit warren of rotting medieval buildings huddled in St Giles-in-the-Fields looked like a miserable collection of rooks' nests, overcrowded with colonies of families. The St Giles 'rookery', as it was known, housed communities of poor Irish labourers: the builders, bricklayers, boatmen, sedan-chair porters, coal heavers and costermongers whose brawn kept the city going.

This small, filthy, ramshackle and violent rookery was one of the worst slums in history. One of its derelict buildings was known as 'Rat's Castle'. The nearby fields were the scenes of bare-knuckle and dog-fighting. Like slums in cities such as Mumbai today, St Giles was a feature of a metropolis whose population was growing faster than its low-cost housing. There were numerous lodging houses, into which crammed hundreds of transients lured to London by the promise of jobs. The St Giles rookery was a closed urban world within the city, a place few dared to tread. Yet it was a stone's throw from one of London's newest and most fashionable districts, Bloomsbury, with its aristocratic squares, large town houses and the British Museum (founded in 1753).

Those parts of the City that had been immolated in the Great Fire of 1666 were rebuilt in brick and stone, with handsome houses, wider streets and grand public buildings, such as St Paul's Cathedral, fifty or so churches built by Christopher Wren, the Bank of England and Mansion House. But among the gleaming brand-new City were streets and alleys that had escaped the ravages of the fire and provided visible memories of the old, rougher London of rickety timbered buildings, narrow courts and fetid alleys. The outer wards of Farringdon and Clerkenwell were typical rookeries in the richest city on earth, with their dank slums, passageway tunnels, and the 'rough games' of their inhabitants. Until the 1750s Hockley-in-the-Hole, in Clerkenwell, was the centre of savage wrestling matches, sword fights, bare-knuckle fighting, bull-baiting and the breeding of vicious fighting dogs.

The London of the eighteenth century was a boisterous, over-crowded city, plagued by gang fights, muggings, petty crime, animal abuse and brutality. It was also a hardworking city. Almost every visitor to London remarked on the incessant press of the crowds, the congested traffic and the tumultuous uproar of the streets that engulfed them as they arrived. Sedan chairs, Hackney carriages, coaches, singing street-food vendors and ballad-mongers added to the cacophony.

The open space of St James's Square, where twenty of the twenty-three houses were homes of aristocrats, was like 'a common dunghill' in the 1720s, a pile of rubbish, soil, ashes, offal and even dead dogs. London was a place where politeness coexisted with grime, both physical and moral. Working-class Soho rubbed up against upper-class Mayfair.

The topography of London made it hard for the 'polite' to insulate themselves from the realities of the city. Big as it was by the standards of the time, it took just one hour to walk north to south and perhaps three at the most east to west. Throughout the eighteenth century, the main shopping streets were the Strand, Fleet Street, Cheapside and Cornhill, meaning that the fashionable West Enders had to force their way through the diverse geography of London to make their purchases. To the shock of foreign visitors, the royal parks were open to all: promenading men and women of the elite mingled with all kinds of Londoners.

Foreigners were amazed by the way in which London had the effect of levelling social distinctions, at least in the public parts of the city. A German tourist noticed how no government minister or aristocrat would dare make the poorest give way on the street, 'yet they daily pass on foot through the best-peopled and most frequented streets of London, where they are pressed and elbowed, and bespattered, without once offering to complain'.[28]

In light of the egalitarian expectations of urban life, the aristocracy and gentry of London began to dress down on the streets, avoiding embellishments of class. 'In former ages,' it was written in the 1780s, 'a Gentleman was easily distinguished from the Multitude by his DRESS. In the present period, all external evidence of rank among men is destroyed.' Swords were swapped for canes and umbrellas. By the end of the century, male fashions were less flamboyant; the wealthy wore darker, plainer clothes that did not stick out. It marked the beginning of the male urban look that would dominate the following centuries: sober suits and ties.[29]

An intricate mosaic of different types of peoples and districts, with poverty and misery living cheek by jowl with opulence and splendour, London was a hectic mix. But if 'politeness' did not conquer this rough and ready city, however, civility was in evidence everywhere. The eighteenth century was the golden age of urban sociability.

Coffee failed to make any dent on the drinking of alcohol, which remained the mainstay of Londoners' sociability. In 1737 there were reckoned to be 531 coffee houses, compared to 207 inns, 447 taverns and 5,975 alehouses. That made for one licensed premises for every 13.4 private houses in London. And that did not include another 7,000 or so places that sold gin between the 1720s and the 1750s. Much like the coffee houses, the London pubs were places of conviviality, conversation and newspapers; they were employment exchanges for all kinds of Londoners, including merchants and professionals, smaller tradesmen and artisans, and working men. One of the key functions of public houses was hosting clubs in back rooms.

The early seventeenth century saw a proliferation of clubs where people of all kinds could associate in pubs and drink heavily. There was the Farting Club, the Ugly Club, the Little Club (for men under five feet), the Tall Club, the Fighting Club, the Fat Men's Club, the One-eyed Men Club, clubs for people with long noses, and so on. There were erudite literary, scientific, political and philosophical clubs. For the less well-off there were punch clubs (drunk as you like for a shilling) and singing clubs. Apprentices and young women met at Cock and Hen clubs, where they danced and paired off. A famous debating society met at the Robin Hood just off the Strand, attracting 'masons, carpenters, smiths, and others' who were allotted five minutes to have their say. They were associations of like-minded people, friends, professions, neighbourhoods, charities and sports. In a city of migrants, clubs of people from, say, Scotland or Staffordshire provided a ready-made form of association to mitigate the loneliness of the teeming metropolis. You name it, there was a club for it in a city defined by its love of association.

Pleasure took place in public, in a crude, bawdy male-dominated drinking culture. Joseph Brasbridge, a silversmith based on Fleet Street, recalled with shame that when he was young and building up his business, he was determined to be a 'jolly fellow', drinking until dawn in a club at the Globe tavern with his buddies: a surgeon, a printer, a parliamentary reporter, a Treasury clerk and the keeper of Newgate Prison. These were not lower-class men by any means; one of them would go on to become lord mayor.

Brasbridge described a city in which high and low pleasures blurred. Take Vauxhall Gardens, the epitome of elegance. In his quest for gentility Jonathan Tyers illuminated the walks. All, that is, except one, the Dark Walk. So-called 'respectable' men could be seen emerging from its protective darkness, buttoning their breeches after an encounter with a prostitute. Tyers the businessman knew better than anyone that, for all the demand for politeness, sex sold, and it sold within ostensibly 'polite' places. Theatres, masquerades and public gardens bustled with prostitutes and pimps.

Caught between savouring the 'elegant pleasures' of polite high society and thirsting for the alternative, rougher world of unrestrained conviviality and 'romantic adventures', James Boswell was not alone in feeling that the metropolis created an impossible tug-of-war in his desires. London was the 'seat of pleasure' but, with its numerous prostitutes and actresses offering continual temptation, it was more precisely the seat of male sexual pleasure. Evident throughout the metropolis, prostitution was especially concentrated in and around Covent Garden, the Strand and Lincoln's Inn Fields. The demand for casual sex was enormous, and it was catered for. The first scene of William Hogarth's series of paintings and prints *A Harlot's Progress* depicts a naive country girl, 'Moll Hackabout', fresh off the coach and hoping for a career as a seamstress in London. Instead her good looks attract the attentions of the notorious procuress Mother Needham, who tempts her with the easy returns and fine clothes of life as a high-class courtesan. As the series progresses Moll briefly prospers as a kept woman living in luxury, before becoming a common prostitute and eventually dying of syphilis at the age of twenty-three. Daniel Defoe's novel *Moll Flanders* shows how a woman survived in an uncaring male city by exchanging sex for cold cash, either in marriage or as a prostitute.

Numbers of prostitutes in London were always exaggerated. An estimate of 50,000 in the late eighteenth century included women who clearly were not sex workers in any sense – tens of thousands of unmarried women living with male partners. But the visibility of prostitution made it seem endemic and the easy availability of sex shaped male behaviour in public.

In eighteenth-century novels London is portrayed again and again as a place of sexual danger for women. In a harrowing episode in Fanny Burney's novel *Evelina* (1778), the eponymous character is very nearly raped in Vauxhall Gardens by a group of drunk men. Unaccompanied women walking the streets were seen by predatory males as fair game. That was one of the unescapable realities of London and other big cities until long into the twentieth century and beyond. The social opportunities permitted to men were not extended to women. A woman of the upper and middle classes risked losing her reputation if she was seen alone on the city's streets. In a horse-powered city, the streets were filthy with animal waste; they were oppressively crowded, smelly and noisy. Women in the city, particularly at night, were not safe from unwanted sexual advances or much worse.

But the idea that women withdrew from public into the privacy of the home is not completely correct. Foreign tourists noted the unusual freedoms given to well-off women compared to other cities in Europe. The ways that leisure was re-forming the eighteenth century metropolis gave middling and upper-class women ways of participating in the social rituals of the city without losing status or respectability. If many foreign visitors found London rather dingy, they were amazed by the opulence of its shops: 'drapers, stationers, confectioners, pastry-cooks, seal-cutters, silver-smiths, booksellers, print-sellers, hosiers, fruiters, china-sellers – one close to another, without intermission, a shop to every house, street after street, and mile after mile; the articles themselves so beautiful and beautifully arranged'. The main shopping thoroughfares of Cornhill, Fleet Street, the Strand and Cheapside in the early eighteenth century were joined by Covent Garden, Regent Street and Oxford Street by the early nineteenth. Behind large plate-glass bow windows, shopkeepers artfully displayed their luxurious wares, illuminating them at night. These high-quality shops were safe and attractive social places for women, who shopped in groups as part of the daily round of activities.[30] In Burney's novel, Evelina noted the 'entertaining' aspect of shopping, the ceremony that accompanied it and its social function: 'At the milliners, the ladies we met were so much dressed, that I should rather have imagined they were making visits than purchases.' Theatres, pleasure gardens, the opera, charities, exhibitions, balls and shops brought elite women into some sort of engagement with the public sphere in the emerging consumer metropolis.

From itinerant street sellers to large-business owners, women had to carve out careers in what was still a very gendered economy; often these jobs – as they are now in many growing cities – were in the informal economy rather than in trade and finance. The networks of information exchange and socialising in coffee houses, pubs and clubs – where vital business connections were forged – were exclusively male. Women had to operate in a different part of the economy; they were entrepreneurs who fed, clothed, cleaned, housed, educated and entertained the metropolis. Most of the street vendors were women; they ran coffee houses, public houses and inns; they cooked, cleaned and laundered. Many of the schools that gave London children a rudimentary education were ventures started by women. The vast dressmaking industry was almost entirely under the control of businesswomen, as was a large chunk of the retail trades. Many women made money by running lodging houses for the thousands of men, women and families who rented a room or two in the city. The boom in popular entertainment opened up new opportunities for women as actors, singers, performers and impresarios. Teresa Cornelys came from Venice to London as a girl in the 1720s. By the 1760s, after a career in the opera, she had become staggeringly wealthy and famous as the organiser of extravagant masquerade balls in Soho Square.

In this, as in many other areas of urban life, London provided the biggest, most exaggerated examples of how cities were changing in the eighteenth century in Europe and America. The shift from court to metropolis was first made evident by the coffee house of the second half of the seventeenth century. They helped sculpt the sociable urban environment that defined cities in the following century, a place where citizen-consumers shaped culture and fashion, where leisure and shopping became key to the urban experience. Theatres and operas, cafés and restaurants, museums and galleries all became absolutely central to the modern urban experience.

★

'Let's go quickly to a café so that I can get my impressions while they are new.' So said the American artist Janice Biala to her lover Ford Madox Ford in 1935 after she saw a particularly striking vista in London and wanted to sketch it. When Ford replied that there were no cafés in London, she was aghast: 'But if London does not provide cafés for her artists how can she expect to have any art? ... Or any letters? Or any civilisation? Or any anything?'[31]

Whereas Italian, German, Spanish and French aristocrats (and in America, 'people of refinement') enjoyed the lively pavement café society of their cities, London – which had led the way in importing the urban phenomena of coffee houses to western Europe – now had nothing comparable. What had happened?[32]

The change had begun long before. White's Chocolate House became the exclusive White's Club in 1736. At Jonathan's Coffee House in the City anyone could be a share trader for a day, for the price of a cup of joe. This became unacceptable to the brokers. In 1761 they paid the owner of Jonathan's £1,500 a year for exclusive use of the coffee room for three hours each day. Tested in the courts, the Lord Chief Justice stated that a coffee house was a free and open market and ruled against the stockbrokers. In response the brokers built their own coffee house-cum-exchange, New Jonathan's on Sweetings Alley. It was soon renamed the London Stock Exchange, open only to those who paid sixpence a day. In 1801 all but bona fide members of the club who paid an annual subscription were excluded.[33] In parallel moves, the underwriters of Lloyd's Coffee House decamped first to their own coffee house, then to the upper floor of the Royal Exchange in 1773.

The informal nature of the coffee house gave way to much more regulated and controlled financial markets. The echoes are still there, however. Although housed in Richard Rogers's stainless-steel tower, Lloyd's of London, the biggest insurance market in the world, retains the kind of face-to-face form of business that goes back to its founda-tion in the hurly-burly of the coffee house. Underwriters still perch on stools and the tail-coated staff are called waiters.

Business and trading moved from the open world of the coffee house to a more regulated and controlled arena, members-only exchanges and – that modern invention – offices. And in numerous other ways the sociability of the eighteenth century was succeeded by a more exclusive form of manners. As Henry James astutely noted, the absence of pavement cafés in London in the 1880s was the telltale sign of a society with a rigid class system. Gentlemen drank coffee; but they did so in the comfortable and secluded environs of their clubs. The poor drank the black stuff from barrows and stalls on the way to work.

As the century wore on and London expanded to 6 million residents, the attraction of a spacious house with a garden sucked even more middle-class citizens out of the centre. Whereas bourgeois Parisians and other urbanites in dense European cities lived in apartments in the city centre, their London peers were suburbanites. Continental cafés were part of the social life of compact European cities. During the nineteenth century London re-formed around modern transport. Railways, horse-buses, trams and the underground allowed people to settle further from the centre. The suburban splurge of London helped kill off the convivial city that had made it so attractive in the eighteenth century when it was still walkable and its population was under a million.

The coffee house's demise followed the decline of gregariousness and the tendency towards exclusivity in social, literary, scientific and business life, a move away from public sociability towards segmentation, institutionalisation and suburbanisation. As the coffee house disappeared, London ascended to unrivalled global power and its triumph as a commercial metropolis. London had, for Henry James writing in the late nineteenth century, an 'intensely commercial character'. Not for this imperial metropolis, business-minded and class-conscious as it was, the frivolity and conviviality of the Parisian café. Those days had gone.

9

The Gates of Hell?

Manchester and Chicago, 1830–1914

'Manchester is the chimney of the world,' wrote General Charles Napier in 1839. 'Rich rascals, poor rogues, drunken ragamuffins and prostitutes form the moral; soot made into paste by rain the physique; and the only view is a long chimney: what a place! the entrance to hell realised!'[1]

In the Manchester of the 1840s over 500 chimneys exhaled a thick blanket of coal smoke, powering new technologies of mass production. Alexis de Tocqueville marvelled in horror at Manchester's 'huge palaces of industry' and the 'noise of furnaces, the whistle of steam'. Such a city had never been seen before. Every day the sound of thousands of power looms reverberated through it, shaking the buildings. The Swedish writer Fredrika Bremer captured the restless force of the industrial urban Frankenstein and its sensory impact: 'Manchester appeared to my eyes like a colossal spider, in the midst of its factories, towns, suburbs and villages, in which everything seemed to be spinning – spinning – spinning clothes for all the people in the world. There she sat, that Queen of spiders, surrounded by a mass of ugly houses and factories, veiled in a thick cloud of rain, not unlike a spider's web. It produced a dark, oppressive impression on me.'[2]

Bremer also visited Chicago. The American colossus, she wrote, was 'one of the most miserable and ugly cities' in the world. It did not deserve the title 'Queen of the Lake', she commented acidly, 'for sitting there on the shore of the lake in wretched dishabille, she resembles rather a huckstress than a queen'.[3]

Like Manchester, Chicago's cityscape, with its ribbons of railroad tracks radiating from the city and tangle of telegraph lines, its monumental grain elevators and lumberyards, its noisome stockyards, steel mills and factory chimneys, was nineteenth-century industrialism made manifest. Visitors commented that Chicago sounded like no other city in the world, with the 'deep hollow roar of the locomotive and the shrill scream from the steamboat' mingling with the clatter of industry, the squeals of thousands of hogs about to be slaughtered and the uproar of the incessant crowds. Others experienced the power of Chicago throbbing 'with an unbridled violence'. A French visitor felt the stench of Chicago grab him by the throat as soon as he arrived.[4]

Size, population growth and sensory assault were one thing. Much more daunting was what these new cities did to humanity. Manchester – 'Cottonopolis' – stood at the heart of the global textile industry, ground zero in the history of worldwide industrialisation. The sight of Manchester's mills was a harbinger of humankind's future: 'Here humanity attains its most complete development and its most brutish,' wrote de Tocqueville, 'here civilisation makes its miracles, and civilised man is turned back almost into a savage.'[5]

On one side of the Atlantic, in the American South, slaves were mobilised to grow, harvest and pack cotton; on the other, an industrial workforce numbering in the hundreds of thousands was coerced to turn it into textiles. They were wage earners, dependent on the factory system. Women and children were favoured because they could be paid less and disciplined more easily, as this questioning of a girl employed in a factory from the age of six testifies:

Question: What were your hours of labour?

Answer: As a child I worked from five in the morning till nine at night.

Q: What time was allowed for meals?

A: We were allowed forty minutes at noon.

Q: Had you any time to get breakfast, or drinking?

A: No, we got it as we could.

Q: Did you have time to eat it?

A: No; we were obliged to leave it or to take it home, and when we did not take it, the overlooker took it, and gave it to the pigs.

Q: Suppose you flagged a little, or were late, what would they do?

A: Strap us.

Q: What work did you do?

A: A weigher in the card-room.

Q: How long did you work there?

A: From half-past five, till eight at night.

Q: What is the carding-room like?

A: Dusty. You cannot see each other for dust.

Q: Did working in the card-room affect your health?

A: Yes; it was so dusty, the dust got up my lungs, and the work was so hard. I got so bad in health, that when I pulled the baskets down, I pulled my bones out of their places.

Q: You are considerably deformed in your person in consequence of this labour?

A: Yes, I am.

Q: At what time did it come on?

A: I was about thirteen years old when it began coming, and it has got worse since. When my mother died I had to look after myself.

Q: Where are you now?

A: In the poorhouse.

Q: You are utterly incapable of working in the factories?

A: Yes.

The greatest proportion of factory workers were aged between sixteen and twenty-four; many of them were Irish, economically vulnerable, discriminated against and therefore easy to control. Alongside the textile mills grew chemical plants and engineering works. But thousands more were employed in casual or seasonal labour outside the factory gates. One survey found that 40% of men were 'irregularly employed' and 60% were on subsistence wages. 'Could there be any kind of life more outraged, more opposed to man's natural instincts?' asked the French philosopher Hippolyte Taine when he visited Manchester.

The Chicago meatpacking houses struck fear into visitors with their squealing animals facing slaughter, the pools of blood, viscera and grease. But even more appalling were the conditions of the humans working there, soaked in blood and gore and half-frozen. Dependent on the pitiful wage, the plant gates were crowded each morning with workers hoping for a day's work. 'These are not packing plants at all; these are packing boxes crammed with wage slaves.'[6]

'All America', wrote a German of Chicago, 'looks with fear at this city that hurls her threat over the country.' The city was the 'storm center of civilisation,' warned Josiah Strong, founder of the Social Gospel movement. 'Here is heaped ... social dynamite.' 'Manchester is a name of deep and even of awful significance,' intoned the civil servant and evangelical Sir James Stephen. For him, the city of industrial wealth and urban degradation was a sign 'that we are approaching a great crisis and catastrophe in human affairs'.[7]

*

In the early years of the nineteenth century a third of Britain's population was urbanised. By 1851, more than half lived in towns and cities, the first human society in the history of the world that was more urban than rural. Within a mere three decades two out of every three Britons were urbanised. The first urban revolution began in Mesopotamia. The second began in Britain towards the end of the eighteenth century and developed at a ferocious pace, first in that country, and then globally.

'What Manchester does today, the rest of the world does tomorrow,' declared Benjamin Disraeli. Manchester's population doubled between 1801 and the 1820s and doubled again by the 1850s, reaching 400,000 in that decade and 700,000 by the end of the century. Chicago's early history was even more explosive; it went from under a hundred people in 1830 to 109,000 in 1860, 503,000 in 1880 and 1.7 million in 1900. No city in the history of the world had grown so quickly.

The Industrial Revolution provided the food, clothing, tools, utensils, building materials, transport networks and power that made rapid mass urbanisation possible. The swagger, newness and modernity of Chicago was made vivid by something entirely different – by the skyscrapers that rose from the prairie in the 1880s. The skyscraper was (and is) a symbol of capitalist triumph and technological mastery. Frontier Chicago, built of wood, burnt to the ground in the Great Fire of 1871. Its central business district was rebuilt quickly, and then rebuilt a second time, this time with the most innovative architecture and engineering in the world, signalling Chicago's status as the iconic global metropolis of the century. Advances in steel achieved by Chicago's advanced railroad industry provided beams that allowed walls to be thinner. Encased in concrete they were fireproof. Electricity gave rise to elevators, light bulbs, telegraphs and telephones, recent inventions that made working in a tower possible, along with heating and ventilation systems. The skyscraper was a machine as much as it was a building, the culmination of nineteenth-century technology. The clean, simple facade of a sixteen-storey building like the Monadnock (1889–92) was frequently described as looking like a machine.[8]

In 1800 barely 5% of the global population was urbanised. Between 1850 and 1950, while the global population expanded two and a half times, the urban population grew twenty times. By the latter date 30% of humans (751 million people) were city-dwellers; today the world's cities are home to 4.2 billion people. Manchester and Chicago were the 'shock cities' of the nineteenth century. They heralded, it appeared, not only the Industrial but the Urban Revolution. As such, they were avidly studied to divine humanity's future.

Three years after General Napier's caustic description of the city, the twenty-two-year-old Friedrich Engels arrived in Manchester from Germany to work in the offices of Ermen & Engels, a cotton-spinning company part-owned by his father. He was sent there to 'cure' him of his communist beliefs. Instead he came face to face with the consequences of industrial capitalism in its city of origin.

He went to Angel Meadow, Manchester's most notorious slum. 'Everywhere one sees heaps of refuse, garbage and filth,' he wrote. 'One walks along a very rough path on the riverbank, in between clothes posts and washing lines to reach a chaotic group of little, one-storeyed, one-room cabins. Most of them have earth floors and working, living and sleeping all takes place in one room.' The centre of the very modern metropolis was a scene of 'filth, ruin, and uninhabitableness'. Engels' observations of the horrific conditions in the world's pioneering industrial city were published in 1845 as *Die Lage der arbeitenden Klasse in England* (*The Condition of the Working Class in England*), one of the most influential books of the century and a glimpse at a new way of living that Engels portrayed as the 'grim future of capitalism and the industrial age'. Angel Meadow, for Engels, was quite simply 'Hell upon Earth'.[9]

If Manchester had Angel Meadow, Chicago had 'Little Hell', an urban island in the centre of the city created by the Chicago River and the North Branch Canal. A place of vast factories, innumerable squalid shanties and trash-filled streets, it got its apocalyptic name from the rain of soot that fell from the sky and the perpetual ball of flame emanating from the People's Gas, Light and Coke Company that illuminated the smoggy sky with an infernal glow. Little Hell gave birth first to Chicago's Irish mafia, then to its Italian successor. This is cursed ground: in the 1940s America's most infamous public housing project, Cabrini–Green, sprouted from its poisoned soil. The high-rises were a new incarnation of Little Hell, places of violence, rat and cockroach infestations, graffiti, clogged trash chutes, gang wars and sniper shootings.

Cities like Manchester and Chicago grew so quickly, and were so obsessed with profit, that they lacked the civic amenities, sanitation, public spaces and communal associations that had defined cities since they first emerged in Mesopotamia 6,000 years before. In slums such as Angel Meadow, houses were built by 'the horrible system of huddling cottages together, back to back, in streets without drains, or any means of carrying away the refuse from the doors of the homes'. Multiple-occupancy was common (the average Irish slum house had 8.7 people); overcrowding forced many casual workers into damp shared cellars in lodging houses where they often slept three to a bed. There were two outdoor toilets for every 250 residents of Angel Meadow.[10]

Low-lying, the Little Ireland slum district of Manchester (of which Angel Meadow formed the core) was a damp environment and its rivers were clogged with excrement and black from pollution. In Chicago the roadside gutters filled up with human and animal waste, 'leaving standing pools of an indescribable liquid'. These ditches were so vile that 'the very swine turn up their noses in supreme disgust'. Privies contaminated backyard wells used for drinking water. Built on level ground over hard clay, Chicago was a damp and polluted city, with so-called 'death fogs' emanating from piles of ordure. The river ran with sewage and industrial effluence. As Chicago rose to become 'Porkopolis' – the meatpacking capital of the world – the blood and offal of over 3 million livestock slaughtered every year exacerbated the hygiene and pollution crises.[11]

This stinking, greasy water made its way into the lake, where it was sucked back into the city through the intake pipe of the water-works. The city was being poisoned by 'the great deeps of mud and slime and unimaginable filth. The breeding beds of miasmas and death-fogs'. Along the banks of the dirty river were 'patches' – shanty towns that housed the city's outcasts and recently arrived migrants in wooden shacks. One of the most notorious of these was Conley's Patch – where the Wrigley and Tribune buildings now stand – a haven of crime, prostitution and Irish gangs, presided over by its hard-drinking matriarch Mother Conley. Between 1862 and 1872 alone Chicago's West Side grew from 57,000 to 214,000. The vast majority had to make do with whatever housing they could find, temporary shacks built on marshland. The largest of the squatter villages was Kilgubbin, an Irish district that sat on a swamp hugging the river and 'numbered ... many thousands of inhabitants, of all ages and habits, besides large droves of geese, goslings, pigs and rats'.[12]

Packingtown, a slum that grew to serve the meat industry, was one of the most depraved slums of nineteenth-century America. The home, over the years, of waves of non-English-speaking immigrant communities whose only opportunities for work lay in the vile meat-packing plants, its horror was immortalised in Upton Sinclair's 1904 novel *The Jungle*. It was bordered on one side by slaughterhouses, on another by an enormous garbage dump, on a third by railroad tracks and on the fourth by Bubbly Creek, named thus because it fizzed with gases released by decomposing blood and entrails. In the summer mosquitoes descended, attracted by the irresistible lure of garbage, offal and shit.

Polluted water, excrement and rats unleashed typhoid fever, typhus, dysentery, diphtheria, smallpox and infant diarrhoea. In rural areas of Britain, 32% of infants died before their fifth birthday and life expectancy was close to forty. In Manchester and Chicago, the figures were 60% and twenty-six; in London and Birmingham, life expectancy was thirty-seven. Nowhere in the mid-nineteenth century had a death rate comparable to these beshitten industrial cities. From the 1830s Asian cholera tore through the slums. In 1854 6% of Chicago's population succumbed to the epidemic, the sixth year in a row that the city had been devastated by disease.[13]

Urban topography made this an urgent problem in the industrial age. As a Manchester newspaper put it, the commercial centre was ringed 'by a huge cordon of beastliness and filth, enough to strike fear into the heart of every civilised inhabitant', leaving it as a small island surrounded by slums. Haunted by fears of contamination from the proletariat, middle-class families fled to the suburbs. And they kept on going: as the working-class population exploded, slums encroached on the suburban utopia, forcing another wave of flight to new, more distant semi-rural escapes. For most of history the word 'suburb' had conjured up the worst of the city; it was the dumping ground for detritus, waste and noxious trades. Now it promised escape.[14]

Manchester clocked up a lot of firsts in urban history, among them the first omnibus service (1824) and first passenger rail station (1830). Buses, trains and, later, trams facilitated the suburban exodus to commuterville. Wide roads lined with shops screened the slums that lay behind. Chicago, after the Great Fire of 1871, developed on a similar pattern, with a depopulated central business district – the Loop – mushrooming with skyscrapers but surrounded, as it were, by a barbarous besieging army of factories and slums; beyond this ring of desolation were yet more rings of housing, getting ever more prosperous as they got further from the Loop. Modern metropolitan transport made this segregation pattern possible: the poor trudged to work and lived with the pollution; the middle class and wealthy could afford to commute from suburbs or, if you were really lucky, picturesque villages overlooking open water on the North Shore.[15]

For observers, this fragmentation of the urban community and the division of the city into hermetically sealed, class-based residential districts added to the nightmare. When the engines stopped and the counting houses closed for the day, they felt that 'moral order' departed the city for the serene suburbs, abnegating civic responsibility and surrendering its centre to vice and crime.

For horrified residents of industrial cities, night-time in the inner city appeared to resemble the zombie apocalypse, with 'a surging mass of humans overflowing' from the slums and taking over the central business district. And there was no shortage of shocked accounts in newspapers and books detailing what happened to the city at night. Angus Bethune Reach penned a series of accounts of nocturnal Manchester in 1849. 'In returning, last Sunday night, by the Oldham Road, from one of my tours, I was somewhat surprised to hear loud sounds of music and jollity which floated out of public house windows. The street was swarming with drunken men and women and with young mill girls shouting, hallooing and romping

with each other.' Reach was 'astonished and grieved' by the 'scene of
... brutal and general intemperance': 'The public houses and gin shops
were roaring full. Rows and fights and scuffles were every moment
taking place within doors and in the streets. The whole street rang
with shouting, screaming and swearing, mingled with the jarring music
of half a dozen bands.'[16]

One Sunday evening in 1854 Temperance Society volunteers sampled
350 pubs and counted 215,000 customers: 120,000 men, 72,000 women
and 23,000 children. In Chicago's Packingtown there were 500 bars
within its sixteen blocks, one saloon for every seventy people. Shocked
at the boisterous Irish whiskey saloons and German beer gardens – so
enthusiastically frequented on the Sabbath – the authorities banned
alcohol sales on Sunday and raised the cost of a liquor licence from
$50 per year to $300. Thousands of working people, mainly Irish and
German, took to the streets in the bloody Lager Beer Riot of 1855 to
defend their way of life.[17]

'Oldham Street on a Sunday night appears to be given up to the
carnival revels of Manchester's vagabonds,' according to an investiga-
tive journalist. 'Here scenes may be witnessed which are unparalleled
in any city or town in England.' On Sunday evenings gaggles of young
working-class men, women and teenagers dressed in their best clothes,
the boys in 'ready-made garments of the most alarming pattern and
extravagant cut' and the factory girls 'gorgeous in cheap jewellery,
feathers and silk'. They streamed out of Ancoats and other slums to
promenade up and down Oldham Street and Market Street, along
Hyde Road and Stretford Road, showing off their finery and pairing
off with each other in a ritual known as the 'Monkey Run'. The
populations in cities such as Chicago and Manchester were young: in
the latter, throughout the nineteenth century, 40% were under twenty.
They had jobs, and hence money to spend on drink, entertainment
and fashion. They were assertive and sexually active.[18]

Drunkenness and sexual pleasure were one thing. Crime was quite
another. Danger stalked the working-class city. 'Like a huge rabbit
warren, it was threaded by a number of narrow and dark passages
and streets,' wrote a charity worker of Angel Meadow. 'It was not
safe for respectably dressed persons to pass through its streets alone,
even at midday.' Manchester had its violent teenage slum gangs, or
'scuttlers'. Armed with knives and bats, they beat up other youths

who wandered into their territory, and invaded other slum areas for pitched battles against rival gangs.[19]

The Irish of both Manchester and Chicago were blamed for slum conditions and the moral degradation of the whole urban community. Tellingly, cholera was labelled 'Irish fever'. According to the press, Irish gangs associated with particular regions of their homeland were notorious for patrolling their streets, keeping out intruders who came from other parts of Ireland. In 1851, for example, a constable came across two Irish clans, the McNeills and the Carrolls, viciously fighting in the street: 'The entire neighbourhood seemed to be engaged in the melee, fighting with pokers, sticks, and axes, like incarnate fiends.'[20]

Chicago's newspapers were as virulently anti-Irish, blaming them for disordering the city and possessing 'a most remarkable and striking fondness and passion for riots and rows'. As in Manchester, territorial Irish gangs such as the Dukies and the Shielders fought each other and intimidated German, Jewish, Polish and black groups who settled in or near their patch. Later, at the beginning of the twentieth century, Polish gangs claimed ownership over whole blocks of the city, fought each other, and battled the Italian gangs of Little Sicily. A ferocious boom town hungry for human muscle power to slaughter hogs, build canals, construct buildings, haul freight and toil in factories, Chicago's population was made up of foreign-born immigrants (59% of the population) and a transient population of visiting businessmen, tourists, farmers, sailors, casual labourers and onward-bound emigrants. The hubbub of people from all over the world drawn to this miracle city attracted swindlers, conmen, hustlers, professional gamblers, pickpockets, pimps and prostitutes in droves.[21]

Vice made up a significant part of Chicago's black economy, its impenetrable shanties and patchwork of ethnic colonies, lying hard by the business district, providing numerous insalubrious but tempting pleasure zones. The profits to be made from illicit pleasures stimulated the growth of organised crime gangs which were hand in glove with the city's politicians, magistrates and police officers. Throughout its history, Chicago has been a city associated with mafia, corruption, vice and illegal drugs, as if it could never outgrow its campsite origins. A study conducted in the 1930s pointed to 1,313 gangs in the metropolis occupying 'that broad twilight zone' of railroads, factories, deteriorating neighbourhoods and shifting immigrant colonies that closely encircled the central business district. There was the official map of Chicago, and also an alternative, imaginary map, an intricate mosaic of blocks, neighbourhoods and slivers of territory that were variously under the absolute sway of a gang like the 'Night Raiders', 'Deadshots', 'South Siders' or 'XXXs'.[22]

In 1869, 125 children under ten were arrested for felony, and 2,404 between the ages of ten and twenty. The teenage crime wave was believed to be the inevitable result of the arrival in the city of thousands of orphaned or abandoned immigrant children who were either left homeless or forced into dosshouses or the security offered by a street gang. The fate of street urchins was the starkest evidence of a sick urban society. As in industrial England, the industrial city was held responsible for the breakdown of the paternally controlled family. Children were abandoned to the streets, to gangs and exploitative adult criminals. Their fate symbolised the ways in which modern cities were undermining the very foundations of society.[23]

As a visitor to Angel Meadows wrote of its inhabitants: 'Their misery, vice and prejudice will prove volcanic elements, by whose explosive violence the structure of society may be destroyed.' You didn't have to be Friedrich Engels or Karl Marx to believe that the misery of slum life and industrial labour would inevitably lead to bitter class conflict. Fear – of the anger Engels saw festering in the squalor of the slums that grew in tandem with industrial capitalism – gnawed at Victorian society. The spatial division of a city like Manchester into commercial centre, benighted slums and middle-class suburbia was vivid physical evidence carved into the cityscape of not only the unbridgeable abyss between proletariat and bourgeoisie, but of the coming violent struggle between the classes.[24]

As Engels wrote, modern urban life, as developed in the sooty giants of Chicago and Manchester, helped 'to weld the proletariat into a compact group with its own ways of life and thought, and its own outlook on society'.[25]

*

Every hour, eighty-five people move to Lagos, and fifty-three get to Shanghai. They are part of the most significant migration in human history. You would have to build eight new cities the size of New York or three new Lagoses to house the growing global urban population every year. Step into an informal settlement in India, say, or Nigeria, or any in the developing world, and you tread ground that would be familiar to Engels: open sewers, shared toilets, cramped spaces, poorly constructed dwellings that let in downpours, air thick with kerosene and rats – lots of rats. These places are claustrophobic, with families forced to live, cook, clean, wash and bring up their children in one small room. They are blighted by crime, gangs, disease and, above all, crippling daily economic anxiety and insecurity of tenure that makes life almost intolerable. Informal settlements appear chaotic, dangerous, miserable – the worst side effect of our urban odyssey.

But they offer hope. Built from the ground up by their communities, they are complex, self-supporting social structures – cities-within-cities – that demonstrate the best of humanity, even among dirt and pollution. 'Slum' might be seen as a pejorative word. But to a lot of people living in such places, the word has come to represent pride rather than despair. And for good reason; they emphasise the unique strength and cohesion of their communities, built as they often are as self-sustaining villages of extended families or migrants sharing origins in a common rural area. In contrast to the alienation and anonymity of many cities, slums and informal settlements are sociable. They are undeniably grim and horrific; but they can be happy places too.

In Mumbai, high property prices, the scarcity of land and the failure of the state to build, has resulted in an acute housing crisis, forcing 55% of its population to live in informal settlements, which are so densely populated that they account for just 12% of the city's total area. Mumbai's slum-dwellers include educated, middle-class people who work in the city's gleaming financial centre but who simply can't find anywhere else to live. They exist alongside people who earn $1 a day doing the menial jobs that keep the city going or simply battling day by day for survival in a metropolis of over 20 million. Inhospitable and lacking infrastructure, slums call upon their inhabitants to be among the most resourceful and toughest people on the planet. As a result, they are places of startling energy and entrepreneurialism. One of Asia's largest slums – Dharavi in Mumbai, home to nearly 1 million people squeezed into 520 acres of land – has an internal economy of $1 billion a year. There are 15,000 single-room factories and 5,000 small enterprises, ranging from small garment and leather workshops to waste-picking and micro-recycling businesses. It is estimated that, thanks to its army of entrepreneurs, Mumbai recycles 80% of its solid waste, compared to just 45% in the UK.[26]

Extreme poverty in Brazil is more prevalent in rural areas (25%) than in urban (5%). Over three generations in Brazilian *favelas* between the 1960s and the early twenty-first century, illiteracy rates plummeted from 79% among first-generation rural migrants to 45% in their children's generation and just 6% for their grandchildren. Healthcare and education are much worse in rural India than for the slum-dweller of Mumbai. Infant mortality rates in a sub-Saharan city of 1 million people or more are a third lower than outside the city. In Pakistani cities 66% of girls aged between seven and twelve whose parents earn $1 a day or less attend school, compared to 31% in villages. The peasants of nineteenth-century Ireland fled misery and famine for better lives in the slums of Manchester and Chicago, taking their chances with cholera and typhoid. As an Irishman put it, living and working in Manchester gave him the chance to eat two meals a day. Slum life might have been rough and unhealthy; but then as now, it offered a better standard of living and opportunities than the countryside. Rural poverty is one of the defining features of our age and one of the main reason cities are growing at breakneck speed: in 1991 44% of the world's population was employed in agriculture; today it is just 28% and continues to fall rapidly.[27]

Cities offer not only material benefits, but excitement and the chance for individual self-reinvention. For many citizens of Manchester and Chicago, the city meant a form of liberty. That was something that critics of the Victorian city never really grasped: the darkness and squalor blinded them to the ways in which community was being reconceived in the modern manufacturing metropolis.

Urban-dwellers could afford a greater range of goods and entertainments than their rural cousins, and – equally importantly at least – choices about how to live their lives and what (if anything) to worship. For all their horrors, Engels recognised that the city slums meant liberation from 'happy vegetation in the countryside' and was essential for political awakening. Hippolyte Taine compared the lot of a French peasant and a Manchester slum-dweller. The former might live longer in 'the most natural and the least constrained form of existence', but the Manchester worker had richer compensations: he 'possesses more ideas and notions of all kinds, more intelligence in social, political, and religious matters; in short, his horizon is more extended'. Taine went on to say that a Manchester millhand read more newspapers and had a broader understanding of the world thanks to the cosmopolitanism of the city. 'A working man who is a unit in a large organisation feels how greatly he is dependent upon others, in consequence of this he associates with his comrades, and thus escapes a life of isolation.'[28]

In industrial urban Britain 90% of working-class homes included extended families and/or lodgers, much more than in the pre-industrial age when households were constructed around married couples and their children. Village life was recreated in the street, with close ties of friendship, marriage, kinship and shared geographical origins forming networks of mutual aid and sociability. While privacy was becoming important in middle-class homes in the nineteenth century, the density and lack of space in working-class districts forced people together. Much working-class life took place in the street – 'that great recreation room', according to Robert Roberts in his book *The Classic Slum*. People sat on their front steps or gathered on the street corner; children played games and kicked footballs; there was dancing when the organ grinder made an appearance, and singing at other times. 'The "Road" was a social centre', remembered Edna Bold of her childhood in Manchester, 'where everyone met, shopped, talked, walked. The butcher, the baker, the grocer, the milliner, the draper, the barber, the greengrocer, the pawnbroker, the undertaker were friends, confidants, and mines of information.' 'The evenings were delicious,' wrote Frank Norris of Chicago. Chairs and carpets were brought onto the stoop, the sidewalks were full of children playing games, young men and women – dressed in their finery – promenaded.[29]

British social reformers expressed their surprise at people's deep attachment to their street, even in the bleakest of slums. After the Great Fire of Chicago, the city council attempted to outlaw flammable timber buildings. Immigrant labourers stormed City Hall, promising bloodshed if they were not allowed to rebuild their homesteads and communities with the only materials they could afford. They did not want to live in apartments in tenements on brownstone canyons like New Yorkers; they wanted their street life back because it gave them independence and solidarity.[30]

In numerous ways working-class people, hurled as they were into a hostile industrial jungle, helped make – from the bottom up – their cities. William Aitken entered the Manchester mills as a child labourer, where he witnessed the horrific cruelties of the early factory system. His life told a very different story from a simple one of misery and victimhood. Industrialisation produced, alongside the hardship, 'wonderful improvements'. Not least was the way in which the industrial city brought working men and women together. In discussion and collaboration, they found practical ways to better their lot. They became a force within Britain, culturally and politically. The working class were not passive victims; they were, according to Aitken, 'sons of freedom', and living in the metropolis, with its expanded opportunities, made them so.[31]

Working-class civic culture saw the creation of hundreds of mutual aid and friendly societies, cooperative shops and savings banks. The most celebrated of these, the Manchester Unity Friendly Society Independent Order of Oddfellows, had 300,000 members by 1860, all of whom contributed a few pence every week in return for sick allowance, out-of-work benefit, medical help, life insurance and funeral costs. Many friendly-society lodges set up libraries, night schools and book clubs, and organised dinners, debates, picnics, railway excursions and other leisure activities for their members.

Working-class mutual aid was based around alcohol and conviviality as much as leisure activities. 'The public house is for the operative, what the public squares were for the ancients,' remarked a French visitor to Manchester in 1844. 'It is where they meet one another, and where they discuss the topics in which they are interested. Their meetings, whether permanent or accidental; their Masonic lodges; their mutual aid societies; their clubs and secret societies, are all held in public houses.'[32]

Many of these groups that flowed into Chicago from the late 1840s were fleeing political repression and economic hardship in Europe, especially after the failed 1848 revolutions and the Irish potato famine. German communists and Irish nationalists, inured to rural deprivation and experienced in revolutionary agitation, faced nativist aggression and hostility.[33] Physically attacked and discriminated against in Chicago, their bonds of ethnicity and past political experience were sharpened by collective self-defence and self-help as they fought to stake their claim in the city. People born in the United States made up the largest single group in Chicago in 1870 – but it was still a modest proportion, just 41%. The remaining 59% of the city was segmented into ethnic groups, with the Germans (23% of the total population) and the Irish (21%) making up the next biggest ethnic communities.

Close to a Shell gas station, at Roosevelt and Western in Chicago's Near West Side, amid a post-industrial cityscape of chain-linked fences, distribution centres, power lines, car-hire lots, drive-thru fast-food outlets, derelict factories clad in ivy and scrubby open ground full of weeds and wild flowers, there is a coffee shop in a strange, stranded Germanic building that looks like a lost European castle. The turreted building is a lonely remnant of a former German neighbourhood that once clustered here. The motto *Gut Heil* – good health – stands out on one gable. The coffee shop is one of the two remaining *Turnverein* halls. *Turnverein* is German for 'gymnastics union', a movement founded during the Napoleonic Wars to instil principles of physical fitness, discipline and political awareness in German youth as a building block for national defence and self-determination. German émigrés, particularly the '48ers, built their first *Turnverein* in Chicago in 1852, each chapter a site for inner-city, slum-dwelling immigrants to get fit, compete in sports, bowl, wash, read, debate, socialise and celebrate their ethnic roots through food, song, drama and drink. On the facade of the hall on Roosevelt and Western are the intertwined letters FFST, standing for *Frisch, Fromm, Stark & Treu* – 'Healthy, Upright, Strong & True' – the principles of urban self-help.[34]

Chicago was the sixth-largest German-speaking city in the world: this was not a minor social organisation but a powerful urban civic network. The *Arbeiterverein* (German workers' club) organised parades, dance parties and lakeside picnics for 20,000 people at a time. As one American sociologist put it: 'The principal thoroughfares of the work-ingmen's districts [of Chicago] are gay all summer with the banners announcing the picnic of one or the other of these lodges. On Sunday, the great gala day for the foreign people, these excursions are numerous.' As in Manchester, collective self-help and alcohol went hand in hand.[35]

The desire to educate the community and to protect it against economic exploitation grew out of, and in turn fed, radical politics. Politics and working-class civic society were interwoven. Chicago's tight-knit Irish community, hardened by outside attacks, became a mobilised force, dominant in city elections, the Democratic Party, municipal government, the police and the organised labour movement. The *Arbeiterverein* was as proficient at organising major strikes as picnics; the *Turnverein* taught socialism alongside gymnastics in their large halls. The latter helped mobilise the fight for the eight-hour working day, improvements to factories, labour-law reform, women's rights and public ownership. Radical they may have been, but they were also patriotically American: members of the *Turnverein* fought and died in great numbers for the Union side during the American Civil War.[36]

Manchester achieved fame in the nineteenth century not just as the shock city of industrialisation and the textile capital of the world, but for its ideology of free-market capitalism. The faith of the 'Manchester School' that unrestrained capitalism would bring peace and harmony to the world has proved a major force in recent global history, an ideology that has shaped all our lives. But for all that, people in Manchester actively promoted an alternative world view. In 1842, during a slump, the city was hit by riots and political rallies calling for universal suffrage. A city of organised labour, unions and strikes, Manchester hosted the first Trades Union Congress in 1868 and the city's radical politics were instrumental in the foundation of the Labour Party at the end of the century. During the American Civil War, the Union's embargo on slave-produced raw cotton caused unemployment and misery in Manchester. Yet the very people who suffered the most were ardent in their support for President Lincoln and the abolition of slavery.

The political culture of Manchester, with its assertive working class and a liberal middle class, helped make the city a breeding ground for new ideas and movements. Mary Fildes (1789–1875), as chair of the Manchester Female Reform Society, was on the hustings at St Peter's Fields in 1819, ready to address the vast crowd demanding political reform, shortly before the cavalry attacked in what became the Peterloo Massacre. Rebecca Moore campaigned on behalf of the Manchester Ladies Anti-Slavery Society before becoming an executive committee member of the Manchester Society for Women's Suffrage. This society was led first by Elizabeth Wolstenholme (1833–1918) and then by Lydia Becker (1827–90), a tireless campaigner, writer, and founder of the Manchester-based *Women's Suffrage Journal*. The succeeding generation of feminist campaigners was led by the Manchester-born Emmeline Pankhurst, and her daughters Christabel and Sylvia. Inspired by tales of her paternal grandfather, who had been at Peterloo, Emmeline's political awakening took place amid the lively socialist milieu of late nineteenth-century Manchester and the city's feminist movement led by Lydia Becker. The Pankhursts' organisation, the Women's Social and Political Union, founded in Manchester in 1903, propelled the cause of women's rights through militant suffragette action.

First-hand experience of the working conditions of Manchester's mills and factories, and the states of housing, sanitation and education, inspired women of working-class backgrounds to campaign for female enfranchisement. This after all was a city and a working class steeped in a long history of resistance, industrial strikes, mass protest and collective action. It was a city of radicalism, be it the radicalism of free-trade liberals assaulting the edifice of aristocratic privilege or the radicalism of workers objecting to their conditions. Esther Roper's father, one of eleven children, started work aged eleven in a factory and worked his way out of the Manchester slums to become a missionary and clergyman. Her mother was the daughter of Irish migrants. Roper became secretary of the Manchester National Society for Women's Suffrage, organising the first political reform movements aimed directly at working women. She recruited volunteers such as Annie Heaton and Selina Cooper (both of whom had worked in the mills since their early childhoods) to distribute leaflets and speak outside factory and mill gates.

Unlike the middle-class ladies who led the suffrage movement, people like Heaton and Cooper spoke the language of northern working-class women. Their route to political awakening had been through the associations, societies and cooperatives built by urban workers. Cooper sat on the committee of her trade union and was a member of the Independent Labour Party. Convincing workers that the ballot box was the best way to secure better wages, working conditions and housing was key to mobilising urban women to campaign for the vote.[37]

For the first time, women were taking active, elected public roles in shaping the city around them. Lydia Roper was elected to

Manchester's first School Board in 1870, a position she used to demand free admission to schools, daily meals, improvements to buildings and equality between boys and girls in the curriculum.

Women, because they ran households and brought up children, were the guardians of the welfare of the city. So argued Jane Addams, co-founder of Chicago's Hull House, a centre for urban reform. Not only should women be given the vote, but they should have public roles in city government, cleaning up the mess – human, industrial, political and moral. Hull House was a dilapidated mansion in a poor multi-ethnic neighbourhood. The female volunteers provided medical treatment and midwifery for the local residents, along with night schools, a gym, a bathhouse, art courses and other vital social services. They made in-depth investigations of the local area, using the most up-to-date methodologies in statistical mapping and sociological surveying to document housing conditions, over-crowding, infant mortality, sweatshops, diseases, drug use, child labour, prostitution and a host of urban social evils. The fiery Florence Kelley (translator into English of Engels's *Condition of the Working Class*) produced a report into conditions in the garment industry's sweatshops. So blistering were the conclusions that the report led to the Illinois Factory Law and to Kelley being appointed as the state's factory inspector with a staff of eleven to enforce the law. No other woman in the world at the time had such power in a city. Jane Addams became the first female sanitary inspector of Chicago's 19th Ward, a position she used to wage war on the city's garbage problem.

The work of Addams, Kelley and other women revealed the grim-ness of slum life and work with precision and statistical rigour. Addams believed that in a diverse city, it was the interaction and shared endeav-ours of different classes and ethnicities that created the community spirit strong enough to effect radical change. Key to achieving this was developing children. As Addams argued in *The Spirit of Youth and the City Streets* (1909), the modern city robbed children of their youth. Only by providing them with proper places to play and exercise could the city do them justice. Children playing and competing in sport, she wrote, showed 'the undoubted power of public recreation [in bringing] together all classes of a community in the modern city, unhappily so full of devices for keeping men apart'.

The movement for outdoor space and recreational programmes
was given its impetus from the grass roots, from second-generation
urban working-class ethnic communities – such as the German
Turnverein, the Czech Sokol Union, the Polish Falcons and the Gaelic
Athletic Club – who put physical education, sport and outdoor excursions at the heart of their lives. A demonstration of gymnastics at a
Turnverein hall in front of the Chicago Board of Health in 1884 led to
one of its members being appointed to devise a physical educational
programme for Chicago's public schools. The *Turnverein* campaigned
for physical recreational facilities in Chicago's public parks – swimming
pools, gymnastics, ball games and playgrounds – so that they would
become places for sport rather than just sedate Sunday strolling.[38]

*

The gates of hell? To outsiders the industrial monsters looked like the
inferno. To slum-dwellers in Angel Meadow or Packingtown it doubtless was perdition. But to many others, this new iteration of the
metropolis offered possibilities, the slum acting as a gateway from
rural poverty and isolation to fresh forms of social life and action.
Workers, women and migrants were instrumental in building new
civic institutions and behaviours in an age of savage urban upheaval.
More often than not, they did it on their own, without help from
above.

And the physical city itself changed around the new working class.
From the middle part of the nineteenth century real wages began to
rise and work shifts got shorter, giving factory workers and labourers
more money to spend on leisure. Businesses moved into the inner
city to cater for this growing market. Over the Whit holiday week of
1850 in Manchester, some 200,000 people paid for railway excursions
out of town; during the same holiday at the end of the decade 95,000
frequented the Belle Vue pleasure gardens. Pubs, as ever, remained
central to life, with Manchester having the greatest concentration of
public houses in the country. In 1852 it was estimated that 25,000
people, mainly young and working class, were attending three large
pub halls (the Casino, Victoria Saloon and Polytechnic Hall) every
week. By the next decade, these saloons had evolved into music halls,
which housed thousands who revelled in the blend of popular songs,

suggestive comedians, drag artists, circus performers and novelty acts, all of which called upon boisterous audience participation. In the 1890s the bawdy, rowdy music hall was changing again and becoming more family-friendly. The luxurious Manchester Palace Theatre of Varieties opened in 1891, aimed at middle- as well as working-class families.[39]

Modern mass entertainment and extravaganza began life in these music halls. Manchester has always been a pioneer of popular culture, from the Victorian music halls to the Hacienda, the legendary night-club that flourished in the 1980s and 90s. Today the city is known best globally for its two giant Premier League football clubs, Manchester United and Manchester City. United began life in 1878 as Newton Heath, the football team of the Lancashire and Yorkshire Railway Company's carriage and wagon department. Its rival was founded two years later by members of St Mark's Church in West Gorton as a way of weaning local youths away from street gangs. Association football emerged from the sporting ethos of elite schools and universities; when it was played by workers in the street or wasteland, it was considered antisocial. Organised teams, however, became a way of forging communities in the city. They emerged from churches, trades unions, neighbourhoods and factories.

Rail and telegraphy made sport on this scale possible: steam power took players and supporters to play against other cities and the tele-graph transmitted back the results to newspapers. The Football Association legitimised professionalism in 1885; three years later the English Football League was founded in Manchester. The old gentle-manly amateur teams could not compete against clubs centred on large concentrations of populations that paid for the best players. The same process happened at roughly the same time in the United States. Begun as an upper-class sport, baseball gained an ascendancy over cricket during the Civil War. In post-war America, professionalised baseball emerged as an urban, working-class sport, eagerly taken up by immigrant communities in the cities. Many of the early stars of baseball were Irish and Germans seeking a way out of poverty. These sporting giants helped attract legions of fans to urban baseball grounds. The connection between packed stands and sporting success became established: those teams with a big weekly revenue and deep pockets could afford the best players.

Fans had to fight for the right to enjoy their leisure time. They met fierce resistance to watching games on a Sunday – their only day off – and to drinking alcohol in the stands. The American Association baseball league was the self-proclaimed 'beer and whiskey league' or 'lower-class league' because it not only sold seats for a cheaper price than its rival, the National League, but it played its games on Sunday and allowed alcoholic refreshments. By the end of the century market forces had made baseball a working-class Sunday game, with crowds of enthusiastic, noisy fans.

The emergence of Sunday mass sport was seen, in America, as a key way in which puritanical Anglo-American culture was reshaped through the spending power of lower-class immigrants, for whom Sunday was a day of booze, relaxation and recreation. Playing at West Side Park, the Chicago White Stockings (later the Chicago Cubs) drew crowds in excess of 12,500 on Sundays in the 1890s. Comiskey Park, built on a former city garbage dump for the Chicago White Sox in 1909, could seat an unprecedented 32,000 fans, earning it the title of 'Baseball Palace of the World'. Such cathedrals of sport focused on nationally prominent teams gave working-class people and ethnic minorities a sense of civic pride and belonging to the city, something that had been conspicuously missing from the older fragmented culture of the Industrial Revolution that centred on the factory, the street, the saloon and the club. The stoic athleticism of middle-class amateur sport gave way to the festive, tribal sport of the working class in cities in Europe and America.

Demand for watching football in English cities exceeded the capacity of urban football pitches, with their rudimentary wooden stands. The only venue big enough for the FA Cup Final contested between Everton and Wolves in 1893 was the Fallowfield athletics stadium in Manchester, which could accommodate an unprecedented 45,000 fans, although 60,000 pushed their way in. The commercial success of the game paved the way for stadiums. West Gorton went professional early; by 1895, renamed City, it was playing in front of 20,000–30,000 people. Newton Heath, meanwhile, narrowly escaped bankruptcy and renamed itself Manchester United in 1902. In 1910, buoyed by a string of victories, United moved to 80,000-seat Old Trafford, 'unrivalled in the world' as the first football stadium built to a masterplan.

Today Old Trafford is nicknamed 'the Theatre of Dreams'. Big stadiums have become totemic features of the cityscape around the globe; supporting a sports team – be it association football, American football, baseball, basketball, rugby, cricket, hockey – defines urban tribalism. Crowds, numbering in the tens of thousands, with their chants, songs, noise and rituals reaffirm shared affinities within a cherished bastion – the tradition-soaked, emotionally charged, hermetically sealed bowl of the stadium. Fans spill out of the enclosed arena and into pubs, bars, cafés, clubs, squares and streets to talk and argue about the game, to dissect tactics and sing songs. Rooted in history and folklore, sport has been one of the most potent binding forces of the modern metropolis, central to the urban experience of millions, particularly – throughout the twentieth century – of working-class males.

Games like football and baseball are seen by their fans as being distinctively working class, sports that emerged from their lifestyles, working lives, communities and wage packets, rather than something that was imposed from above. The stadium is symbolic in many ways of the modern city. The rapid development of these cities, with their pollution, slums and disease, forced out the middle classes to the sylvan suburbs, leaving the inner city to become almost exclusively working class and multi-ethnic. 'Within the looming shadow of the skyscraper, in Chicago as in every great city,' wrote the urban sociologist Harvey Warren Zorbaugh in 1929, 'is found a zone of instability and change – the tidelands of city life.' Sports stadiums, along with working-class shops, markets, restaurants, snooker halls, small businesses, workshops, nightclubs, pubs, bars, betting shops, dance halls and fast-food joints, came to dominate the inner metropolis. For long into the twentieth century, the metropolis *was* a working-class and migrant city, characterised by urban ways of life that were markedly different from the suburbs, the high-end residential zones and the business district. To be urban meant, in popular parlance, to be part of this hardscrabble existence, near the geographical heart of the city, but remote from its power and wealth.[40]

Over time these inner-city 'tidelands' have undergone constant change as working people have themselves moved out to suburbs, their places taken by new immigrant communities with their own particular tastes, foods and ways of life. Like their nineteenth-century forebears – the rural migrants to Manchester, the Irish and Germans of Chicago – the new residents of the inner city have survived the shock, alienation and hostility of the city by constructing their own urban communities. The unloved, grimy inner city has been the place of resilience, where incomers have forged their communal identities and sought individual self-betterment. They are like tidelands because different ethnicities have washed through them, moving in and moving on up the housing ladder. The ingenuity and instinct for self-survival in these urban wastelands have profoundly shaped popular culture – from radical politics and feminism to baseball, association football and hip hop.

Yet these communities in the tidelands are the most vulnerable to the ebbs and flows of history, victims of economic depressions, 'slum clearance', public housing experiments, road-building, deindustrialisation and gentrification. The horrors of the industrial city as revealed in cities such as Manchester and Chicago provoked a powerful, visceral response. The industrial hell-city was Babylon reborn, a soul-crushing place of sin and exploitation. In Fritz Lang's 1927 film *Metropolis* the city of the future is depicted as one where a pampered elite live in sun-bathed skyscrapers, while, underground and unseen, a vast class of workers toil ceaselessly in the dark to operate the machines that power the hyper-advanced metropolis. In one of the most powerful scenes in the movie, we are shown a hallucination in which the city's machine becomes Moloch, the Canaanite god who devoured his children. In *Metropolis*, the workers are fed to the jaws of the machine, sacrificed to the uncontrollable chaos of modern urbanisation.

The film, one of the most famous in movie history, drew heavily on biblical myths and on the recurrent imagery of Babylon that runs through history. It reflected the mood of the age, which was heavily disillusioned with urban life. The city had failed. The unremitting bleakness of Lang's vision was nothing new. Literature and art were suffused with the misery of modern urban life. The emphasis was firmly on the squalid, hopeless, deviant, corrupting and criminal.

The light in which the city is cast by writers, poets and artists helps determine the kind of cities we get. The deeply ingrained hostility towards urban life – especially in the two dominant cultures of the last 300 years, British and American – meant that the cities that emerged in the frenetic period of urbanisation were all too often badly planned and ill-governed. The salacious always trumped anything positive. Slums are always places of nightmare and social breakdown, not of self-reliance, self-organisation, community and innovation. The story told in this chapter, of social networks, political activism and fun, is always buried beneath a slag heap of misery.

If the urban poor are vulnerable to economic shocks, they are also vulnerable to the utopian dreams of others. They are the ingenious survivors of cities; but they are more often than not presented as helpless. Cities and city-dwellers are incredibly resilient; but they are often seen as on the brink of collapse. Left to their own devices, people are very good at constructing their own communities. But that rarely happens. The urbanisation that emerged in the wake of industrialisation and in opposition to it – the City Beautiful movement, the Garden City movement, the modernist movement – sought alike to impose order and cleanliness on the jerry-built nineteenth-century city. Babylonian confusion would be replaced by rational order; top-down planning would take over from grass-roots self-organisation. As later chapters will show, much of this desire to create the New Jerusalem was profoundly anti-urban. It meant, in many cases, rejecting the traditional city – with its jumble of activities mixed together, its improvised housing, its street vendors and ad hoc markets – in favour of suburbs, or constructing superblocks and 'towers in the park' in the place of the incoherent human ant heap. It meant undoing the traditional metropolis.

The emotional reaction against the mess of industrialisation would dominate thinking about cities in the twentieth century and beyond, with its utopian schemes for new ways of living and its desire to sanitise the urban environment. The rejection of the old city in favour of semi-rural tranquillity became deeply ingrained. But the old urban ideal was not dead. Two major metropolises launched a rear-guard action against the suburbanisation of the world and offered an alternative view of the modern city. The antidote to the shock cities of Manchester and Chicago took physical form in the pre-eminent metropolises of the nineteenth and early twentieth centuries: Paris and New York.

Paris Syndrome

Paris, 1830–1914

In 2006 the BBC ran a report on a mysterious modern disease. Every year a dozen or so Japanese tourists had to be evacuated from Paris. Intoxicated by the romantic, idealised cityscape for most of their lives, the reality of indifferent locals, crowded boulevards, dirty metro stations and rude waiters was such a shock that it sent them into 'psychiatric breakdown'. The Japanese embassy opened a twenty-four-hour hotline for sufferers of Paris Syndrome.[1]

I was prepared to laugh off Paris Syndrome as an urban myth until I read about Sigmund Freud's similar mental crisis. 'Paris had been for many years the goal of my longings,' he wrote in 1885, 'and the bliss with which I first set foot on its pavements I took as a guarantee that I should attain the fulfilment of other wishes too.' Elation soon wore off; on his first day in the city it was all he could do to stop himself crying in the streets, so disappointed and isolated did he feel. The crowds were terrifying; Parisians were unapproachable and arrogant. Freud suffered with paranoid delusions, checking the curtains round his hotel bed for traces of arsenic.[2]

Today almost 18 million people make the pilgrimage to Paris from abroad every year, collectively contributing $17 billion to its economy and keeping 18% of the population in employment. Only Bangkok (21 million) and London (20 million) have more international visitors. At any one moment there could be 50,000 foreign tourists on the boulevards. They are part of a pilgrimage that goes deep into history. Even before the advent of mass tourism in the 1860s, Paris was visited every year by 100,000 international visitors. In Offenbach's *La Vie Parisienne* the chorus is made up of tourists: 'We are going to invade', they sing, 'The sovereign city, / The resort of pleasure.'

The American Emma Willard approached Paris by coach on a November night in 1830 unable to sleep because she was so full of excitement. When she was told they had arrived, 'I looked in vain ... for the imposing objects of which I had fancied.' Her first experience of Paris was waiting while her luggage was searched by customs officers. 'We were amidst dirt and disorder – fatigued, without even a place to sit down – and strange eyes seemed to glare upon us.' The dingy streets seemed 'anything but the elegant Paris of my imagination'.[3]

In the nineteenth century the great cathedral of Notre-Dame shared the tiny Île de la Cité with some 15,000 poor Parisian workers living in a congested squalor of ancient houses. Almost everywhere in the metropolis, more people were cramming into the dwindling available space. The streets and alleys of Paris, dark and dank, resembled 'the tortuous paths of insects in the heart of a piece of fruit'. Overcrowded and with poor sanitation, the city was hit hard by cholera; in 1832 20,000 of the city's 861,000 residents were killed by the disease. Early nineteenth-century Paris represented 'the primitive city in all of its original dirt ... the Middle Ages in a state of agony'.[4]

Only when they walked the Rue de Rivoli, the Tuileries, the Boulevard des Italiens and the Place de la Révolution did tourists discover, wedged into the ugly, congested, ramshackle medieval city, 'a new world of ultra-civilised' urban living unobtainable anywhere else on the planet. There was, of course, the largest collection of art available to the public in the Louvre, complemented by galleries at the Luxembourg Palace, Versailles and Saint-Cloud. Fashion, shopping and gastronomy were unrivalled. Balzac wrote that the 'great poem of display chants its stanzas of colour from the Église de la Madeleine to the Porte Saint-Denis'.

The true glory of Paris was not its physical appearance, but the use its human population made of it; the theatricality of the streets – a 'landscape built of sheer life' – made it the most seductive city on the planet and the holy grail for tourists. An anonymous English resident wrote that walking the streets was exhilarating: 'It is the reflex of the life and movement that surrounds us ... for general intensity of life ... Paris has no parallel.'[5]

An antidote to Paris Syndrome was to immerse yourself in the performance and become a connoisseur of the urban drama. As a visiting American reverend remarked, the boulevard 'is certainly the best place in the world to amuse oneself in ... You only have to put on your hat and walk into the street to find entertainment.' Paris offered an unparalleled banquet for all the senses. According to Balzac, the city had become a 'vast metropolitan workshop for the manufacture of enjoyment'. Paris, he wrote, 'is endlessly on the march ... never taking a rest'; it is 'a monstrous miracle, an astonishing assemblage of movements, machines and ideas, the city of a thousand different romances ... a restless queen of cities'.[6]

Parisians took their pleasures in public, in cafés, gardens and parks, dances, open-air concerts, theatres and shops. The dangers of street traffic gave rise to some 300 arcades. As Balzac captures so deftly in his novels, Paris was a city of constant, jarring movement. The early part of the nineteenth century saw a flowering of literature written by urban explorers picking out the sights, sounds, contrasts and variety of Paris. They are like guidebooks written not for tourists but for the city's inhabitants, revealing the mysteries of the hidden city so that they could be understood or feared. The city itself became a character in a book, a complex living organism that had to be analysed and explained.

Parisians had words for the spectators of urban life. There was the *badaud*, a 'gawker' who strolled amid the crowds enjoying the unfolding theatre of daily life. 'In Paris, everything becomes an event,' wrote the dramatist de Jouy: 'a train of wood being floated down the river, two coaches running into each other, a man dressed differently from others, an armoured car, a dog fight, if they are noticed by two people, there will soon be a thousand, and the crowd will always grow, until some other circumstance, just as remarkable, pulls it away.' In *Les Plaisirs de Paris* Alfred Delvau wrote that for a Parisian to live at home, think at home, eat or drink at home, to suffer at home or to die at home was as unthinkable as it was boring: 'We need publicity, daylight, the street, the cabaret, the café, the restaurant.'[7]

Whereas Londoners strode 'with a grave collected air', noted Anna Jameson (another American tourist of the 1830s), Parisians sauntered and stared 'as if they had no other purpose in life but to look about them'. If the word *badaud* encapsulated the attitude of the Parisian mob to their streets, which they regarded as their salon or theatre, there was another term that came to define the modern urbane figure: the *flâneur*.[8]

'The *flâneur* is to the *badaud* what the gourmet is to the glutton,' wrote Auguste de Lacroix in 1842. The word *flâneur* has no exact English translation. Whereas the *badaud* greedily consumed the city, the *flâneur* was a discriminating connoisseur, a secret, detached observer who investigated the city from the middle of the urban crowd without ever being part of it. Balzac described *flânerie* as 'the gastronomy of the eye'. Charles Baudelaire depicted the character like this: 'For the perfect *flâneur*, for the passionate spectator, it is an immense joy to set up house in the heart of the multitude, amid the ebb and flow of movement, in the midst of the fugitive and the infinite.'⁹

The Parisian *flâneur* was the creation of journalists and writers in the early decades of the nineteenth century. Before then, a *flâneur* meant an idle loiterer with nothing much to do but gaze. By the 1820s and 30s, the middle-class *flâneur* had become a person of serious intent. He symbolised the triumph of the bourgeoisie as owners of the streets. 'What oddities you can find when you know how to stroll and look,' wrote Baudelaire. 'To saunter is a science,' declared Balzac, capturing the Parisian passion for *flânerie*.¹⁰

That's what made Paris unique: the sensibility of its people in their appreciation of the everyday life of the city and its peculiar rhythm.

British and American visitors to Paris learnt to adapt themselves to its rhythms, slowing their pace and dropping their reserve so that they began to look straight at other people in the street, the café and the arcades. That's what we do in a strange city where we don't know the language: we try and immerse ourselves by becoming detached observers amid the cacophony of urban life. An English description of the *flâneur* likened the urban wanderer to the newly invented photography: 'His mind is like a sensitive blank photograph plate, ready for any impression which may present itself.' The modern habit of hiding behind a camera or phone is a version of the detached *flâneur*, who is there but not there, an anonymous bystander recording impressions and framing the scene, like a tourist. 'The photographer', wrote Susan Sontag, 'is an armed version of the solitary walker recon- noitring, stalking, cruising the urban inferno, the voyeuristic stroller who discovers the city as landscape of voluptuous extremes.'¹¹

Modern art, literature, photography and, later, cinema were influ- enced by *flânerie*. More profoundly, it has helped us mine deeper into the psychology of city-living, posing and helping to answer questions about modern urban life. But before we get there, we arrive at the point that the Parisian *flâneur*'s world came under violent assault.

*

You don't have to ascend a skyscraper, as you do in many other cities, to appreciate the panorama of Paris and make it legible. Because Paris is set in a wide, flat basin, the wanderer of its streets is presented with an extensive horizontal urban skyline that showcases its historic buildings. Seen from up high, from the hills of Montmartre and Belleville or from the Eiffel Tower, you can see the splendid geometric street plan – a masterpiece of city-building – laid out in glory in front of you, adorned with the foliage of trees.

The Paris that conquers the imagination this way is a creation of the 1850s and of the modern world's greatest urban visionary, Georges-Eugène Haussmann. The circulatory system of the city had become clogged; it had to be decongested, letting in light and air to the darkness and allowing its citizens to move about the metropolis more freely. Europe was facing an urban apocalypse of disease, revolution and social breakdown. Manifest in places like Manchester, it was reaching its culmination in Paris.

Fastidious in everything, he had no affection for medieval Paris, which he associated with dirt. In all aspects of his life he wanted to impose order on chaos and cleanliness on muck. A 'tall, strong, vigorous, energetic' man who was at the same time 'clever and devious', Haussmann was an experienced forty-four-year-old public administrator when in 1853 he was recommended to the emperor Napoleon III as candidate for the prefecture of the Seine.[12]

In December 1851, facing the expiration of his term in office as president, Napoleon had seized power in a *coup d'état*. 'Paris is the heart of France,' he declared a few months later in a speech. 'Let us apply our efforts to embellishing this great city. Let us open new streets, make the working-class quarters, which lack air and light, healthier, and let the beneficial sunlight reach everywhere within our walls.'[13]

But still the project limped on. In December 1852, Napoleon declared himself emperor. Now, with absolute power, he could put his vision into motion without political constraint. Within days of Haussmann's appointment the emperor showed him a map of Paris, with wide, straight new boulevards marked over the medieval street plan, the arteries that would pump life into decaying Paris. Napoleon III wanted a modern city, beautiful, hygienic and navigable, a city fit for an emperor. And he wanted it quickly.

The Paris that emerged was a product both of Napoleonic imperial power and of Haussmann's systematic brain. It reflected the modern need for mobility and its master planner's deep-seated need for order and uniformity. Paris's renewal began with the *grande croisée de Paris*, a crossroads designed to facilitate movement east–west along the Rue de Rivoli and the Rue Saint-Antoine, and north–south along two new boulevards, Strasbourg and Sébastopol. On the Île de la Cité, the ancient cradle of Paris, Notre-Dame was hacked free of the ancient buildings that clustered round it and most of the population departed the island. In their place came buildings of municipal power and administration. 'It was the gutting of old Paris,' wrote Haussmann.[14]

From the Arc de Triomphe radiated a star of avenues; three boulevards stretched out from the Place du Château-d'Eau (the modern Place de la République); new streets connected the system to the city's railway stations. Impenetrable, narrow lanes that spewed this way and that were swept away. Many historic buildings were destroyed along with the jumble of homes. Even deep history was not exempt. Today those who climb the steps of the churches of Saint-Gervais and Saint-Jacques de la Boucherie in the Marais probably do not realise that they conceal Paris's two last remaining hillocks known as *monceaux*, on which once sat Merovingian settlements. The rest of the *monceaux*, along with much of the prehistoric and historic topography of Paris, were levelled by Haussmann to make a flat surface for his new city. 'Another week or two, and another leaf will have been torn out of the book of historical Paris,' bemoaned an English resident. The clutter of juxtaposing buildings, styles and ages, so characteristic of cities, lost out to Haussmann's beloved geometric streets, lined with a uniform parade of buildings that were faced with the city's distinctive butter-yellow Lutetian limestone.[15]

While many were horrified at the destruction of their homes, streets, neighbourhoods and landmarks – and of historic Paris – Haussmann remained the dispassionate technocrat, hardly bothering about the human cost as he set about his drastic surgery. 'In order to make the vast spaces at the extremities of the city, which remained unproductive, inaccessible and uninhabitable,' he wrote, 'the first job was to cut streets right through the city from one side to the other, by tearing open the central districts.' Gutting, cutting, tearing: Haussmann's language was that of brutal creative destruction.[16]

As a sickly and fragile child with weak lungs, Haussmann had to walk from home to school through a maze of narrow streets and alleys, his senses assaulted by noxious smells and dirt. It is little wonder that as a fastidious adult, remembering the traumatised schoolboy he once was, lost in the medieval warren, he craved a sanitised and rational city.[17]

Paris, for Haussmann, was like a human body, a system of arteries, veins, organs and lungs. It also had intestines and bowels. Haussmann's true masterpiece lay beneath the streets, in his sewerage system. In London – whose 200,000 cesspools and stinking river overflowed with the waste of more than 2.6 million humans – the civil engineer Joseph Bazalgette constructed an enormous network of over eighty-two miles of underground sewers and 1,000 miles of street sewers from 1858, complete with intercepting sewers, pumping stations and outflow systems. Famously, Bazalgette made the sewers so wide that his system can still, by and large, cope with London's effluence today. Unable to put sewage pipes under Chicago, Chicago was raised to make room for the pipes. From 1858 entire brick buildings were lifted six feet on hydraulic jacks and jackscrews. By 1860, 600 labourers using 6,000 jacks were lifting half a city block at a time. While they hauled up an entire row of shops, offices, businesses and hotels weighing 35,000 tons and occupying an acre, street life went on exactly as if nothing was happening. While the streets were suspended, new foundations were put in place, complete with sewage pipes.[18]

Chicago and London had their miracles of underground modernisation in the 1850s and 60s. Haussmann surpassed even these triumphs of sanitation and technology. His network of sewers replicated his rectilinear street plan and they were as rational, grand and well lit as the boulevards above; the pipes and galleries were large enough to walk in or even take a boat through and its walkways were kept scrupulously clean. The sewers expressed Haussmann's view of the city not first and foremost as a multigenerational, multilayered human construct, but as a machine. Or, to put it another way, he was concerned more with the arteries and organs, less with the connective tissue that binds the body together.[19]

The lungs of the city were as important as the digestive system. Haussmann wrote in his memoirs that the emperor instructed him: 'Do not miss an opportunity to build in all arrondissements of Paris the greatest number of squares, in order to offer Parisians, as they have done in London, places for relaxation and recreation for all the families and all the children, rich and poor.' Haussmann created four huge and magnificent parks, adding 600,000 trees and 4,500 acres of open space to the city, and incorporated twenty-four new squares into his plan. No Parisian would be more than ten minutes' walk from open space.[20]

In a century of urban decay and of flight from the cramped, dirty city centre, Paris stood as a beacon of modernity and progress, the metropolis resurrected in the industrial age. Opened up to light and air, embellished with order and elegance, and cleansed beyond recognition, Paris attracted tourists like never before. The Grand Hôtel du Louvre opened in 1855 to coincide with the International Exhibition. France's first luxury hotel and the largest in Europe, it was the pinnacle of elegant tourism with 1,250 staff, 700 deluxe bedrooms and two steam-powered elevators. The Grand Hôtel, opened in 1862 near the Opéra, was so magnificently opulent that the empress Eugénie said that it felt 'absolutely like home. I feel like I am at Compiègne or Fontainebleau'. Occupying an entire triangular city block, it had 800 luxury bedrooms, sixty-five salons, hydraulic lifts, Turkish baths, a telegraph service, theatre ticket desk and wine cellar with 1 million bottles.[21]

Grand hotels were complemented by *grands magasins*, shimmering new department stores built on a monumental scale. Le Bon Marché, built between 1867 and 1876 with the engineering assistance of Gustave Eiffel, was a breakaway multistorey, iron-framed department store designed so that its massive interior – 50,000 square metres – was filled with light. Along its four sides enormous plate-glass windows offered glimpses into the gorgeous stage set of consumerism. Every day an army of 3,500 employees catered to 16,000 customers. The grand hotels and *grands magasins* were not simply bigger than their predecessors; they were deliberately designed, at huge cost, to resemble public buildings and monuments, visitor attractions in their own rights.[22]

The reconstruction of Paris also created room for bigger, more luxurious boulevard cafés such as the El Dorado on the Boulevard de Sébastopol and the Café de la Paix on the ground floor of the Grand Hôtel. As a travel guide described these new creations: 'When lighted up at night, the effect … is perfectly dazzling. Chairs and small tables are placed outside, where both sexes can enjoy the cool of the evening, and witness the animated scenes around them … The eye is dazzled with gorgeousness, and the effect is heightened by the degree of taste and luxury displayed in the fitting-up.'[23]

Marx acidly commented that Haussmann had bulldozed the historic city 'to make a place for the sightseer!' Imposing neoclassical railway stations, grand hotels, grand department stores, *grands boulevards*, grand cafés, opera houses, theatres, museums, art galleries, Gothic cathedrals, parks and promenades – the Paris tourist trail was laid out as a glamorous tour through an urban pleasure zone for international visitors, sightseers, weekenders and shoppers, offering them the opportunity to partake of an urbane lifestyle once exclusively reserved for the aristocracy and super-rich.

And they came in great numbers as the tourism industry took off with the advent of the railway. In 1840 there were 87,000 passages across the English Channel; this rose to 344,719 in 1869 and 951,078 in 1899. The tour operator Thomas Cook took Britons to Paris's Exposition Universelle in 1867 for the low cost of thirty-six shillings each, for which customers got four days all inclusive. Between 9 million and 11 million people from France and around the world went to this World Fair; that of 1876 attracted 13 million and in 1889 (when the Eiffel Tower was unveiled to the world) attendance was over 30 million.[24]

The age of mass tourism had arrived with a bang. Cities caught in the vortex of this revolution have changed immeasurably. Between 2000 and 2015 the number of global tourists doubled to reach 1.3 billion; by 2030 there will be 2 billion people heading off on holiday every year. There are many cities where the central district seems less like a living habitation or business centre than a tourist theme park; imagine New Orleans or Bangkok without their legions of tourists. Even big financial centres like London, New York, Paris and Shanghai give over much of their central districts to tourists, providing them with bars, restaurants, fast food and entertainment, housing them in hotels, hostels and Airbnb apartments. The balance tips away from the full-time citizenry; these hundreds of millions of pleasure seekers are surely one of the major forces reshaping modern metropolises.

This is hardly a surprise when the transient population of a metropolis dwarves the resident population. London, with close to 10 million inhabitants, received 274 million domestic day trippers in 2014, 11.4 million domestic overnight visitors and 17.4 million international visitors. Shanghai had 300 million visitors, mainly domestic, earning itself $35 billion in the process.[25]

Paris anticipated the sanitisation of metropolitan city centres over the last century and a half or so, as they became places for shopping and leisure. The newspaper Le Temps snorted with fury in 1867 that the geographic centre of Haussmann's Paris was the Opéra, a place of frivolity, not a cathedral, a civic edifice or a parliament: 'Are we no longer anything more than the capital of elegance and pleasure?'[26]

★

'Cruel demolisher,' wrote the poet Charles Valette of Haussmann, 'what have you done with my past? / I search in vain for Paris; I search for myself.' During Haussmann's whirlwind renovations 350,000 Parisians were displaced. No city had ever been transformed so quickly in peacetime. 'Old' Paris was vanquished, leaving many traumatised by its new incarnation. 'No more anarchic streets, running freely, crammed full,' lamented Victor Hugo. 'No more caprice; no more meandering crossroads.'[27]

The craquelure of streets that gave Paris life and made it a city of 'flâneurs, badauds, and pleasure seekers' had been replaced by ruthless geometry and boulevards disappearing into the distance. The regimented vistas of the boulevards, in other words, fixed the gaze forward, rather than encouraging the wandering eye of flânerie. Many more saw the street plan as the manifestation of tyrannical control, a massive urban barracks designed to discipline the masses.[28]

If Manchester and Chicago suggested a new trend of cities to turn themselves inside out, with the centre dominated by industry and slums, and the suburbs as semi-pastoral retreat, new Paris spectacularly reversed that. There was a gentrified, cleansed centre, and working-class, industrial periphery. 'Artisans and workers', wrote Louis Lazare,

'are shut up in veritable Siberias, criss-crossed with winding, unpaved paths, without lights, without shops, with no water laid on, where everything is lacking ... We have sown rags onto the purple robe of a queen; we have built within Paris two cities, quite different and hostile: the city of luxury, surrounded, besieged by the city of misery.'[29]

In a famous painting of the new Paris – the monumental *Paris Street, A Rainy Day* (1877) – Gustave Caillebotte depicts one of Haussmann's most characteristic innovations, a star-shaped intersection from which streets radiate. The triangular point of the central apartment block is as vast and as intimidatingly impersonal as the prow of an ocean liner surging towards a helpless lifeboat. In the far distance there is scaffolding: this is a city still being Haussmannised, even though Haussmann was no longer in power in 1877. Umbrellas are up, the cobbles gleam with rain, and there are people on the street. But the pedestrians in this wide-open urban expanse are separated by distance. No one talks, even those walking in pairs. The main figures are fashionably dressed bourgeoisie, denizens of the expensive *appartements* that fill the scene; workers are distant and alone, mere servants of the metropolitan elite, not active participants in the life of the street.

The spatial separation of the Parisian strollers is extenuated by their umbrellas, a device that creates a physical circle of privacy. The elegant central couple look away from the bulky man approaching them – of whom we only see half – but the imminent collision of their umbrellas is going to have to result in a pirouette of avoidance – another distancing act – within seconds. Or else they are going to jostle for space.

The setting is different in Van Gogh's *On the Outskirts of Paris*, one of a series of works that he painted in 1887 depicting places where the city met the countryside. Here is the 'bastard countryside', the edgelands of Paris. The working people of the *banlieue*, displaced from the centre of the metropolis, are rendered as grey smudges. As in Caillebotte's painting, there is a solitary lamp post in the centre. But in this case it is an urban artefact strangely misplaced in the fields of this eerie liminal zone. The people walk in separate directions down different muddy paths, emphasising their alienation from each other and from Paris. Here in these paintings by Caillebotte and Van Gogh, starkly presented, is the loneliness of the modern city.

Manchester and Chicago, with their industry and poverty, were the shock cities of the nineteenth century. Paris was no less shocking. The suddenness of Haussmann's transformation of the metropolis, the razing of the old intimate city, dramatised the alienating effects of urban life. Caillebotte's paintings of urban loneliness are commentaries on the psychology of modern city life, not necessarily representations of the reality of Paris. In most written accounts and impressionist paintings, the new Paris is a swirl of pleasure, noise, hubbub, crowds and wild energy.

An American tourist described Parisians as 'nomadic cosmopolites', at home only to sleep and restlessly on the move between cafés, restaurants, parks, theatres, dances and the myriad places of entertainment from waking until late at night. Haussmann's gas street lights meant that pavement culture could continue into the dark. The city's theatres, operas, ballets and music halls could accommodate 54,000 people every night. In addition, there were café-concerts and gaslit dancing gardens. According to Alfred Delvau, Parisians 'like to *pose*, to make a spectacle of ourselves, to have a public, a *gallery*, witnesses to our life'.[30]

The fast brushstrokes of impressionist painters are the rapid eye movements of the urbanite assaulted by a barrage of sensory data. The painters of the Haussmannised Paris – Manet, Degas, Renoir, Caillebotte and Monet chief among them – plug themselves directly into the nervous system of the modern city. A close friend of Baudelaire, Édouard Manet brought the sensibility of the *flâneur* to modern art. Manet walked and walked, making quick sketches of city life as he went, alert to the seemingly transient and trivial. Like the *flâneur*, he observed and painted as a detached observer, from the centre of the crowd but apart from it too.[31]

In the foreground of his *Corner of a Café-Concert* (1878–9), Manet shows a worker in a blue smock puffing on a pipe, his wine before him, as he looks at a dancer on the stage. Next to him is the back of a middle-class man in a grey bowler hat, and, further along, an elegantly dressed woman; all are looking up at the stage. These three different spectators are still and alone. Around them is activity. The dancer is in the middle of her performance; the musicians are playing away. Mirroring the dancer, a waitress is frozen in a moment of almost balletic movement, leaning forward to place down a glass of beer with one hand while holding two more in the other. Even as she disposes of one order, and is about to fulfil others, she is scanning the room for more thirsty customers or a bill to settle or a spill to mop up. In a second she will be somewhere else. Her focus is away from the stage, on a crowded café full of conversation and clatter we can't see but can imagine all too vividly. She almost envelops the worker as she leans across him; but they gaze in different directions and have no awareness of each other. The four principal figures occupy a tiny space together, but are in their own private, disconnected worlds.[32]

Manet's *A Bar at the Folies-Bergère* (1882) is one of the greatest artistic commentaries on modern urban life. Bottles of champagne, flowers and fruit, enticingly placed on a marble bar, separate us from a *verseuse*, a server of drinks. Behind her is a large mirror, reflecting an enormous chandelier and the crowd in the Folies-Bergère, Paris's most famous nightclub and music hall. At venues like the Folies-Bergère, a mixed clientele was able to sit at tables or in the *loges*; they could mingle and walk about. That is what we see in the reflection. Manet relegates the circus performance to the tiny legs of a trapeze artist in the top left. For him, as for the patrons, the real entertainment was the urban crowd. Manet's brushstrokes turn the crowd into a confused, smudged morass of top hats and indistinct figures; but the cacophony and animation of the crowd is palpable.

Our relationship with the *verseuse* is much less clear. The mirror reveals that she is being approached by a figure in a top hat. Is he ordering a drink? Is he propositioning her? Waitresses and barmaids were assumed to be prostitutes or sexually available. But this *verseuse* is leaning forward assertively; her eyes are sad, but her lips are forming something like a sneer. Hers is the gaze of the *flâneuse* turned right back on the voyeuristic *flâneur*.

It is a troubling image. Manet puts his finger right on anxieties about the modern city. In *Corner at a Café-Concert*, the patrons are together but separate. In *A Bar at the Folies-Bergère*, we are thrust into an urban world where human relationships are just as uncertain and unreadable. For Manet the modern city, like his paintbrush, has blurred all these certainties.

'There is perhaps no psychic phenomenon which is so uncondition-ally reserved to the city as the blasé outlook,' wrote the German sociologist Georg Simmel in his essay 'The Metropolis and Mental

Life' (1903). For Simmel, the modern urban personality was formed in part by 'the swift and continuous shift of external and internal stimuli'. If you had to engage with every piece of the blizzard of information, you 'would be completely atomised internally and come to an unimaginable psychic state'. The other force that moulded the 'general psychic trait of the metropolis' was the money economy and advanced division of labour that depersonalised relations between people and undid the traditional bonds that held society together. In his exploration of industrial Manchester back in the 1840s, Engels had glimpsed the same psychological crisis. The 'very turmoil of the streets' was revolting to human nature: 'The greater the number of people that are packed into a tiny space, the more repulsive and offensive becomes the brutal indifference, the unfeeling concentration of each person on his private affairs.' In the big city the isolating effects of capitalism were pushed to excess: 'The dissolution of mankind into monads, of which each one has a separate principle, the world of atoms, is here carried to the utmost extreme.'

The result was that, according to Simmel, the city-dweller had to find ways to construct 'protection of the inner life against the domination of the metropolis'. This manifested itself in a 'blasé' attitude and a default suspicious, reserved demeanour. In another work, 'The Stranger' of 1908, Simmel developed this notion of reserve. It came, he said, from the simultaneous 'nearness and remoteness' that was at the essence of urban life: 'nearness' from the claustrophobia of city-living, and 'remoteness' from anonymous strangers.

Caillebotte's Paris is an impersonal realm of atomised individuals made all the more vivid by the hyper-modern rectilinear boulevards that have replaced the conviviality of the ancient streets and erased historical memory. Degas, Renoir and Manet brilliantly captured not only the 'swift and continuous shift ... of stimuli' of the modern city but the 'nearness and remoteness' of commercialised leisure in the new Paris. Manet's figures are pressed close together; but they are worlds apart, spectators and customers of a show that is unfolding around them. They are in the middle of crowded Paris; but the scenes are haunted by loneliness. They – like the city they inhabit – are impossible to read. The legibility of the city, and its citizens, has been rubbed away into an impressionist's smudge by the forces of modernity.[33]

The tension between the nearness and remoteness of city life, as well as the blasé and reserved attitudes of urbanites, is expressed nowhere better than in the face and posture of Manet's enigmatic *verseuse* at the Folies-Bergère. Her 'fuck you' face is the external defence mechanism of the city-dweller forced into continual interactions with anonymous strangers, people you can't know and don't trust.

She is also a figure that expresses deep anxieties about the position of women in the city. She is dressed fashionably, like a bourgeois lady; but, working at a bar, she can't be bourgeoise. She is like a *flâneuse*, in disguise and distancing herself from the crowd while gazing at the scene of urban life. The point is reinforced by the visual distortion of the reflected scene. The male *flâneur* attempting to converse with her is pushed to the side; he does not possess mastery.[34]

The omnipresence of *flâneurs* in nineteenth-century Paris asks the question – where are the *flâneuses*? Men had the privilege of being able to blend into the crowd and move freely through the city. Women in public – particularly alone in cafés and bars and on the street – always carried the suspicion that they were available for sex. In another Manet painting, *The Plum* (1878), a working-class girl sits alone in a café. In front of her is a glass of plum brandy, but the girl sits bored and alone with an unlit cigarette between her fingers. She lacks both spoon for the plum and light for the cigarette, emphasising her awkwardness in this public space. In *The Café-Concert* (1878–9) a girl, this time with lit cigarette and a beer, sits pensively. Beside her is a smartly dressed man. Where she is uncertain, he radiates confidence and self-possession. Both the women in these two paintings are lonely and ill at ease. Their smoking proclaims their liberation from the constraints of society. Manet gives no clue if they are out to sell their bodies. The point is that, out in public enjoying the pleasures of Paris, the assumption will always be that they *are* prostitutes. Hence their unease. If anyone has a right to feel alienated, caught between 'nearness and remoteness', it is these women trying to claim a place in the city. The men have no such social anxiety.[35]

Manet's *verseuse* does not give any hint of being for sale. Protected by her attitude and by the slab of the bar, working at the Folies-Bergère has given her a vantage point and access to public life. Similarly, in Zola's realist novel *Au bonheur des dames*, published a year after Manet's famous painting but set in the 1860s, Denise Baudu works as a salesgirl in one of the new Parisian department stores. Like the *verseuse*, Baudu observes life from behind the counter. Both salesgirls, in the bar and the shop, are part of this exhilarating new world of commercialised leisure. But then, working-class girls and women always had access to the city, especially in the fields of retail and entertainment, even if it made them prey to continual male attention. Commercialised leisure, however, allowed 'respectable' women, members of the bourgeoisie, to begin to re-enter city life on their own terms.[36]

George Sand said she relished the boulevards because she could walk 'for a long time, hands in pocket, without getting lost, without having constantly to ask directions ... it is a blessing to follow a wide sidewalk'. An appalled man visited the Folies-Bergère: 'for the first time I had seen women in a café with smoking permitted. All around us were not just women, but *Ladies* ... the ladies themselves seemed hardly out of their element.' The management of the Folies-Bergère, for their part, were happy to encourage women customers, advertising in the feminist newspaper *La Gazette des Femmes* in 1882.[37]

The large store became a destination for a day trip, a microcosm of the city, or at least of an idealised city. By providing lunches and cakes, tea and coffee, reading rooms and lavatories (a facility in short supply for women in the city), they presented themselves as places of public assembly and shopping as a social activity. In London, unchaperoned women could meet at Lyons' Corner Houses and ABC tearooms. By 1909 Lyons was serving over 300,000 customers a day, many of them shoppers and also an increasing number of women employed in office jobs. Like the department stores, Lyons offered an answer to a very basic, but very real barrier to women's mobility in the city: they had WCs.[38]

Shopping has, throughout history, thrown people together into dynamic interaction in the city. It has been at the heart of urban life since Uruk, although its forms change. In late twentieth-century United States – as in parts of the Middle East, Europe and Asia – malls provided places for people-watching and mingling for those who, like middle-class women in the nineteenth century, were excluded by the crime, poor planning, traffic and the inaccessibility of their city centres: teenagers. The language and aims of *flânerie* still inform how we conceive the urban experience, even if the setting is radically different from Paris. According to the architect Jon Jerde, commissioned to rethink the mall in the 1980s: 'Urban and suburban Americans seldom stroll aimlessly, as Europeans do, to parade and rub shoulders in a crowd. We need a destination, a sense of arrival at a definite location. My aim, in developments such as Horton Plaza [San Diego] and the Westside Pavilion [LA], is to provide a destination which is also a public parade and a communal centre.' The mall made up for the emptiness of American city centres, focal points – with their shops, displays, fountains, benches, public squares, foliage, cafés, food courts, cinemas and crowds – in the ocean expanse of car-based suburbia, where *flânerie* is virtually a criminal act.[39]

The department store (later the mall) represented a bastardised, impoverished form of engagement with city life for writers such as Georg Simmel and Walter Benjamin. They saw a radical change in urban life – symbolised by the replanning of Paris – occurring in the middle of the nineteenth century, driven by the impersonalising force of capitalism. In the past shopping forced people to traverse the entire central city, going to places of specialisation: it was how you inhabited the city. Haggling and conversing with shopkeepers – often the same craftsmen who had made what you wanted to buy – made it a richly engaging social activity. The enemies of department stores took the view that by forcing these places out of business and centralising shopping in one place, customers became distanced from production; now you dealt, over a counter, with a salesperson, paying a fixed price. Commercialised leisure similarly turned people into detached, passive observers of the 'society of the spectacle', caught between 'nearness and remoteness'.

The resulting alienation, loneliness and anxiety are brilliantly captured in impressionist art, itself a manifestation of the ultra-modern. This is a world of compulsive consumption and emotional impoverishment – an age of urban crisis. But is this reading correct?

*

The impressionist painters identified the malaise of city life – a kind of version of Paris Syndrome – but also suggested its cure. By absorbing ourselves into the city, we become *flâneurs* or *badauds*, decipherers of the city and observers of the theatre of urban life. The best psychological self-defence for the urbanite is not to be 'reserved' or 'blasé'; it is in immersion in the sights, sounds, emotions and sensations of the city as it unfolds around us.

We can be discriminating *flâneurs*, rubbernecking *badauds* or aimless boulevardiers, passive spectators or active participants. We can be gluttons *and* gourmets. We can enjoy 'remoteness' as we melt into the anonymous, formless crowd; but we can also revel in 'nearness' when we form the self-chosen bonds of association and subcultures so readily available in the metropolis – neighbourhood, club, pub, bar, café, team, church or whatever group tickles your fancy. Alienation and sociability lie side by side in the city, two faces of the same coin. You can be one of Manet's solitary drinkers in a crowded bar or a lonely stroller in a Caillebotte canvas, enjoying (for a moment) the privacy of urban alienation; but the next moment you can be immersed in your self-chosen community. As Virginia Woolf wrote, when we step alone into the streets 'we shed the self our friends know us by and become part of that vast republican army of anonymous trampers'.

In Elizabeth Gaskell's *John Barton*, as the protagonist is jostled and pushed in the crowded streets of Manchester, he invents stories for the people milling round him: 'But … you cannot … read the lot of those who daily pass you on the street. How do you know the wild romances of their lives; the trials, the temptations they are even now enduring, resisting, sinking under? … Errands of mercy – errands of sin – did you ever think where all the thousands of people you daily meet are bound?'

Baudelaire wrote that the *flâneur* was 'like a kaleidoscope gifted with consciousness' that responds to all the movements and elements of life around him. Grasping these fragments, telling ourselves stories is the essence of urban life. The city-dweller as a collector of tiny incidents is put beautifully by Charlie Chaplin: 'This was the London of my childhood, of my moods and my awakening: memories of Lambeth in the spring; of trivial incidents and things: of riding with my mother on top of a horse-bus trying to touch lilac trees – of the many coloured bus-tickets, orange, blue, pink and green, that bestrewed the pavement where the trams and buses stopped … of melancholy Sundays and pale-faced parents and children escorting toy windmills and coloured balloons over Westminster Bridge: and the maternal penny steamers that lowered their funnels as they glided under it … From such trivia I believe my soul was born.'

The city becomes as much a construct of our imagination and experience as it is an actual engorging physical presence. Going by bus, train or underground, driving or walking, we make our own mental maps of the city. If you travel by public transport your private city might consist of a few clusters of geographically distant places, little pockets that you know among the vast blank of the rest of the city. If you drive, your city is unveiled in an entirely different, linear way prescribed by the road system. Urban walkers know the city more intimately because they depart from established routes, discovering the connective tissue that knits together the very different districts of a city but which remain unknown to the majority.

The adaptive human mind wants to take control of the immense, mysterious built environment. It wants to impose order onto chaos, to make the illegible legible. Walking the city, and writing it, are important ways of fulfilling that need. The history of constructing subjective urban topographies runs deep. Before the sixteenth century, artistic representations of cities were formulaic, often based on biblical imagery. But that century saw the beginning of bird's-eye views of cities, giving viewers the impression of looking down on real buildings and people. It presents an illusion of coherence that is impossible at street level. The novel inherited these panoptic ambitions, but shifted the perspective. This new form, which feeds on mistaken and concealed identities, serendipitous meetings, intertwined lives and random encounters, is a creation of urban complexity. The tangled topography of the city is reflected in the intricate pathways of plot as the novel emerged in the eighteenth century.

Dickens became one of the greatest interpreters of urban life because he was a prodigious walker; his visceral encounters with the physical and human cityscape run through all his work. Urban literature is bound up with walking, because walking takes you away from the familiar, down 'long perplexing lanes untrod before', as John Gay put it in his 1716 poem 'Trivia; or, the Art of Walking the Streets of London'. Gay's poem was not so much a tour of the streets as a guide to the 'art' of walking round a dirty, dangerous, messy city – offering practical advice on footwear as well as saying *how* one should look at the city. Much later, in his influential book *The London Adventure; or the art of wandering* (1924), Arthur Machen wrote that everyone knew the historic centre of the city, or if you didn't, a guidebook could help you out. The real life of the city, and its true wonder, lay off the beaten track where the peculiarities of life are glimpsed by pure chance, out of the corner of one's eye. This is where you see how the city *really* works; how it knits together; how people live, survive and respond to their built environment.

Both Gay and Machen, writing at different times, highlight that real life happens off the beaten track, away from the rat runs and established routes that dominate our lives. Writers in London and Paris in the eighteenth century and beyond churned out immense numbers of walking guides, rambling narratives and 'spy' stories that purported to expose the secret underbelly of the city to an audience hungry to understand and mentally map their fast-changing, turbulent metropolises.

London and Paris have spawned voluminous literature on urban walking; there is a dialogue between the two cities. Edgar Allan Poe's story 'The Man in the Crowd' (1840) – in which the narrator follows a stranger obsessively through the crowds of London – influenced Baudelaire, the patron saint of *flânerie*. Walter Benjamin, who formulated *flânerie* into a theory and remains one of the most acute observers of urban life, wrote that Paris, with its long associations with street exploration and its theatricality, taught him the 'art of straying'. In the twentieth century, the surrealists and, later, the situationists, took up the baton of *flânerie*. Louis Aragon's *Le Paysan de Paris* (*Paris Peasant*, 1926) is a forensic examination of two small areas, the Passage de l'Opéra – an arcade facing demolition – and the Parc des Buttes-Chaumont, in which every minute detail comes under microscopic scrutiny. The surrealist André Breton described a walk in Aragon's company: 'The localities that we passed through ... even the most colourless ones, were positively transformed by a spellbinding romantic inventiveness that never faltered and that needed only a street-turning or a shop window to inspire a fresh outpouring ... no one else could have been carried away by such intoxicating reveries about a sort of secret life of the city.'[40]

Paris and London are rich in urban literature in part because they became the world's leading cultural metropolises at a time when people were absorbing the shock of modern industrial urbanisation. The outpouring catered to a need to comprehend the monstrously gigantic city.

'The city's streets can be read as can the geological record in the rock.' So wrote Harvey W. Zorbaugh in his sociological study of Chicago, *The Gold Coast and the Slum* (1929). By walking from the central city through the slums you could 'read' the buildings, detecting not only the physical traces left by ebbs and flows of economic history but the changes in ownership and use as immigrant communities had arrived, claimed the territory, and moved on, ceding neighbourhoods to newcomers. Each group left its traces on the cityscape, to be deciphered by the urban excavator. In a state of constant change, cities often entomb or erase their history; but history and forgotten folkways remain to be rediscovered. Zorbaugh belonged to the Chicago School of urban sociologists, who saw cities as complex ecologies that could be studied scientifically.

Zorbaugh's walk encompassed an area no more than a mile and half long and a mile wide. Yet within this space were not only dozens of micro-communities whose members hailed from all over the world, but extremes of wealth and poverty – a whole ecosystem to be uncovered by observation, a zone – although very new – already saturated in history. This was a world of inordinate complexity that forces you to reconceive your sense of geography:

As one walks from the Drake Hotel and the Lake Shore Drive west along Oak Street, through the world of rooming houses, into the slum and the streets of the Italian Colony one has a sense of distance … Distance that is not geographical but social. There are distances of language and custom. There are distances represented by wealth … There are distances of horizon – the Gold Coast living throughout the world while Little Hell is still only slowly emerging out of its old Sicilian villages … It is one world that revolves about the Lake Shore Drive, with its mansions, clubs, and motors, its benefits and assemblies. It is another world that revolves about the Dill Pickle Club, the soapboxes of Washington Square, or the shop of Romano the Barber. And each little world is absorbed in its own affairs.

Every built environment, even relatively young ones, yields stories as you peel away the layers and reveal its rich strata of history, myth, folklore, memories, topography. When Henry James came to London in the 1870s, then the biggest and most powerful city in the history of the world, he found it 'not a pleasant place'; it was so big and formless that he experienced himself as 'an impersonal black hole in the huge general blackness'. But there was a cure: 'I used to take long walks in the rain. I took possession of London.'[41]

James gives us an important insight. The freedom and pleasure of traversing the city gives us intimacy with it. There are cities today where walking is simply too dangerous and inhospitable. Few would walk for pleasure through Lagos, Caracas or Los Angeles. And there have been groups who have been excluded from walking. Those who have cast the city in their imagination, who have mediated the experience of the streets for others in novels, paintings, photographs and non-fiction, have predominantly been men – and middle- or upper-class men at that. Baudelaire wrote that walking in the metropolis was as dangerous as exploring the jungle or a prairie: taking possession of the city by navigating its social layers and disparate geographies was an act of masculinity. Until the twentieth century, in Western cities, women wanderers were considered to be soliciting or prey for sexual advances: walkers of the street were literally street walkers and subject to the gaze of voyeuristic *flâneurs*. Mary Higgs, who masqueraded as a down-and-out woman to conduct social research in the opening years of the twentieth century, wrote that 'The bold, free look of a man at a destitute woman must be felt to be realised.' The problem has not gone away: cities are still often places of danger and unwanted attention for women.[42]

'What I long for is the freedom of going about alone, of coming and going, of sitting in the seats of the Tuileries ... of stopping and looking at the artistic shops, of entering churches and museums, of walking about the old streets at night; that's what I long for.' This is the plaintive sigh of the artist Marie Bashkirtseff in the 1880s. When George Sand walked the streets of Paris dressed as a man in 1831 it was not just an act of rebellion, it was illegal: women were forbidden to wear trousers. Sand captured the exhilaration of being able to see without being looked at, a male privilege: 'I flew from one end of Paris to the other ... No one knew me, no one looked at me, no one found fault with me; I was an atom lost in that immense crowd.'[43]

Lily Gair Wilkinson, writing in a series of articles in 1913, said that the only way to understand the realities of modern urban life was to walk it like a *flâneur*. Wilkinson, an anarchist feminist, attempts to uncover the city by conducting us on a walking tour. This was a time when women were beginning to enter the city again, as office workers, shoppers and strollers; when the stigma attached to solo, unchaperoned women was beginning to ebb. But then she asks her female readers: 'If you being a woman, resolved to be free in this social sense, to go out into the world as a woman in freedom, how would it fare with you? ... For a time you might wander unhindered, elated by thoughts of liberty, but very soon you would find that you cannot dwell forever on the heights.' The only respite from the 'dreary grey buildings and endless discomfort' is a 'dingy' tea shop. 'You settle yourself in your uncomfortable corner, sip some of the nasty tea, taste a bun, and ruminate dubiously about your determination to be free.' A woman cannot be a *flâneur*, she concludes, not in the same way as a middle-class man who has untrammelled access to the city and, most importantly, opportunity to lose all sense of time while wandering. You hear the clock ticking as you forlornly sip your tea: 'In half an hour you are due at the office. Now, then, be free for a day if you dare!' Entering the world as 'a woman in freedom', an anonymous explorer of the city, is impossible for a working woman, bound by time and hampered by an inhospitable cityscape.[44]

Wilkinson's is a pessimistic take on walking, to be sure. But she expresses the longing to take 'possession' of the city in the way Henry James suggests, and get the same pleasure from it. Walking the city is a right; accessing it is political. One of the greatest writings on urban perambulation is Virginia Woolf's 'Street Haunting', an account of her early evening winter's walk across London to buy a pencil. 'The evening hour ... gives us the irresponsibility which darkness and lamplight bestow. We are no longer quite ourselves.' Published in 1930, 'Street Haunting' is a masterpiece of *flânerie* written at a time when it was a relatively new thing for women of Woolf's class to enjoy such freedom.

In Agnès Varda's film *Cléo de 5 à 7* (1962), the protagonist, a beautiful singer, learns to see Paris in a new way and in turn is changed by Paris while she anxiously awaits the result of a biopsy. Varda's shots of Parisian cafés and streets recall the stolen glimpses of life in Manet's paintings, the fragmented viewpoint of the *flâneur/flâneuse* brought to cinematic life. Cléo begins the film as a self-absorbed and vain woman; by allowing herself to be absorbed into the fabric of her city, by melting into the crowd, she is transformed. But, before she can do that, she has to anonymise herself. A performer and an object of male desire, she is more used to being looked *at* rather than doing the looking. By taking off her wig, replacing her chic clothes with a simple black dress and wearing dark glasses, she can achieve a degree of anonymity. It is a reminder that a woman still has to wear a disguise to traverse the city. Unwanted male attention is still a threat in 1962, as it still is today. Like the barmaid in Manet's *Folies-Bergère*, she has to put on her game face.[45]

Distilled in Woolf's essay and Varda's film is not only the intense pleasure of moving about the city on foot, but the degree to which walking intensifies our relationship with the built environment. Like Henry James, we take 'possession' over where we live when we find ways to mentally map it. As territorial, pattern-forming creatures, humans are good at imposing their own kind of order on their environment, humanising the forbiddingly vast urban landscape in the imagination so that it becomes habitable. The experiences of George Sand, Lily Wilkinson, Virginia Woolf and Agnès Varda show just how powerful that urge is, but also how fraught with barriers and dangers. The arrival of the *flâneuse* coincided with the proliferation of cars and their attendant road systems, making the city even less of a hospitable terrain for the pedestrian.

Georg Simmel – along with countless writers and sociologists – might have seen the modern city as a Babylon of soul-crushing dimensions. But that was to ignore the human capacity to cut Babylon down to size, and make it habitable.

The profound sense of alienation felt by sufferers of Paris Syndrome – that cocktail of anticlimax and loneliness – is an exaggerated version of how we might all feel in a city. It is also an extreme manifestation of how we all, to varying extents, fictionalise places and imbue them with meaning. That we thrive amid the uproar and transience of the modern metropolis is a testament to our coping strategies.

Sigmund Freud was almost crushed by Paris. But he came to terms with it by total immersion in the city, sketching it and describing its topography in detail in letters to his fiancée. After a few months he came to love it, a result of becoming intimately acquainted with it.

The history and literature of *flânerie*, psychogeography, deep topography – call it what you will – teaches us a lot about how to enjoy city life and urban tourism. Great buildings and monuments give a city the illusion of being static and timeless. But cities are best seen in movement, in the everyday life of their people, and in the sinews and connective tissue that hold the organism together. Walking is what makes a city liveable and, above all, pleasurable. That is the way to survive a city, whether you are a resident or a visitor.

II

Skyscraper Souls

New York, 1899–1939

The clarinet begins and we see the craggy skyline of Manhattan, followed by a series of iconic images in high-contrast black and white: the Queensboro Bridge, Broadway, blinking neon signs, diners, fire escapes, crowds, and skyscrapers, skyscrapers, skyscrapers dominating the skyline, a momentous assemblage by day, by night a glittering fantasy land of a million light bulbs. 'Chapter One. He adored New York City,' the voiceover begins. 'He idolised it all out of proportion. Uh, no, make that: He ... he ... *romanticised* it all out of proportion. Better. To him ... no matter what the season was, this was still a town that existed in black and white and pulsated to the great tunes of George Gershwin.'

So begins Woody Allen's film *Manhattan* (1979). As his character, Ike, speaks aloud his various versions of the first words of his New York novel, we see the city in its towering glory and neon-lit night time to the exhilarating soundtrack of *Rhapsody in Blue*. The concrete outcrop of Manhattan is as hard and forbidding as it is bewitching. It is a fortress to be stormed. Ike worries that his first sentence is too corny. Can the city ever be romanticised enough, or is it 'a metaphor for the decay of contemporary culture'? Is it an ethereal, dream city, or one of garbage and gangs? Is it one of high culture or of 'beautiful women and street-smart guys who seemed to know all the angles'? In the end, Ike settles on the idea that his character mirrors the crenellated city that he adores and which has shaped him: tough *and* romantic.

The opening sequence takes us directly back to the early days of cinema: from its very beginning, cinema's gaze was directed up at the soaring buildings of the twentieth century. The hyper-modernity of cinema was transfixed by the hyper-modernity of the high-rise. For early Hollywood, the city was New York, and New York was the city – the symbol and synecdoche of everything urban and futuristic.

The new vertical buildings of Manhattan were perfect subject matter for the camera. They fill the screen. The camera's love of the vertical axis is displayed beautifully in a short film from 8 October 1902. It starts with a 5th Avenue scene, the moustachioed men wearing bowler and top hats, the women long skirts; there are horse-drawn carriages and wagons, trams and a motor car, with an apparently normal office building in the background. But then the camera pans up ... and up ... and up ... leaving the nineteenth century far behind to reveal, one storey at a time, a cloud-piercing twentieth-century skyscraper, the recently completed Fuller Building. As the film shows in its stunning reveal, the Flatiron (as the building became better known) was bombastically futuristic and at radical odds with the traditional street below, a harbinger of the vertical city of the new century.

For viewers in 1902 – particularly those who did not live in New York – the footage must have been both unsettling and breathtaking; when will the camera ever get to the top of this incredible tower? What is perhaps most interesting, over a century later, is the behaviour of the crowd. They stare at the camera. Probably they have never seen one before. Here then, immortalised in little more than a minute of film, is the meeting of two sensational new technologies, the movie camera and the skyscraper.

Another short documentary filmed by Thomas A. Edison Inc. a few months later, *Skyscrapers of New York City, from the North River, May 10 1903*, reveals a different story: the combination of the vertical and horizontal axes caught in the lens. Filmed from a moving boat, the awesome outline of Manhattan gradually unfolds, one giant building after another, an urban vista like no other on earth. The spire of Trinity Church, only a few years before the tallest building in the city, is barely visible amid the forest of towers. The skyscrapers fill the screen with their monumentality. When this panorama was filmed, 1.5 million New Yorkers were commuting every day to Lower Manhattan and filling these offices. The tallest, the 391-feet-high Park Row Building, had a daytime population comparable to a medium-sized town, 4,000.

In *The Skyscrapers of New York* (1906), one of the earliest dramatic pictures, you can see nothing but the tops of high-rise buildings in the background. Apart from two internal scenes, the movie was shot entirely on the bare steel girders of a vertigo-inducing uncompleted skyscraper at Broadway and 12th. The brick masons dextrously negotiate the narrow scaffolding, and at one point an unfeasibly large group of them cling onto a chain dangled from an unseen crane and disappear over the edge into the void. The plot is driven by a dispute between the foreman and a worker, which leads to the film's climax, billed as 'a thrilling hand-to-hand encounter on one of the highest buildings ever erected in New York'.

Manhattan's mushrooming office blocks were an apt symbol for the city. The push for the heavens at the turn of the century made strikingly visible the city's problems: in New York people competed for space. The island's geographical limitations, its booming success and its laissez-faire attitude towards planning had the effect of thrusting people, businesses and economic activities into intolerable proximity. The docks were an uncoordinated chaos, with intense competition for waterfront. The water supply was inadequate. Every working day by 1920 the 2 million people who lived in Manhattan were joined by another 2 million commuters who packed onto the city's poorly developed public transit systems to reach downtown, where corporate headquarters, banks, law firms, factories, sweatshops, fashionable department stores and rotten tenements jostled and squirmed together. In parts of the Lower East Side population densities were 1,000 people per acre, a situation comparable to Dharavi in Mumbai in the twenty-first century. Squeezed by all these pressures, the city responded by bulging upwards.[1]

For the critics of skyscrapers, their sudden emergence was the unwelcome triumph of unfettered capitalism over public space. 'New York has no skyline at all,' grumbled the critic Montgomery Schuyler. 'It is all interruptions, of various heights, shapes and sizes ... scattered or huddled towers which have nothing to do with each other or with what is below.' Burgeoning sixteen-storey skyscrapers made people fear that streets would become little more than 'obscure trails half-lost between the bases of perpendicular precipices'.[2]

The hijacking of the city by speculative finance turned New York into a volatile zone. Skyscrapers built in the 1880s and 90s were already being torn down by the 1900s and 1910s to make way for bigger, better and more profitable versions. Dictated by the market, by land values and by fashion, skyscrapers were every bit a disposable commodity. The new vertical city, with its corporate skyline, seemed to reflect the economy: unstable, impermanent and in constant flux.[3]

And what happened up in these exclusive urban eyries anyway? In his short story from 1905 'Psyche and the Pskyscraper', O. Henry puts himself in the shoes of a skyscraper-dwelling man. If you are up 'you can ... look down upon your fellow men 300 feet below, and despise them as insects'. From that 'impossible perspective' the city takes on a new outlook, 'degraded to an unintelligible mass of distorted buildings'. Safely ensconced in wealth and luxury, the city recedes to insignificance. So too do its people: 'What are the ambitions, the achievements, the paltry conquests and loves of those restless black insects below compared with the serene and awful immensity of the universe that lies above and around their insignificant city?'

The skyscraper seemed to distance its fortunate inhabitants – the lords of finance – from the city and the people who lived there. What cared they about the city they were trampling under foot?

Despite voices of opposition, the towers continued to rise. The Singer Tower, completed in 1908 for the sewing-machine company, became the tallest building in the world at 612 feet. Its reign lasted only a few months, before it was surpassed by the Metropolitan Life Insurance Company's 700-foot-high, fifty-storey tower modelled on an Italian Renaissance campanile. The soaring Gothic 792-foot marvel that was the Woolworth Building of 1913 then stole the mantle. Lit up at night by searchlights, the Woolworth Building – with its numerous high-profile companies as tenants, its luxurious entrance halls, restaurants, shops, the fastest elevators in the world and a swimming pool – epitomised urban glamour.

The Singer, Metropolitan Life and Woolworth buildings show the megalomaniacal forces driving the vertical city. For all three companies, their buildings were financial assets and advertisements on a stupendous scale. They featured in newspapers, magazines, photographs and films distributed around the world; they appeared on cereal boxes, coffee packaging, postcards and more.[4]

In 1914 Mayor John Purroy announced the death of the skyscraper. At the laying of the cornerstone of the new Equitable Building the mayor remarked that it might be the last skyscraper ever built in New York. The biggest office building on the planet, the building sat on a plot of less than an acre but provided 1.2 million square feet of floor space over thirty-six storeys for 15,000 workers. Although not the tallest building in the city, it occupied an entire block and cast its shadow over 7.5 acres, condemning nearby buildings with fewer than twenty-one floors to permanent darkness. When the Equitable opened in 1915 the economy was in a downturn, with high office-vacancy rates. In this kind of market, renters chose the newest, highest, brightest offices. The Equitable was seen as a thief not just of sunlight and air from its neighbours, but of their tenants too. Skyscraper speculation was a ruthless business.[5]

Here was the supreme example of how the free market was ruining cities in a chaos of capitalism. But neither law nor the city could do much to prevent further high-rises like this. More skyscrapers like the Equitable were promised, and they would turn Manhattan's streets into dark, narrow canyons as speculators fought each other for light and space up in the sky. In the pioneering short film *Manhatta* (1921) the camera greedily consumes New York. But it is a disconcerting experience. The camera looks down menacingly from atop high-rises, as from an eyrie or a sniper's nest, at the minuscule people far below. This is a metropolis of stark geometric lines, spectral towers and cage-like steel girders. Steam belches out of the giant buildings, and from engines and ships; vehicles, made to look like toys, and identikit people move with ant-like regularity. This is more machine than metropolis, a cubist's paradise of dramatic vertical lines and light/dark contrasts.

If this is the future metropolis, it is a bleak prospect. The disillusionment with the vertical city was widespread. New York seemed to be running out of control, burying its citizens under concrete and steel. The villain of the piece, the Equitable Building, forced the traditionally laissez-faire and unplanned city to pass its first Zoning Law in 1916, regulating the height, size and arrangement of the city's buildings. It prevented factories from invading retail and residential districts, and also protected the latter from the encroachment of businesses. It outlawed the construction of outsized buildings in most parts of the city. Where they were allowed, in Lower Manhattan, skyscrapers had to conform to new restrictions. Any part of a building above a height of two and a half times the width of the street in front of it had to taper away from the street so that light and air could reach the pedestrian. No more would skyscrapers rise sheer and monotonous, stealing sunshine from the city.

But rather than bring the experiment with vertical urbanism to a halt, the Zoning Law accidently unleashed a golden age of skyscraper building, creating the city that continued to fascinate filmmakers.

*

'New York – city of enchantment, of delirium – terrifying, alluring, magnetic.' These are the words that start the 1927 silent masterpiece *East Side, West Side*, directed by Allan Dwan. Then the first image: Manhattan's towers at dawn behind the Brooklyn Bridge. The camera reveals more great skyscrapers; then the words appear: 'City eternally building; greedily demanding steel and stone, concrete and brick, the bodies and souls of men: tearing down the skyscraper of yesterday to rear tomorrow's dreams against the sky.' The camera returns to the waterfront, where a handsome, muscular young man, John Breen (played by George O'Brien), sits studying the incredible scene across the river.

The rippling water makes it look like the skyscraper city is somehow alive; it is an incredible illusion. John has been brought up on an aged barge that carries bricks to building sites on Manhattan Island. He reaches down and seizes a brick. The screen is then filled with a vast skyscraper, its tower exactly fitting the brick. The single brick has become the building John dreams of constructing for New York.

The vision fades. He stands and faces the city in a power pose, the wind billowing his raggedy clothes. Energised, he runs along the pier, Manhattan's glorious skyline hulking over him.

East Side, West Side is notable for its striking cinematography of the city. After the deaths of his parents in an accident, John crosses the river to Manhattan, where he is thrown into the vortex of the Lower East Side. He works as a boxer and a construction worker, labouring deep underground on the foundations of new skyscrapers. After a series of adventures, he realises his dream of becoming an architect, the master builder of the city he idolises. In the final scene, filmed on top of a skyscraper, John's love interest, Becka, comments: 'Building, John – always building. We tear down and build up. When is it going

to stop?' John replies: 'When we have built the perfect city, Becka ...
The city of our dreams!'

'The remaking of New York is at full tide,' remarked the *New York
Times* in November 1925, capturing the exhilaration and bombastic
self-confidence of Gotham City at this time. 'Upon every hand power-
driven hammers split the air. Donkey engines whistle and shriek.
Bundles of steel beams ascend to the startling heights, often with a
steel worker standing amidships, his hand upon the fall of the derrick.
No human agency could keep count of the unmeasured tons in steel,
stone and brick that are raised day by day, ton upon ton, until a new
skyscraper stands in the place of some lowly structure.' The building
boom created new cinematic possibilities. Films like *The Shock Punch*
(1925), filmed with a handheld camera high on the bare steel girders
of the Barclay-Vesey Building while it was under construction, sit
alongside the numerous and very famous photographs of workers
balanced hundreds of feet in the air having lunch, playing golf and
so on. The film features an Ivy League graduate who wants to prove
his masculinity by working as a riveter high above the city. 'A skyscraper
under construction is one of the most thrilling sights in the modern
city,' wrote a journalist. 'Perhaps you caught sight of the men who
worked in and about the naked steel ... he is a workman with the
poise of an acrobat, the skill of a juggler, the strength of a blacksmith,
and the teamwork of a ball-player.' In the bonanza phase of skyscraper
building, the new metropolis – and the men risking their lives to build
it – were worshipped as superhuman.[6]

The world's centre of gravity was shifting to the United States.
New York had displaced London not only as the world's biggest city,
but also as the financial, commercial and cultural capital of the globe.
Just as Shanghai's profusion of skyscrapers crowned China's rapid
urbanisation at the beginning of the twenty-first century as hundreds
of millions transferred from rural poverty to cities, the soaring ascent
of Gotham marked America's emergence as an urban society: by 1920
more than 50% of US citizens lived in cities for the first time. By the
end of the decade there were 2,479 high-rise buildings in New York,
2,000 more than its nearest rival in verticality, Chicago.

The way Gotham developed had everything to do with the restrictions of the 1916 Zoning Law, which forced skyscraper architects to
find creative ways to preserve light and air at street level. As one

skyscraper builder put it, zoning gave 'architectural design in high buildings the greatest impetus it has ever known', producing 'a new and beautiful pyramidical skyline'. The skyscrapers of the 1920s – the kind John Breen dreamed of building in *East Side, West Side* – taper away from the street in a series of steps or setbacks like mountain ranges, crenellated castles or Mesopotamian ziggurats. (The base of the Empire State, for example, is just five storeys before the building starts to taper.) Appropriately in a decade of American triumphs, this radical style was hailed as uniquely American; it was 'born of a new spirit which is neither Greek nor Roman or classical or Renaissance, but which is distinctly of today'. Some called the new skyscrapers 'neo-American', connecting them to Mesoamerican pyramids and marking a departure from slavish obedience to the Old World.[7]

The camera made New York a futuristic city, a place of romance and desire, and displayed to the world what the metropolitan world would look like. 'When we were twenty,' remembered Jean-Paul Sartre of the late 1920s, 'we heard about skyscrapers. We discovered them in amazement in the movies. They were the architecture of the future, just as cinema was the art of the future.' Manhattan's towers were not simply buildings. The architectural designer and promoter of skyscrapers Hugh Ferriss wrote in 1922 that 'we are not contemplating the new architecture of a city, we are contemplating the new architecture of a civilisation'.[8]

The success of the new wave of skyscrapers caused that rare thing – an outbreak of optimism about all things urban. In his book *The Metropolis of Tomorrow* (1929), Ferriss provided illustrations depicting the cities of the future, dominated by evenly spaced New York-style ziggurats. Where pre-1916 skyscrapers threatened chaos, those of the 1920s promised order and beauty – the building blocks of a new kind of metropolis in the congested twentieth century and an answer to humankind's problems.

The benign relationship between lowly street and dizzying height was the supreme achievement of New York's skyscraper ascendancy in the 1920s. Its monumentality did not lose touch with the human. In the twenty-first century, Hong Kong and Tokyo are examples of cities that have managed to combine skyscrapers with a pulsating street life, retaining a mix of shops and activities at ground level, in striking contrast to the sanitising and deadening effect of other skyscraper cities.

The importance of the psychological connection between person on the street and towering new building was central to the thinking of many of the architects of the 1920s. Ralph Walker, the architect of some of New York's most stunning skyscrapers of that decade, believed that vast modern urban edifices should be works of art that not only fitted harmoniously with the cityscape but which made people 'physically comfortable and mentally happy'. His skyscrapers, he argued, should serve not just the owners and the people who worked in them, but the hundreds of thousands of people who saw them every day and constituted their audience. 'The architect of the future', he said, 'will have to be a psychologist.'[9]

Inspired by Ferriss's drawings, Walker's first major work was the Barclay-Vesey Building. Walker softened what would otherwise be an austere mass of a building with numerous carved reliefs: vines, tendrils, seahorses, birds, squirrels and elephant heads. Walker's later Western Union Building steps up through nineteen different colours of brick, from dark to light, suggesting growth. The stone curtain walls of his skyscraper built for the Irving Trust Company at 1 Wall Street were carved to resemble real curtains. The terraces formed by the setbacks provided space for greenery and gardens. Exterior decoration and ornament humanised a vast building making it part of the collective skyline and a civil member of the street.[10]

Walker put as much effort into the interiors of his skyscrapers, to make them humane, emotionally enriching workplaces. Hildreth Meière, the artist who worked on many of Walker's skyscraper interiors, wrote: 'Upon the architects who design our buildings rests the responsibility of giving us what we demand – something beautiful as well as efficient.' When work on the Irving Trust Building was complete, Ralph Walker commented: 'We all feel that we have created something that is modern, spiritually and mentally, rather than modern for the physically modern ... The skyscraper ... is the only means of living ... in this age of the machine. It is an expression and reflection of the age.'[11]

The German filmmaker Fritz Lang, arriving in New York in 1924, was detained on his ship overnight by immigration officers. He gazed spellbound on the city: 'the buildings seemed to be a vertical veil, scintillating and very light, a luxurious backdrop, suspended in the dark sky to dazzle, distract and hypnotise ... The sight of New York alone should be enough to turn this beacon of beauty into the centre of a film.'[12]

Lang took back his memories of the New York skyline to Berlin, where he and his team built a miniature city. The resulting city in *Metropolis* (1927) is astounding. A breakthrough in special effects, it brought to the screens the city of the future – of 2026 to be precise. The ethereal beauty of Lang's vertical city is complemented by its volcanic energy and sustained by a slave army of zombie-like proletarians who toil in a drab subterranean city far below the majestic skyscrapers.

The moral lesson of *Metropolis* is rooted in history and very ancient critiques of the urban world; it is the story of the Tower of Babel and of Babylon retold for the twentieth century. Its main attraction for viewers in 1927, however, was its futuristic sci-fi vision of New York and its advanced special effects. Here is the city of tomorrow: it is only a small jump from New York in the 1920s. Lang used stop–start animation to show vast skyscrapers, aircraft, cars on multi-lane motorways, skybridges and trains criss-crossing aerial viaducts between the towers.

The lavish Hollywood musical comedy *Just Imagine* (1930) conjures up a New York in 1980. Inspired by the utopian visions of Hugh Ferriss and Harvey Wiley Corbett, a team of 205 designers and technicians created a gigantic model city at the stupendous cost of $168,000. Whereas *Metropolis* showed urban nightmare, *Just Imagine* depicts a New York of vast art deco towers linked by roads and walkways; people fly between buildings in personal airplanes. It turned the urban theories of Ferriss and others into 3D and gave people a glance at the future. 'In the future when the evolution of the city is accomplished', wrote Ferriss, 'the people of New York will actually live in the sky.'[13] Whether it is the metropolis of *Just Imagine* or of *Blade Runner*, our sense of the future is bound up with our hopes and fears about the city.

*

In the twenty-first century, every night thousands gather on Shanghai's Bund to see the skyscrapers of the Lujiazui financial district of Pudong across the river illuminated in lights of all colours, a stirring, futuristic, unrivalled sight. Filmmakers are as attracted to Shanghai as their forebears were to Manhattan. The city's ultramodern skyscrapers were used in *Mission: Impossible V* (2006) and *Skyfall* (2012). In the film *Her* (2013) a futuristic Los Angeles was created using footage of Shanghai's already existing hyper-modern buildings.

Even its advocates called it a 'Third World backwater' as the twentieth century drew to a close. Shrouded in pollution and disfigured by neglect, Shanghai's glory days belonged to the distant pre-communist period when it had been dubbed the 'Paris of the East'. In the early 1990s there were no modern high-rises, shopping centres, overpasses or subways; the grandest buildings were the decaying art deco marble masterpieces of the jazz age, and even the light switches were pre-war. Until 1983, the tallest building was the Park Hotel on Nanjing West Road, built in 1934 and standing at 275 feet.[14]

But then in 1991 Jiang Zemin announced that Shanghai would be the 'dragon's head' of China's modernisation and its point of contact with the world. Almost overnight the dowdy, dilapidated city became a frenetic boom town, with a million construction workers and 20% of the world's cranes ceaselessly at work on 23,000 building sites. A strip of swampy farmland called Pudong was turned into one of the most fantastic cityscapes on the planet – a steel and glass jungle that contains some of the twenty-first century's most iconic buildings, including the twisting, tapering Shanghai Tower. Opened in 2016, it is the second-tallest building in the world at 2,073 feet. With over 25,000 buildings of twelve storeys or more, Shanghai has more high-rises than any other city on the planet. Its nearest rival, Seoul, has 17,000. Shanghai possesses almost 1,000 buildings over a hundred metres, and 157 taller than 150 metres.

Like Tokyo, Hong Kong, Singapore, Bangkok and Dubai before it, Shanghai has used the power of its skyline not just to underline its rise to economic dominance, but also to create the conditions for global success. From the 1980s, Shanghai and a host of other Chinese cities have undergone a frenzy of skyscraper and high-rise construction. The velocity of urbanisation meant that between 2011 and 2013 China consumed more concrete than the United States did in the entire twentieth century.[15]

The distinctive skyscraper profiles in Asian cities, more than anything else, established the rebalancing of the global economy towards Asia. City battled city in an expensive all-out architectural war. The urban age of the twenty-first century has been defined by this intense competition, with cities becoming ever-changing stage sets for the performance of global capitalism. As with New York in the early twentieth century, the history of capitalism can be read in the sculpted outline of the city. What you see is not so much office buildings as hyper-expensive missile launchers aimed at rival cities.

Where once Asian cities borrowed Western ideas about city building, now Western cities are becoming more Asian. Perhaps nowhere exemplifies this better than London, a capital which had mostly resisted the encroachment of skyscrapers for decades. The need to build big, to rebrand itself with an outsized skyline, conquered central London in the early twenty-first century as planning regulations were relaxed. Skyscrapers and expensive residential high-rises proliferated with no less astonishing speed than in Shanghai. In the first eighteen years of this century, the number of supertall skyscrapers in cities around the world went from around 600 to 3,251; the modern metropolis is reaching upwards at speed. Aspirations and financial power – not to say virility – are firmly connected to skyscrapers, to offices and luxury apartments with expansive views, to the photogenic qualities of a city.[16]

Looking across the Huangpu river towards Pudong is one of the most stirring sights in the world, a triumph of urban ambition and supercharged renewal. But standing among the towers is like being in a soulless, desolate business park on the edge of town. The towers seem more spaced out from each other than they do from afar, far less impressive. Go into one of those towers, however, and take the elevator to the viewing platform and the whole city unfolds before you in an unforgettable panorama. Pudong is little different from hundreds of other skyscraper districts the world over. They are part of a show, enjoyable only either from a distance or from inside. The effect on the city itself, from street level, is deadening. Modern skyscrapers are often set in empty plazas; their reflective glass shuts out onlookers. The rapid 'Shanghai-ification' of the world's metropolises in recent years has impacted on how we live and work in cities, how they look and feel.

The city that gave birth to the vision of the modern global vertical city is quite different. New York's urban skyline is still the most beloved

in the world. But at street level downtown Manhattan is not as sanitised as Pudong or Singapore. Why this is the case has everything to
do with the way its skyscrapers were built in the boom period of the
1920s. In Manhattan, things, people and activities are stacked one on
top of another in a way that is very different from the sanitised twenty-
first-century skyscraper metropolis. The skyline is as raucous as George
Gershwin; tumultuous rather than ordered; random and experimental,
not planned.

The magnificent outline of a skyscraper city always sets the pulse
racing. But they can also make a city look like a bastion of privilege,
unobtainable to outsiders. Alfred Kazin, in the 1920s a small boy
living in the poverty of the Russian Jewish immigrant district of
Brownsville in eastern Brooklyn, wrote: 'We were of the city, but
somehow not in it. Whenever I went off on my favourite walk ...
and climbed to the hill to the old reservoir from which I could look
straight across to the skyscrapers of Manhattan, I saw New York as
a foreign city. There, brilliant and unreal, the city had its life, as
Brownsville was ours.'[17]

*

There is an economic theory that you can predict that an economic
crash is about to happen when a new skyscraper rises to claim the
title of tallest building in the world. The Singer Building and the Met
Life coincided with the Panic of 1907. The Woolworth Building arrived
in time for the depression of 1913. The World Trade Center and the
Sears Tower opened during the 1973 oil crisis and the 1973–4 stock-
market crash. Kuala Lumpur's Petronas Towers became the world's
tallest buildings just before the Asian financial crisis of 1997. The
subprime mortgage disaster has its monument: the Burj Khalifa
skyscraper, opened in October 2009. The very day that the Shanghai
Tower was finished, the Chinese stock market plunged 7% in half an
hour.

The skyscraper boom of the 1920s was brought to halt by the crash
of 1929 and the Great Depression. Its monuments were the Bank of
Manhattan Trust Building, which overtook the Woolworth to become
the world's tallest building in 1930; the ethereal Chrysler Building,
which stole the record a few months later; and the mighty Empire

State, the next holder of the world record. A journalist wrote that the skyscrapers of the 1920s, particularly the last three giants, were 'the material embodiment of the late bull market'. They soared above lesser buildings like the graph of equity prices. By 1930, however, they stood as 'ironic witnesses of collapsed hopes'.[18]

Investment in building collapsed from $4 billion in 1925 to $1.5 billion in 1930 and just $400 million in 1933. When the Empire State was completed, a workforce of 3,500 found themselves jobless overnight. During the Depression 80% of all those working in the building industry were out of work, making up 30% of total unemployed. The world's tallest tower, short of tenants, was nicknamed 'The Empty State Building'. The belief that New York would become an entirely vertical city disappeared at a stroke as the incredible pace of high-rise building came to a sudden halt. Like paper gains from the stock market, it turned out they had been the product of rampant speculation, not the manifestation of some brave new urban dream. The movies registered the changed mood.[19]

A Shriek in the Night (1933) opens with the brooding presence of a skyscraper in the night sky. The first thing we hear is a horrendous scream, followed by the body of a millionaire plunging to his death. This is payback time. The adage went that every storey of a skyscraper cost the life of a workman who had fallen as it was being constructed. These construction workers were, it seems, doomed to fall by the same corporate greed and lust for power that had doomed the country.

This attitude is expressed with powerful darkness in the film *Skyscraper Souls* of 1932, directed by Edgar Selwyn and adapted from the novel of the same name by Faith Baldwin. It centres on a fictional skyscraper – taller than the Empire State – and follows the intertwined lives of the workers and residents. Its owner, David Dwight (Warren William), sums up the attitude of the 1920s when he describes his skyscraper as 'this marvel of engineering, this spirit of the age crystallised in steel and stone'. The building is a city in itself; people mingle and meet in the public areas; there are numerous small shops, drug stores, cafés, restaurants, small businesses, gyms, a swimming pool, saunas and apartments. Career women try and make their way, living independently in apartments, even as they fend off predatory men at every turn.

The building is presided over by its megalomaniac Dwight, who uses his position to get all the power and sex he wants. His assistant and equally hard-edged business partner, Sarah Dennis (Verree Teasdale), is also his mistress. He seduces Sarah's secretary, the naive Lynn Harding (Maureen O'Sullivan). The only problem is that Dwight doesn't in fact own the Dwight Building, 'the great monument to his ego', as one character puts it. He has used his position as president of a major bank to fund the building with the savings of depositors. When the $30 million debt becomes due, he refuses to sell the building, even though to do so would mean making a profit and saving his bank and its small-fry investors. Driven by his obsession with the skyscraper he manipulates the stock market and orchestrates a crash, bringing ruin to everyone around him: his business partners, the women he has seduced, his bank, small investors – many of them residents of the tower – who have borrowed to buy his overpriced stock. They are all bankrupted, their lives destroyed, so that Dwight can have his skyscraper. They wheedle, bargain, offer their bodies in the ensuing apocalyptic scenario.

But success has driven Dwight to madness. They laughed, he says, when he said he wanted to build a hundred-storey building. 'But I had the courage, the vision, and it's *mine*, and I own it! It goes halfway to hell, and right up to heaven, and it's beautiful.' He boasts about its indestructability. Then he raves on: 'A million men sweated to build it. Mines, quarries, factories, forests! Men gave their lives to it ... I'd hate to tell you how many men dropped off the girders while they were going up. But it was worth it! Nothing's created without pain and suffering – a child that's born, a cause that's won, a building that's built!'

Safe in his penthouse, secluded from the chaos he has caused, Dwight thinks he is invincible. But he meets his fate at the hands of his discarded assistant/mistress, Sarah, who shoots him dead. She has halted his mad desire for flesh and power, but consumed with grief, she staggers to the balcony. There again is that wonderous Manhattan skyline; rarely before has it looked so beautiful in cinema. Only now we hear the chill winds screaming menacingly on this lonely ledge. Sarah stands tall far above hundreds of skyscrapers. Then she's gone, straight over the parapet. In a truly horrific moment of cinema, we see her body disappear to a speck as it plunges towards the street. The scream of the wind becomes the screams of pedestrian witnesses.

In the Depression-scarred America of 1932, *Skyscraper Souls* exposes the malevolent passions that had sculpted the city. Sublime beauty confronts rampant greed and exploitation. The skyscraper is a machine that minces its human prey, turning them into savages. In 1920s films such as *East Side, West Side*, getting to the top of a skyscraper represented the fulfilment of earthly dreams. Five years later, in *Skyscraper Souls*, the same location is the place where ambition meets hubris. The creator of the tower is impaled by his lust for power and sex in the Olympian paradise he has made for himself. Sarah Dennis, the strong, determined female who has scaled the heights and climbed her way to the top of New York, becomes – in every sense – the fallen woman, punished for defying convention.[20]

Sarah Dennis's fall prefigures a much more famous descent from a skyscraper in a film released a year later. In *King Kong* (1933), one of the greatest blockbuster movies ever made, Manhattan Island becomes a kind of mountainous landscape, the man-made mirror image of King Kong's native craggy domain, Skull Island. Captured and brought to New York City, Kong goes on the rampage, capturing Ann Darrow (Fay Wray) and scaling the Empire State Building, which he considers to be the simulacrum of his mountaintop throne on Skull Island. As he breaks free and finds himself in the dense, noisy canyons of the city streets, Kong smashes up the 6th Avenue elevated railroad. As a child the director of *King Kong*, Merian C. Cooper had been kept awake by those trains: 'I used to think I'd like to rip the damn thing down.'[21]

Kong fulfils that fantasy. He is an elemental life force let loose on the city, exacting revenge. His primeval potency threatens the very fabric of the financial centre of the world, the epicentre of the Depression. King Kong's ascent of New York's buildings, culminating in the Empire State, is still thrilling to watch. As he smashes up the train and shimmies up the greatest tower constructed by mortals, he fulfils our desire to overmaster these inhuman creations, to run amok in an artificial environment, and to conquer the mountain peak.

But, as in *Skyscraper Souls*, the price for daring to reach for the ultimate height is death. Like other would-be masters of the city, Kong's perilous climb to the top results in a catastrophic fall.

King Kong's vertiginous encounter with New York illustrates the point that the skyscraper skyline was increasingly troubled in the 1930s. Encoded in the 1930s Hollywood vision of NYC – particularly the dramatic parade of towers, barely a decade old – were multiple layers of meaning. 1933 was a vintage year for celluloid New York. *King Kong* was a smash hit. So too was *42nd Street*, in which everyone is poor as the Great Depression bites, but there is more than enough energy to keep things going on 'naughty, bawdy, gaudy, sporty 42nd Street'. The city's foundational myth – that the outsider can succeed if she or he works hard enough to get a break – is affirmed in director Julian Marsh's words to chorus girl Peggy Sawyer (Ruby Keeler): 'You're going out a youngster but you've got to come back a star!'

In the sensational closing number, the chorus girls are turned into skyscrapers, creating the Manhattan skyline as an enormous single tower is revealed with Peggy and the male lead (Dick Powell) triumphantly on top. A place of ambition, a place of greed and cruelty, a place of fantasy, an embodiment of either rampant capitalism or social mobility – the concrete escarpment of Manhattan became the perfect backdrop for the projection of Hollywood's fantasies in the jaded 1930s. Irresistibly drawn back to the lure of the skyscraper, New York once again became a place of glamour and dreams, a symbol of America's recovery. On 2 March 1933, *King Kong* premiered in New York. Two days later Franklin D. Roosevelt was sworn in as thirty-second president of the United States. On 11 March, *42nd Street* opened.

There was another New York that Hollywood liked to depict: the one of crowded tenements, endemic crime and dirty streets, with their cast of fast-talking, wise-cracking, ethnically mixed city-dwellers and streetwise kids. The tenement street became the dark reflection of *42nd Street*'s glimmering skyscraper fantasy land. And like the skyscraper, the tenement was an ideal filmic stage, where life is played out; both are iconic of New York and instantly recognisable. One of the most influential films in establishing the New York tenement as staple of Hollywood was King Vidor's *Street Scene* (1931), set on one city block over the course of twenty-four hours. As in so many movies, the camera pans down from the nearby Chrysler and Empire State buildings, over a dense sea of tenement roofs (the Lower East Side: home to 400,000 overcrowded people) and focuses on children playing out on the street on a sweltering summer's evening. The street swarms with life: this is life lived outdoors, a place of gossip, petty spats, illicit romances and play.[22]

Here we are again at the heart of the problem facing America. If Wall Street took its share of the blame, so too did the tenement street. There were over fifty gangster films produced in Hollywood in 1931 alone. Where did this criminal epidemic come from, the movies seem to be saying, if not from the built environment itself?[23]

The subtitle of *Dead End* (1937) is 'Cradle of Crime', the cradle being the bleak tenement street by the river, East 53rd Street, in the shadow of the Rockefeller Center. With slum conditions at home and nowhere to play, the street has turned its kids into brawling, fighting, bullying, gambling, foul-mouthed thugs, the gangsters of tomorrow and the victims of the Depression. Their inevitable path to a life of crime is aided by notorious mobster Hugh 'Baby Face' Martin (Humphrey Bogart) – returned to the street of his birth for the day – who teaches them how to use a knife. The 'dead end' teenagers in turn indoctrinate the younger neighbourhood kids. The urban street – an assemblage of delinquents, criminals, prostitutes, drunks and deadbeats – is a place of danger and no hope. Bogart's character escaped it by becoming a ruthless gangster. His childhood friend Dave (Joel McCrea) studies for years to become an architect, but still can't get away. Even the virtuous Drina (Sylvia Sidney) can only imagine leaving the slum through sex – by marrying a millionaire. The block is hell on earth; but as one cop remarks, it's better than Harlem, reminding the viewer that this is one of countless no-hope, dead-end streets.

In one powerful scene, Drina tells the would-be architect Dave that she has tried to bring her little brother up well, but he has been sucked into the mire of the street. 'He's not a bad kid,' she says.

'Oh, what chance have they got against all this?' replies Dave casting his eye round the tenement, his voice choked with bitterness and rage. 'You've got to fight for a place to play ... They get used to fighting ... I spend my life dreaming about tearing these places down.'

'Yeah, you always talked about that,' murmurs Drina; 'how you're going to tear all this down, and all the other places like them. How you're going to build a decent world, where people could live decent and be decent.'

The guest of honour at *Dead End*'s premiere was Robert F. Wagner Sr, the New York senator whose Housing Act, providing for slum clearance and public housing, would come into law a mere five days later. Hollywood played a vital role in preparing the public for New Deal housing reform: as the Housing Act came into force thousands were sitting in movie theatres listening to Dave fantasising about demolishing the slums. In another hugely influential film attacking the inner-city street, *One-Third of a Nation* (1939), we again hear Sylvia Sidney's voice promising her crippled brother that the city is going to tear down the tenements and build 'decent' new houses: 'you won't have to play in the streets anymore. There'll be grass and trees, and regular playgrounds for kids, with swings and a handball court.'[24]

Tenements were a screenwriter's dream – lively, interesting places that lent themselves to narrative. Of course, Hollywood loved them, especially when the kind of narrative attached to them was one that dovetailed with the all-popular gangster movie. In visceral films like *Street Scene*, *Dead End* and *One-Third*, the idea of working-class neighbourhoods being places of community and sociability is entirely absent. They are nightmare zones. Tough and unpleasant as they were, the poorest streets of New York were in reality richly textured, multiethnic places of resilience, entrepreneurism and, occasionally, joy.

But you wouldn't get that from Hollywood. The films are in lockstep with the reformers. Like Dave, they wanted to tear it all down and build anew. The conclusion of *One-Third* shows the tenement being demolished and a new housing development built: multistorey apartment blocks spaced out amid greenery – an oasis away from the street. Babylon has fallen; the New Jerusalem is being built.[25]

The revolution had already started when the film hit the nation's screens: the Harlem River Houses were completed in 1937, the Williamsburg Houses and the Red Hook Houses, both in Brooklyn, a year later, and the Y-shaped Queensbridge Houses in 1939, to this day the largest housing project in the United States: six superblocks with 3,149 apartments and 10,000 residents.

The movie industry was as harsh in its critique of the modern city – of its hectic streets, its built environment, its promiscuous mixing of ethnicities, the filth of crime, prostitution and juvenile delinquency, and the state of its morals – as any social reformer or modernist. The brooding menace of *film noir* further reflected the pessimism regarding the traditional city. Tear it down!

New York had been dealing in visions of the future for decades. The Depression put paid to the glamour of the city's dreamscape – but only briefly. The modernist high-rises of the housing projects competed with downtown skyscrapers as symbols of twentieth century urban utopia. *One-Third of a Nation* and the opening of the Queensbridge Houses both coincided with the 1939 New York World's Fair, which gave its 45 million visitors a preview of 'the Metropolis City of 1960', designed by the film set and industrial designer Norman Bel Geddes for the Futurama exhibit. Every day during the Fair, 30,000 people travelled on chairlifts over Geddes's vast animated model city containing 500,000 buildings, a million trees, fourteen-lane highways, airports and, most significantly of all, 50,000 moving model cars.

Futurama's accompanying Technicolor film, *To New Horizons*, tells us that humankind's cultural evolution has been determined by the freedom that movement has given us. The invention and popularisation of the motor car has accelerated and democratised that progress, the voiceover proclaims. Geddes imagined interstate highways connecting US cities and reshaping them. Huge highways would also slash through the city, connecting its residential, business and industrial areas. 'A quarter of a mile high,' intones the narrator dramatically, 'skyscrapers tower, with convenient rest and recreational facilities for all. On many of the buildings are landing decks for helicopters and autogyros. Rich in sunshine is the city of 1960. Fresh air, fine green parkways, recreational and civic centres. Modern and efficient city planning. Breathtaking architecture. Each city block a unit in itself.' Gone is the messy street. Pedestrians hurry high above the speeding traffic, on elevated walkways. The camera soars over busy roads, shopping malls and high-rises set in verdant parkland.

This is urban utopia imagined for the age of the car. It is the city as foreseen and promoted by Le Corbusier. 'A city made for speed is a city made for success,' he wrote. The traditional city street was to him a 'relic', 'non-functioning', 'obsolete', 'disgusting'. Modern life depended on speed – and on the 'pure geometry' of an ordered, coherent city. Le Corbusier loved skyscrapers; but he wanted vast uniform towers – for both working and living – spaced apart in a park-like setting, connected by car-filled elevated highways.

The projects starting in the 1930s, such as the Harlem River, Williamsburg, Red Hook and Queensbridge houses, were mini-towers in the park hived off from the street. Many of the architects who worked on them were either disciples of or heavily influenced by European modernism. The unelected 'master planner' of New York, Robert Moses – an admirer of Le Corbusier – believed that 'cities are created by and for traffic', which should go through them, not around them. 'His vision of a city of highways and towers', wrote the *New York Times*, 'influenced the planning of cities around the nation' and made New York the first city of the automobile age.[26]

In the future, most Americans would be car-owners; the traditional city and its streets and neighbourhoods would not do for them. Moses oversaw the construction of 416 miles of parkways, thirteen expressways that sabred through the city and thirteen new bridges. Thousands were displaced and their neighbourhoods carved up and isolated by massive new roads. He cleared slums and moved 200,000 New Yorkers to high-rise public housing, the majority far from the neighbourhoods of their birth. When you redesign a city for the modern age, he said, 'you have to hack your way with a meat axe'.

With 110 redbrick high-rises and 11,250 apartments, Stuyvesant Town–Peter Cooper Village was built to allow New Yorkers 'to live in a park – to live in the country in the heart of New York' and to show what city life could and would become. As it happened 11,000 working-class members of the neighbourhood had to pack their belongings and move out in what the *New York Times* called 'the greatest and most significant mass movement of families in New York's history'. The new high-rise, gated garden suburb in the heart of the city was intended so that 'families of moderate means might live in health, comfort and dignity in park-like communities'. And 'moderate means' meant white, middle-class people.[27] The working class would have to wait for their 'towers in the park'. When they eventually came, they were built at considerably lower cost than the $50 million lavished on Stuyvesant Town. They were also pushed to the periphery. Concrete projects like the Queensbridge Houses were just the start of the high-rise concrete drama of public housing.

The vertical automobile city was taking shape in all its various forms. The combination of private cars and towers entranced urban planners the world over, especially when it was seen through the medium of the big screen. New York remained the beacon of metropolitan progress.

*

In an age and a city overshadowed by big buildings, congestion, crime, social breakdown and economic turmoil, one beset by alienation, loneliness and anomie, it was lucky that there were still heroes able to overcome the superhuman scale of the mid-twentieth century metropolis. Such men saw skyscrapers not as forbidding monuments, but as mere playthings; undaunted by the concrete jungle and the crowds of humanity, they remained individuals, albeit hidden behind the kind of dual identity assumed by other denizens of the teeming metropolis.

First appearing in March and April 1939 respectively, Bruce Wayne and Clark Kent are lonely men dedicated to cleaning up their fictional home cities, Gotham and Metropolis, both based on New York. As their alter egos Batman and Superman they are figures of escapism and wish-fulfilment. They are vigilantes taking on the bogeymen of urban life: big business, organised crime, crooked politicians, corrupt policemen and muggers.

The skyscraper is reduced to human scale as Superman bounds over it with a single leap or Batman scales it with laughable ease. Both melt into the crowd and become anonymous when it suits them. As Clark Kent, Superman is an unassuming, mild-mannered, spectacle-wearing professional who goes about the city unnoticed. It is no accident that the Kent side of his character is based on Harold Lloyd, the ordinary-looking silent movie actor who had adventures on skyscrapers. As well as taking on the usual suspects, Superman is an urban warrior. His X-ray vision unpeels the city's secrets, and in a very early comic strip, like an omnipotent town planner he razes slums to prompt the government to create better housing for the working poor.

Batman and Superman came into being at the right moment. The city was dwarfing individuals in terms of physical size and population:

both characters take on the forces that crush the city-dweller in the twentieth century. The high-rise was set to become the norm not just as a place of work, but of home. No wonder they became so popular so quickly. Batman and Superman were the products of the Depression and organised crime, of urban utopianism and anxiety about the high-rise future. But in 1939, they also represented escapism from bigger threats facing the city.

12

Annihilation

Warsaw, 1939–45

Shanghai: this was where the Second World War began. W. H. Auden and Christopher Isherwood visited the legendary neon-lit, glitzy, bawdy International Settlement at Shanghai in May 1938 and found it marooned amid 'a cratered and barren moon-landscape' which had recently been the biggest city in China. The full horror of Blitzkrieg, aerial bombardment, protracted siege, snipers and house-to-house fighting had been visited upon China's megacity, well before European cities confronted the same nightmare. Only a few months before the battle, German bombers had levelled the Basque town of Guernica in support of General Franco during the Spanish Civil War. The world was on notice after Guernica and Shanghai: modern aerial warfare was capable of obliterating entire cities.[1]

The blood-soaked siege and battle of Shanghai was the opening encounter in the war between Japan and China that had been simmering for years. After three months of bombardment and intense urban warfare, the Chinese forces were broken. A Pathé newsreel shows Japanese troops advancing, house by ruined house, through the mauled carcass of Shanghai against a hail of machine-gun fire; plumes of smoke billowing above tiled roofs; tanks forcing their way over bare twisted metal and bricks; and, according to the grim narrative, 'bombs falling through the air like raindrops from an April shower'. The most shocking photograph of the 1930s, 'Bloody Saturday', shows a crying baby in the ruins of Shanghai South Station after sixteen Japanese planes had bombed refugees trying to flee the destroyed city. The photographer, H. S. Wong, wrote that his shoes were soaked in blood as he recorded the carnage; the platform and tracks were strewn with limbs. This was the torture inflicted on the world's fifth largest metropolis and its population of 3.5 million.[2]

'The International Settlement and the French Concession form an island, an oasis in the midst of the stark, frightful wilderness which was once the Chinese city,' wrote Auden and Isherwood in May 1938. 'In this city – conquered, yet unoccupied by its conquerors – the mechanism of the old life is still ticking, but seems doomed to stop, like a watch dropped in the desert.'[3]

What had happened to Shanghai in 1937 was the fulfilment of fears that had been building up since the end of the First World War. Novels, films, defence reports, military strategists, academic theses and urban planners had become obsessed with the fate of cities in the next war. At the heart of this thinking was the notion that modern, technological metropolises were inherently fragile: damage the precious and intricate life-support system of a city – its power, food and water supplies, transportation, civil administration – and it would quickly descend into primitive chaos. It did not take an enormous leap of the imagination to envisage the sheer hell of millions of urban people deprived of water, food, healthcare and shelter. Statesmen were desperate to avoid war at all costs.[4]

The history of mankind's attempt to eradicate cities tells us more about how cities function than almost anything else. Tested to their limits, cities reveal themselves. Even in the face of Armageddon, the clock keeps ticking in the urban wasteland, somehow.

How to Kill a City, Part 1: Occupation

Long before the German invasion of Poland, plans had been drawn up for converting Warsaw into a Nazi model city for 130,000 Aryan Germans. It would have wooden-framed medieval houses and narrow streets, set in extensive parkland. Relegated to a suburb on the east bank of the Vistula would be the only Poles allowed, 80,000 slaves to minister to their German overlords.[5]

Planning the campaign before the war, generals had suggested that Warsaw need not be attacked because, once the Polish army had been defeated, the Germans could simply walk in. 'No!' Hitler had shrieked. 'Warsaw must be attacked.' He reserved a particular loathing for the

Polish capital. According to a witness Hitler elaborated 'how the skies would be darkened, how millions of tons of shells would rain down on Warsaw, how people would drown in blood. Then his eyes nearly popped out of his head and he became a different person. He was suddenly seized by a lust for blood.'[6]

What does it take to destroy a city? Humankind has devised numerous means. Between 1939 and 1945 almost every one of these tactics was visited on the Polish capital.

Warsaw experienced the terror of air raids on the very first day of the Second World War, 1 September 1939. Over the next few weeks, as the German army pushed back Polish defence forces and bewildered refugees streamed into Warsaw, the city was subject to continual air raids. They got more ferocious as the Wehrmacht closed in on the capital. Unrestricted aerial bombardment was combined with artillery assault. 'The damage in Warsaw is colossal,' reported the *Warsaw Courier* on 28 September. 'Electricity, plumbing, filters and telephones are out of operation. All the hospitals have been bombed ... there is not one historical building or monument which is not totally or seriously damaged. Whole streets have ceased to exist.' That was the day Warsaw capitulated to the Nazis. People emerged from cellars into the smoking ruins, bewildered that the city had surrendered; left to themselves Varsovians would likely have fought on. The Germans entered and occupied Warsaw on 1 October. On the 15th the city was handed over to the Nazi colonial administration, headed by Heinrich Himmler.[7]

In a war against urban life, the Nazis tore the heart out of the city, systematically stripping it of its cultural, political and economic significance and suppressing ordinary citizens in a campaign of terror. Universities and schools were closed; textbooks, history books and foreign-language literature were confiscated; opera and theatre were banned; bookshops were shut down; cinemas showed 'ancient' movies or propaganda pieces; printing presses fell silent. It was forbidden to play any music by Poland's favourite composer, Chopin. His statue in Lazienki Park was blasted off its pedestal and the bronze presented to Hitler; that of Copernicus was removed, the Nazis claiming he was German.[8]

Bit by bit the memory of Warsaw's culture and history was erased; the Germans partially destroyed both the National Museum and the

Zacheta Fine Arts Gallery and confiscated what was left. The only books published were on the subjects of cookery, preserving food, growing vegetables and rearing domestic animals. On the grounds that slaves should not understand their masters' language, Poles were forbidden from learning German.[9]

A campaign of extermination against Warsaw's intelligentsia – Operation Intelligenzaktion – began as soon as Poland was taken. Hitler told Hans Frank, the head of the General Government in Poland, that the occupied lands were 'a Polish reservation, a great Polish labour camp'. And labour camps did not need intellectuals or artists. 'The covered Gestapo truck is the scourge of Warsaw,' wrote Thaddeus Chylinski, US vice consul. 'People shudder when these trucks careen down the streets. At night conditions become worse; everyone prays that the trucks will not stop in front of their home. The sound of grinding brakes is often the forerunner of tragedy for those within earshot.' By 1944, 10,000 members of the Warsaw intelligentsia had been murdered.[10]

Those middle-class professionals who survived mass arrests and killings were forced either to seek work as manual labourers, or to become beggars. Their jobs were taken by German colonists. The most salubrious districts were reserved for German colonists, bureaucrats and soldiers. The new overlords of Warsaw – many of them low-status before the war – could not believe their luck, taking their pick from the best apartments, along with art, jewellery, rugs and furniture. Signs saying *Nur für Deutsche* (Germans only) and *Kein Zutritt für Polen* (No Entry for Poles) appeared on trams, parks, playgrounds and restaurants.[11]

With most of the windows having been shattered in the opening weeks of the war, windows were boarded up with cardboard. Varsovians and refugees decamped to the suburbs, where houses were divided and subdivided again into ever smaller flats. By 1941 just 15% of the population lived in a dwelling with three or more rooms. During the exceptionally cold first winter of occupation, when the daily temperature plummeted to under −20°C, there was almost no coal available for heating.[12]

The population went hungry, surviving on the most meagre rations. The monthly allowance was 4.3 kilos of bread, 400 grams of flour, 400 grams of meat, seventy-five grams of coffee and one egg. Beer, wine, butter, cheese and cigarettes were off the menu entirely, and sugar in short supply. Facing starvation, Varsovians turned to the black market, food smugglers and vodka sellers, all of whom were ruthlessly repressed by the Gestapo. 'The Poles have gorged themselves for twenty years,' they would say, 'now they must live on bread and water.' A Pole remembered his childhood in occupied Warsaw, collecting potato peelings from the kitchen of a nearby hospital. 'Once … we managed to get hold of mouldy bread, which had already been eaten by mice, but it tasted very good.'[13]

The people of Warsaw were deliberately reduced to a slave population in preparation for the eventual demolition of their city. There were plenty of jobs – but they were in factories making munitions for the German military or in constructing airfields, fortifications and railways. Life on the streets became grim. They echoed to the sound of wooden clogs – people could no longer afford leather. Varsovians dressed in shabby clothes; no one wanted to attract attention. People sold their belongings on the side of the road. With no private cars, taxis or horse-drawn vehicles any more, many unemployed white-collar workers became rickshaw drivers.

At night the curfew emptied the streets. By day loudspeakers blared out German military music and propaganda in Polish. Gestapo patrolled the city, keeping the population in terror by sporadically rounding up men and boys at random and taking them to forced-labour camps. Women and girls were kidnapped and raped. The Gestapo raided apartment buildings at dawn, making arrests of those suspected of resisting the occupation.[14]

A schoolgirl aged sixteen was accused of tearing down German posters; she was executed the next day and her schoolmates arrested and never seen again. A boy scout of fifteen was shot on the spot for criticising the Gestapo. An old woman was shot point-blank by a Gestapo officer because he thought she had motioned to a young man to escape a dragnet operation … These are just three examples of daily terror. The population wore a mask of servility and indifference on their faces. They had to.[15]

'Life takes place in silence,' wrote Zofia Nałkowska. With most of the glue of urban society dissolved – newspapers, clubs, schools, trades unions, universities, books – Varsovians retreated into silence. Many turned to heavy drinking. The desire to stay alive, find warmth, get enough food, consumed people. The writer Andrzej Trzebiński burst out: 'I am being devoured by my fucking life.'[16]

From September 1943 Governor Frank ordered random executions of thirty or forty people at a time on the streets of Warsaw every day. Between 1941 and August 1944, 40,000 ethnically Polish Varsovians were shot in public and 160,000 were deported to forced-labour camps. Warsaw became a prison city ruled by fear with a slave population kept in near starvation. But within that urban prison was another one far, far worse. In the months following occupation, the German authorities imposed forced labour on the 400,000-strong Jewish community, making them clear bomb damage; their savings were seized and communal worship forbidden. On 1 April 1940 work began building a wall around 1.3 square miles of the city in the northern part of midtown. Clearly intended as a closed Jewish residential district, there was confusion about what was going to happen. Only in August 1940 were the Gentile Poles ordered out and the Varsovian Jews ordered in. As both groups began to move, the city descended into chaos. 'Everywhere there was wild panic, unashamed hysterical terror,' remembered Bernard Goldstein. 'The multitude filled the streets, a nation on the march.'[17]

On 15 November the gates were closed; 30% of Warsaw's population were confined within 2.4% of the land area of the city, completely sealed off from the outside world behind three metres of bricks and barbed wire. The captive population in the ghetto was a gold mine for German entrepreneurs. From May 1941 the city within a city was full of small factories, workshops and warehouses, producing mattresses and clothing, and repairing equipment for the German army.

Food supplies were kept at starvation levels, 184 calories per person per day compared to the (still meagre) 699 calories allotted to Gentile Poles. (A person uses about 3,000 calories during a day's hard physical labour.) Children became adept at wriggling out of the ghetto to obtain supplies; Jewish and Gentile entrepreneurs profited from smuggling provisions in. The ghetto imported 1.8 million zlotys' worth of food legally in 1941, but received contraband worth 80 million. Those who could afford it – those with businesses, jobs, savings or possessions to sell – obtained nutritionally better food. The poor, unemployed, orphans, refugees and the elderly relied on thin soup.[18]

Between 1940 and 1942, over 80,000 people, 10,000 of them children, died from disease and maltreatment at the hands of the Germans. Bernard Goldstein wrote that 'sick children lay, half dead, almost naked, swollen from hunger, with running sores, parchment-like skin, comatose eyes, breathing heavily with a rattle in their throats ... Yellow and gaunt, whimpering in their weakness, "A piece of bread ... A piece of bread ..."'[19]

How to Kill a City, Part 2: Bombs

Soon after the city fell, Hitler visited Warsaw. He toured the bombed ruins with a group of foreign correspondents. 'Gentlemen,' he said to them, 'you have seen for yourselves what criminal folly it was to try to defend this city ... I only wish that certain statesmen in other countries who seem to want to turn all of Europe into a second Warsaw could have the opportunity to see, as you have, the real meaning of war.'[20]

Western Europe experienced the urban inferno from 1940. The centre of Rotterdam was devastated on 14 May. When the Germans threatened to mete out the same punishment on Utrecht, the Netherlands surrendered. The next day British bombers attacked German military targets in the Rhineland. They went on to bomb targets in Hamburg, Bremen, Essen and other north German cities.

In reality, the damage done to Warsaw had been caused by artillery as much as aerial attack. The British bombing campaign against German industrial and military infrastructure had been woefully inadequate. The Luftwaffe had been designed to support military ground operations, not destroy cities. The Royal Air Force was focused on defence. Nonetheless, the British raids on German cities, although desultory in 1940, caused millions to flee underground in terror. On the night of 25 August, ninety-five aircraft bombed Berlin. Hitler was outraged: 'When they declare they will attack our cities in great measure, we will eradicate their cities. The hour will come when one of us will break – and it will not be National Socialist Germany.'[21]

The Luftwaffe's offensive against Britain began as the spearhead of an amphibious landing. When the possibility of ground operations receded, aerial bombardment of British cities became a strategic campaign, aimed at destroying industry, breaking civilian morale and forcing Britain to negotiate. London got it first: 13,685 tons of high explosives and 13,000 incendiary devices rained down on the capital in September and October 1940. Then cities in the Midlands and Merseyside were hit. The raid against Coventry (Operation Moonlight Sonata) was devastating: 503 tons of bombs, including 139 one-ton mines. The target was an industrial area that made aircraft engines and components; cloud and smoke obscured the target zone and the heavy bombs and incendiaries fell on residential areas, the city centre and the cathedral. The raid destroyed 4,300 homes and two-thirds of Coventry's buildings, killing 568 people.

The British counter-attack was even more ferocious. Air Marshal Sir Arthur Harris stated bluntly that the aim of the bombing offensive 'should be unambiguously stated … [as] the destruction of German cities, the killing of German workers, and disruption of civilised life throughout Germany'. Bombing should concentrate on the life-support mechanism of cities – the public utilities – and housing; it should create millions of homeless refugees and eviscerate German morale. So total was the envisaged destruction of cities that Harris and other strategists believed Germany would be knocked out of the war within months.[22]

By 1942 it was clear that bombing cities had not provided the knockout blow people had predicted. But many believed that was because the campaigns had not been effective enough. The war on cities escalated even as air raids failed to achieve the desired results. Bombing factories was not enough: Britain moved to a deliberate policy of flattening cities in order to reduce manpower and demoralise the people. In a typically vile wartime euphemism, the new policy was known as 'de-housing'.[23]

The test run for area-bombing was made on the ancient Hanseatic capital, Lübeck. But getting the same kind of results in a large metropolis was harder. The first 1,000-bomber raid unleashed was against Cologne in May, obliterating just 5.2% of the city's buildings. Attacks of the same magnitude on Essen and Bremen destroyed a mere eleven buildings in the former and 572 in the latter. But from March 1943, the British had enough heavy bombers, bigger bombs, improved navigation, and ways of baffling enemy radar operators to mount serious raids and area-bombings of German cities.

They also had the USAAF. Models of German streets were constructed at Porton Down in Wiltshire and at the Dugway Proving Ground, Utah, to simulate incendiary attacks and test the optimal conditions for firestorms. Research, technical improvements and statistical surveys investigated every possible means of honing the city-killing machine. More importantly, any moral qualms about indiscriminate slaughter of civilians and wholescale destruction of their urban habitat had eroded. In May and June 1943 vast bomber fleets wiped out 80% of the urban area of Barmen and 94% of Wuppertal and devastated Cologne once again.

The full demonstration of British urban bombing, however, came in July with Operation Gomorrah, targeting Germany's second city, Hamburg. The code name came from the Old Testament: 'Then the Lord rained brimstone and fire on Sodom and Gomorrah, from the Lord out of the heavens. Thus, He destroyed these cities and the entire plain, including all the inhabitants of the cities and everything that grew on the ground.'

Hot summer temperatures and low humidity made for the ideal conditions as far as the bombers were concerned. The incendiaries created enormous fires that merged together and sent a plume of hot air into the sky. The heat sucked in air at hurricane-force speeds from the surrounding areas, pushing temperatures up to 800°. So strong was this wind of death that it collapsed buildings, sucked oxygen out of packed air-raid shelters, uprooted trees and swept people into the inferno. By the end of the eight-day assault on the city, 37,000 had died, 900,000 evacuated and 61% of Hamburg's buildings were destroyed.

With every apparent successful bombing raid, officers such as Harris – further convinced by improved bombing technology – demanded escalation, claiming that more of the same would bring about 'inevitable' German surrender. By 1945 the huge air fleets were capable of pounding cities to lunar landscapes. Some 25,000 people were incinerated in Dresden on the night of 13/14 February and fifteen square miles immolated. The next day it was blind-bombed again. A few days later 83% of Pforzheim was burnt, killing 17,600; 89% of Würzburg went as well. As late as April, when the war was almost over, Potsdam was destroyed.

By the end of the war, 158 German cities had been heavily bombed. Some like Cologne, Munich and Berlin had been raided on numerous

Between 2002 and 2005 the Cheonggyecheon freeway was ripped out to reveal a long-buried stream. The green oasis in the heart of Seoul shows what can happen when cars are diverted from city centres.

One of the most striking results of greening a city: Rua Gonçalo de Carvalho in Porto Alegre, Brazil.

Left: Tomorrow's city today: Los Angeles set the pace for car-dominated suburbia and sprawl in the middle of the twentieth century.

Hyper-modernity and
street life in Tokyo.

One of the most successful megacities of the twentieth century, Tokyo was built up from the wreckage of the Second World War. Skyscrapers coexist with neighbourhood street life.

Once the murder capital of the world, Comuna 13 in the Colombian city of Medellin was transformed from a benighted slum by a series of far-sighted reforms.

A tale of two cities in Lagos: a surfer looks across at the building site which will become Eko Atlantic, a kind of African Dubai thick with gleaming skyscrapers, expensive hotels and luxury yachts.

powerful thermal currents that buffeted our plane severely, bringing with it the horrible smell of burning flesh.'[28]

In the most destructive air raid in history around 100,000 people were killed that night in Tokyo, many of them incinerated; 267,171 buildings were destroyed, sixteen square miles of city wiped out, and 1 million people made homeless. From then until June almost every Japanese city was assaulted with incendiaries.

The bombs fell on one of the most resilient urban cultures in history. In Tokyo, in particular, living on the edge of disaster was a way of life; before 1945 it had experienced repeated cycles of destruction and recovery, devastated as it was by regular fires, floods, typhoons and earthquakes. Woven into the urban culture was preparedness and the capacity to recover. Tokyo is also a city that has never had a strong tradition of urban planning, growing instead haphazardly neighbourhood by neighbourhood, building by building. After the fires that swept through Tokyo in the nineteenth century, districts were rebuilt by their residents. The same was true after the 7.9-magnitude Great Kantō Earthquake of 1 September 1923 which killed 143,000 and destroyed the greater part of the city. At the time of the earthquake Tokyo had 452 voluntary, self-organised neighbourhood societies called chōnaikai, covering about half the city. When disaster struck, they provided the bedrock for recovery. After the earthquake chōnaikai were established across the whole of Tokyo.[29]

Rebuilding traditional wooden structures always happened with stunning speed after a disaster. Even after the cataclysmic firebombing of March 1945, the homeless survivors continued to inhabit the wreckage of their city, building hundreds of thousands of flimsy wooden structures, much as their forebears had done after Tokyo's periodic conflagrations. In the immediate aftermath, many people lived in subways, tunnels or holes in the ground; they turned the carcasses of trams and buses into homes. These people did not desert the city; they remained in its ruins and began the work of rebuilding.

In one flash of apocalyptic light at 8.15 a.m. on 6 August 1945, sixty-four kilograms of uranium detonated above Hiroshima releasing the equivalent of sixteen kilotons of TNT. The heat, 4,000°C, caused buildings in the hypocentre to spontaneously combust and eviscerated thousands. The shock wave erupted at a speed of two miles per second, flattening buildings in its path; gamma rays and 'black rain' spread radiation even further. The blast and shock wave wiped out everything within a two-kilometre radius, killing 80,000 out of 420,000 people; a further 60,000 died from injuries and radiation poisoning by the end of the year. Thousands would suffer from wounds and psychological trauma for the rest of their lives. The area around ground zero was turned into a scorched wilderness, 'an atomic desert'.

But the city was not dead, despite the destruction of 70% of its buildings. Even amid the horror of what had been visited on Hiroshima, hospitals were set up in schools and warehouses within hours, and emergency food supplies organised. As the fires raged, girls from the high school helped tear down buildings to create firebreaks. On the day of the attack, Tetsuro Mukai was working in the head-quarters of the electric power company, about 700 metres from the hypocentre. He survived and spent the day fighting the fires at the power station. 'Looking back now [in 2015], it wouldn't have been difficult to escape the situation,' he remembered. 'But I stayed because I was driven by a sense of duty to see electricity restored to the city.' The next day power was back on in some areas. Despite suffering radiation sickness, Mukai helped raise telegraph poles throughout the devastated area. Within a week and a half 30% of homes had electricity and by November it extended across the entire city. Kuro Horino, a fifty-one-year-old engineer in the Water Supply Division, managed to repair the city's water pumps on the afternoon of the explosion, despite suffering from severe burns.[30]

As a result of the extraordinary efforts of Hiroshima's citizens, a semblance of normal life began to appear alongside basic services. A radio station began broadcasting from the suburbs the day after the attack. The Bank of Japan reopened within two days. An unofficial market began trading on the south side of Hiroshima Station. Schools resumed teaching children, many of them bald from radiation sick-ness, in warehouses or in the streets. Just as important was establishing links with relatives outside the city. Five days after the A-bomb, a temporary post office was set up and postal workers walked through the debris, using their memory to locate destroyed houses. As soon as they could, people began building makeshift huts in and around ground zero. Knowing the critical importance of communication, postal workers brought letters to people in their address-less temporary homes. Postboxes began to appear. 'Those red postboxes standing in the ruins were like a symbol of a peaceful life,' remembered a postman decades later.[31]

It is a cliché of writing about cities to quote the tribune Sicinius in Shakespeare's *Coriolanus*: 'What is the city but the people?' Its true meaning only becomes apparent in the history of the Second World War. The resilience exhibited in Hiroshima was part of a global phenomenon, one that revealed the incredible strengths, often ignored or underestimated, that large-scale human settlements possess.

How to Kill a City, Part 3: Total War

Hitler recognised the limitations of aerial bombardment. But he had other more terrifying methods of destroying cities. Capturing a great metropolis often means the war is won. What you do afterwards is another matter. In regard to cities like Paris, Brussels or London, Hitler did not want to unleash total destruction: 'In the end victor or vanquished, we shall all be buried in the same ruins.' But total war and wars of annihilation are different.[32]

'The city of Sennacherib, son of Sargon, offspring of a house slave, conqueror of Babylon, plunderer of Babylonia, its roots I shall pluck out of the foundations of the land I shall obliterate.' These were the chill words of King Nabopolassar of Babylon, ordering the complete destruction of Nineveh in 612 BC. *Delenda est Carthago*: Carthage must be destroyed. In its conquest for imperial control over the Mediterranean, Rome knew it must wipe its rival, Carthage, off the face of the earth. After a three-year siege, in 146 BC, the Roman general Scipio Africanus systematically demolished the great metropolis of the ancient world. Fires raged for seventeen days, leaving ashes a metre deep. The place was deserted: 140,000 women and children had been evacuated; 150,000 died in the siege and the survivors – 55,000 – were sold into slavery. The site of the city was sown with salt and a plough was symbolically drawn over the bare ground: all that was urban had become rural. Every single record of the city's existence was eliminated.

Cities are so resilient that a conqueror must obliterate every part of its life-support system. Nothing can remain, least of all its memories. The then second-largest city in the world, Vijayanagara in southern India, was burnt to the ground by its enemies in 1565. The Thai metropolis Phra Nakhon Si Ayutthaya, which flourished in the seventeenth century and grew to one of the biggest cities on the planet with a million people, joined the list of vanished cities when it was demolished by the Burmese in 1767.

In June 1941 Hitler launched Operation Barbarossa, the largest military operation in history. Once complete, Germany would seize the agricultural resources of the Soviet Union and use the bounty to feed its people. Deprived of food supplies, the Germans estimated that 30 million people in the Soviet Union would die. The Russian urban population had grown by 30 million between the First World War and 1939. By using Russian lands as a food and fuel source, therefore, Germany would knock Russia back into its pre-urban past by wiping out its 'superfluous' population. In the place of ruined Soviet metropolises would come German colonial cities surrounded by productive fields, the Aryan 'Garden of Eden'.

The Wehrmacht had three points of attack: Leningrad, Moscow and Ukraine. The invasion began in June; by autumn Army Group North had encircled Leningrad, and Army Group South was triumphant in Ukraine. The flanks of the main attack secure, the 1.9 million men, 1,000 tanks and 1,390 aircraft of Army Group Centre could advance east to inflict the decisive blow on Moscow. Some 70,000–80,000 citizens of Kharkov starved to death, a grim foretaste of what the Nazis intended to happen to countless cities in their new empire. There, and in countless other towns and cities, the Jewish populations were rounded up and shot or methodically exterminated in gas vans, known to the Soviets as 'Soul Destroyers'. After the capture of Minsk 20,000 Jews were murdered and another 100,000 forced into a newly created ghetto. Like Warsaw, Hitler had plans to level the Byelorussian capital and build a new city called 'Asgard' for the German elite. In Norse mythology Asgard was the celestial city of the gods.

Expecting a direct attack, the citizens of Leningrad dug huge defensive works around their city. But the Germans had other plans: the city was to be besieged and starved into submission. Following the defeat of the Soviet Union, Hitler said, 'there can be no interest in the continued existence of this large urban centre'. No quarter should be given, no surrender allowed, because Nazi Germany should not have to deal with relocating and feeding homeless city people: 'we can have no interest in maintaining even a part of this very large urban population'. The great metropolis and its people, Hitler said, 'must vanish from the earth's surface'. The Germans expected a quick victory. The aim was 'to level Moscow and Leningrad and make them uninhabitable'.[33]

Hitler's command was that no German would die storming Leningrad in pointless street fighting. Victory would come by acting like a boa constrictor: by strangling the city to death. Only dribbles of food could come into Leningrad by boat across Lake Ladoga or by parachute. The city's food warehouses, power stations and water-works were destroyed. Three million people were sealed in Leningrad awaiting death as the winter approached. 'We have returned to prehis-toric times,' wrote Elena Skryabina from inside Leningrad. 'Life has been reduced to one thing – the hunt for food.'[34]

Nerves were shredded by the constant bombardments from artillery and bomber planes. Leningraders ate cats, pigeons, crows, gulls and then pets and zoo animals; wallpaper was boiled to extract the paste, and shoe leather and Vaseline were eaten. Soup and bread made from grass went on sale. 'When you walk out of your house in the morning, you bump into dead bodies,' Skryabina wrote in her diary. 'They are every-where: on the streets, in the courtyards. The bodies lie for a long time. There is nobody to pick them up.' Scurvy gripped the population; people became frenzied in their hunt for scraps of food. Flour dust was scraped from the walls and floorboards of mills. Cotton-seed cakes, usually burnt in ship's furnaces, were used to make bread. Sheep guts and calf skins were boiled down to make 'meat jelly'. In October the bread ration was cut to 250 grams a day for workers and 125 for everyone else.[35]

Deprived of food supplies, electricity and fuel, Leningrad went from being a functioning city to a deadly trap within weeks. Leningraders likened themselves to starved wolves, preoccupied with the thought of survival and indifferent to everything else that was going on around them. People lost interest in family life, in sex, even in the bombs that rained down every day; they became suspicious of others. With no schools open, few jobs to go to and little in the way of entertainment, life became a monotony of queuing for bread and water and scavenging for food. In December the first instances of cannibalism were reported. Corpses were discovered with lumps of flesh hacked out. Within a year, 2,015 people had been arrested for 'the use of human meat for food', as the police called it.[36]

While Leningrad starved in the autumn and early winter of 1941, Army Group Centre began Operation Typhoon, its all-out assault on the Russian capital. Moscow panicked, expecting a bloody battle or Stalin's abandonment of the city. As the air raids began and the panzer divisions rolled onward, officials burnt documents in great bonfires, refugees inundated railway stations, and law and order began to break down on the streets. Stalin ordered the evacuation of the Communist Party and the government to Kuibyshev; he was about to follow. His belongings were packed; trains and planes were on standby; the Kremlin was eerily empty.

Then on 19 October Stalin made one of the most fateful decisions of the war. He announced he was going to stay; Moscow would be held at all costs. In a feat of logistics, 400,000 fresh troops, 1,500 planes and 1,700 tanks were rushed almost 4,000 miles from the Far East to Moscow. With the Germans closing in on the metropolis and air raids causing widespread damage, the annual military parade on Red Square was held on 7 November – a show of considerable bravado that was filmed and shown around the Soviet Union.

In the intense cold of the winter of 1941/2, Hitler's military machine ground to a halt outside Moscow. On 5 December the Russians began their counteroffensive. Within a month Hitler's mighty Wehrmacht had been pushed back 150 miles from the capital of communism. Although Moscow remained in peril, Barbarossa was over. In this deadly struggle for a city, 7 million men were involved for six hellish months. If Tsar Alexander I had sacrificed the built fabric of Moscow to save the city from Napoleon, Stalin sacrificed 926,000 lives. Like other would-be conquerors throughout history, Hitler impaled himself on a city.

Meanwhile in Leningrad, temperatures sank to -30° in the coldest winter of the twentieth century. Weakened by malnourishment, freezing conditions and the piling up of human ordure, people succumbed to dysentery. Others simply starved to death. By February 1942, the worst month of the siege, 20,000 people were dying every day. Orphaned children were surviving in a liminal world of bombed-out buildings. But winter also brought some relief. When Lake Ladoga froze sufficiently in January, the 'Road of Life' opened, a six-lane ice highway that ran the German blockade. Lorries brought in food and evacuated half a million people, mainly children, women and the elderly, before April.

Although the siege, with its continual bombardments and subsistence food levels, lasted until January 1944, the worst was over. By the end of 1942 the population of Leningrad had fallen from 3 million to 637,000, giving the ruined city the feeling of a ghost town. Over three-quarters of the population were women by then, employed in munitions factories and shipyards. Deaths from bombardment, disease and starvation amounted to at least a million; 1.4 million were evacuated. The numbers of Axis and Russian combatants and the civilians of Leningrad who died in the apocalyptic struggle for the metropolis far exceeded the total number of people killed in air raids across the entire world.

For an army, a city determined to resist to the last man, woman and child is perhaps the most formidable obstacle in the world, a vortex of destruction. Cities can chew up entire armies. They are the graveyards of military ambitions. Napoleon foundered in Moscow in 1812 and in Leipzig a year later. Hitler was defied in Leningrad, Moscow and, most disastrously, Stalingrad.

By 1942 the Wehrmacht was in desperate need of fuel. Capturing the oilfields of the Caucasus, Operation Case Blue, was essential if Germany was to win the war. Taking the unlovely industrial southern city of Stalingrad, however, was secondary to that target. But once again, Hitler was obsessed with razing a symbolically significant Russian city, diverting vital oil and aircraft away from the Caucasus to the campaign against Stalingrad. Many Russian cities and towns had surrendered or been abandoned in the face of Blitzkrieg. But Stalin would not yield any inch of the city named in his honour.

The German 6th Army under Friedrich Paulus reached Stalingrad in late August 1942. On the 23rd and for a further five days the air fleet Luftflotte IV subjected Stalingrad and its 400,000 residents to heavy attack, reducing the industrial city to an urban wasteland.

This terrain of ruins and rubble became one of the most pivotal battlefields in history. What usually gave the Wehrmacht their superiority – devastatingly fast attacks and manoeuvrability – was denied them in urban warfare. Blitzkrieg descended into what German soldiers called *Rattenkrieg* – rat war. Every inch of street, every mound of rubble, every building and room in it had to be contested in close-range combat. Fighting took place in sewers; the Wehrmacht and the

Red Army battled for ruined, roofless buildings floor by floor. In some places the front line was a corridor between rooms. The carcasses of tractor factories and grain elevators became battlefields within a battle-field. According to Stalin's Order No. 227, the defenders and civilians of Stalingrad were mandated to take 'not one step back'. A Soviet platoon under the command of Sergeant Yakov Pavlov fortified and defended a bombed-out four-storey apartment building for sixty days against repeated German attacks. Vasily Chuikov, commander of the Russian forces in Stalingrad, joked that the Germans lost more men trying to take 'Pavlov's House' than they had capturing Paris.

'Approaching this place, soldiers used to say: "We are entering hell." And after spending one or two days here, they said: "No, this isn't hell, this is ten times worse than hell."' Many of the snipers, tank drivers, soldiers and civilians defending Stalingrad and fighting through the man-made ravines, caves and canyons were women; they endured one of the most terrible of all battles. NKVD detachments blocked the outskirts of the city, shooting deserters from the Armageddon of Stalingrad. The Germans hammered through the city, house by house, until most of Stalingrad was in their hands by mid-November, with only pockets of Russian resistance. At that point, before the Germans could claim possession of the city, the Soviets unleashed Operation Uranus, their massive counter-attack that encircled Stalingrad.[37]

The German 6th Army – 270,000 men – were trapped inside. Back in September Hitler had vowed never to leave Stalingrad. General Paulus was forbidden either to try and break out or to surrender. Food was airlifted into the city for a bit. But by late December the German forces in the Caucasus and Russia were in full retreat, leaving the 6th Army to hold out. With dwindling stocks of food and ammunition, the Germans faced a renewed bout of urban warfare. They experienced what the citizens of Leningrad and the Warsaw ghetto had suffered at the hands of the Germans: starvation and ravaging disease. On 31 January 1943, what remained of the 6th Army surrendered.

The self-proclaimed destroyer of cities, Hitler was destroyed by cities. During the Second World War 1,710 Russian towns and cities and 70,000 villages were smashed to rubble. As the Red Army pushed the Germans back westwards in 1943 and 1944, more violence was meted out on cities and civilians. During the great Russian offensive in 1944 – Operation Bagration – an enormous Russian army took the

German Army Group Centre in Byelorussia completely by surprise. First the city of Vitebsk was attacked and encircled by the Red Army. The German units in the city wanted to retreat. Hitler reacted furiously. Vitebsk was one of several *Fester Platz*, fortified cities that would be held at all costs, down to the last man, to delay the Russian offensive. But rather than hold up the attack, these cities became deadly traps for the beleaguered and outnumbered Germans. Encircled by Russian tanks and infantry, bombed by planes, the smaller German forces stood no chance. The 3rd Panzer Army was destroyed at Vitebsk. At the fortress cities of Orsha and Mogilev, thousands of Germans were taken prisoner or killed. After air raids and brief, futile street fights, 70,000 Germans were taken prisoner at Babruysk and another 100,000 when Minsk – so recently designated as the future Nazi 'city of the gods' – was attacked and captured.[38]

Hitler's insane idea of making his soldiers stand and fight in fortified cities led to half a million casualties and the capture of 150,000 men, including twelve generals, in a mere two weeks. By the end of the war, 209 Byelorussian towns and cities, out of 270 in the country, had been wholly or partly destroyed. As the Soviets advanced into Lithuania and Poland, the same fate awaited yet more cities – such as Vilnius, Białystok, Lublin and Königsberg – designated by Hitler as 'fortresses'; their civilians and garrisons faced slaughter, imprisonment, homelessness, privation and rape as they were forced into the disintegrating front line.

Facing the inevitability of defeat as the Red Army progressed towards Berlin, Hitler was prepared to unleash the apocalypse on urban Europe, making every city a battlefield. On Christmas Eve 1944 Budapest joined the list of cities sacrificed and ruined by Hitler when it came under siege from the Red Army. Thousands of towns and cities lay smouldering between Stalingrad and Berlin.

How to Kill a City, Part 4: Genocide, Deportation, Pillage and Demolition

The atomic-bomb-scorched earth of Hiroshima was supposed to be incapable of supporting plant life for seventy-five years. The survival of giant camphor trees and the flowering of oleanders symbolised the persistence of life. Human life too always seemed to reassert itself, even in the face of apocalypse. In Stalingrad, the city's inhabitants returned to live in basements below the rubble as soon as the Germans surrendered.

In Warsaw, for much of the war citizens faced not bombs but an apparatus of terror that undermined the very thing that kept war-ravaged and bombed cities together – civic spirit and solidarity. Warsaw was slated for destruction by the Nazis; but only once the last drops of energy could be wrung out of its population producing munitions and materiel for the Eastern Front.

Yet even in these circumstances, a secret Warsaw existed in parallel to the Nazi-controlled Warsaw. When the Nazis banned universities, the underground University of Western Lands was founded, with 250 teachers who awarded 2,000 degrees at the risk of their lives. Teachers illegally taught thousands of secondary-school pupils; those adults who were caught were sent to Auschwitz and the children to factories in Germany. Newspapers were printed and radio stations broadcast from secret basements. Clandestine theatre, poetry readings, political debates and literary meetings kept alive Poland's culture and the soul of the city. People relished travelling by tram, for it was there that jokes and rumours were whispered between passengers. 'The streetcar sympathised with us', remembered one Varsovian, 'and shared our hate and disdain.' For a few brave people there was the solace of planning armed resistance.[39]

Urban life reasserted itself, with all its vices and virtues, even in the misery and squalor of the Warsaw ghetto. It was, after all, a city of 400,000 residents. The foulness, indignity and fear made many people incarcerated there more determined than ever to live with purpose and decency. The municipal council organised waste disposal, utilities, postal services, healthcare, labour, trade and policing, levying taxes to pay for it. Numerous charities provided food and welfare for the poorest members of the community; around 2,000 tenement and house committees organised childcare and oversaw sanitation. As well as the illegal schools, there were clinics, orphanages, libraries, soup kitchens, day-care centres, vocational training schemes and gymnasia. At one point the ghetto had forty-seven underground newspapers. Politics also survived, with active left-wing Zionist youth groups and trades unions operating clandestinely. They were to evolve into armed resistance movements.[40]

Entrepreneurs founded businesses catering to the needs of the city. A specially created sandy 'beach' where you could sunbathe in swimming costume cost two zlotys to enter. The rich ate well in cafés and restaurants and wore fashionable clothes made by tailors and dressmakers. Impresarios thrived: the ghetto had a full symphony orchestra which played at the Melody House, and several theatres in which 300 professional actors, musicians and singers performed. As one ghetto resident put it, 'Every dance is a protest against our oppressors.'[41]

Under the intense pressure of ghettoisation, the extremes of urban life were magnified in the city within a city. According to one survivor, 'no city in the world had as many beautiful and elegant women serving in cafés as did the short-lived ghetto, with its Cafés des Arts, Splendide, Negresco, etc. But right in front of these display windows, hordes of wretched beggars would pass, often collapsing from inanition.' Crime and prostitution proliferated; there was rampant inequality, profiteering and exploitation. The council and the police had to deal with the Nazis, straining community relations even further. And while many tried to maintain urban life, the constant influx of deportees from all over Europe exacerbated the hunger and intensified slum conditions.[42]

In meetings held between 7 and 18 December 1941, Hitler made it clear that the Jews would be punished for the war. The Final Solution would be visited on European Jewry. In early 1942 conditions in the Warsaw ghetto were deteriorating fast, with 39,719 dying from starvation and disease in the first six months of the year. On 21 July an edict arrived ordering the evacuation of all Jews, except those employed by the Germans or who were fit to work. The next day, on the fast of Tisha B'Av, 7,200 Jews were taken to the *Umschlagplatz* holding station. Over the next eight weeks, the Germans sealed off designated sections of the ghetto every day and rounded up between 5,000 and 10,000 in these blocks.

'The ghetto has been turned into an inferno,' Chaim Kaplan wrote in his diary as the vast prison city was systematically liquidated over the summer of 1942. 'Men have become beasts.' The Jewish Ghetto Police, charged with fulfilling the German evacuation quotas, were forced to fight their fellow Jews and root them out of hiding places in order to remove them to the *Umschlagplatz*. People scrambled over roofs and walls to escape; they begged, bribed and bargained; women offered their bodies in order to be spared. Those who remained looted the ghetto. The will to survive became a personal battle in which ties of community, faith, friendship and family broke down. Some members of the police, sickened by what they had to do, deserted or committed suicide. By the middle of September, 254,000 people had been removed to the *Umschlagplatz*. From there, every day, they were taken to the Treblinka death camp and slaughtered.[43]

The 36,000 Jews who remained in Warsaw as slave labourers after the removals inhabited a ghost town. Many of their wives, children, family members and friends had been wrenched away to Treblinka. They suffered agonies of guilt and shame. The population of an entire city had been destroyed by a handful of Germans and their coerced Jewish police helpers within a matter of weeks. The only thing to do was to resist. The survivors began hoarding food. The Żydowska Organizacja Bojowa (Jewish Combat Organisation) and Żydowski Związek Wojskowy (Jewish Military Union) built bunkers and fighting posts equipped with gas, electricity and toilets. They smuggled in weapons and made Molotov cocktails. When the next, final round of deportations began in January 1943, the SS unexpectedly found themselves in a guerrilla warzone. They retreated.[44]

The resistance fighters knew they would die; they wanted, however, to choose the manner of their death and rescue the honour of the Jewish people. Some Jews managed to slip out and seek refuge as best they could in the Polish city. The SS were back in force on 19 April, reinforced with tanks, armoured cars and light cannon. Only by destroying the ghetto block by block with flamethrowers, blowing up basements and sewers, and dropping smoke bombs into bunkers, were the Germans able to subdue the revolt. Even so, the fierce guerrilla resistance of the 'bunker wars' lasted a month.

By the end, the Germans had removed 53,667 Jews, the majority shipped to Majdanek and Treblinka. The entire ghetto was a ruin of rubble. A concentration camp was built on the wreckage, and new groups of Jews brought in from elsewhere in Europe compelled to clear tens of millions of bricks until any trace of the city within a city was no more.

A year after the ghetto rose up against the Germans, the rest of Warsaw rebelled. The circumstances were entirely different. With the

Red Army approaching the city after the stunning successes of Operation Bagration, the Polish leadership felt it had to claim its stake in its country's future before it fell under Soviet domination.

Lightly armed and wielding Molotov cocktails, Polish resistance fighters rose up at 5 p.m. on 1 August 1944. 'Within fifteen minutes our city, one million strong, had joined the fight,' wrote Tadeusz Bór-Komorowski, commander of the Polish Home Army. Much of Warsaw was in Polish hands for the first time in almost five years. Loudspeakers, so long used to batter Varsovians with propaganda, threats and orders, played the Polish national anthem, which people had not heard since 1939. The Polish flag flew high on the Prudential Building, Europe's third-tallest skyscraper. The mood was euphoric. Men, women and children of all ages rushed to help build barricades, make Molotov cocktails and dig tunnels between buildings.[45]

When Hitler was told of the uprising his whole body trembled as he raised his fists in anger. 'He was almost screaming, his eyes seemed about to pop out of his head and the veins stood out on his temples.' But Himmler calmed him down: the uprising was a 'blessing'. 'After five, six weeks we shall leave,' Himmler said. 'But by then Warsaw ... will be extinguished.' At first Hitler wanted to remove German forces, encircle the city and bomb it to dust. But that was militarily unfeasible. Instead Hitler and Himmler issued their Order for Warsaw on 1 August: 'Every citizen of Warsaw is to be killed including men, women and children. Warsaw has to be levelled to the ground in order to set a terrifying example to the rest of Europe.'[46]

What happened next was the systematic destruction of an entire city.

The reconquest and destruction of Warsaw was under the command of SS Obergruppenführer Erich von dem Bach-Zelewski, a man who had overseen the mass murder of Jews during Operation Barbarossa and genocidal operations against partisans. Himmler sent him a collection of the most feared and bloodstained SS units from all over the Reich. Among them were the troops led by Oscar Dirlewanger, made up of dangerous prisoners released from German jails, soldiers considered too deranged for the regular army, deserters from the Red Army, Azerbaijanis and Muslim fighters from the Caucasus. The Dirlewanger Brigade had looted, raped, tortured and slaughtered its way through eastern Europe, massacring Jews, suspected partisans and innocent women and children in stomach-churning numbers.[47]

These rapists and mass-murderers were unleashed on the Wola district of Warsaw on 5 August with orders to kill and destroy everyone and everything in their path. Apartment buildings were surrounded. Then hand grenades were thrown in and the buildings set on fire. The men, women and children who emerged were machine-gunned. This was repeated one building at time. But it took too long. Tactics changed, so that crowds of civilians were taken to execution sites in factories, tram depots and railway viaducts, where they were gunned down on en masse.

The *modus operandi* of the Dirlewanger Brigade was to rape before they killed; they thought nothing of massacring children. By the time the Germans took Wolwa the SS had killed 40,000 Poles. At the same time, the equally genocidal Russian People's Liberation Army (RONA), a ragtag brigade of anti-Bolshevik Russians who served with the Germans, were inflicting similar gruesome scenes in the Ochota district. At Marie Curie's Radium Institute, drunken RONA thugs raped staff and patients alike, including terminally ill cancer victims, before dousing them in petrol and setting them alight. They moved on to other hospitals. Hitler's and Himmler's orders were being followed: first the citizens of Warsaw were murdered, then their buildings were destroyed. Indiscriminate slaughter eventually stopped, however. Nazi leaders decided they wanted the city's entire population as slave labourers. Now columns of citizens were marched out of their districts and sent to concentration camps.[48]

Out went the Dirlewanger Brigade and RONA. In came some of the most devastating military equipment deployed on the streets of a city. The narrow streets of Warsaw's Old Town were too narrow for ordinary tanks. Thousands of Poles were holed up there, seemingly impregnable in a fortress of buildings and alleys. On Hitler's orders a deadly arsenal of weaponry was dispatched from far and wide to help in the elimination of Warsaw. The military value of subduing the Warsaw Uprising was slight. But Hitler was on a messianic crusade to level the metropolis at all costs. His best equipment was withdrawn from the front and sent to wreak carnage.

These weapons had been specifically designed after Stalingrad for urban warfare. In came four supersized Karl-Gerät mortars, some of the biggest siege weapons in history, which fired 1,577-kg shells capable of destroying an entire building. An enormous armoured train arrived to bombard the Old Town. They were joined by fixed rocket launchers and an array of heavy howitzers. The latest mobile assault weapons were also rushed to Warsaw: ten Sturmpanzer IVs armed with short-range howitzers; two gigantic Sturmtigers armed with rocket launchers; and ninety remote-controlled Goliath tanks that could smash down walls. The most terrifying weapon, however, was the Nebelwerfer six-barrel rocket launchers, capable of firing numerous incendiary bombs in swift succession. The Poles called them *krowy*, cows, because they sounded like a herd bellowing in agony. This, the full might of Nazi siege technology, was used to destroy Warsaw building by building. The artillery and Stuka dive bombers ground the Old Town to rubble. Then in came the Goliaths to remove barricades and pull down the remaining walls. After them came Sturmtigers, followed by infantry and flamethrowers. After lastly, the Dirlewanger Brigade and other SS units.

The Poles fought valiantly, threatening the Germans with another Stalingrad. But no one could defy the German superguns. The entire Old Town was devastated, with 30,000 buried under millions of bricks. Many Poles fled through the sewers. But thousands remained, and faced the genocidal rapists of the Dirlewanger Brigade.

After that the Stukas and superguns were turned on the central city, where 250,000 Poles were forced into basements. Outside, buildings were destroyed 'from the top down, chunk by chunk or blown to smithereens by one direct hit'. Still the resistance fought on, engaged in some of the fiercest fighting of the entire war. For sixty-three days the Germans struggled to regain the city. Finally, on 2 October, when it was clear the Red Army was not coming to their rescue, the Polish capitulated. As they emerged from their bunkers, Varsovians took a last look at their city: 'It was a terrible sight, with huge burned-out blocks ... in front of me was an unbelievable sight, an endless line of people with luggage and other strange things like bicycles and prams.'[49]

At the beginning of the uprising there were more than 700,000 people left living in Warsaw. Civilian deaths in the uprising accounted for 150,000. Of the survivors, 55,000 were transferred to Auschwitz and other concentration camps; 150,000 went as slaves to the Reich; 17,000 were imprisoned as POWs; and 350,000 were dispatched elsewhere in Poland. According to the novelist Zofia Nałkowska, Warsaw became 'one of the many dead cities of history', its people the 'new down-and-outs'.[50]

'The city must completely disappear from the surface of the earth,' ordered Himmler. 'No stone can remain standing. Every building must be razed to its foundation.' All that could be stripped from the city was loaded onto over 40,000 railway carriages and sent to Germany. Everything was taken, from treasures and artwork to rope, paper, candles and scraps of metal. Then the specialist demolition crews called *Verbrennungskommandos* (annihilation commandos) moved in. What remained of the city was destroyed methodically. Sappers set buildings on fire with flamethrowers and dynamite; tanks opened fire on empty structures. The Krasiński Palace, the Załuski Library, the National Archives, the National Museum, the University of Warsaw, the Royal Castle, palaces, churches, monuments, hospitals, apartment blocks, schools – everything was erased. By January 93% of the city was no more.[51]

Only by resorting to genocide, mass deportation and total demolition could a city be destroyed. But even so, was Warsaw really dead?

*

When Soviet troops arrived in Warsaw on 17 January 1945 they entered 'a phantom city'. 'I have seen many towns destroyed,' said General Eisenhower, 'but nowhere have I been faced with such extent of destruction executed with such bestiality.'[52]

The war against Nazi Germany climaxed in the *Götterdämmerung* of urban warfare in April as the Red Army fought, pillaged and raped house by house through Berlin, already wrecked by sustained Allied air raids and Russian artillery. On 30 April the Russians captured the Reichstag. That night Hitler killed himself in his bunker. On 2/3 May the Germans surrendered. 'A full moon shone from a cloudless sky', wrote a Red Cross representative, 'so you could see the awful extent of the damage. A ghost town of cave-dwellers was all that was left of this world metropolis.'

The belief before the war was that cities were fragile things, vulnerable to modern weapons. Anyone surveying the stark burnt-out buildings and mounds of rubble in cities the length and breadth of continental Europe in May 1945 might fairly ask how the damage could ever be repaired. Berlin lay under 55 million cubic metres of rubble; Hamburg under 35 million. But the story of the Second World War is the story of the incredible resilience of cities, even in the most extreme circumstances.

The fate meted out to Warsaw was beyond anything that any city had experienced in modern war. If Berlin looked like a post-apocalyptic city, the capital of Poland had experienced damage on a different magnitude. It lay entombed under 700 million cubic metres of rubble. Some 81% of Berlin was destroyed; but of this, 11% of buildings were obliterated and 70% damaged. In Warsaw, by contrast, over 80% of its buildings had been completely eradicated.[53]

Yet even in the midst of total destruction, traces of life remained. While the *Verbrennungskommandos* demolished the city's buildings, small groups of Jews and Poles burrowed deep under the ruins in concealed bunkers and sewers. They were known as 'Robinson Crusoes', 'Cavemen', and, by the Germans who hunted them down, 'Rats'. One group even produced a magazine with a spoof advertisement for tourists: 'Why go to Egypt to see the pyramids – there are so many ruins in Warsaw.'[54] The 'Robinsons' lived in what one survivor, Helena Midler, called 'the city of eternal night', hidden beneath an urban wasteland, where any food or water had to be scavenged at the risk of death. Many starved, froze to death or were discovered and shot by the Germans. When Warsaw was liberated by the Russians, these few people emerged into the light.

The pianist Władysław Szpilman described entering streets that had once teemed with people and traffic. Now it was a sea of bricks, and he had to climb over mountains of rubble 'as if they were scree slopes. My feet became entangled in a confused mess of ripped telephone wires and tramlines, and scraps of fabric that had once decorated flats or clothed human beings, long since dead.'[55]

When the Russian war correspondent Vasily Grossman arrived in Warsaw on 17 January, so bad was the damage that he had to clamber in by an improvised route: 'It was the first time in my life that I've used a fire ladder to enter a city.' He was followed over the scree slopes: 'A file of old and young men in crumpled hats, berets, autumn coats or macintoshes were walking and pushing in front of them little pushcarts with thick tyres loaded with bundles, bags and suitcases. Girls and young women were walking, blowing on their frozen fingers,

and looking at the ruins with sorrow filled eyes. There were already
hundreds and thousands of them.'[56]

The people of Warsaw were back in their city the very first moment
they could after the Nazis were pushed out. At first they camped amid
the desolation. But their presence meant that the most extreme
modern example of city-murder had failed.

The influx of returnees breathed oxygen into the dying embers of
Warsaw. They kick-started the reconstruction of the city on their own,
rebuilding houses in the centre. They arrived as a debate raged about
the future of the ruins. Opinion in the government was divided. Some
wanted to abandon Warsaw and move the capital to Krakow or Łódź,
leaving its forlorn wreckage to be preserved as a lasting monument
to the crimes committed against Poland. Others believed it should be
reconstructed as it was before September 1939, both as an act of defiance against the Nazis and as a way of restoring the cherished and
familiar to those traumatised Varsovians who had survived the war.
For a handful of town planners and architects, such as Jan Chmielewski,
newly escaped from a concentration camp, the sight of destroyed
Warsaw came not as a horrible shock but as 'relief': here was a golden
chance to build a radical new city now that the irrational chaos of
the old metropolis had been obliterated.[57]

The dilemmas facing Warsaw were a version of those confronting
populations in other destroyed or partially destroyed cities – from
London to Tokyo, Minsk to Hamburg, Kiev to Coventry. Within days
of the liberation of Warsaw, the Biuro Odbudowy Stolicy (BOS, Office
for the Reconstruction of the Capital) was formed. If Warsaw's
annihilation was unprecedented in modern warfare, so too was the
scale and speed of the reconstruction of its historical monuments.
The effort of will was remarkable, given the comprehensive level of
destruction, the murder of 60% of Warsaw's pre-war population, and
the poverty of the country. Funds were set up and donations came
from all over Poland, as did labourers volunteering their services. By
1952 almost all of Warsaw's historic Old Town had been restored from
scratch.

No effort was spared in ensuring every detail was authentic.
Eighteenth-century paintings, drawings, documents, postcards, photographs – traces from all round the world were sought to help the
conservators of Poland's past. There was another source. Incredibly,

during the occupation a number of architects had secretly collated documents and made drawings of Warsaw's historic buildings in anticipation of its destruction. Risking death, these people had encoded the memories of the city so that it could never be killed, smuggling out and hiding in monasteries and POW camps the fragmentary records of the city and a vision of what it could be.[58]

Warsaw's Old Town is one of the world's supreme monuments to the resilience of cities and the reverence people hold to their built environment: while a city exists in scraps of smuggled drawings and in human memories it can never truly be destroyed. All over Europe something similar happened. In city after city, town centres were rebuilt as monuments to a time before barbarism and genocide. People's attachment to the old, to the familiar and historic is evident in hundreds of cities. Lübeck's Hanseatic glories were slowly and painstakingly restored in the city's core; in Frankfurt half-timbered houses replaced those which had been bombed.

'The Whole Nation Builds its Capital.' That was the slogan given to the incredible work of renovation. Nothing came close to the extent of Warsaw's reconstruction. But it was highly significant that the historical part of the city chosen to be memorialised was the baroque Old Town of the seventeenth and eighteenth centuries. Elsewhere, people who had started to reconstruct their homes and bring to life the pretty alleys that criss-crossed the city centre found they were slated for destruction again. In the place of these tenements came monumental new structures, designed to awe. The most famous is the skyscraper originally known as the Joseph Stalin Palace of Culture and Science, a gift from the Soviet Union. Modelled on Moscow's 'Seven Sisters' skyscrapers, but incorporating Polish design features, it rose out of the ruins of Warsaw as a visual statement of communist power. While work was underway on constructing such Soviet monstrosities, ordinary Varsovians lived in their shadows, in huts, ruined buildings and shanty towns.

With gargantuan symbols of communist power plonked in the centre, Warsaw resembled dozens of Stalinist cities. But Warsaw wanted to be different. Many of the leading lights of the BOS were left-wing modernists who, during the interwar period, had put Warsaw in the avant-garde of architectural radicalism. During the dark night of Nazi occupation, they went underground, awarding degrees and doctorates and secretly planning a new, modern metropolis that would emerge once the Germans had been expelled. After 1945 they wanted Warsaw to reclaim its place at the centre of Europe, as a cosmopolitan, progressive metropolis.

And, in a ruined city awaiting recovery, they had a lot of power – as did radical architects in cities across Europe. They saw the nineteenth-century city – with its tenements, alleys and boulevards – as a hideous jumble. Their radical urbanism would be the midwife of a new social world, more egalitarian and collective than anything that had gone before. Warsaw's planners wanted to construct large pioneering housing estates in place of the old-fashioned tenements and streets.

The head of the BOS believed that through architecture a 'new form of coexistence' would occur, a more democratic, equal society based on collectivist principles. Large housing estates, with their green spaces, schools, surgeries, shops and means of association, would forge self-sufficient working-class urban communities. For Polish architects 'life, work [and] recreation today, from cradle to the grave, evolves within architecture. Good architecture constantly teaches orderliness, logical and consequential thinking, develops imagination, without which no achievements are possible.' The modern city was to be one of concrete high-rise housing set in parks, office blocks and car parks; it would be criss-crossed by urban expressways and encircled by ring roads. According to the modernist architects Szymon and Helena Syrkus, designers of many of the initial post-war housing estates in Warsaw, the new form of mass metropolitan housing gave urbanised workers access to the basic pleasures of life: 'sun, greenery, and air'.[59]

In a few short years, the urban face of Europe was utterly trans-formed by the violence of war and the tide of idealism that succeeded it. As in Warsaw, much of what had not been destroyed in conflict was levelled by bulldozer. Areas labelled as 'slum' or 'blighted' were cleared and their communities relocated to hyper-modern housing. In France, thousands of *grands ensembles* – massive apartment blocks made of pre-cast reinforced concrete – were built on the outskirts of towns. In British cities, war was waged on 'the ugly, distorting mirror of humanity' evident in working-class inner-city areas, and on 'nine-teenth- and twentieth-century muddle and meanness' in favour of order, efficiency, spaciousness and self-sufficient urban communities embodied by the new multistorey concrete blocks, large estates and 'new towns' created outside cities. It felt like a revolution, exhilarating and full of possibility and optimism after the darkest hour of human history. In the late 1940s and 50s, cities were in the process of fast-moving radical reinvention during which, like Warsaw, selected areas were preserved as heritage while others, familiar neighbourhoods and historic streets, were swept away in the name of progress. According to the Belgian socialist architect Renaat Braem: 'This will be total war, with urbanism as a weapon to realise the liberating living framework.' For planners such as Braem, total war of 1939–45 would give way to 'total architecture' as a means of reorganising society along rational, scientific lines.[60]

Warsaw is the Phoenix City, one which keeps rising out of the ashes of destruction. There was, of course, a gaping hole in the culture of the city and cities throughout Europe: the entire Jewish population that had once made up a third of the population of Warsaw was gone. Of close to 400,000 Jewish citizens, no more than 5,000 made it back to the city after the war. That kind of damage was irreparable.

The history of Warsaw also reveals something else. If it owed its survival to anything it was the spirit of its people, those who resisted and those who returned to remake their city. City-dwellers all over the world showed this kind of determination, in different circumstances. Yet no sooner had the Poles escaped one tyranny than they got another. This new reality became manifest on the cityscape. While Varsovians showed their preference for the old, familiar city of streets, alleys and tenements, what they got was Stalinist monumentality and drab, grey concrete housing estates.

The striking contrast between the intimate streets of the restored baroque Old Town and the austere new developments made visible Poland's predicament, caught between Europe and the USSR. It was also an exaggerated example of what was going on throughout the world. In Germany, Britain and elsewhere there was real tension between people's desire to return to the familiar cityscape and the authorities' concept of what the modern city should be in the brave new post-war world. In the cold light of history, the uniformity and universalism of modernist architecture and its fervent desire to radically reshape society was an attack on the very idea of the city and on urbanity itself: the longing for order at war with the mess, chaos and individuality inherent in urban life.

In Tokyo, by contrast, with its strong traditions of self-reliance and neighbourhood organisation, reconstruction was left to a large degree in the hands of individuals. Most new development in residential areas was carried out by householders themselves, who utilised traditional construction methods, vernacular architecture and local constructors. The unplanned, incremental redevelopment of Tokyo laid the foundations for the city's rise from devastation to become the great global metropolis of the second half of the twentieth century. Informal settlements and high-density emergency shanty towns became the platform for urban growth, giving Tokyo its intoxicatingly dense and differentiated urban fabric. The contrast with cities elsewhere – particularly (but not exclusively) Warsaw, where authoritarianism and paternalism denied a role to individuals and urban micro-communities in deciding the future of their cities – is glaring.[61]

13

Sounds of the Suburbs

Los Angeles, 1945–99

Broken glass strewn everywhere, the stench of urine on communal stairwells, rat infestations and cockroaches, junkies wielding baseball bats in the alley. This is the urban inferno cast into life in 'The Message', a 1982 electro-rap single by Grandmaster Flash & the Furious Five. The protagonist would get out, leaving behind the incessant noise, noxious smells, gangs, police brutality, rapacious debt collectors and drugs that have pushed him to the edge of sanity; but he's got no choice because he has no money. 'The Message' was named the most influential hip-hop single of all time by *Rolling Stone* thirty years after it was released. It changed the direction of hip hop as it was emerging from the block parties of New York City and taking its place in the global mainstream.

The birth of hip hop is commonly agreed to have occurred at 1520 Sedgwick Avenue, in the Bronx, New York City, on 11 August 1973 when DJ Kool Herc was emceeing at a party in the building's recreation room. The unremarkable high-rise dating from 1967 sits in a cluster of high-rises wedged between two thundering freeways – Interstate 81 and the Cross Bronx Expressway. 'As I came up from the subway I saw a dreadful sight: a row of splendid redbrick apartment houses ... turned into an enormous mass of ruins. The facades were charred black, some of the upper walls had collapsed, the windows were smashed and the sidewalks were still strewn with debris. As I ... walked downhill for about half a mile east I saw a great panorama of recent ruins unfold before me.' This devastated cityscape had been deserted by 300,000 of its inhabitants.[1]

This was not an account of a bombed-out city in 1945. This was Marshall Berman's account of visiting the Bronx, where he grew up, in 1980. The Bronx had become 'a symbol of every disaster that could happen to a city'. The Cross Bronx Expressway scythed through neighbourhoods, dispersing rooted communities and throwing up impenetrable traffic-filled asphalt barriers between parts of the district. As in many cities in the world in the 1960s and 70s, the poorest residents were relocated into concrete high-rise housing projects. Although untouched by the war, American cities embraced the post-war urge to smash down and rebuild as readily as anywhere else. Between 1950 and 1970, 6 million housing units were demolished in the US. Of these, half were in city centres and they disproportionately affected renters and non-whites. Berman was writing of the people of the Bronx, but it could have been about working-class people all over the urban world, from Paris to Glasgow, the East End of London to Warsaw: 'They were prepared for grinding poverty, but not for the rupture and collapse of their rough world.'²

High-rise housing and multi-lane roads tore out the best defence against inner-city poverty – the street-based community. Like many other inner-city zones, these concrete slabs in the Bronx became infested with crime gangs and drug-dealing. Already scarred by housing projects, poverty and unemployment, the Bronx was hit by a wave of arson in the 1970s as landlords burnt their low-value tenements in order to claim the insurance money. Berman looked with sympathy on the folk he had grown up with and who remained loyal to the neighbourhood. 'These stricken people belong to one of the largest shadow communities in the world, victims of a great crime without a name. Let us give it a name now: *urbicide*, the murder of a city.'

Writing in 1968, a retired US intelligence colonel, comparing 'the cement-block jungles of high-rise buildings' of US inner-city ghettos – with their alleys and rooftops – to the jungles of Vietnam, wondered if American troops would fare any better in the urban environment than they did in the tropical one. He answered in the negative. But inner-city meltdown was making urban counter-insurgency tactics a pressing matter for the military. Between 1964 and 1968, 52,629 people were arrested in major riots that burst out in 257 US cities. In May 1968, in the aftermath of the assassination of Martin Luther

King, the FBI secretly warned that the United States 'must fully expect to be confronted with virtual rebellion in its urban areas in months to come'.[3]

Hip hop – one of the dominant cultural forms on the planet today – came out of the urban nightmare of the Bronx in the 1970s. Don't push me too far, goes the impassioned staccato rap of 'The Message', 'Cause I'm close to the edge'. This was an anthem of survival and defiance, and a warning.

Hip hop emerged as the voice of marginalised black youth trapped in the ravaged post-industrial inner city. A voice of positivity, the genre, with its inventive lyrical dexterity, was in part an exuberant response to the grimness of the urban environment but also a riposte to those who had written off the youth as criminals and drug addicts. It offered them an alternative to gang life and an outlet of creativity in the otherwise bleak inner city.

The ephemeral music of neighbourhood parties and nightclubs, hip hop and rap went commercial from 1979. Over the next decades it became part of the cultural mainstream, transforming pop music in the process and leaving its mark on fashion, design and art. 'The Message' is significant in hip-hop history, signalling its move towards protest and social commentary. The meteoric global success of the genre gave back dignity to the ghetto, but also seared the image of the neglected urban no-go areas onto the public consciousness.

The Queensbridge Houses in Queens – the innovative and celebrated concrete housing blocks considered in Chapter 11 – had become by the 1980s an urban hellhole of poverty and degradation, and was the centre of the crack-cocaine trade. The scene of gang warfare, it had more murders than any other project in New York City. But it also became one of the hotbeds of hip-hop innovation under the direction of Marley Marl. A radio DJ, Marl revolutionised the sound of hip hop and helped found the Juice Crew in 1983, an artistic collective comprising some of the emerging talents of the 1980s, including Roxanne Shanté, Biz Markie and Big Daddy Kane. The creative energy of the troubled project inspired a teenage school dropout, Nas – 'the poetic sage of the Queensbridge projects' – who became one of the most successful rap artists of the 1990s. 'Growing up in Queensbridge,' Nas recalled in 1998, 'it was Marley Marl and the Juice Crew that gave rap niggas like myself hope that there was another life beyond our hood ... He made us believe that although we came from those wild streets, we still had a chance to change our lives.'⁴

Rooted in the sounds and feel of the streets, hip hop is informed by the specificity of place. It is also versatile, embracing word play and slang, outrageous boasting, lyrical flights of fancy, comedy, social activism and protest framed by autobiography. That intimate connection to the local, coupled with its myriad forms, has helped make hip hop a universal, global movement, the articulation of frustrations felt in dilapidated inner cities everywhere. Nas's debut album *Illmatic* (1994), released when he was twenty, was a first-person narrative detailing a teenager's experience growing up in one of the most notorious projects in the United States. 'When I made *Illmatic* I was a little kid in Queensbridge trapped in the ghetto,' he remembered a few years later. 'My soul was trapped in the Queensbridge projects.'⁵

In his stream of consciousness, Nas became the poet-chronicler of one particular place. His lyrics are entangled in his own autobiography and the physicality of Queensbridge, referring to its street names, its gangs and his friends; the slang he uses is specific to this small corner of New York. 'I want you to know who I am: what the streets taste like, feel like, smell like,' Nas said. 'What the cops talk like, walk like, think like. What the crackheads do – I wanted you to smell it, feel it. It was important to me that I told the story that way because I thought that it wouldn't be told if I didn't tell it.'⁶

Illmatic is a damningly eloquent denunciation of the utopian modernist housing experiment inflicted on people all over the world. Like other hip-hop records, it testifies to the fall not only of the city in the second half of the twentieth century but the gutting of the urban ideal itself. The teenage Nas dreams of escaping, but he can't.

New York – the supreme example of the twentieth-century metropolis – was in decay. The 1964 New York World's Fair (with the meaningless slogan 'Man's Achievements on a Shrinking Globe in an Expanding Universe') was an embarrassing and costly failure, a symbol of a troubled city. In the 1970s it came close to bankruptcy. Its fabric was decaying, its streets haunted by muggers, drug dealers and the homeless. In the 1990s a poll of New Yorkers showed that 60% would rather live somewhere else.

The tide pulled violently away from the city in the years following the Second World War, leaving millions stranded and trapped in the wreckage. The industries that had sustained city life moved. So too did millions of people, sucking the life out of their former neighbourhoods.

They left the city for somewhere else. For a new kind of metropolis.

*

'Tomorrow's City Today', they called it, as the City of Lakewood sprouted out of 3,500 acres of lima-bean fields in the southern part of Los Angeles County in 1950. Every day 4,000 workers completed at least fifty homes in a giant outdoor assembly line. That was roughly one dwelling completed every ten minutes. The workers divided into thirty different crews, each responsible for a specific task. On one block workers poured concrete, while on another carpenters put up prefabricated walls and rafters. Shingles were nailed to a roof while painters finished the interior.[7]

By 1953, 17,500 modest ranch-style stuccoed bungalows and 140 miles of road had been built and Lakewood's residents, mostly young families totalling 70,000 people, took up residence. At its heart was the Lakewood Center, a gigantic shopping mall surrounded by a 10,000-space car park.

Here indeed was tomorrow's city. The young couples were buying into a modern lifestyle centred around the privacy of a detached family home with a garden, around recreation and consumerism. With a sunny climate, a relaxed ethos, easy access to beaches, countryside and mountains, good schools, tasty food and high-paying jobs, they were sold Eden and eagerly took it.

The lure of California attracted families from all over the United States to Lakewood – and also, in smaller numbers, from places like Canada, Germany and Britain. According to a documentary from the time, 'They loved the way the homes and streets were laid out so neatly around the super-modern shopping centres, with acres of free parking. Their whole pattern of living, working and shopping became that of modern suburbia. To many, Lakewood was paradise.'

The Lakewood model of mass-produced housing anchored to a mega-mall was replicated all over LA County, the country, and indeed the world. In the two decades after Lakewood broke ground in 1950,

America's major cities got 10 million new residents while the suburbs gained 85 million. The exodus from cities continued: during the Second World War just 13% of Americans were suburbanised but by the 1990s over half of the entire population had migrated to join them. Just as significant were the geographic realities of this kind of living. While the urban and suburban population of America grew by 75% the built footprint of urban and suburban metropolises expanded by 300%. Car-based urbanism created a new kind of city, revolutionising lifestyles in the process. American civilisation was forming around the private realm of the individual household, rather than the public life of the city.[8]

But it wasn't just the physical layout, lifestyles and social aspirations of Lakewood that was pioneering. In 1953 the nearby city of Long Beach decided to annex the new development. Fearful that Long Beach would burden their utopia with industries and housing they did not like, Lakewood's residents incorporated their boxfresh development as a municipality.

Under the arrangement Lakewood contracted out the provision of road maintenance, education, health and policing services to LA County, but received a share of sales taxes from shopping centres and retained control over zoning. In other words, Lakewood became a self-governing city, able to keep out things – such as industry and cheap housing – it did not like, and by implication the undesirable people that came with them. By securing power over future housing development, Lakewood could exclude renters, who were more likely to be dependent on welfare; and by decreeing the lot size and design of new dwellings, it could indirectly determine that house prices would remain high enough to retain their exclusivity.

That power over the physical environment became, alongside its lifestyle opportunities, one of the chief attractions of Lakeside. A city within a city, it was a world unto itself full of like-minded people: white, lower-middle-class and well-paid blue-collar homeowners. Studied closely across the US, the Lakewood Plan became a template for hundreds of other communities. In the Los Angeles Basin, dozens of autonomous incorporated municipalities sprang up with fiercely defended demarcated boundaries, covering hundreds of square miles of former countryside with innumerable acres of tract housing and shopping centres.[9]

Lakewood, and the cities that modelled themselves on it, aspired to keep things just as they were. The original pioneers who settled in this virgin land were escaping *to* a world of new beginnings and enviable lifestyles. But they were fleeing *from* something else as well – the worn-out, old city with its polluting industries, grime, crime, immorality, overcrowding and polyglot mix of ethnicities. Working- and middle-class families of European descent who came from congested districts in New York, Chicago, Houston, St Louis and so on, hunting for an idyllic lifestyle in sun-drenched, palm-fringed California, did not want the downtown inner city, oozing with vice, to pursue them to their new-found Shangri-La; they bolted the door behind them and triple-locked it.

Today, seventy years since its founding, Lakewood has replaced its 1950s futuristic motto with a new one. As I drove into the city along Del Amo Boulevard one August morning I was greeted by a sign on a pedestrian overpass reading: 'Lakewood. Times Change. Values Don't.' The slogan becomes real as I drove through twenty-first-century Lakewood's residential streets. It is beautiful: tranquil tree-shaded avenues reveal neat bungalows one after another, most with picket fences, immaculate lawns and lovingly tended, bounteous plants. Many homes display Stars and Stripes; SUVs and large pickup trucks are ubiquitous. Decades on from the initial utopian dreams, this seems as quintessential a blue-collar and middle-class American suburb as it is possible to get, true to its founding spirit.

*

Today we talk about living in an urban world. But the reality is that, for most of us, it is a *sub*-urban world, a world of sprawl.

From the end of the Second World War the city, as it had been known for millennia, underwent rapid and radical change. Towards the closing of the twentieth century it was predicted that the traditional city would dissolve into endlessly expanding megalopolises. The gargantuan urban conglomeration of Greater Los Angeles, which today drapes itself over 33,954 square miles of southern California, is in many ways the metropolis, or mother city, of runaway growth.

The aerial view of the Los Angeles Basin is one of the most imposing sights on earth, a gargantuan concentration of people, activity and energy. Bigger than the Republic of Ireland and with a population of 19 million people, it is not a city but a metroverse: a constellation of cities, oversized residential areas, industrial zones, malls, office parks, distribution centres, connected by mile upon mile of freeway that seemingly has no end or limit. For many visitors in the post-war years this supersized megacity region was a monstrous, revolting thing, incomprehensible for those used to the traditional, compact city with a definable centre.

But in the twenty-first century cities of this type, and urban regions of this scale, are commonplace on all inhabited continents. The power-houses of the global economy are no longer cities but twenty-nine urban mega-regions of combined metropolitan areas; together these conurbations produce more than half the world's wealth. There is the Boston–New York–Washington corridor (BosWash), with 47.6 million people and an output of \$3.6 trillion; Greater Tokyo with 40 million and \$1.8 trillion; Hong-Shen (Hong Kong and Shenzhen) with 19.5 million and \$1 trillion. Hong-Shen is in turn part of the Pearl River Delta, a dense network of cities with over 100 million people. China is planning to build high-speed rail networks which will bind even more city clusters into vast, hyper-urban regions. In 2014 the Chinese government announced the creation of Jing-Jin-Ji, a 132,000-square-mile megacity region encompassing Beijing, Hebei and Tianjin and containing 112 million people. Welcome to the endless city.

Southern California experienced this phenomenon, the decentral-ised metropolis, first. And if this historical revolution has a spiritual home amid LA's roiling ocean of housing it is the city of Lakewood, which lies twenty miles or so south of downtown LA.

Dorothy Parker supposedly quipped that Los Angeles was 'seventy-two suburbs in search of a city'. It is a perception of LA repeated in various forms by its many detractors. But that would be true only if Los Angeles was a traditional city, with a business/industrial core and rings of residential suburbs that radiated out as the city grew. Long before Lakewood was built, LA was deliberately developed as a new kind of city for the twentieth century: a decentralised city.

With a population under 10,000 in the 1870s, LA surged to become a global metropolis at a time when technologies were reshaping the urban world – particularly technologies of mobility. By the 1920s, Greater Los Angeles had the most developed intra-urban rail system in the world, 1,100 miles of line that bound hundreds of cities, towns and villages into a regional urban network. It also extended its tentacles into undeveloped areas, its vast spider web the skeleton of a future city yet to grow flesh. By that time, an Angeleno was four times more likely to own a car than a fellow American. This was a city based on mobility, not concentration like a traditional city. And the industries that sustained the metropolis – oil, rubber, car-making, entertainment and aircraft manufacture – needed considerable elbow room.

By their nature these giant plants, hungry for space, dispersed. LA's numerous cities looked and felt suburban, to be sure. But they were not in search of a central city. Jobs were not concentrated in one area, but spread out. The Greater LA region was not a collection of suburbs feeding a nucleated hub, but a patchwork of interrelated cities that were beginning to merge together. The city of South Gate, seven miles south of downtown LA, developed as a blue-collar suburb, with a General Motors car factory and tract housing developments. South Gate had the air of countryside, with jerry-built homesteads and gardens with chicken runs and vegetable patches. Utilising the sprawling transit lines and metropolitan road system, working-class residents were able to commute to manufacturing jobs across the region.[10]

LA did not explode as a result of thoughtless sprawl or zombie-like suburban accretion. Its expansion was dictated by the industries it supported – but also by a utopian conception of what a modern city should be.

According to Dana Bartlett, a Congregationalist minister who came to LA in 1896, 'Climate has a cash value.' It had value because it attracted wealthy tourists to the 'national playground'. 'But to none has the climate such a cash value as to the working man,' wrote Bartlett in his book The Better City. Living in the southern Californian climate would benefit the working class: it would imbue them with health, save them from excessive winter fuel bills and allow them to build their own cheap houses, grow vegetables and flowers and keep chickens. 'Here even the pauper lives like a king.'

Writing in 1907 when LA was still very small, Bartlett imagined a future where working-class families spent their leisure time in the mountains or at the beach. They would own their own home, complete with garden, and work in factories dispersed around the area. Bartlett

called this 'nobler living', in which beauty and health coexisted in a
city without oppressive overcrowding. Bartlett articulated an idea
widely shared about how LA should develop. He tapped into the urban
future envisaged by the Englishman Ebenezer Howard, whose 1902
book *Garden Cities of Tomorrow* is one of the most influential works
of urban planning. Modestly sized garden cities, in this formulation,
would be built in the countryside, surrounded by fields and forests,
as an antidote to the poison of the contemporary industrial city. The
dispersed, semi-rural metropolises envisaged for the twentieth century
were direct responses to the vile, deathly Babylons of the nineteenth
– Chicago, Manchester, New York and a host of other cities.

Under the direction of chief engineer William Mulholland, LA built
the longest aqueduct in the world, conveying water 233 miles from
the Owens Valley to the city. The profusion of water opened up large
areas to productive farmland; it generated electricity; and most importantly it supplied more liquid than the city needed. The offer of cheap
water allowed LA to expand by annexing neighbouring communities.
LA got itself a port in 1909 by gaining Wilmington and San Pedro and
creating a land corridor from city to sea. It annexed Hollywood in
1910, the San Fernando Valley in 1915, Sawtelle, Hyde Park, Eagle Rock,
Venice, Watts and Tujunga in the 1920s and 30s. In the 1890s, the city
of Los Angeles occupied twenty-eight square miles and had a population under 100,000; by 1932 it had swollen to 469 square miles (an
increase of 1,575%, bringing it to the same area as New York City)
and had 1.3 million residents (compared to the 7 million New Yorkers
occupying the same amount of land). Its extent and low density are
explained by the fact that two-thirds of Angelenos lived in a detached
home, an extraordinary proportion for a city of its size – in New York
it was 20% and in Philadelphia 15%. The area of LA County covered
by the lawns of suburban bungalows, meanwhile increased to ninety-
five square miles, four times the size of Manhattan. And that's not
counting extensive country clubs, golf clubs and parking lots. The
ideal lifestyle requires a heck of a lot of room. Suburbanisation was
a cause of sprawl, therefore; and sprawl caused suburbanisation as
people sought to get closer to the desirable rural fringe.[11]

In the early part of the twentieth century, Los Angeles cultivated
the image of the city of the future, one where nature and human
activity coexisted, where the problems that beset the overcrowded

industrial city were solved. Based on mass transit, cars, highways, dispersed industry and single-family homes, Greater LA seemed to presage the future of all metropolises. This cut against contemporary notions of futuristic urbanism. Wasn't the city of tomorrow supposed to be vertical, a glittering array of skyscrapers? Apparently not. Cities seemed to be going horizontal instead.

'A city with all the personality of a paper cup,' sneered Raymond Chandler of LA. The city's downtown and central area became progressively more run-down as people sought jobs and homes in the wider region. What many saw as abysmal, characterless sprawl, others saw as a welcome escape from the confines of decaying cities. Even as it grew, large parts of LA County seemed to keep true to the boosters' myth of the city as arcadian. The lure of owning a detached home set in pleasant surroundings drew over 2 million people to LA County before the Second World War to work in the city's booming aircraft, rubber, automobile and oil industries.

The massive San Fernando Valley, part of the city since 1913, was transformed from parched area to a verdant paradise as a result of Mulholland's great aqueduct, a patchwork of suburban cities, irrigated fields, ranches, groves, orchards and golf courses bound to the rest of the city by rail lines. The valley's rural splendour, its cliffs and rock formations, provided the setting for many of the numerous westerns that graced cinema screens in the 1920s and 30s; its ranches were snapped up by Hollywood stars. The historian Catherine Mulholland recalled her childhood: 'When I think of growing up in the Valley during the 1930s, I remember solitude: the lone sound of the train whistle disrupting the country stillness, the howl of a coyote, the solitary jackrabbit darting across my path and loping ahead as I biked to school over bumpy dirt roads.'[12]

*

The rural splendour could not last. A tidal wave of suburban development engulfed the San Fernando Valley from the 1940s with tens of thousands of ranch-style homes that washed away real ranches, dirt tracks and jackrabbits. This became 'America's Suburb', a desirable fantasy world of sparkling swimming pools, citrus trees, mini-malls, drive-in cinemas, famed globally as the ultimate manifestation of the

Californian dream and the epicentre of car-based youth culture. The mega-suburban region gave birth to the stereotype of the materialistic, airheaded 'Valley Girl' whose upward inflection at the end of the sentence has like totally conquered the world.

The San Fernando Valley was the fastest-growing region in the United States, the population doubling in the 1940s, doubling again in the 1950s, and exceeding a million by the 1960s as monotonous suburban tract houses sprawled the length of the valley.

The British and Americans have never taken to cities in the way that people in Asia or continental Europe did. The tendency has been to seek to escape from the city as soon as one could, pushing instinctively for the rural fringe. The ability to do so depended on wealth. Only those who could afford to commute could escape the overcrowding, disease, pollution and crime of the city centre. Railways and trams created picturesque and expensive suburbs on the fringe of cities for the wealthy in the nineteenth century.

Beginning in Britain, suburbia gathered speed in the nineteenth century and accelerated in the twentieth, changing the very nature of the city as it did so. The drive for 'Homes for Heroes' and slum clearance in Britain after the First World War saw the creation of vast suburban council estates on the edges of large cities. Manchester built a satellite 'garden city', Wythenshawe, planned to have 25,000 houses for 100,000 people. London County Council developed eight 'cottage estates' in the 1920s, places where large numbers of inner-city 'slum'-dwellers could be relocated. The Becontree Estate in Dagenham became the largest housing development in the world, with 25,769 mainly semi-detached dwellings and a population in 1939 of 116,000. To the west of London, the Metropolitan Railway Company created a string of idyllic commuter estates for middle-class people along its lines. Characterised by Tudor revival semis, this expansive suburban area radiating out of London became known as 'Metroland'. London's ever-advancing interwar Metroland was the most pronounced example of the unstoppable city seeping ever further in search of an arcadian dream, voraciously eating up fields and villages in the process. Although the population of London between 1921 and 1931 grew by 10%, its footprint increased by 200%. LA's San Fernando Valley showed the same process at work – but this time on steroids as the suburban monster greedily consumed the things it loved the most.

The dream of suburban living – of a single-family home in semi-rural settings – was shared in the Anglo-American world. The deep-rooted desire to escape the bloated leviathan that was the modern metropolis existed across the industrial world. But the form post-war suburbia took was dictated by powerful, and often invisible forces.

Southern California is in the business of manufacturing dreams, spinning its own myths. It is the global capital of laid-back values, alternative lifestyles and carefree beach culture. But modern LA is the creation of war. A good proportion of the people who lived in Lakewood worked at the Douglas Aircraft Company facilities in and around Long Beach. They assembled military jets, including the Skyknight, one of which sits on a concrete spike in a public park in the heart of the community. Similarly, there was a concentration of defence industries in the San Fernando Valley. The Lockheed Aircraft Company became the biggest employer in the valley during the Second World War, producing thousands of Flying Fortresses and fighter planes. After the war it moved into advanced jet aircraft, producing, among others, the U2 spyplane.

The suburban utopia unveiled at Lakewood might not have seemed like it, but it was a product of the Cold War, a dormitory for thousands of bodies needed to construct the artefacts of modern conflict. Not only did the suburban pioneers of Lakewood have desirable homes, they enjoyed pay packets way in excess of the national average.[13]

They benefited from the Cold War, but they also sat on its front line. As a high-tech military manufacturing and research centre, LA was a prime target for Soviet nuclear missiles. The suburban cities of the San Fernando Valley may have typified 1950s aspirations and social change, but even as children rode their bikes through suburbia and teenagers went to drive-in cinemas, the tranquillity was frequently interrupted by sonic booms as Lockheed tested hyper-advanced planes in the skies above. This 1950s leafy Eden was defended by batteries of Nike surface-to-air missiles fitted with nuclear warheads. They were among the missile sites that surrounded Greater LA, the 'Ring of Supersonic Steel' that made LA one of the most fortified cities in the world.[14]

Suburban sprawl and the atomic age were intimately connected. The apocalyptic literature and films of the 1950s made city-living scary enough, imbuing suburbia, exurbs and commuter towns with a sense of psychological security, distant as they seemed to be from any future ground zero in a major city. But the process of exodus was given its impetus by federal government. Military strategists and urban planners were coming to believe that a policy of dispersal of people and industries from vulnerable compact cities was a pre-emptive form of defence against nuclear strike. Forcibly dispersing cities was impossible in a democratic country. But it could be done indirectly. Tax incentives determined where industry located. Large-scale road-building programmes in the 1950s allowed settlements to spring up in places previously considered too remote. And then there was the federal government's control over the housing market.[15]

House-hunting couples might have believed they were making free choices, but the path guiding them towards suburbia was predetermined at the highest levels. The American suburbs, with their distinctive look and feel, were not the manifestation of national taste or individual choices; they were largely the creation of the state. Founded in the wake of the Great Depression, the Federal Housing Authority (FHA) provided billions of dollars insuring the mortgage market. Before the 1930s if you wanted a loan you had to provide a deposit of around 50%, and the mortgage was payable within ten years. The ginormous safety net for investors provided by the FHA changed everything. It meant that deposits were minimal or zero; that interest rates were low; and the mortgage period could be extended to thirty years. The mortgage market exploded, giving easy access to homeownership to everyone with the median 1950 household income, $4,000.[16]

But the FHA was not going to insure any old house. It gave priority to detached new-built houses on wide streets and cul-de-sacs. It mandated that houses be set back at least fifteen feet from the road and be entirely surrounded by garden. The FHA approved of homogeneous housing developments and disapproved of mixed-use districts, where there were shops or commerce. It preferred expansiveness over density, and disapproved of rental properties or the presence of old housing stock, believing that such things would 'accelerate the tendency to lower-class occupancy'. It favoured places near arterial roads, rather than public transit lines. These, after all, were standardised, fungible home loans traded on a nationwide market; therefore, there was a need for standardised, fungible homes.[17]

In other words, you could have whatever home you liked, as long as it was a brand-new bungalow in suburbia. You might have wanted to live in a city, but you would struggle to get a mortgage for an inner-city dwelling. None of this was obvious to the buyer; real-estate agents and mortgage brokers directed them towards the ideal FHA home, which was typically in a new out-of-town development. The reason suburbia exploded in the 1950s was because the government wanted it to, and subsidised it with billions of dollars. The company that built Lakewood did so knowing they had to provide homes that were afford-able to people who earned the median wage. Its three-bedroom ranch-style bungalows were sold for $8,255. They were purchasable by people who could obtain thirty-year mortgages at $50 a month with no down payment. Building within these restraints, and competing in the lucra-tive mortgage market, meant mass-producing prefabricated homes at speed. Uniform houses within a development – with the same finishes, appliances, materials and hardware – meant that its builders could leverage economies of scale; Lakewood, for example, was supplied with 200,000 identical interior doors. When you drive around Lakewood or the San Fernando Valley the uniformity of housing is overpowering. The reason is not because people wanted it that way: it is because this was federally subsidised housing, even if that fact was concealed from house-hunters who enjoyed the illusion of freedom.

The wholesome suburban life was celebrated in countless TV programmes and films, making it highly desirable, even idealistic. But the actual aesthetics of suburbia were dictated by FHA investment policies and by national security considerations of 'defensive dispersal'. The 1954 Housing Act mandated federal agencies, including the FHA, to facilitate the reduction of cities' vulnerability to enemy attack. In practice, this meant dispersal through suburbanisation. The law also enjoined that loans should only be given to housing that was 'subject to urban defence standards'. When various types of homes were exposed to atomic-test blasts in Operation Cue in the Nevada desert, it was discovered that the ranch-style bungalow stood up the best. In addition, those with venetian blinds suffered the least damage to their interiors. Not coincidentally, nine out of every ten new-built houses in southern California in the 1950s were ranch bungalows.[18]

The anarchic blue-collar suburbs of South Gate, where working people built their own homes from the ground up, gave way to the manicured lawns of FHA-backed, cookie-cut Lakewood. Suburbia came to mean conformity. But it was a conformity enjoined by the housing market and political priorities, not necessarily by individual choice. And it was unanswerable. Mortgage payments of $50 a month on a ranch-style three-bedroom bungalow in the 'burbs were considerably cheaper than renting a dilapidated city-centre apartment. Becoming a homeowner also put you on the path to financial security.

Government policies were explicitly intended to direct people away from the urban core to the suburban periphery. The enormous wealth of America that came in the wake of the Second World War was invested in transforming lives through the growth of the automobile suburb. The 1950s is often described as a period of 'white flight' from messy, ethnically mixed inner cities to the racially segregated middle-class suburban Shangri-La. It is not quite as simple as that. There was a policy of deliberate dispersal from cities to suburbs. It chimed with people's genuine desires to raise their families in homes they owned, away from cities that they were continually told cowered under the shadow of nuclear war and the pervasive threat of 'urban blight'.

Federal housing policies accelerated the rapid outward spread of metropolitan areas and sucked populations out of urban cores. Think of the affluence of 1950s America and you automatically think of leafy suburban streets and wholesome suburban family values. And that image is overwhelmingly white and middle class. The stereotype accords with reality. Barriers of segregation criss-crossed LA, as they did in other horizontally expanding US cities. Until 1948 homeowners in new suburban tracts could refuse to sell houses to black families; the Supreme Court ruling in *Shelley* v. *Kraemer* of that year outlawed restrictive covenants that prevented homeowners from selling or renting their properties to minorities. But there were other ways of keeping a suburb white. Real-estate agents steered prospective minority purchasers away from their development. The FHA used its power to favour housing developments that were racially and socially homogeneous, creating suburbs with predominantly similar income levels and racial complexions. The presence of even a few families not of European heritage in a suburban district was enough to drive down house prices because the FHA refused to insure mortgages in racially mixed neighbourhoods. Given this blunt economic fact – and added to already endemic racism – it is hardly surprising that in many suburban areas of LA, prospective black or Latino residents were intimidated by armed vigilante homeowner gangs.

The idyllic suburbs were lily-white and segregated by class: as racially and socially monotonous as the houses were uniform. In 1960, Lakewood numbered seven African Americans out of its 70,000 residents. And while the San Fernando Valley's population rocketed from 300,000 to 700,000 in the 1950s, its African American population declined from 1,100 to 900. This is hardly surprising given that although the federal government underwrote $120 billion worth of new housing by 1960, just 2% of this went to non-whites. The courts might have outlawed segregation; but the housing market made it as fearsome as ever.[19]

As middle- and lower-class families of European backgrounds deserted the city, their places were taken by new migrants. During the Second Great Migration, more than 5 million African Americans moved from the rural South to the cities of the north-east, Midwest and west. As white America was becoming thoroughly suburbanised, black Americans became 80% urbanised. The cities they moved into were near crisis point. Much of the old housing stock was facing demolition in favour of high-rise projects and freeways. Public housing was squeezed into former slum districts. Mortgages and insurance were hard to come by in these areas. Jobs were scarce as industry followed the exodus out of town. In Britain, France, the Netherlands and elsewhere the picture was similar: the decaying inner city became the home of immigrant communities as their middle- and working-class communities trekked out to more salubrious suburbs, satellite towns and planned new towns.

In LA, like other American cities, African American migrants were confined to a small inner-city area with ageing buildings and large substandard housing projects – South Central, the South Side and Watts – at a time when the metropolitan area as a whole was mushrooming with suburban housing. The decay of the inner city – with its poor-quality housing, unemployment, violence and crime – was in part caused by turbocharged suburbanisation and in turn fuelled the limitless growth of suburbia as more and more people wanted to flee the urban trap and never look back. The urban nightmare also made people in communities such as Lakewood more determined than ever to preserve the paradise they had created, to keep out the polluting influences of the inner city by erecting virtual and real fences against undesirables.

*

Suburbia: the very word is loaded with meaning. In literature, music and film, suburbia is the *anti*-urban space, the polar opposite of the thrill, freedom and complexity of the city: a built-up wilderness of supreme blandness, stultifying conformity, hollowed-out alienation, compulsive consumerism and monotone bourgeois whiteness. The boredom and sameness of suburbia was one of its overriding attractions: a safe space from the tumult of the chaotic city; an Anywheresville drained of history in a dangerous world of nuclear weapons. 'Do you know the road I live in – Ellesmere Road, West Bletchley?' George Orwell's protagonist in his novel *Coming Up for Air* (1939) asks. 'Even if you don't, you know fifty others exactly like it. You know how these streets fester all over the inner-outer suburbs. Always the same. Long, long rows of little semi-detached houses ... The stucco front, the creosoted gate, the privet hedge, the green front door. The Laurels, The Myrtles, The Hawthorns, Mon Abri, Mon Repos, Belle Vue.'

There is a long tradition of literary depictions of the stultifying atmosphere, middle-brow intellectual ambitions and prosaic values of suburbia: from George and Weedon Grossmith's *Diary of a Nobody* (1892) to Richard Yates's *Revolutionary Road* (1961) and John Updike's *Couples* (1968), from Hanif Kureishi's *The Buddha of Suburbia* (1990) to Jonathan Franzen's *The Corrections* (2001). The suburbs have been the beloved muse of filmmakers, attracted to the darkness that apparently lurks behind the superficial sameness and sterility. David Lynch's *Blue Velvet* (1986), Sam Mendes' *American Beauty* (1999) and Bryan Forbes's *The Stepford Wives* (1975) immediately spring to mind as undisputed classics of the genre. Horror movies feast on suburbia with indecent zombie-like relish: *A Nightmare on Elm Street* (1984), *Dawn of the Dead* (1978). It is a place that conceals domestic struggles, mysteries and crime – *Desperate Housewives*, *The Sopranos*. Unlike city life, suburban life takes place behind closed doors, offering scope for myriad narratives but at the same time making them frustratingly unknowable. What exactly is going on beyond the manicured lawn?

Time and again, suburbs are presented as a heaven that turns into hell. They come in for criticism, not least for imprisoning women in domestic drudgery while their husbands commute to work. They are a juicy prospect for the artist: all that neatness, rigid family hierarchies and uniformity must just be the cover for all-day drinking, pill-popping, swingers' parties and worse, surely?

It is in pop music that the suburbs come in for the most sustained and unnuanced drubbing. In the 1962 song by Malvina Reynolds, suburbia is made up of 'little boxes made of ticky-tacky'. And, like their homes, the people 'put in' boxes have similar backgrounds, education, jobs and hobbies.

The boredom, self-satisfaction, homogeneity and hypocrisy of the suburbs are a natural target for pop music. And why not? Marketed, after all, at teenagers, pop music speaks to their daily experiences of drudgery in a purposively sanitised and safe child-friendly environment and gives them a sense of release. In Green Day's masterpiece 'Jesus of Suburbia' (2005), the suburb is an apocalyptically hollow, artificial construct; it exists at the end of some forlorn highway, a Nowheresville. It is a place of hypocrites, therapy and antidepressants, where the centre of the world is the 7-Eleven.

The Pet Shop Boys' 'Suburbia' (1986) is about the ennui of suburban living: all you can do is indulge in pointless acts of graffiti for release. In the video dreary ranch homes in LA are juxtaposed with dreary mock-Tudor semi-detached houses in London: the experience of global suburbia is interchangeable. Similarly, in 'Suburban Dreams' (1980), Martha and the Muffins capture the universal experience of modern life: strolling aimlessly through a fluorescent-lit mall drinking synthetic shakes and avoiding the clumsy advances of high-school boys. Adult life in the suburbs is all mind-numbing conversations about the weather, who's bought a new pool or a state-of-the-art car, while adolescents nihilistically listen to heavy metal and cruise the mall.

All adolescents want to escape from home into the world, not vice versa as adults do. The suburbs naturally mark a front line of conflict between teenagers and parents, a clash of values and aspirations. The only option is to escape. But where to? In Arcade Fire's haunting 'Sprawl II' from their 2010 album *The Suburbs*, suburbia has spread so completely that it has conquered the world; run away if you want, but it is the same everywhere. What are rock and punk but howls of anger at conformity and consumerism? Shocking bourgeois values is what teenagers do, and kicking at suburbia – the embodiment of conventional lifestyles – is a recurrent theme of pop.

But while popular perceptions of the suburbs are firmly rooted, the suburbs themselves have, over the last seventy years, been places of dynamic change. While city centres have remained stable, suburbs have undergone rapid, momentous evolution. They are where history has happened since the Second World War. If a drive through Lakewood seems like stepping back into the 1950s, it is a carefully crafted illusion. The tides of history have washed through places like this, reshaping everything. To understand modern urbanism, to see how the metropolis is developing, you have to leave the museum/tourist attraction city centre and venture into the mysterious edgelands.

★

Although it is a ten-minute drive from Lakewood to Compton, it is a journey into another world. The dwellings look the same – yet more ranch-style bungalows – but this is one of the most infamous addresses in the world. Its global notoriety came from the debut of the LA hip-hop group N.W.A. (Niggaz Wit Attitudes), *Straight Outta Compton* (1988), a seminal gangsta rap album which revelled in the gang violence and brutality of Los Angeles's most violent neighbourhoods. Even without any radio play or exposure on MTV, the album quickly went platinum.

The incredible commercial success of *Straight Outta Compton* came in large part because N.W.A. purported to be participants in the savage gang wars of LA, not merely reporters. Immensely popular with teenagers in white middle-class suburbia (80% of the fan base, according to the record label), the album – with its sounds of gunshots and wailing sirens, its explicit lyrics, and the furious rage at the police – shocked America. N.W.A. boasted of their flash cars as well as their AK-47s. In the single 'Fuck Tha Police', group member Ice Cube attacks the LAPD for its brutality and racism. Ice Cube spits out his rage at officers wrongly arresting him for dealing narcotics just because he has expensive jewellery and a pager, responding with revenge fantasies. The chorus is a chant of the single's explicit title.

Straight Outta Compton's impact came in part because it gave suburban teenagers everywhere a voyeuristic encounter with the ghetto, and also because it expressed rage at what parts of LA had become in the 1980s. It also made the city of Compton internationally famous as the symbol of urban breakdown and nihilism. The media referred to Compton as a 'slum'; its notoriety after *Straight Outta Compton* made it a no-go area.

This was guerrilla gang warfare being enacted not in the grim modernist tower blocks like Queensbridge, but in what had been suburbia. The Second Great Migration had brought thousands of African American families to southern California during and immediately after the Second World War. Stuck in substandard housing in South Central and Watts, they aspired to a pleasant home in the suburbs no less than anyone else.

The barriers to fulfilling this dream were so great for African Americans, and life in South Central so unpleasant, that they were prepared to pay more for a home in places like Compton and Crenshaw than members of the white working class. Compton in the late 1940s and 50s was as white as most suburbs. (It was briefly home to George H. W. Bush and his family in 1949 when the future president was working as an oil-bit salesman for Dresser Industries.) Some white homeowners were beaten by their white neighbours for listing their properties with realtors who sold to black buyers. When Alfred and Luquella Jackson were unloading their moving van in Compton in May 1953 they were assailed by a white mob. They had to defend themselves with a pair of Colt .45 pistols and a twelve-gauge shotgun. Elsewhere, white vigilante gangs burnt crosses on lawns, vandalised homes and beat up prospective African American home buyers.[20]

As soon as African Americans moved into an LA neighbourhood a particular dynamic played out. The idea that African American buyers depressed property prices became a self-fulfilling prophecy as white residents began to panic-sell. This in turn opened up house-buying opportunities to more black families eager to escape the inner city. By 1960 African Americans made up 40% of Compton. Horrified observers saw suburbs like this as experiencing 'ghetto sprawl' as the inner city seeped into white enclaves. But the opposite was the case: Compton represented escape from the inner city for African Americans as much as it had done for white working-class people. They were

professionals and clerical workers, craftsmen, nurses and factory opera-
tives. Their children went to integrated high schools and on to universities such as UCLA and Berkeley. Their homes were spacious with
well-tended gardens; they were as likely to have motorboats or camper
vans on their drives as their white neighbours. To the genuine astonishment of many white residents and visitors, black suburbanites acted
and behaved like any other suburbanites. In the 1960s, Compton
showed what a mixed-race suburb could be at a time when 95% of
people living in American suburbia were of European descent. 'For
once,' said one African American in Compton, 'the Negro did not
move into slums; for once he came into good housing.'[21]

The background of N.W.A.'s founders is striking. Arabian Prince's
father was an author and his mother a piano teacher. Eazy-E's mother
was a grade school administrator and his father a postal worker. MC
Ren's father owned a barber shop. Ice Cube's mother was a hospital
clerk, and before becoming a rapper he studied architecture. They
were products of a successful African American suburb, yet they
chronicled gang war and social breakdown less than three decades
after Compton had been described as the 'Beverly Hills of the Black
Belt'. What had gone wrong?[22]

The mixed-race nature of Compton came to a swift end in 1965. In
nearby Watts, police maltreatment of an African American brought
to a head simmering discontent at heavy-handed policing and slum
conditions. During the ensuing Watts Riots, there were thirty-four
deaths; $40 million worth of damage was caused, with 977 buildings
burnt or destroyed. The violence prompted the flight of white residents and affluent African Americans. They took with them their
businesses, leaving Compton's commercial district a ghost town. This
disaster hit at a time when industry was relocating to new sites further
away as well. By the early 1980s, most of the big manufacturing firms
were gone, leaving mass unemployment and an eroded tax base.[23]

Eazy-E, Ice Cube, MS Ren and Arabian Prince were children of the
1960s. When they were born, over half the population of Compton
was under eighteen. They watched as their city and its schools fell
into dilapidation and their parents were laid off and became dependent
on welfare. The collapse of public transportation meant that the
population was unable to go in search of jobs. Utopian suburbia gave
way, very quickly, to a disaster zone where there was no hope of a

good job; shops were boarded up and public services were in freefall. Deprived of a future, young African American males joined street gangs. The Crips were founded at Freemont High School in South Central in 1969; their deadly rivals, the Bloods, began in Compton, taking their distinguishing red colour from their local high school. Gangs affiliated to the Crips and Bloods proliferated, their membership totalling between 70,000 and 90,000 criminals and drug dealers. Their territorial battles intensified in the 1980s, fuelled by the fortunes being made from the crack-cocaine epidemic.

From being the black Beverly Hills in the 1960s, Compton became the centre of LA County's vicious gang war in the 1980s where drive-bys and gunfights were horrifyingly commonplace. For rapper Ice-T, in the LA of the 1980s crack cocaine and money made life meaningless. Hip hop played up to the gang affinities of the city, the supposed glamour of street life and conflict with the LAPD, but also represented the dangers and bleakness of life. The menace of the beat and the hard-hitting, confrontational lyrics of West Coast hip hop reflected the grim reality of life in Compton, even if the actual storylines were inventions. It spoke to a generation brought up since the 1960s in an environment saturated with casual violence, lives characterised by a brutish daily struggle for survival. 'Colors' (1988) vividly denounces the warlike atmosphere of LA's streets, and the struggle for survival that is beyond the comprehension of most Americans. The effect of drugs and violence is brutalising: what's left but a nihilistic urge for violence?

Tracks such as 'Fuck Tha Police' were cries of angst and pain, and warnings of what happened when the suburbs became urbanised ghettos. They were attacks on the heavy-handedness of the LAPD and its militarised gang sweeps. Four years later LA exploded into riots once again after the acquittal of LAPD officers accused of beating Rodney King in a suburban district of the San Fernando Valley.

The dark light cast on Compton highlighted an issue that was little discussed in the 1980s. By 1980 8.2% of American suburbanites (7.4 million people) lived below the poverty line; over the next two decades the figure doubled, meaning that impoverished suburbanites outnumbered poor people in the inner city. Murders fell in American cities by 16.7% but rose by 16.9% in the suburbs. Like Compton (but to a lesser degree) many suburbs were beset by problems common to cities. They were not the polar opposite of the city; they were now woven into the fabric of the expanding metropolis: this was made clear by the spread of crime, drugs and unemployment to suburbs. They got steadily more ethnically diverse, mirroring the trajectory of traditional cities. The distinction between urban and suburban began to dissolve. It meant the creation of a new kind of metropolis.[24]

★

In the opening sequence of *The Sopranos*, Tony Soprano drives out of the Lincoln Tunnel. In his rear-view mirror is the skyline of Manhattan. The city disappears as Tony continues along the Jersey Turnpike. Like any commuter retreading the same old stretch of road, he moodily snatches the ticket from the toll plaza. And like any commuter he is probably oblivious by now to the scenery of his journey: the out-of-town business parks, the decaying industry, the spirals of highway, the airport, the shopping streets of a suburban town, the fading homes of 1950s suburbia. The older buildings give way to row upon row of more modern suburban dwellings, until finally Tony pulls up at his spacious 1990s family McMansion, which looks like it has only just been plonked onto the countryside.

The Sopranos' opening sequence is what urban geographers call a transect, a slice taken from city centre to periphery that reveals a range of social and physical habitats. Tony's journey through the sprawl is a drive through layers of history. Every city can be read like this, a landscape that reveals the passage of recent history and the ways in which our cities are in a state of constant, violent flux.

On the August day I visited Lakewood and Compton, I drove through a cityscape made and remade during the turbulent late twentieth century. Lakewood, once the quintessentially white blue-collar neighbourhood, is now one of the most racially balanced suburbs in America: 41% non-Hispanic white; 8.7% African American, 16% Asian and 30% Latino.

The history of Lakewood was shaped by the geopolitics of the second half of the twentieth century. Brought into life by the economic boom of the 1950s and sustained by high federal spending on defence in the Cold War, the fall of the Berlin Wall spelt the end of plum jobs in the defence industries. The spectre of unemployment fell over the whole of Greater LA as a result of the collapse of the Soviet Union;

it was felt acutely in Lakewood. The city leapt to fame as suburban utopia in the 1950s. It achieved celebrity again in 1993, but this time as a symbol of suburban dystopia when a gang of high-school boys known as the Spur Posse were arrested for numerous sexual crimes and rapes. Suddenly Lakewood became symbolic of social breakdown in suburbia – of family dysfunction, feral teenagers and sexual promiscuity – as the boys involved did the rounds of the tabloid TV talk-show circuit.[25]

Lakewood reflects the roller-coaster ride of America since the Second World War, its boom, busts, deindustrialisation, diversity and its fraying suburban idealism. The urban topography of LA is like an evolving organism, adapting itself to the external stimuli of geopolitics and globalisation. Or it is like a giant beach, where the ebb and flow of tides continually re-forms the shoreline, creating a patchwork of ever-changing communities. The force of these powerful tides is evident in the suburban landscape. The consequences of the deindustrialisation of the global West, the dismantling of the Soviet Union and the rise of Asia are made visible from the car window.

Compton, stereotyped as an African American ghetto, saw a massive increase in its Latino population in the 1980s; it became the majority in the late 1990s. Drive further north to Huntington Park and the signs are in Spanish, reflecting the suburb's dramatic transition between 1975 and 1985 from being almost entirely white working class to 97% Latino. Many of those who moved into Huntington Park came from the barrios of East LA and inner-city public housing, seeking a better life as suburban homeowners. The range of businesses catering to the city's Latino communities is a startling example of entrepreneurship.

There is a pattern: the continual flow of people out of declining suburbs to new ones to improve their socio-economic position and achieve a better standard of living. African Americans moved out of places like Compton to ethnically diverse suburbs offering better opportunities, such as in the San Fernando Valley, San Bernardino or Riverside. Their places in the post-war inner suburbs were taken by migrants attracted since the 1960s, like so many before them, to LA: people from Mexico, Central America and South America.

All this was made possible by the changes that ripped through the global economy. LA became the hub of the Asia-Pacific economy, providing the headquarters for global financial corporations. As its manufacturing declined, its service and high-tech industries roared into life, and the ports of Los Angeles and Long Beach became the gateways for the importation of cars, electronic parts and plastics from China, Hong Kong, Japan, Vietnam, South Korea and Taiwan. In the post-industrial economy, the social structure of the city took on an hourglass shape: lots of rich people at the top, not many in the middle, and a vast low-wage immigrant population making up the base. The new economy demanded low-wage, low-skilled, deunionised labour: gardeners, cleaners, drivers, nannies and workers in garment factories. By the 2010 census, 47.7% of the population of LA County was Hispanic; non-Hispanic whites made up just 27.8%.[26]

The changes that reshaped LA's population were not unique to that city. Across the United States, suburbs were becoming more diverse. By the end of the twentieth century, the fastest-growing suburban populations were Latinos, African Americans and Asians. In addition, 50% of immigrants leapfrogged straight into suburbs. In other words, suburbs became more urban in character, reflecting the diversity of the globalised metropolis.

The metropolitan landscape is sculpted by the various people who have occupied it, lived in it, and moved on. In the late twentieth century this gradual process became frenetic. From Huntington Park it is a short drive to Monterey Park in the San Gabriel Valley. This quiet, low-density place has the small-town appeal of many American suburbs; but its familiar form belies its critical importance to understanding how cities have undergone rapid change. Monterey Park – and most of the San Gabriel Valley – represents a microcosm not only of our contemporary urban revolution but of modern globalisation.

Like so many suburbs, it was overwhelmingly white in the immediate post-war years. But during the 1960s the white composition declined from 85% to 50%, with Latinos making up 34% and Asian Americans 15%. Many of the new Asian-origin residents were upwardly mobile families making their way out of traditional urban enclaves downtown – Little Tokyo and Chinatown – for a better standard of living in the suburbs. Over the next two decades the young real-estate investor Frederic Hsieh used the modest Asian presence to promote the suburb to prospective Asian immigrants as the 'Chinese Beverly Hills'.[27]

Hsieh saw the potential in Monterey Park. Close to downtown LA, it offered easy access to the financial centre at a time when it was reorientating itself to the Asia-Pacific economy. Hsieh compared the rolling hills of the San Gabriel Valley to Taipei; he marketed the suburb in Asian newspapers, making an address in Monterey Park synonymous with success in America. Even the city's then area code – 818 – helped, because in Chinese numerology 8 is believed to bring wealth. It worked: during the 1970s and 80s tens of thousands of affluent and well-educated migrants from Hong Kong, Taiwan, Vietnam and China began to buy property there. By 1990 it became the only Asian-majority city in the US, or as some dubbed it, the 'First Suburban Chinatown'.[28]

But that moniker was misleading. Monterey Park differed from monoethnic urban Chinatowns the world over. Although people of Chinese origin accounted for 63% of the by-now majority Asian American population, they came from all over mainland China as well as Hong Kong and Taiwan, and lived alongside families from Japan, Vietnam, Korea, the Philippines and elsewhere in south-east Asia; there was also a strong Latino make-up (30%), while the white component was 12%. Few suburbs have changed so rapidly – or so visibly. Many of the new Chinese suburbanites were highly educated engineers, computer programmers, lawyers and other professionals, who were able to buy properties in cash.[29]

Like the preceding generations of professional white Americans, they were attracted to Monterey Park because it offered an attractive lifestyle, affordable housing and business opportunities in a suburb that was well connected to all the major southern California freeways. Significantly, these entrepreneurs bypassed the city centre and made a beeline for the 'burbs, bucking the historical trend whereby immigrant communities gained a foothold in a foreign port or major city.

The suburbs, in 1970s and 80s America, offered the best place to start a business and investment in property. As a result of the influx not just of people but of cash, Monterey Park changed rapidly to the disquiet of many of its older residents. A local doughnut shop and a tyre shop became Chinese banks; familiar chain shops and strip malls were replaced with Asian stores and supermarkets. Old-fashioned American restaurants changed ownership and began selling some of the best Cantonese, Szechuan, Shanxi, Shanghai and Taiwanese food in the US. By the early 1990s there were over sixty Chinese restaurants within the city's 7.7 square miles; suburban malls became a mecca for foodies. Chinese signs appeared in abundance on Garvey Avenue, the commercial centre of the city, announcing Chinese accountants, lawyers, realtors, hair salons, medical practices, supermarkets, travel agents and, of course, eateries. Such businesses served the local community and revitalised the city during a time of deindustrialisation, to be sure; they also gave people escaping political uncertainty in Hong Kong, Taiwan and mainland China a way of bringing money out of Asia and into the US. But the significance went far beyond that.

At the time when personal and business life was being revolutionised by information technology, some 65% of the personal-computer products imported into the US came through LA. The majority of the Chinese companies that assembled and distributed computers were based in the San Gabriel Valley. As the international flows of people, capital and products intensified in the late twentieth century, the suburban cities of the valley glowed red hot. The San Gabriel Valley, on the surface an unassuming, classically suburban area, was at the centre of globalisation, with not only high-tech industries, but financial, legal and insurance services managing the tides of capital and consumer goods streaming between Asia and the United States. The booming Pacific Rim economy had its focal point among the acres of wooden bungalows. We know about the global city: the global suburb is much less heralded.[30]

The economic vitality of the SGV in the 1980s and 90s as it became a hub of computer technology was a microcosm of what was happening throughout metropolitan areas. Until the last quarter of the twentieth century most cities were like giant vortexes, sucking in commuters, money, business and shoppers every day. But things went into sudden reverse as cities copied the centrifugal tendencies of LA.

By the 1980s over 50% of American companies had relocated to the periphery and more than 80% of jobs were now beyond the old central business district. The post-war decades saw cities turned inside out. Like the computer industry in the SGV, suburbs went from being dormitories to places of business, eroding any simple distinction between suburb and city. Some suburbs had morphed into so-called 'technoburbs', named because modern technologies – such as cars, telephones and computers – liberated satellite suburbs from dependence on their urban mother planet. These suburbs became more like cities; in turn they were rendering useless many of the things that made dense city centres so indispensable throughout history: face-to-face contact, the provision of unique specialised functions, and the need to concentrate them within walking distance. Take Atlanta, Georgia. In 1960, 90% of its office space was concentrated downtown. By 1980 that share had plummeted to 42% as almost a hundred industrial parks proliferated on its periphery. Today, Atlanta is the least dense major city in the world with just 630 people per square mile (Dhaka, the densest city, packs 115,000 into each square mile; the global median is 14,000). Throughout the world, cities have become more like LA, amorphous places with not one but many centres, where businesses and urban functions spread out. The kinds of businesses in the post-industrial, globalised economy – high-tech, research and services – by their nature preferred suburban business parks over city centres.

The most famous example, of course, is the constellation of towns in northern California between San Jose and San Francisco that centre on Stanford University. No area in the world has had such an impact on our lives over the last few decades. This string of suburbia, research campuses and business parks is home to Google, Apple, Twitter, Facebook, Netflix, Yahoo, Uber, Airbnb, Oracle, eBay and LinkedIn. Silicon Valley is no city; it is not suburbia either. With its unprecedented global power, it epitomises the modern formless, decentralised city.

Back in LA, the story of the SGV is not just the story of successful Taiwanese and Chinese international businessmen forging trans-Pacific trade links. Immigrants to Monterey Park included the wealthy and skilled as well as the poor and unskilled. It is also the familiar story of white resistance to incursions into suburbia. Attempts were made by residents' groups to ban Chinese signage and declare English the city's official language. But the front line of the battle was the humble Californian bungalow. Newly affluent Asian homebuyers wanted to convert old wooden bungalows intended for small nuclear families into larger, grander homes that reflected their wealth, status and family size. In order to accommodate single and lower-income immigrants, speculators also started building apartment blocks in suburbia. They met resistance from local preservationist groups who wanted to save what they saw as suburban heritage from Asian 'mansionisation' and urbanisation in a last-ditch attempt to retain the original character of the place.[31]

Driving east through the SGV, pre-war suburbs give way to eclectic, modest pre-war bungalows, then to the more uniform suburbs of the post-war years. As the twentieth century wore on, LA became the densest urban area in the United States with 6,000 people per square mile (which is still not very dense: the density of both Greater London and Shanghai is 14,500; that of central Paris over 52,000). While suburbia in the eastern part of the United States was characterised by open spaces, LA built over most of its area, leaving little in the way of parks or countryside. Asian families have progressed east through the valley as they have grown richer, in exactly the same way that white and African American families have leapfrogged from suburb to suburb, chasing the dream to the fringes of the metropolis as the older suburbs become more crowded, more run-down and ever more enclosed by new housing from the mythic semi-rural sweet spot that marks the desirable edge of the city.

The progress east towards ever more affluent suburbs also mirrors the rebalancing of the global economy towards Asia. Chinese home-buyers began moving into some of the wealthiest and most exclusive of all LA suburban districts, San Marino and Arcadia, beautiful, oak-shaded towns that lie beneath the San Gabriel Mountains. Previously favoured by white American CEOs and executives, they have become majority Asian since the beginning of the twenty-first century. The Asian incomers are typically not upwardly mobile businesspeople who made their fortunes in LA and moved out as their incomes rose. They are freshly minted multimillionaire and billionaire Chinese CEOs and government officials who have come direct to Arcadia from Shanghai and Beijing.

They are chasing the same dream as their American suburban predecessors: a large, prestigious home in pleasant surroundings where the schools are good, the mall is groaning with luxury goodies, and their money is safely tied up in American assets. Arcadia, the archetypal upper-middle-class American small town which oozes affluence on every oak-shaded street, is no longer a suburb simply of LA or Pasadena, but of the globalised world. Many old 1940s split-level, ranch-style homes with big gardens were bought, demolished and rebuilt as enormous, extravagant Chinese mansions, complete with crystal chandeliers, marble interiors, big wine cellars, wok kitchens, circular drives and everything a super-rich expatriate Chinese family could want.[32]

Every year in the 2010s, between 150 and 250 2,000-square-foot 1940s houses became 12,000-square-foot twenty-first-century mega-mansions. These hulking, blingy monsters overshadowing the remaining traditional homes are symbolic of the power Chinese tastes and money have over the modern world. They also show the power of American suburbia: for generations millions have come to southern California, of different backgrounds and means, lured by the siren song of the Californian suburban lifestyle.

The millionaire mega-mansions of Arcadia tell one story of globalisation. I drove further east to tell another one, a forty-minute drive through contiguous suburban sprawl to the dispiriting McMansions of a new city called Eastvale in the Jurupa Valley. A few years ago this pancake-flat, dusty, half-desert spot was all cattle farms and vineyards. Now it is a vast planned suburb. This is no longer LA, which is forty-six miles to the west; this is the Inland Empire. It is, however, part of the unending sprawl of the Greater Los Angeles/southern California megacity region.

The lifeless supersized suburbs here are the twenty-first-century version of Lakewood – thousands of prefabricated suburban homes built in recent years around box malls. Eastvale, like Lakewood was in the 1950s, is emblematic of the steroid-fuelled hyper-suburbanisation of America and other parts of the world at the turn of the millennium. Houses were getting bigger, pressing further into the countryside; subdivisions were sprawling ever further along highways and around intersections; 100% mortgages were making these dwellings affordable to even more people. Eastvale, like so many other places, is almost city-sized, but lacks many of the things that enrich city-living – a downtown with shops, cafés and restaurants; walkable, lively streets; diversity of architecture; a nightlife.

Traditional notions of urbanisation and suburbanisation have broken down. We have 'edge cities' or 'stealth cities' – settlements that provide housing and employment but which are not urban. The late twentieth century saw the creation of 'boomburbs' in America – vast suburbs of over 100,000 people that had long-term population-growth figures in double digits. Their population increase and economic vitality outpaced cities. Mesa, a suburb of Phoenix, Arizona, for example, has a population of over half a million, making it bigger than the cities of Miami, St Louis and Minneapolis. It has businesses and industries, but no definable centre. Eastvale shares the same essential features: it is a city that doesn't want to be a city.[33]

Its population swelled in the first decade of the millennium from 6,000 to 53,668 as the rural valley was inundated with a deluge of tract housing. Yet even so, this anonymous Anywheresville is already saturated in history. Eastvale came into being during a blizzard of new housing in America: across the country 6.3 million low-density housing units (equivalent to the size of the entire LA metro area) were built between 2003 and 2006 alone. This massive explosion was possible because of investment money – much of it from China – flowing into the US housing market and buying mortgage-backed securities. During this period of easy credit, large luxury suburban mansions became available to people who could not normally afford them. (There is more than a road which connects the Chinese mansions of Arcadia with the McMansions of Eastvale.) Built by the subprime mortgage industry, the new residents of Eastvale were particularly badly hit when the American housing bubble burst in 2008, seeing the value of their overpriced properties halve. Although only a few years old, Eastvale went from being a shiny new suburb to a half-deserted ghost town with vast, deserted foreclosed houses. For a number of years after the financial crisis, gangs moved in, turning McMansions into crystal-meth labs and indoor marijuana farms.

People went to Lakewood in the 1950s to work in the most modern and politically driven industries of the time – making planes and missiles for the Cold War. The people of Eastvale have jobs that are no less cutting-edge. They live near some of the most startling buildings in the world.

For miles and miles these featureless mega-boxes – some the size of a small town, the more modest the extent of a village – sprawl over land where you can still see vines struggling to break through. They carry names that are familiar the world over: UPS, FedEx, Costco, Walmart, Amazon. These gargantuan 1 million-square-foot (twenty-three acre) fulfilment centres sit amid the surviving cattle farms, dairies and forlorn wineries, at the centre of a complex web of freeways, airports, rail lines and suburbs. During the 2010s an extra 20 million square feet of warehousing were being leased year on year in this part of California. This is a massive modern inland port, where millions of tons of cheap imports from Asia are warehoused and redistributed across the United States to fulfil the all-important promise of next-day delivery. Millions of mouse clicks or fingers jabbed at smartphone screens keep the machinery in continual motion. The significance of this inland port is cloaked by the homely feel of suburbia that pervades the area.[34]

Eastvale is a suburb that exists because it is bound up with the global marketplace. The forces that brought millions of Mexicans, Central and South Americans to LA, thousands of Taiwanese entrepreneurs to the San Gabriel Valley, and hundreds of brand-new Chinese millionaires and billionaires to Arcadia, have enticed people to Eastvale to play out a new chapter of the suburban dream. They live at the crossroads of the twenty-first-century economy, just as people in sleepy Lakewood lived at the epicentre of the Cold War. And like their suburban forebears in Lakewood and Compton, they are as vulnerable to shifts in geopolitics, global economics and technology: if the torrent of cargo reaching the inland port dries up, or when automation takes over, the jobs will go.[35]

The trucks streamed towards this huge area of warehouses along the freeway hauling their containers of smartphones, plastic toys, underwear, car parts, frying pans, tools and gadgets that were made 12,000 miles away. I headed in the opposite direction, south-west to where they had come from, a sixty-two-mile journey past yet more sprawling settlements with mind-blurringly identical housing, back past Lakewood and Compton, to the Port of Long Beach, one of Asia's premier gateways to the American market. My 160-mile loop (not counting diversions) circumnavigated a landscape rich in history and meaning, a drive-by narrative that began in the atomic age of the 1950s and concluded at twenty-first-century globalisation's ground zero. The monotonous, history-erasing sameness of suburbia, although it concealed the magnitude of the story, dramatised it as well. Sometimes history happens in boring places. In fact, they often turn out not to be so boring after all.

At Long Beach, huge container ships were unloading. They connect the mega-urban region of LA and southern California to the other major nodes of the global economy, trading megalopolises that have boomed since the 1970s – the 55 million people of the Guangdong–Hong Kong–Macau Greater Bay Area; the Yangtze River Delta Megalopolis (Shanghai, Nanjing, Hangzhou, Suzhou, Jinjiang, Wuxi) with 88 million; Seoul–Incheon, 25 million; Mega Manila, 41 million. Standing on the water's edge at Long Beach amid the flow of goods and capital, is as good a place as any to take a moment to contemplate the forces that have urbanised – and suburbanised – incalculable areas of land all over the world.

*

This is an age defined by monstrous sprawling urban giants. Although this chapter has focused on Los Angeles and its contiguous urban region, it is a story that applies more widely to cities across the globe that have morphed into massive, polycentric megalopolises. The history of LA is the history not of suburbanisation, but the history of how the sharp division between suburb and city has faded. It is about how the city has taken on a new form, but yet is in a continual process of metamorphosis.

As suburbs became more complex and economically vital, they spread even further and faster, chewing up an incredible 43 million acres of American countryside (the size of Washington State) between 1982 and 2012. By 2002, during the housing boom, the United States was losing two acres of farmland, forests and open space every minute to suburban expansion.[36]

From LA to Atlanta, Phoenix to Kansas City, America was the leading exemplar of runaway car-dependent, low-density urban sprawl in the late twentieth century. With widespread car use, spiralling freeways, cheap money, abundant fossil fuels, plenty of land, declining city centres, dispersing businesses and increasing population, people's craving for low-density, out-of-town family homes could be indulged. Perhaps even more significant was the vast fortune spent by central government subsidising the sprawl with tax incentives, mortgages and 68,000 miles of expressway. Car-based, sprawling suburbia, the defining feature of American urbanism in the twentieth century, became the blueprint for other societies undergoing rapid urbanisation. In Asian cities such as Bangkok, Jakarta, Manila and Kuala Lumpur, the hunger among the growing middle classes for LA-style suburban developments was evident in the 1980s. In Tokyo, rising house prices forced 10 million people from the central city to the outer suburbs between 1975 and 1995.

In China, however, few households had cars in the 1980s; walking, cycling and buses were the main forms of transport and cities remained compact. It is easy to associate the rapid urbanisation of China with its eye-catching skyscrapers. But the real story is not vertical, but horizontal, as Chinese cities melted into the countryside. In the 1990s, suburbanisation began in earnest as car-ownership increased. Large urban centres have expanded their footprint by an average of 450 square kilometres since 1978. Some 60% of new middle-class housing was built in the outer suburbs and 70% of cheap housing in the inner suburbs. China seemed bound on the American trajectory, and it was powered by many of the same forces.

Mass suburbanisation occurred on two fronts. The populations of incredibly dense, lively *lilong* and *hutong* neighbourhoods in Beijing and Shanghai, centred on webs of lanes and alleys, were relocated compulsorily to monotonous suburban superblock developments. The reorientation of China's economy towards export markets called for the same kind of restructuring that had turned LA – and cities the world over – inside out. High-tech business parks and export-orientated manufactures were dispersed into suburban development zones; malls and retail parks mushroomed. The correlation between globalisation and suburbanisation is pronounced. On the other front, China's burgeoning middle class decamped to luxury low-density suburban communities. Some of their names attest to the fantasy that inspired them: Orange County, Park Springs and Longbeach (outside Beijing) or Rancho Santa Fe (Shanghai) were built with replicas of southern Californian suburban homes. The dreamy lifestyle offered by American suburbia (like American skyscrapers) has been powerful, broadcast globally as it has been by one of LA's greatest manufactures – its film and TV industry.[37]

The rage for land-gobbling, space-craving suburban living was apparent everywhere. In Britain the built environment doubled in the last two decades of the millennium even though the population grew only modestly. Those years were characterised by sprawl of all kinds. Between 1980 and 1990 the urban population of developing countries increased from 972 million to 1.385 billion. In 1950 only London and

New York were megacities with over 8 million residents each, and there were eighty-three cities with a million or more people. By 1990 there were twenty megacities, and 198 with over a million people. The sheer velocity at which many Asian, African and South American cities grew forced millions of poor rural migrants into suburban shanty towns. Like richer cities, the movement was outwards, not upwards. Lagos, one of the fastest-growing cities, expanded from 762,418 people in 1960 to over 13 million by the close of the century. At the same time, its urban area went from 124 to 708 square miles.

At no point in human history have cities and urban life undergone such momentous changes. The polycentric, sprawling global megacity region which became apparent in LA in the 1950s has since conquered the world. Driven by post-war capitalism, the suburban metropolis has pushed both the concept of the city and humankind's relationship with the natural world to their limits.

Suburbia is an apt monument to the triumph of capitalism and globalisation. Its luxurious expansiveness mirrors our ferocious consumer culture, which promises to fulfil all our desires and runs on the principle of growth without limits. It transforms a natural environment into a controlled, artificial one. In the post-war golden age of suburbia, LA led the way, not least in the startling growth of its gardening industry. Jacarandas, native to the Amazon, were popular in Lakewood for their incredible blossom. Lakewooders also planted dichondra in place of grass on their lawns, because it did not require much mowing. Those two were among an abundance of trees, plants, flowers, shrubs, grasses and fruits imported from every corner of the planet and liberally planted in Los Angeles, transforming suburbia into a fully human-made landscape that is maintained by millions of water sprinklers and gallons of pesticides.[38]

What could be more eloquent an expression of the world at the dawn of the third millennium than the suburban garden? It is a microcosm of the way we dominate the planet. But the real danger of sprawl is not the reordering of our immediate environment. Our species' rejection of the compact city in favour of lavish living space has resulted in metropolises insatiably hungry for ever more electric power, gas, oil, water, concrete and road systems. Sprawl consumes countryside, to be sure; it also squanders resources on a monumental scale. Modern car-based urbanism has ripped the life out of city streets and encouraged nature-devouring low-density expansion. The car has been the great enemy of the urban. It needs more space than anything else, accounting for over 50% of land use in most cities, and much more in LA. We have reshaped our cities around the needs of the car.

The dispersed metropolis requires a lot of driving to navigate; the result is ever-worse congestion and pollution. As metropolitan areas ran outward like a ripe camembert, the average individual American's yearly drive lengthened to 12,000 miles, and commuting times tripled between the 1960s and the end of the century. At the same time, the proportion of household income spent on cars doubled to 20%. During a period of turbocharged suburbanisation and rapid sprawl, it was found that between 1990 and 1995 alone, the time spent driving by mothers of young children rose by 11%; hours spent behind the wheel were greater than those devoted to dressing, bathing and feeding an infant combined. Some 87% of journeys are made by car, hardly a surprising statistic in a country where the automobile is king and rules the city. The price to pay is 40,000 people killed every year in road accidents. It is also paid in the body size of Americans – in the 1970s one in ten were obese; now it is one in three. Deaths from asthma have tripled since the 1990s. Elsewhere, Lagos is the scene of daily gridlock, with commuters spending an average thirty hours a week stuck in slow-moving traffic; in Mexico City 200,000 new cars enter the streets every year. Both Lagos and Mexico City live under the threat of catastrophic environmental collapse. And now that China has become a nation of sprawl, suburbanisation and car-ownership from the 1990s, the problem has gone global.

Low-density urban sprawl, automobile-centric cities and the everyday lifestyles that go with it are the product of cheap oil, and utterly dependent upon it. It is therefore a finite metropolitan form. But in the meantime, car-dependence has made the modern city an engine of poisoning smog, environmental fragmentation and climate change.

14

Megacity

Lagos, 1999–2020

The city is full of predators. It is an environment suited for the tough, who are equipped to adapt and prosper. They thrive in the urban world – much more so than in the countryside. But at the same time, city life tames them, providing a haven for the weak, allowing them to survive the metropolis too.

This may be true for humans; but it is apparent across the urban ecosystem as well. Coyotes, foxes, raccoons, magpies and goshawks, among others, can reach higher densities and populations in cities than in their natural habitat. The city is good for them, it seems. Reintroduced into the UK only twenty-five years ago, the red kite is now a common urban visitor in south-east England. Accustomed to perching on cliffs and using their height to stoop on prey, the craggy cityscape of New York is ideal for peregrine falcons. A pair moved there in 1983; now the city has the highest density of peregrines. Found in cities all over the world, the peregrine has reinvented itself as an urban bird.

Yet, despite the increase in mammalian hunters and avian raptors, the populations of small animals and birds they prey upon also increase. This is known as the urban 'predation paradox'. Enjoying a superabundance of food left by humans, they turn their attention away from small mammals and birds' nests towards picnic sites, bins and roadkill. Prey species – such as song birds – benefit from new food sources in the anthropic environment and from relief from predatory pressures. Even urban cats hunt less. The heat-island effect of the city and the predation paradox has acted as a magnet for swallows and blackbirds seeking warmth and safety. Since the 1980s, the fortunes spent by urbanites and suburbanites on bird food – over £200 million a year in the UK and $4 billion in the US – has increased the bird population and attracted new species to the urban melting pot. The Eurasian blackcap warbler has altered its habitual migration route from central Europe to Spain and North Africa, preferring to head west to enjoy the bounteous feasts laid on in British suburban gardens. Urban bird populations have increased and diversified. No wonder the peregrine falcon, surveying the concrete canyons from its skyscraper cliff, likes its new environment.[1]

Animals behave very differently in cities. Those species that can adapt to a totally different environment thrive. These are known as synanthropic species – ones that benefit from association with human populations. Urban raccoons in Chicago, with a super-rich clumping of reliable food sources in bins, reduce the extent of their roaming ranges and produce more offspring. In Los Angeles, mountain lions have managed to limit themselves to twenty-five square miles instead of the 370 square miles they are accustomed to in the wilderness. Chicago's coyotes have learnt how to cross the road safely. Like the peregrine, the city provides them with refuge from the hunting and trapping they suffer in the wild. The average life expectancy of a coyote in rural America is two and a half years; in cities they can live to twelve or thirteen and raise more pups. Chacma baboons in Cape Town, hanuman langur monkeys in Jodhpur, white-footed tamarin monkeys in Medellín and macaques in Kuala Lumpur are among many simian species that embrace the urban lifestyle, with its inviting roof-tops, wasteful humans and absence of predators. Flamingos started migrating to Mumbai in the 1980s, attracted by the abundance of blue-green algae caused by sewage; by 2019 their numbers reached 120,000, creating patches of pink amid the high-rises. In the informal settlements skirting Mumbai, elusive leopards use the dense urban jungle to hunt for feral dogs in the dead of night.[2]

The challenge of the human-made environment forces animals to learn new problem-solving behaviours. They become streetwise. A crow in the Japanese city of Sendai learnt, at some point in the 1980s, that the wheels of a slow-moving car are ideal for cracking walnuts. Crows throughout the city learnt to do the same. In Vienna spiders that overcame their preference for the dark and wove webs in sections of a bridge illuminated by fluorescent tubes caught four times more prey. North American city raccoons are quicker at solving problems – such as opening doors and windows – than their country cousins. In laboratory experiments finches captured in cities proved more adept at opening lids or pulling on drawers to get food than ones from rural environments. City-raised animals are noticeably bolder and more curious. Some are also less aggressive as a result of living at greater densities. Animals existing in noisy, energetic places – such as mice near underground railway lines – mute their stress responses. A study of small urbanised mammals such as shrews, voles, bats and squirrels found they had bigger brain sizes, much like the brains of London cab drivers, who have greater grey matter in the posterior hippocampus as a result of years spent navigating the complex city labyrinth.[3]

Cities have taken control of their animal residents' evolution in startling and rapid ways. Famously, the peppered moth became dark in response to the polluted environment of the Industrial Revolution. The London Underground mosquito is an entirely new species that has evolved recently in subterranean areas rich in human blood. It has continued to do so: mosquitos on the Piccadilly line are genetically different from those on the Bakerloo. The urban heat-island effect allows blackbirds to remain over winter rather than migrate. They are becoming a separate species to the forest blackbird, mating earlier, developing a shorter beak because the city provides an abundance of easily obtainable food, and singing at a higher pitch to be heard over the traffic. Natural selection is favouring birds with shorter wings that can avoid traffic, smaller mammals, fatter fish, and larger insects capable of travelling further in search of fragmented food sources. In Tucson, Arizona, house finches are evolving longer and fatter beaks because their main food source now comes from garden birdfeeders. In Puerto Rican cities, lizards' toes have evolved to grip bricks and concrete.[4]

*

Evolution is supposed to happen at glacial pace, over millions of years. The incredible story of the adaptation of animals to this radically altered environment is one of the many consequences for the planet of our mushrooming urbanisation over recent decades. The global urban population has surged from a billion in 1960 to in excess of 4 billion in 2020. The growth rates of urban land area were *faster* than population growth in a period when low-density sprawl became endemic. Cities consumed 58,000 square kilometres of the planet between 1970 and 2000; they will gobble up another 1.2 million square kilometres by 2030, tripling the urban area while the urban population doubles. That means adding an urban area bigger than Manhattan to the world's land surface every single day. By 2030, 65% of the world's built environment will have been constructed since 2000. The new global city built in these three decades will, if lumped together, cover an area the size of South Africa. We are living at a time of planetary upheaval.[5] The push of cities into wild habitats and previously untouched ecosystems has increased the likelihood of the transmission of infectious diseases from animals to humans. From the expanding edge of the city, new zoonotic diseases are brought into densely packed metropolises and transferred via the global network to other cities where they wreak havoc.

Although the terrestrial proportion of the planet covered by cities will remain low – about 3% – the key point is *where* we are urbanising. We tend to build our cities in exactly the same spots favoured by animals and plants – lush, well-watered places near coasts, deltas, rivers, grasslands and forests. Present and projected urban growth is concentrated on the world's thirty-six biodiversity hotspots, places with the richest ecologies, such as the Guinean forests of West Africa, the Eastern Afromontane, the Western Ghats in India, the coastal regions of China, Sumatra, and Atlantic Forest in South America. Some 423 fast-growing cities are sprawling into these hotspots, critically threatening the habitats of over 3,000 endangered species.[6]

Megacities and mega urban regions are also taking large chunks out of the world's most fertile croplands. Urbanisation by its very nature releases vast amounts of carbon through deforestation and loss of vegetation biomass, especially when it occurs in the ecologically vital biodiversity hotspots and fertile agricultural regions. Cities change weather patterns and climate in their vicinity; their radiating road systems fragment local species and landscapes. And added to that, the ecological footprint of a city is much larger than the city itself, hungry as it is for electricity, food, water and fuel. The amount of land needed to sustain London – its ecological footprint – is 125 times greater than the metropolis's size.[7]

The successes of urban exploiter species like raccoons, garden birds and peregrines are rare. Every year between 100 million and 600 million migrating birds are killed colliding with skyscrapers in American cities. Their fate represents a microcosm of the ecological damage caused by cities. Rampant urban growth has been responsible for climate change, species extinction and irreparable damage to biodiversity. While cities contain 50% of the human species, they account for 75% of carbon emissions. Los Angeles's thundering freeways prevent gene flow between communities of bobcats and mountain lions near the Ventura Freeway. A bobcat on one side of the freeway is now genetically different from one across the road as inbreeding becomes common in groups trapped by urban sprawl. As cities spread into the planet's precious biodiversity hotspots, more endangered species will suffer the fate of the LA bobcat, their ranges and gene pools shrunk by the world's most dangerous invasive species – *Homo urbanus*.[8]

The shock of our sudden breakneck urbanisation is seen nowhere better in the changing body shapes of some of the world's animals as they race to adapt to the new world or their genetic make-ups suffer as a result of disruption to their habitat.

We welcome our new neighbours – the stirring peregrine falcons, the stalking leopard, crowds of flamingos, new bird species, immigrant badgers – with delight and amazement. Here is nature sharing the artificial city against the odds; here is life in the concrete expanse. News items about evolving blackbirds, wily coyotes and streetwise foxes tell us that cities are part of the ecosystem, not separate from it. Most importantly, it reminds us that we can share the city with nature despite the damage we have done if we make modifications to our built environment.

Until very recent times we saw the city and the countryside as two distinct and incompatible things. There was, after all, a lot of nature and not a lot of city. For much of history the urban has been seen as the enemy of the natural, a destructive force that gobbled up the countryside. The shock of mass urbanisation and resulting climate change has altered that psychological perception; now the city is becoming dominant over nature. This has changed how we see the metropolis. It is startling to consider that 47% of London is green space and that it contains within its bounds the largest urban forest in the world – there are as many trees as people (over 8 million) and they cover 21% of the city's area. In addition, London has at least 14,000 species of plants, animals and fungi and 1,500 sites of ecological importance, with 10% of its metropolitan area designated for nature conservation. Brussels has 50% of the floral species found in Belgium, while Cape Town preserves 50% of South Africa's critically endangered vegetation types. The highly urbanised city state of Singapore is one of the most biodiverse places on the planet, with half of its 716 square kilometres given over to forests, nature reserves and networks of green corridors that connect habitats. It is hungry for more foliage, with hundreds of lush green roofs and vertical gardens cascading down skyscrapers.[9]

We are only just starting to wake up to the fact that cities support rich biodiversity and that this ecology is vital to our survival. Tropical cities emerging in the planet's biodiversity hotspots are capable of sustaining plant and animal species if their citizens plan accordingly, as Singapore shows. Indeed, the recent evolutionary history of animals and plants in the city might herald the future not only of the planet's biodiversity, but of the city itself.

Every day 60,000 people walk alongside an urban stream fringed with greenery in the heart of one of the world's biggest metropolises. At the beginning of this century it was a hideous elevated freeway cutting through Seoul; cars criss-crossed over it while underneath criminals consorted and people dumped garbage. Between 2002 and 2005 the Cheonggyecheon freeway was ripped out and a stream, long buried beneath concrete, was revived. It is harder to drive your car into downtown Seoul now there is no freeway. But that is no bad thing – the loss of road has encouraged use of, and investment in, public transport. Today the Cheonggyecheon creek is a remarkable oasis of greenery and water in the middle of the city. It reduces air-pollution levels and mitigates the heat-island effect with temperatures 5.9°C cooler than elsewhere in the metropolis. More importantly, its foliage increases biodiversity and improves quality of human life in the city.[10]

The Cheonggyecheon project was expensive, with a price tag in the hundreds of millions of dollars, and mired in controversy. Nonetheless it stands as an international symbol of green urban renewal. One of the defining aspects of modern urbanism is the attempt to strike a balance between cities and nature in a way that has never been contemplated before. In part this is because wildlife is good for human health and mental well-being. Cities have had parks, trees and open spaces for centuries, to be sure. But today many cities are coming to see that nature does not have to be hived off in particular areas; it can be woven throughout the urban fabric. Not all projects have to be as lavish as the Cheonggyecheon megaproject. The micro level is even more important for local biodiversity. Creating green corridors linking railway sidings, road verges, pocket parks, vacant spaces, private gardens and open areas has become a part of town planning across the world. Encouraging pollinators and keeping bees has also become a priority in cities as people become more conscious of the urban ecosystem.

In common with peregrine falcons, bees are finding the twenty-first-century metropolis a congenial environment because its diversity of plants makes it a foraging paradise compared to intensively farmed land, where monoculture prevails. Analysis of honey showed that an urban bee in Boston, Massachusetts, takes pollen from 411 different species of plant compared to nearby rural bees, whose honey had traces from just eighty-two. What other species can thrive under these changing urban conditions? And how will they evolve? A large metropolis can become a patchwork of almost imperceptible micro-habitats that exist alongside larger public parks that can attract colonisers to the city.[11]

Mexico City has installed more than 226,000 square feet of roof gardens since 2008. Barcelona, one of Europe's most densely populated cities, is creating green corridors through the city, a network of linked parks, gardens, roof gardens, trees, green walls and creepers that will squeeze an extra 400 acres of green space into the city. Tiny, dense Singapore managed to create green space equivalent to the size of Regent's Park in London – 400 acres – in the sky, on rooftops, walls and balconies. Mexico City, Barcelona and Singapore's efforts are examples of how a city can add greenery without carving space out of the urban fabric. Perhaps the most striking result of greening a city is Rue Gonçalo de Carvalho in Porto Alegre, Brazil. The street's tall rosewood trees, with their lavish canopies, cut a green swathe through the urban environment. This street is one of seventy green tunnels that burrow through the city.[12]

The view of Rue Gonçalo de Carvalho could well be a vision of the future metropolis. We'd better hope it is. Trees are not being planted in their millions in cities around the world just for crowd-pleasing aesthetic reasons or to benefit bees and butterflies. Humans seem to value things with a price tag. In this case it is known as 'treeconomics'. The presence of trees can boost a property's price by 20%. Cape Town valued its urban ecology at between $5.13 billion and $9.78 billion. The 2,789-hectare urban forest in Lanzhou provides an economic service to the city estimated to be $14 million a year; New York's trees provide annual benefits put at $120 million. Where once urban trees were seen as ornamental, they are now regarded as essential. One large tree can suck 150 kilograms of carbon out of the atmosphere. They also filter out airborne pollutants (between 20% and 50% of particulate-matter concentrations) and cool overheated cities by between 2°C and 8°C, reducing air conditioning use by 30%. If trees can have this effect, they will be vital not so much in halting climate change as helping us survive its effects. Since 2000, as urban temperatures have surged, use of air conditioning has doubled and will triple again by 2050. The power required to keep us cool will equal the *total* electricity demand of the USA and Germany combined – 10% of all global consumption. If roof gardens in Mexico City and green walls in Cairo can cool buildings, they offer an alternative to this self-destructive reliance on air conditioning.[13]

When we monetise nature, we begin to see its value. Or else we learn the hard way the dependence of cities on their ecology. New Orleans paid for the loss of its wetlands in 2005 when it suffered catastrophic flooding. In the same year Mumbai came to regret the destruction of forty square kilometres of mangrove forests – nature's barrier between land and sea – when it too flooded. During Bangalore's rapid urbanisation, its temperature went up by 2.5°C and it experiences frequent flooding, both as a result of the destruction of 88% of its vegetation and 79% of its wetlands. Louisville, Kentucky, is one of the most heat-stressed cities in the US, where downtown temperatures can be 10°C hotter than in the suburbs, in large part because vegetation cover in the urban core is pitifully low at about 8%. The city needs to plant hundreds of thousands of trees a year to restrain its galloping temperatures; so far, its private sector has been reluctant to do anything about it.

Faced with a future of superstorms, the vast impermeable concrete layering of modern cities and suburbs has made them unable to absorb excess water. Chicago, Berlin and Shanghai are learning (or relearning) how to mimic natural hydrology as an urgent flood-prevention tactic. Trees are vital because they are capable of absorbing large amounts of water. But, like the Lingang district of Shanghai, cities are also using roof gardens, urban wetlands, porous pavements, bioswales and rain gardens as giant sponges that soak up excess rainwater and gradually release it. The water is filtered into aquifers and rivers or eventually evaporates into the atmosphere, cooling the city as it does so.

The need is to get rid of floodwater; the by-products are more trees and flower beds, water features and urban wetlands that are beneficial to human well-being and biodiversity. In many developing parts of the world, biodiversity has to some extent been maintained by an expansion in city agriculture that has paralleled urban growth, particularly where rural food production has not kept up with the pace of change. In Havana, 90% of fruit and vegetables are grown in 200 *organopónicos*, organic urban farms, that have been established since the fall of the Soviet bloc in 1991 meant a collapse of Cuba's food and fertiliser imports. *Organopónicos* occupy 12% of the metropolitan area, often wedged between ugly tower blocks in densely populated parts of the city.[14]

Across the globe there are 100–200 million urban farmers, 65% of them women, operating in everything from back gardens, abandoned plots and rooftops to established city farms. The United Nations estimates that between 15% and 20% of food production now comes from metropolitan areas. In Kenyan cities 29% of families are employed in agriculture; in Vietnamese and Nicaraguan cities 70% of households make some kind of money from food production.[15]

Since the turn of the millennium, urban farming has become a part of the survival strategies of people in fast-growing megacities in Africa, Latin America and Asia. Millions grow fruit and vegetables simply to earn enough to stay alive. Urban farms will never satisfy the needs of a city. But they are important for local economies and even more so for augmenting the urban environment and its biodiversity, providing habitat for a variety of arthropods, microbes, birds and small mammals.

The greener city sounds utopian. But it is happening in different ways around the world, sometimes without us really noticing. In Seattle invasive species are being replaced by native evergreens because they are better at storm-water retention. Between 2007 and 2015 New York City planted a million additional trees. Shanghai's tree coverage increased from 3% in 1990 to 13% in 2009 and 23% by 2020; its latest city plan promises to increase it to 50% by the middle of this century. In Salvador, Brazil, a large garbage dump is being turned into an extensive urban forest, using treated sludge from the city's sewerage system as fertiliser. Previously barren, car-filled streets in Amsterdam are being transformed with trees, gardens, rose bushes, composters and play equipment as 1,500 parking spaces are eliminated every year. Since 2011 Los Angeles – a park-poor city – has turned abandoned lots and foreclosed building sites into tiny pocket parks. There are also new 'parklets', tiny green extensions from the sidewalk into the street that reclaim parking spaces for pedestrians.

The LA parklet is a small symbolic victory in a city once called 'autopia', a metropolis built around the car. Cars will not be a permanent feature of our cities: history surely teaches that technologies are superseded one way or another. Already, cities are battling against the automobile, restricting and taxing their rights of access. As in Amsterdam, trees and plants may come in the place of land-greedy cars. Chennai allocated a whopping 60% of its transportation budget to walking and cycling. In the United States there are plans to convert several enormous multi-lane urban freeways – the monsters that slashed through neighbourhoods in the 1960s, isolating them and condemning them to terminal decline – into tree-lined boulevards with parks running down the middle. A vivid example of this transition from cars to vegetation is Seoullo 7017, a once-busy city flyover in Seoul that was closed to traffic in 2015 and converted into a one-kilometre-long pedestrianised sky garden with 24,000 plants and trees.

*

Cities are complex adaptive systems. As history shows, they are supremely good at ensuring their own survival. The greening of twenty-first-century cities is an aspect of this age-old instinct for self-preservation, defensive and pre-emptive as surely as walls, watchtowers, citadels and air-raid shelters once were. Cities are the leading actors in combating climate change, more so than nation states. Shanghai, Osaka, Lagos, Ho Chi Minh City, Dhaka and Miami are among many cities that will be submerged by a 1.5-metre rise in sea levels. Today, two-thirds of metropolises with populations exceeding 5 million people lie in areas that are no more than ten metres above sea level. If cities are at the forefront of combating climate change, it is because they are on its front line.

In 2017 $394 billion was invested in green tech around the world and almost $2 trillion in renewal energy. San Francisco, Frankfurt, Vancouver and San Diego are on their way to becoming cities that get 100% of their electricity through renewable energy. Companies in cities such as Newark and Singapore are experimenting with computer-controlled hydroponic agriculture. These skyscraper farms use just 10% of the water required in conventional farming, with hardly any nitrates and pesticides.

The city-builders of the twenty-first century have familiar names: Google, Cisco, Apple, Microsoft, Panasonic, IBM, Siemens, Huawei. True to their backgrounds, such companies see the twenty-first-century metropolis as a system that can be made more efficient – and hence more sustainable – by using Big Data and artificial intelligence. Just as cities adapted to technological change – such as the Industrial Revolution and the internal combustion engine – they will reshape around the computer.

In this vision of the city of the future, sensors are embedded every-where while smartphones beam back yet more data to a central computer that allows the city to monitor and respond in real time to traffic and public transport flows, energy use and pollution levels, and detect crime and accidents. In Rio de Janeiro a force of 400 staffs the city's NASA-like operational control centre, measuring everything from congestion and pollution to keeping watch on CCTV camera streams and keywords being used in local social media.

Santander, Europe's smartest city, already has 20,000 sensors keeping eternal watch on the activities of the human hive. Sensors in bins report to garbage trucks when they need to be emptied; those embedded in parks monitor moisture in the soil and switch sprinklers on and off according to need; street lights dim and brighten in response to pedestrian and traffic volume. Artificial intelligence used in this way can cut energy and water costs by 50%. It can also make the city more efficient in other ways. Acoustic sensors detect the sirens of an approaching ambulance and link up with traffic lights to clear the way to the emergency. It has been calculated that 30% of driving time is spent looking for a place to park; wireless sensors can detect an unused space and direct a motorist straight to it.

Driven by data, this model is known as 'IoT towns' ('IoT' standing for 'Internet of Things'), 'the ubiquitous city', the 'sentient city' and, most commonly, the 'smart city', where information is continually devoured by AI for predictive modelling and real-time responsiveness. Meta-analysis of smartphone use, for instance, can be used to see how and when citizens move about a city, changing bus routes accordingly. It can also be used to track the spread of infectious diseases through compulsory digital surveillance of entire urban populations. The monitoring of behaviour within the metropolis, done in the name of efficiency and crisis management, will surely become one of the salient features of urban life in the present century.

The authoritarianism implied by smart cities, and enforced by fears of deadly pandemics, is deeply troubling. Yet while cities are weaving digital technologies into their infrastructure, one of the most eye-catching and significant aspects of contemporary urbanism is the ways in which we have come to see cities as woven into their ecosystems, not as places apart from the natural world. We are able to appreciate how trees and open spaces, mangrove forests and wetlands, bees and birds interact with the urban environment and make it healthier and more resilient. We are coming, slowly, to see our cities as natural as well as man-made environments where all their facets – including transport, waste management, housing, water, food, biodiversity, animal habitations, insect life, wetlands, fuel needs and so on – are part of complex, mutually dependent ecosystems.

In an unstable world, it is becoming increasingly urgent for other cities, particularly in developing areas in biodiversity hotspots, to avoid the mistakes made during the urbanising history of more mature cities. Curitiba provides inspiration. Since the 1970s, this poor, fast-growing, flood-prone Brazilian city that lies within one of the biodiversity hotspots has added 1.5 million trees, 154 square miles of parks and several artificial lakes, and has built an ecological corridor alongside the river Barigui. While the population tripled, the amount of green space went from 0.5 square metres per person to an astonishing fifty square metres. Curitiba did not simply plant trees; it developed a plan that integrated sustainability policies into every almost every aspect of urban planning.

While cities in the 1960s and 70s were tearing up chunks of down-town and putting in roads, Curitiba did the opposite, preserving its historic core and pedestrianising its streets. The city developed an extensive and innovative bus rapid transit (BRT) network used by 70% of the population, despite the city having more cars per capita than any other Brazilian city. Copied by 150 cities around the world, the BRT cut traffic by 30% and has resulted in the city having remarkably low levels of air pollution. Curitiba also pioneered a 'green exchange' whereby recyclable trash was exchanged for bus tickets and food; today 70% of garbage is recycled. The interweaving of urban planning and environmentalism has had an economic impact: Curitiba's thirty-year economic growth rate is 7.1% compared to the national average of 4.2% and its per capita income is 66% higher. A large and growing proportion of the population lives in unplanned *favelas*. But at the very least its successes show how creative, low-budget policies that link human-made and natural ecosystems can transform a city.

A 'smart city' is not simply one with thousands of sensors and a digital infrastructure. It is one that is designed to provide a resilient human and natural habitat. The effort going into enhancing the biodi-versity of cities is not primarily about being kind to wildlife for its own sake; it is a survival strategy. Imagining the city of the future is always a futile exercise. But based on current trends, it will probably be less like the LA of *Blade Runner* and more like present-day Singapore, with wall gardens tumbling down skyscrapers, urban forests, sky gardens, farms, green streets, biodiversity corridors, inner-city nature reserves, animal life and canopies of trees. It may look nice: but it is a direct consequence of our fight to adapt to man-made climate change.

A solution to our present crisis is evidently to bring nature back into the city. Paradoxical as it may sound, is also imperative to make the world more urban.

★

Places don't get more urban than Lagos and the host of other megaci-ties with extensive, congested informal settlements – Mumbai, Manila, Mexico City, São Paulo, Dhaka. They are complex human ecosystems to be sure – perhaps some of the most complex societies ever created by our species. To many they are the pre-eminent disaster sites of the modern world. They demonstrate a world gone horribly wrong.

To others, however, they are testament to our species' incredible ability to adapt to the urban environment and make it home, however inhospitable and daunting it seems. They reveal humankind's capacity for self-organisation, self-reliance and self-survival in the face of extreme disorder.

In Lagos, a population almost three times greater than London's squeezes into an area two-thirds the size of London. It is predicted to be the largest city in the world by the middle of this century, its population set to double to over 40 million people by 2040 and then keep on growing at a phenomenal rate. In 2018 the number of urban Nigerians overtook the number of rural Nigerians. By 2030 Africa will be the final inhabitable continent to become majority urban – a seminal and fateful moment in our history as a species.

Vast, unfathomable, noisy, dirty, chaotic, overcrowded, energetic, dangerous, Lagos represents the very worst features of modern urbanisation. It also evinces some of the best.

Whatever the case, what happens in Lagos and other megacities in developing states matters because they are home to unprecedented concentrations of humanity. They push everything to the limits – human endurance as well as their own sustainability in an age of climatic instability.

This vast African megacity is infamous for its sprawling slums, corruption and crime, its appalling infrastructure and the worst traffic jams in the world. The sight of back-to-back lorries queueing through the city's potholed roads for weeks on end waiting to deliver and collect containers at the port is an incredible sight. Even more striking are the oil tankers and container ships backed up at sea, queuing for a docking slot at the Apapa Port. Many ships give up the ghost long before they make a berth; the shoreline is littered with abandoned freighters and shipwrecks. On land, the quintessential sound of Lagos is the incessant scream of private diesel electricity generators at night. The city's sprawl into the wetlands, mangrove forests and floodplains has severely disrupted the natural hydrology, making the urban poor vulnerable to increasingly severe rainfall and storm surges. This is a city that cannot ensure continuous electricity for its people, supply them with adequate water or deal with the 10,000 tons of waste produced each day.

In this overwhelmingly dense urban realm, there are few cars that *don't* have dents and scrapes. For every car per kilometre of road in New York, there are ten times more in Lagos. In their battered state, battling hard for space on the disorderly roads in a never-ending war, Lagosian cars are moving symbols of the stresses of megacity life (even if they can rarely move very fast) and the vicious principle of survival of the fittest that is hardwired into the daily experience of Lagos. Fighting through the brutish roads one day, my Lagosian friend apologised in exasperation. If, he said, this brawling mass of motorists could be transposed to an English town all the anger would drain away and they would become civilised. It was the city, he said with bitterness and frustration in his voice, that made them so angry and aggressive.

He had a point; Lagos had just been declared the world's second worst city to live in, just behind war-torn Damascus. I asked the people in the car – who had all spent extensive time working abroad, in the United States and Europe – why they lived in Lagos and loved it. The collective reply was instantaneous and unequivocal: 'This is the funnest city in the world!'

It was Saturday evening, and it was hard to disagree. As darkness fell, the traffic jams built up, music began to blare, food sizzled along every street, and millions of people started to surge through the urban honeycomb, began turning Lagos into the biggest party city on the planet.

No doubt this lust for life is a reaction to, and respite from, the harshness of the city and the demands of its manic energy. Two-thirds of the population live in 200 informal settlements. Most clearly visible for all visitors to Lagos is Makoko, a huge 'floating' slum of between 100,000 and 300,000 people, where wooden shacks perch on stilts in the stinking lagoon. In his novel *The Carnivorous City* (2016), the self-styled 'mayor of Lagos', Toni Kan, wrote: 'Lagos is a beast with bared fangs and a voracious appetite for human flesh. Walk through its neighbourhoods, from the gated communities of Ikoyi and Victoria Island to Lekki and beyond to the riotous warrens of streets and alleyways on the mainland and you can tell this is a carnivorous city. Life is not just brutish – it is short ... Yet, like crazed moths disdaining the rage of the flame, we keep gravitating towards Lagos, compelled by the same centrifugal force that defies reason and willpower.'[16]

Those words, with the names changed, could be written about Uruk in the third millennium BC, or about Baghdad in the tenth century AD, or about Manchester, Chicago, or about thousands of cities through history. Big, brutal and dangerous, cities have always acted as magnets, even if they don't care about their human fuel. And there are very compelling reasons why a Nigerian would want to live in Lagos. It is an oil-rich city, a banking, financial and commercial powerhouse, Nigeria's main manufacturing centre and – with three ports and one of Africa's major international airports – a transportation hub in which over 70% of Nigeria's foreign trade funnels slowly through the congested city. If Lagos was a country it would be the fifth-richest in Africa.

This single city generates more than a third of Nigeria's gross domestic product and per capita incomes are double the national average: of course people keep coming in their thousands every day. The Lagos of 2020 is very different from the Lagos of 2000, when it appeared to be careening towards disaster. Today its economy is booming; so too are its music, fashions, movie-making, literature and arts. Lagos-based Nollywood is the second-biggest film industry in the world in terms of output, after Bollywood. In the 2010s a highly innovative tech start-up business sector also gained a foothold in the city. Foreign investment has poured into the 'Yabacon Valley' – named after Lagos's start-up hub in the Yaba district – because the likes of Google and Facebook see the city as the gateway to what is called 'the next billion' – young people in poorer countries who are yet to embrace mobile Internet. A city dominated by young people (60% are under thirty), its youth culture and entrepreneurialism have created a massive market for music, entertainment, fashion and tech. Mega in every sense, Lagos pulsates with a crazy energy; its dynamism is intoxicating. In the words of a Nigerian journalist, a journey on an iconic dilapidated yellow *danfo* minibus, the prime means of getting about the city, is a microcosm of Lagos itself: 'crazy and funny, breathtaking and intriguing, and of course, risky and life-threatening'.[17]

You feel the weight and energy of 25 million people pressing down on you when you stand on the side of Ahmadu Bello Way on the southern tip of Lagos's Victoria Island and look through a chain-link fence and out across a vast expanse of sand and gravel. This is land only recently reclaimed from the Atlantic Ocean; it sits behind 'the

Great Wall of Lagos', 100,000 five-ton concrete blocks that defend it from the churning sea. Already a few skyscrapers are poking out of the sand, the first of a futuristic smart, sustainable city called Eko Atlantic. It is promoted as Lagos's version of Pudong in Shanghai or of Dubai – an African Manhattan that will catapult Nigeria's megacity to the status of financial capital of Africa and major global hub.

There is something surreal about imagining the gleaming skyscrapers, luxury holiday resorts and marinas full of superyachts that will emerge here, on the tip of one of the biggest, poorest and most dysfunctional cities on earth, where the majority survive in the informal economy on a dollar a day. It is the best possible place to sit and contemplate the forces that have reshaped our metropolises over the last few years. Eko Atlantic is an exaggerated version of what is happening around the world.

At the close of the twentieth century it was supposed that the city as it had always been known was dead or at least in an advanced state of decay. Suburbanisation had turned it inside out; the Internet would complete the process, rendering obsolete the need for physical proximity. The opposite happened. The parallel revolutions in global finance and the knowledge economy encouraged not dispersal, but the clustering of money, assets, ideas, talent and power in a small group of turbocharged global metropolises.[18]

All of which was, of course, to intensify something that had always been the case in cities. Uruk developed so quickly as humanity's first city not least because its home-based craftsmen clustered in its neighbourhoods, sharing knowledge, specialisms and tools. Together they could achieve economies of scale and information networks totally unknown before. The mind-baffling complexity of urban life led to the encoding of knowledge in writing. The coffee-house culture of eighteenth-century London provided informal meeting places and knowledge exchanges for merchants, craftsmen, scientists, explorers, bankers, investors and writers, who together forged the first great capitalist economy through their fluid associations. In twentieth-century New York, the concentration of big banks, small investment firms, lawyers, insurers and advertisers within walking distance fostered intense competition and rapid innovation within the market. In all these cases – and many more through history and around the world – the city, with its dynamism and complex, intermeshed networks, took the organising function of a large corporation or university, providing the framework for informal divisions – and subdivisions – of labour, knowledge-sharing, networking and economies of scale.

The twenty-first-century knowledge economy is similarly urban. The companies and industries that power the modern world – start-ups, tech firms, R&D, media, fashion, fin-tech, advertising – concentrate and cluster even more intensely, feasting off the physical proximity that only a city can provide, even in an age of superfast digital connectivity. Creativity is generated, in large part, by spontaneity and chance encounters; it is bound up with the interaction of work and sociability.

If the forces effecting urbanisation were centrifugal in the twentieth century – forcing the iron filings to scatter apart – in the twenty-first century they are strongly centripetal, drawing those iron filings straight back to the magnet. A handful of city regions spread over the world – containing just under 20% of the world's population – produce 75% of global economic output. And these same cities monopolise new technological, digital and pharmaceutical patents, software innovations, entertainment, finance, insurance and research. With so much of the globe's wealth clustered in a few urban areas, cities have once again become the engines of global prosperity.

Cities prospered in the past because – like Lisbon, Lübeck, Baghdad or Amsterdam – they drew trade routes into their orbit; today they become staggeringly successful if they can attract, and keep on attracting, the intangible: talented individuals, tech start-ups, financial services, streams of data and investors in real estate. The energy that drives the twenty-first-century economy comes from connectivity – fast Internet download speeds and airport capacity, both of which determine a city's access to the lucrative and fickle global flows of knowledge, people, capital and data. One of the most powerful places on earth is Silicon Valley, a place that prospers because of minds, not things. And what makes it successful is the entrepreneurialism generated by face-to-face contact and personal networks. Despite Silicon Valley being in the business of manufacturing technologies of long-distance virtual communication, cyberspace has not supplanted city-space.

The competition for talent has required cities to create an urban ecosystem adapted specifically to the knowledge economy. They need to be able to offer coffee shops and world-class restaurants as much as superfast fibre optics and efficient airports. They need boutique shops, street food, cultural vibrancy, farmers' markets, high-profile sporting events, non-stop entertainment and intoxicating nightlife; they must offer stylish neighbourhoods, a beautified cityscape, good schools, efficient transport, clean air and dynamic universities. Cities have to market themselves aggressively as desirable, exciting places in which to live and work, flaunting their assets in glossy photos, promotional videos and movies, in order to poach the greatest of all commodities – human capital.

Today's spectacular urban renaissance is written in the skyline as much as anywhere else. The astonishing speed of China's urban-led growth was broadcast to the world in a series of iconic skyscraper cities that were built explicitly as visual representations of the country's urban success story. The shiny towers tell the world that their city is a member of the elite club of global powerhouses. They are there as a magnet to attract capital, investment and human resources. It is a branding strategy that Chinese cities borrowed from places such as Tokyo, Kuala Lumpur, Hong Kong and Dubai, and which has been transmitted to London and Lagos.

Lagos's Eko Atlantic is being built over what was once the most popular beach in Lagos. The public space has been taken away from the people to make a city within a city for 250,000 people. It will be a private city, intended for the headquarters of banks, financial companies, law firms and other multinational corporations, the skyscraper apartments of the super-rich, and luxury hotels catering for elite tourists: a mini-Dubai in an African megacity.

Eko Atlantic represents in stark terms the desire to escape from the messy, chaotic city to a well-defended private bastion even if it means colonising the ocean, staking a bet against rising sea levels. The impatience among the wealthy and middle class to transform Lagos into 'Africa's model megacity and [a] global, economic and financial hub' is acute. The priority seems to be to sculpt sections of the city into something that befits its aspirations. By 2017 it was claimed that several aquatic informal settlements in the lagoon – the homes of 300,000 people – had been or were about to be cleared, the government citing environmental and security concerns. The real reason became clear when the sites of these ancient villages were turned into luxury waterside apartments. Similarly, the famous raucous Oshodi market was demolished and replaced with a multi-lane highway and transport terminal. Highly visible to visitors, standing as it did near the airport, the market's sprawling activities seemed to represent the kind of spontaneous urban chaos that conflicted with the official desire for orderliness. The poor seem to be an affront to the new image being created for Lagos.

This is not necessarily to criticise Eko Atlantic or Lagos, merely to argue that what is happening is part of the larger picture of how cities are changing in the early part of this century. Urbanisation has in Africa, as well as in China and across Asia, resulted in the fast expansion of the middle class. The urban renaissance is not being shared equally in terms either of income or of geography. The skylines of cities reflect the divisions that run through contemporary metropolises, with those who can afford it occupying exclusive residential enclaves or retiring to their islands in the sky.

Lagos also attests to another feature of modern urbanism: the incredible success of megacities. Its expansion from 288,000 people in 1950 to 20-something million in 2020 is extraordinary by any measure. It is a metropolis shaped by the urban revolution that has engulfed the world. Lagos shows that individual and national fortunes are tightly bound up with mass urbanisation. The success of the city has been transformative for Nigeria and for millions upon millions of individuals escaping the miseries of rural poverty. But like many other cities, its vertiginous growth has far outpaced its capacity to build the necessary infrastructure or house the newcomers. It came immediately after its freedom from British imperial control and the resulting civil disorder, military dictatorships, corruption and political instability. Lagos's class segmentation today is a legacy, in large part, of racial segregation under colonialism.

Segmentation is undoubtedly the curse of megacities in the developing world. It blocks the flow of the lifeblood through the arteries of metropolises; mobility of all kinds gets impeded. In Lagos the daily commute is known as the 'Go Slow'. It begins at 4 a.m. as people head off for a relatively short journey to the office that can take as much as three hours at a snail's pace through gridlock. In 2010 it was estimated that 3 billion work hours were lost to congestion every year, and it is likely to be a lot more a decade on. That's an awful lot of energy consumed by queuing. Attempts to connect the city through light rail and bus rapid transit have faltered. Traffic congestion is the most glaring symptom of a much wider problem stifling the city. Metropolitan development is slowed down by inadequate infrastructure, schooling, healthcare and policing and by the absence of basic services and social security. These real and metaphorical congestions in the urban circulatory system counteract one of the megacity's greatest advantages: its sheer magnitude and density.[19]

Lagos is a city of millions of entrepreneurs and thousands of micro-economies that flourish between the cracks. Everywhere in the city, people are doing business incessantly, getting by, surviving; they form intricate networks beyond the control and oversight of the formal economy. In Lagos between 50% and 70% of people sustain themselves in the informal sector that services the multifarious needs of the fastest-growing metropolis on earth. There are an estimated 11 million 'micro-enterprises' in Lagos. Most obvious are the hawkers. When traffic slows, they appear out of nowhere selling everything possible, from the immediately useful – cold drinks, groundnuts, yams, Agege bread, roasted corn, phone cards and chargers – to the opportunistic and often bizarre – hat stands, inflatable toys, lilos, ironing boards, brooms, board games. Lagos's 'Go Slow' gridlock is a nightmare for many, a tremendous business opportunity for others, many of them recent migrants seeking an income to get started in the city. The streets of Lagos are like a drive-thru mall served by the ubiquitous hawkers and never-ending roadside markets, shacks, umbrella stalls, kiosks and barbecues.

As cities have sucked in billions of new residents, 61% of the world's workers – 2 billion people – now work in micro-businesses or for themselves, surviving the megacity on their wits. The amount of money generated worldwide off the books is estimated by A. T. Kearney to be $10.7 trillion a year, or 23% of global GDP. The shadow economy is vital to the urban world, providing income (however precarious) for recent migrants. The opportunities available, even at the bottom of the heap, are better than for those living in rural poverty. The DIY sector satisfies 75% of the needs of African cities. It feeds and transports Lagos. Thousands of beaten-up, dangerous yellow *danfo* minibuses ply the routes of the city, moving people about in complex patterns that could not be replicated by a regular, centralised bus service. As one driver told a Nigerian newspaper, *danfos* 'go deep into the interior of Lagos to pull people out' and take them where they need to be.[20]

People have always moved into the city and eked out a living in the unofficial, unrecognised 'grey zone'; the difference today is its magnitude and intensity. Where there are millions packed together, the scale of activity and innovation increases exponentially. Slums in Lagos, Mumbai, Manila, Dhaka, Rio and elsewhere are some of the most innovative and creative human ecosystems on the planet. Survival depends on it: no one else is going to help them.

The symbol of Lagos's slums, Makoko with its shacks on sticks above the polluted lagoon, looks appalling and is used to illustrate countless articles on urban dystopia. But less well known is the fact that it is home to a lucrative timber transhipment market and numerous sawmill businesses. Makoko is on the water for a reason: to take advantage of a business opportunity. One sawyer told the Nigerian *Guardian*: 'Many of us have built houses, sent kids to university, have jeeps.' Many more are poor beyond belief and very recent immigrants in the city; but the sawmills of Makoko at least offer them a route into the city and a place where they can afford to live.[21]

One of the best examples of the vitality of the informal sector is the amazing Otigba Computer Village, a warren of streets in the Lagosian district of Ikeja near Murtala Muhammed Airport, a claustrophobic area of one square kilometre, packed with touts, traders, scammers, technicians, software engineers, freelance IT specialists, cars, *danfos*, food vendors, hawkers and piles of keyboards, coils of cables and mountains of screens. It looks at first sight like any other lively informal African commodities market. But it is much more than that.

In this bustling unregulated tech village, the largest gadget market in West Africa, over 8,000 big, small and individual businesses and 24,000 traders and geeks offer the latest smartphones, laptops and accessories for sale alongside repaired and repurposed devices. They fix screens, upgrade your software, perform data recovery and repair motherboards. The competition is insanely fierce: big tech companies compete alongside individual traders and artisans to offer the best prices and capture a slice of the eye-popping $2 billion annual turnover in the market. Business activity spills out of offices and shacks into the street to capture the attention of the throngs of customers with creative sales patter. There are smart, state-of-the-art showrooms alongside tiny shops, umbrella stands and techies who will fix your device on the bonnet of a car. Customers come from all over the city, Nigeria and Africa; haggling is intense as deals are struck over the latest iPhone or an aged mouse.[22]

No one planned Otigba Computer Village and certainly no one anticipated its staggering daily turnover of over $5 million. Originally a residential area, it attracted typewriter repairers in the 1990s. These technicians made the jump into IT towards the end of the decade. The clustering effect took off quickly at the turn of millennium, as people went there to exchange gadgets, software and ideas. With the growth in personal computers and the arrival of Global System for Mobile (GSM) in Nigeria in 2001 the market exploded.

The GSM multinationals could not compete with Ikeja's hustlers or its home-grown repair and upgrade industry, made up of young entrepreneurs armed with a few tools who scented a massive business opportunity at the advent of the mobile communications boom. The Otigba market sourced materials much cheaper than the technology industry, ensuring that high tech remained a thing of the streets and markets, not corporations. The other rocket fuel injected into Otigba was the deluge of e-waste emanating from the developed world. If you ever wonder where your old laptop or phone goes, it might well be Lagos's Computer Village. The West's profligacy and its disposable culture meant boom time for e-waste brokers in Lagos, who import discarded devices. We don't talk about it much, but our sleek and shiny devices, which look so clean and innocent, are producing one of the fastest-growing and most polluting forms of waste in the world.

Every month half a million used electric devices and parts enter Nigeria from the US, Europe and Asia, many of them illegally. Self-taught, freelance repairers get to work on them, using their skills to get them on sale in the market. Most of them can't be used. The dumping of electronics has created other booming businesses. Scavengers purchase cartloads of broken devices, which they strip down, selling the parts and materials to manufacturers. Then they are tipped at places like the enormous Olusosun dump – one of the biggest in the world – where yet more scavengers mine the mountains of garbage, burning cables for their copper wires and extracting precious materials from computers. In the process, large amounts of lead and mercury are released into the soil and into the water system.[23]

Otigba Computer Village is unregulated, but it has its own trade associations, internal government and justice system. It works on collaboration. Most valuably, the more experienced traders and technicians – many of whom started on the streets at the beginning of the mobile tech era as itinerant geeks before buying shops and showrooms – take on apprentices. When they 'graduate', these young men and women go on to set up their own businesses with their own apprentices either in Otigba or in towns and cities elsewhere in Nigeria. It is a similar story at the enormous Alaba International Market, where hundreds of thousands of entrepreneurs sell and distribute goods imported from around the world to a million daily customers from Nigeria, Ghana, Benin, Togo and elsewhere. The congested informal market, with an annual turnover of $4 billion, is often described as Nigeria's biggest employer and one of the largest commercial centres in Africa; it has its own administration, elected council, sanitary inspectors, security officers, traffic management, complaints team, courts, public relations section and a system of apprenticeship. Around it has grown an ecosystem of cooperative banking and insurance services, micro-financing companies, accountants, craftsmen and technicians. Among the scavengers and scrap traders at the Olusosun dump, the same principles applied. The 4,000 self-employed workers built their own community, with a cinema, barber shops and eateries; its self-agreed rules and mutual trust were overseen by an elected chairman.[24]

The DIY urbanism that keeps Lagos going shows how good humans are at building cities from the ground up; what looks like chaos is often self-organised in an intricate and invisible way. The informal sector steps into the chasm left by the state. Every Sunday Lagos transforms into perhaps the best-dressed city on earth as the population heads down potholed streets, skirting puddles, on the way to mega-churches, many of which hold tens of thousands of people at a time, and to mosques. Many of the Pentecostal churches are entrepreneurial ventures that rake in fortunes and turn their superstar pastors into multimillionaires. When people are left to sink or swim, it is hardly surprising that businesses of all kinds step forward to fill the void. Pastors profit from the absence of the state. But at the same time churches provide community in a city where civic cohesion is in short supply. The creation of faith and free markets, they offer religion as well as things that are lacking elsewhere – solidarity, political commentary, leadership training, business advice and social networks.

When human beings come together, they are capable of organising, one way or another, functional societies. But in ambitious cities like Lagos, informal settlements and the informal economy are often seen as shameful and evidence of backwardness, something to be swept away. The official city is in a perpetual war against its shadowy unofficial counterpart. One newspaper attacked the 'audacity of anarchy' that plagues the city. The millions of Lagosian street hawkers face months in jail for their entrepreneurialism. Impromptu markets and informal 'mechanic villages', where technicians and artisans cluster, are disrupted and torn down. Tens of thousands of Lagosians who made their living scavenging waste dumps for recyclable materials lost their livelihoods when private companies took over. The unofficial symbol of Lagos itself – the smelly *danfo* minibus that keeps the populace moving – is being phased out, to be replaced by what is promised to be a 'world-class mass-transportation system'. For Lagos state governor Akinwunmi Ambode, the *danfos* stand for everything he hates about the chaotic city and the image it presents to the world: 'My dream of ensuring that Lagos becomes a true megacity will not be actualised with the presence of these yellow buses on Lagos roads.'[25]

Even the highly innovative Otigba Computer Village is facing closure, the state government preferring to relocate its functions to a bland out-of-town business park near an expressway as befits a global city. The great superstar of Afrobeat and hero of Lagos, Fela Kuti, sang about the deep distrust of Nigeria's elites: 'Them dey break, yes, them dey steal, yes, them dey loot, yes.' It is still felt today, particularly in regard to the state's attitude to the entrepreneurialism of ordinary Lagosians. Why trust the state to lay on buses when it can't provide electricity or water effectively? As one *danfo* bus driver put it: 'I am CEO on my own, having worked on my own for ten years; telling me to work under someone, and especially government, would not be palatable.' Or as a phone-accessory seller in Computer Village complained: '*Wetin you want make I talk now? Government nor dey do wetin we like. Na wetin dem like dem dey give us*' ('What do you want me to say? Government hardly gives us what we want but instead imposes their will and interests on us').[26]

Throughout history there has been a deep distrust of those who build the city from the bottom up by those who want to impose order from the top down. It's as if people fear that the city will fall apart if it isn't kept under tight control. The dynamism of Lagos's informal economy suggests otherwise. It also shows how megacities across the world can develop in the age of mass urbanisation. That can happen when informal settlements and the informal sector are not seen as problems, but as reservoirs of talent and ingenuity.

Lagos's energy and creativity emerges in large part from its apparent chaos and its people's ingenuity in innovating their way out of the city's pitfalls. 'I no come Lagos com count bridge!' goes a Lagosian expression: 'I didn't come to Lagos to count bridges!' It refers to a 'Johnny Just Come' – a JJC – or an immigrant straight off the bus from a village who supposedly can't help but gape at the huge number of bridges in Lagos. It really means: 'I didn't come to Lagos to waste time, but to make money.' The relentless pursuit of wealth at all levels of society helps create an urban ecosystem that incubates innovation. It was the competitive environment of the streets and market stalls of Otigba that sparked Nigeria's technology revolution, not the state or venture capital. The vibrant start-up culture in the city stems in large part from the early adopters who seized on technology and software as soon as it came on the market at the beginning of this millennium. Similarly, the commercial success that is Nollywood came into life on the streets of Surulere in Lagos, using basic technology and a lot of ingenuity. The city's markets and home-based seamstresses power Lagos's highly successful global fashion industry. Hip hop and dance, drawing its distinctively Lagosian idiom and rollicking energy from the street culture of the megacity's mainland districts, has become a global force, influencing the look and style of rap everywhere, including the US.

The interplay between the informal and formal economies, between clusters of different kinds of activities dispersed throughout the city, produces this kind of creativity. One of the main problems is the barriers that prevent this from happening. There's the barrier of transport, to be sure, but other less visible barriers, such as corruption and lack of services that hinder mobility and connectivity within the city. There is the most impenetrable of all barriers – the barrier of insecurity and lack of ownership. Drawing on the resources of the streets can't simply be an exercise in plundering the best and discarding the rest; it has to be bidirectional.

Around the world – in China, Indonesia, India, South America and elsewhere – megacities and metropolises have grappled with the problems of superfast mass urbanisation. Developing megacities look with envy to the miracle of China's urban-led 9.5% economic growth rate over the last three decades, with nearly a billion people (so far) pulled out of poverty. Chinese money is pouring into African infrastructure projects. The Chinese blueprint is becoming the paramount model in Africa, the fastest-urbanising continent in human history, with rulers dreaming of converting their messy megacities into an African Shanghai. There are housing developments all over the continent that look like they have been lifted straight from the suburbs of a Chinese city. There are also Special Economic Zones – high-tech cities-within-cities like Lekki and Eko Atlantic in Lagos – built with Chinese money and by Chinese architects.

And there is good reason to look towards the world's new great superpower for inspiration. Chinese cities, with their colossal infrastructure projects and strong centralised bureaucratic control, have avoided many of the pitfalls of fast growth. Then there is the draconian *hukou* system, which strictly regulates where people live. Regulation has allowed Shanghai to cap its population at 25 million and Beijing's at 23 million and to redistribute urban growth into cluster cities and mega-regions. Strong central authority has resulted in neat cities, with dramatic skylines in the business district ringed by uniform housing blocks.

China's instantaneous economic transformation and urbanisation is unique in world history not only for its stupendous scale, but for its choreography. But countries with democratic political systems, private property and the rule of law simply cannot stage-manage mass urbanisation in the way China has done. In any case, states with weak central authority and corruption are hamstrung in their attempt to urbanise systematically.

Latin America's equally dramatic urbanisation in the second half of the twentieth century offers Africa another model and many warnings. Famously, Colombia's second-largest metropolis, Medellín, was the most violent city in the world in the 1980s, the global capital of the cocaine trade. The drug lord Pablo Escobar drew his strength from the city's *comunas* – its slums that cling to the steep hillsides. Escobar promised the excluded and despised people a 'Medellín Without Slums', offering to rescue them from the 'inferno of garbage' in which they lived. The Medellín nightmare was the most notorious example of what happens when the social fabric of cities is pulled apart. For many members of the urban poor, the drug cartels that ruled most of the city were the only things offering employment, protection and hope. Escobar pitted the informal city against the formal one in a vicious intra-city civil war; it continued long after his death on a Medellín rooftop in 1993.

Today, after years of military operations to subdue the iron grip of the cartels, the city is a model of urban recovery. Under the leadership of Sergio Fajardo, who was elected mayor in 2004, Medellín began to break down the stark dividing line separating the formal and the informal city. Citizens had to see their poorer neighbours as equal members of the city; the authorities had to gain the trust of the marginalised. Residents of the *comunas* were given a degree of control over planning and organising their neighbourhoods. The erosion of mind-forged barriers went alongside demolishing physical barriers as the city radically rethought its public space. Architecturally significant public buildings such as libraries and community centres were constructed in the *comunas* as a powerful statement that they were an equal part of the city. These marginal settlements were integrated into the city with bus routes and cable cars. Comuna 13, once the most dangerous district in the world's most dangerous city, was connected to the rest of the city by escalator. Its young residents were given paint and encouraged to decorate their community with graffiti and street art. Medellín has by no means solved all its problems. But its radical 'social urbanism', combined with ecological urbanism, has made it more prosperous, more peaceful and globally famous.

Medellín's success depended on changing attitudes towards the urban poor as much as it did on paying for new infrastructure. It relied upon giving people ownership over their lives and neighbourhood. It's a vital lesson for African cities as they attempt to wrestle with runaway growth over the next three decades. As Africa becomes the final inhabited continent to become majority urban in the coming years its megacities will have to do a lot with a fraction of the resources that China had to throw at the problem. If African cities are poor in

investment capital and infrastructure, the immense energy and ingenuity of their populations may be their most valuable assets as their
growth accelerates out of control.

The example of China's top-down urbanisation transfixes policy-
makers. But simply razing informal settlements and moving people
to superblocks is the surest, time-tested way of obliterating the
precious social capital and dynamism that thrives in the urban
ecosystem. There is an alternative model of how megacities can grow
and remain resilient. Fewer than three generations ago, Tokyo was a
rubble of bombed buildings. Today it is the biggest metropolitan
region the world has known with nearly 40 million people and the
most successful megacity ever created. In large part, Tokyo flourished
because its citizens rebuilt their destroyed city in the wake of the
Second World War in a triumph of self-organisation over the kind of
top-down planning that predominated in Europe and America, and
latterly China.

Tokyo in the immediate post-war years looked like a gigantic shanty
town, with improvised housing and few services. Today, much of
Tokyo's dense, low-rise urban core, with its mix of businesses and
housing jostling for space in narrow labyrinthine streets, still has a
passing resemblance to a Mumbai slum, even if its inhabitants are
many times wealthier. For most people in the West – and latterly in
places like China – the urban experience is now a very ordered, sanitised one, in which industry, retail, business, leisure and housing are
separated and sorted into distinct, discrete zones by planners. In a
sense, the wild urban ecosystem becomes a managed zoo, drained
of the dynamism engendered by disorder. Tokyo (like Lagos or
Mumbai) looks chaotic and, well, messy to Western eyes. But this
has been 'informal' or organic urbanisation at its most successful and
vital.[27]

By that I mean a blurring of residential, working, commercial,
industrial, retail and eating spaces that makes streets feel like living,
evolving things. The informal, unplanned neighbourhoods of Tokyo
remained under the control of its inhabitants, not Olympian master
planners. The city feels like a collection of interconnected but self-
sustaining villages, with mixed economic, social and residential functions. Small businesses, family-run restaurants, laundries, tiny *izakaya*
bars, artisans' workshops, car repair yards and street markets rub

shoulders with gleaming banks and offices; jerry-built houses with skyscrapers. Urban development – the transition from huge war-shattered shanty town to hyper-modern megacity – took place incrementally, as buildings were progressively rebuilt, upgraded and repurposed. Individual, autonomous neighbourhoods gradually merged into the wider city without losing their local character and diversity of street-level activity.[28]

Tokyo is not an anarchic, completely unplanned city, however. But its growth was never governed by a masterplan in the way that Singapore or Shanghai experienced. The world's most extensive and intensive intra-city transport system, along with other vital infrastructure, was fitted around the existing city, not vice versa. Working-class districts got the same world-class urban services and amenities as any other. In other words, the city government provided and maintained the circulatory system – the metropolis's arteries, veins and nerves, leaving the connective tissue to develop independently.

In contrast to the Western idea of a city as a place of permanence, in Japan buildings have a short lifespan. The effect is what is often called a high rate of urban metabolism – an ongoing process of city-wide metamorphosis. The metropolis is therefore reconceptualised as provisional, or as a palimpsest, the original words of which remain legible even after continual erasure and rewriting. Or it could be seen as an ever-evolving organism, never reaching its final form but growing, shrinking, changing shape and appearance in response to external environmental stimuli.

Metaphors are important not only in how we *see* the city, but in how we plan it, manage it and live in it. The idea of a city as being in a state of flux is important. The most dynamic cities have been like Tokyo in the post-war decades, in a state of restless metamorphosis. That kind of inbuilt flexibility and adaptiveness allows cities to respond to changing economic conditions and to external shocks. In its period of explosive growth, Uruk demolished and rebuilt constantly, with bigger and better structures feasting on the rubble of the old. Cities such as Rome and London have grown incrementally as well, giving them the layering of historical memory that makes them feel so alive and interesting. Tokyo, like other Asian cities, is of critical importance because it went through this historical process at warp speed as it recovered from near-total destruction and appalling poverty in 1945 with a population of 3.49 million to a futuristic megacity-region and economic powerhouse today. Its fast metabolic rate allowed it to absorb all these changes while remaining fundamentally the same. According to the architect Kisho Kurokawa:

> [Tokyo] is an agglomeration of three hundred cities ... At first there seems to be no order, but the energy, freedom, and the multiplicity that comes from the parts are there. The creation of this new hierarchy is a process that makes use of spontaneously occurring forces. For this reason, it is probably most accurate to say that Tokyo today ... finds itself set somewhere between true chaos and a new hidden order.[29]

In an age when urban planning has become all-important, Tokyo's development in the forty years after WWII is both a reprise of the bigger history of urbanisation over the last 7,000 years and a lesson for megacities elsewhere. Whether it is Amsterdam in the seventeenth century, London in the eighteenth or New York in the twentieth, cities thrive when there is a dynamic interplay between the unplanned, informal city and the official, planned city – where there is room for spontaneity and experimentation. Metaphors of a city as a metabolic system or evolving organism are more than just colourful: they remind us that cities are places that change rapidly as economies boom and bust, new technologies arrive, wars break out and the climate changes. Allowing local self-organisation gives a city room to respond to violent change in a way that strict planning does not. The vitality of Tokyo's informal neighbourhoods provided the preconditions for economic take-off.[30]

In Lagos the messiness of the informal city is often seen as a sign of poverty and shame. But messiness is something to be embraced, especially for a fast-growing city: it is a dynamic feature of urban development. Attempting to regulate and formalise this activity can have a deadening effect on creativity. By providing the conditions and infrastructure for the poorest to construct their own communities, both Medellín and Tokyo achieved success by integrating informal settlements into the wider city and investing in their social capital. It means ceasing to see informal economies and settlements as part of the problem, and instead seeing them as essential to the solution of managing hyper-urbanisation. The provision of basic services, along with security of tenure, are key to turning dysfunctional and marginal places into functional assets.[31]

Tokyo resides in one of the most dangerous places in the world. Throughout its history it has been destroyed not just by fire and bombs, but by violent seismic activity. Self-reliance and self-organisation have long been hardwired into its DNA. Building the city from the street up rather than from the top down has conferred enormous benefits. Tokyo's citizens have been able to absorb every disaster and rebound from them. In the present century many of the global south's emerging megacities are likely to experience similar catastrophes. The resilience that comes from the neighbourhood is one of the surest defences against disaster.

*

We are very good at living in cities, even in extreme circumstances of near-destruction or overcrowding. History tells us that much. On a very simple level, concentrating human brains in proximity with other brains is the best way of igniting ideas, art and social change. Our extraordinary capacity to create settlements of inordinate complexity means that we are becoming a fully urbanised species.

Metropolis began with the sensuality of cities – the delights of sociability and intimacy that enlivened them and gave them their collective power. City-living was made pleasurable by sex, food, shopping, looking, smelling, bathing, walking and festivities. The rituals of urban life took place in agoras, markets, souks and bazaars, on street corners, plazas and bathhouses, in cafés, pubs, parks and stadiums. Later chapters described the concentrations of power that allowed relatively small cities to fundamentally change the world around them. The history of cities from the eighteenth century showed the ways in which humans have learnt to live with the strains of modern urban existence.

From Uruk onwards, the urban ecosystem has been in a constant state of evolution. We build our environment to suit our needs, but then it begins to shape us in a multigenerational process of interaction between us, our buildings and our layers of history. Uruk is a particularly good example. The first city, and one of the longest-existing, its form and the lives of its citizens were shaped by climate change that occurred over millennia. As the marshes receded, rainfall patterns changed, temperatures climbed and river systems became unpredictable, Uruk adapted with the environment. Its durability and adaptability, and that of the urban culture it created, was remarkable.

Rising temperatures and unpredictable storms are already changing cities in the third millennium AD. Cities are noticeably greener and more biodiverse. The New Urban movement has, over the last few decades, argued that we need to combat car-dependent sprawl by making cities and suburbs more compact, pedestrian- and bike-friendly, and economically diverse. Even more recently, the green movement has come to embrace the city as a solution to combat climate change rather than seeing it as its enemy. Cities that are built around street life rather than cars and have advanced transit systems, reduce motorised traffic. Households in dispersed suburbs have a carbon footprint between two and four times greater than households in densely populated city centres. People living in urbanised neighbourhoods – where you walk or use public transport and don't reside in lavish homes – emit less carbon, consume fewer resources such as water and fuel, produce less waste and are more energy efficient. As the world population reaches 10 billion it makes better sense to herd people together, taking pressure off the natural world.

Smaller, compact cities built around people rather than cars are also proven to be better for humans as well as the environment. The closer you live to a city centre the less obese you are. You are also happier. According to scientific research, people living in tightly packed row houses, terraces and apartments where they walk and socialise enjoy better physical and mental health than people in even the most affluent suburbs. The car allowed us to escape the city when industrialisation and deindustrialisation pushed the urban world to breaking point; but now the car – with its personal, social and environmental costs – is degrading the quality of life in suburbia. This is not so much New Urbanism as very, very old urbanism. We decamped to the city for good reasons 5,000 years ago – for the proximity, opportunities, sociability and sensual pleasures it offered – and continued the process over the millennia.[32]

Cities will change. But it won't be born out of idealism, but of necessity. Cities are not only resilient, they are also adaptive systems. If and when we face a resource crunch or an ecological catastrophe that forces energy prices up, cities will change as they always have done. With fewer cars, vans and trucks, urban areas will likely return to higher densities and busy streets – that is to say, return to how they were for most of history.

That doesn't mean we will suddenly crowd back into cities or take up residence in space-saving high-rises. Nor will we hurriedly build new cities. No – it means making suburbia more urban, offering places to walk and socialise, shop and work. This is not a utopian dream of nice neighbourhoods; it is a description of the way that people and places respond to changed conditions. When you can't drive to the city, the mall or the leisure centre, you have to bring them to your doorstep. Already there is a move towards what are called 'urbanburbs' in the United States: compact districts that offer millennials a more metropolitan lifestyle in suburbia, with street life, cafés, restaurants, bars, parks and schools within walking distance. We are an urban species: our desire to live communally will keep on evolving and take new forms.[33]

The new metropolitan form will become one of many local urban centres, rather than a few – a city of self-sufficient villages. It is an irony that one of the cities that best exemplifies this is Los Angeles. LA developed as a quintessential twentieth-century metropolis. Not only was it low-density, car-based and designed to facilitate mobility, but its complexity was organised. That is to say, it was conceived as the antidote to the chaotic, messy metropolis of the Industrial Revolution, in which housing, industry, commerce, retail and leisure would be separated into distinct, tidy, monolithic zones. The metropolis formed around the freeway and the private house. The characterlessness that critics detected was a result of this tendency – by no means confined to LA – of sanitising cities by untangling the jumble.

But from being the standard-bearer of twentieth-century urbanisation, LA is becoming, in curious ways, the pioneer of the changes assailing the twenty-first-century city. Many of its suburbs have become steadily more urban and denser. This was not decreed by central planners; it was the result of informal activity at street and neighbourhood level.

By the second decade of the twenty-first century LA had become majority Latino. The millions of new Angelenos brought with them an entirely different conception of how to inhabit a city. Latin American immigrants and their descendants have significantly lower rates of car-ownership than the rest of the population. They also put a much greater emphasis on the public life of the street and on sociability. They adapted themselves to LA, but adapted their neighbourhoods to their own needs. Latino Urbanism, as it is called, has transformed parts of LA to having the flavour of outdoor, face-to-face public spaces where people stroll, talk and gather. It manifests itself in front yards, which become part of the social life of the street, turning the introverted Californian bungalow into an extroverted Latinised home that serves as a place of public/private interaction. It finds expression in colourful discount stores lining streets, in graffiti art, taco stands, *loncheros* trucks and parties in parks. There are 50,000 informal vendors in LA, who turn streets and parks into impromptu public markets and de facto plazas – places where people want to linger rather than hurry through.[34]

Latino Urbanism cuts across established notions of what LA should be like, and it has been much resisted as messy. But the energy it has brought has forced city government to reconceive urban planning, putting greater emphasis on pedestrianisation and informal retail. It made people realise that streets were not just about mobility; they are places to inhabit, places to play in as well as move through. They are the soul of the city. Almost invisibly, the theoretical principles of New Urbanism – with its advocacy of compact cities, high-density neighbourhoods, mixed use and lively street life – was being put into practice at street level in LA and a series of other US cities by Latino residents responding to urban life in their own way and often in defiance of official disapproval. So successful has it been that some of these neighbourhoods are being gentrified by richer people attracted by their urban, and urbane, character.

Latino Urbanism is an example of what might be called 'messy urbanism', a reminder of how cities used to be. It shows also the way in which the informal character of the megacity of the global south can – and is – asserting itself across the planet. Rebuilding microcommunities within cities and suburbs is one of the most important ways in which cities will become more resilient and sustainable in the coming century. Confined to home, or a small radius around it, during the global lockdown of 2020, having reliable sources of food, medicine and daily necessities in one's immediate locale became critically important; so too did sites of recreation and fresh air. The health of one's neighbourhood, in every sense, took on a fresh significance. Cities across the globe saw mutual-aid societies emerging spontaneously within communities as people reaffirmed the value they put on human connection and neighbourhood sociability, even under stringent conditions of social distancing.

From the Uruk of a few thousand pioneers to the Lagos of over 20 million people, the basic principles of urban life have not changed all that much. Throughout that time, people have dreamed of urban utopias. Very often these visions of the perfect city have led to tragic experiments being enacted on people whose communities have been ripped up in the process. But, as the entrepreneurs of the Otigba Computer Village in Lagos or Latinos in LA show, humans are very good at constructing their own communities and improvising order. History demonstrates this constant tension between those who thrive in the messy human city, and those who want to impose some kind of artificial coherence upon it.

Our survival as a species depends on the next chapter of our urban odyssey. That story will not be made in gleaming global cities. It will not be determined by technocrats designing digital answers to our problems or master planners remaking the city from Olympian heights. It will be made, and experienced most acutely, by billions of people living in megacities and fast-growing metropolises in developing countries. The majority of humans will live in informal settlements and work in the DIY economy, as has been the case for countless urbanites over the last 5,000 years. They are the people who build cities and keep them going, surviving on their ingenuity and resourcefulness and responding to changes in the wider environment. When the energy runs low, and cities become hotter and harsher, they will be the ones who improvise solutions, if they are allowed.

If history is any guide, it tells us they will succeed.

Acknowledgements

I would like to thank the following for their generosity, insights and immense kindness: Claire Ashworth, Clare Conville, Suzanne Dean, Chijioke Dozie, Jeff Fisher, Wade Graham, Bea Hemming, Sanjeev Kanoria, Mark Lobel, David Maxwell, David Milner, Natasha Moreno-Roberts, Birgitta Rabe, Roisin Robothan-Jones, Nicholas Rose, Charmaine Roy, Nishi Sehgal, Daisy Watt, Marney and Chris Wilson.

Notes

Introduction: The Metropolitan Century

1 UN Habitat, *State of the World's Cities 2008/9: harmonious cities* (London, 2008), p. 11; UN Habitat, *State of the World's Cities 2012/2013: prosperity of cities* (NY, 2013), p. 29 • 2 Jaison R. Abel, Ishita Dey and Todd M. Gabe, 'Productivity and the Density of Human Capital', Federal Reserve Bank of New York Staff Reports, 440 (March 2010); OECD, *The Metropolitan Century: understanding urbanisation and its consequences* (Paris, 2015), pp. 35ff; Maria P. Roche, 'Taking Innovation to the Streets: microgeography, physical structure and innovation', *Review of Economics and Statistics*, 21/8/2019, https://www.mitpressjournals.org/doi/abs/10.1162/rest_a_00866 • 3 Jonathan Auerbach and Phyllis Wan, 'Forecasting the Urban Skyline with Extreme Value Theory', 29/10/2018, https://arxiv.org/abs/1808.01514 • 4 A. T. Kearney, *Digital Payments and the Global Informal Economy* (2018), pp. 6, 7 • 5 Janice E. Perlman, 'The Metamorphosis of Marginality: four generations in the *favelas* of Rio de Janeiro', *Annals of the American Academy of Political and Social Science*, 606 (July 2006), 167; Sanni Yaya et al., 'Decomposing the Rural–Urban Gap in the Factors of Under-Five Mortality Rate in Sub-Saharan Africa? Evidence from 35 countries', *BMC Public Health*, 19 (May 2019); Abhijit V. Banerjee and Esther Duflo, 'The Economic Lives of the Poor', *Journal of Economic Perspectives*, 21:1 (Winter 2007), table 9; Maigeng Zhou et al., 'Cause-Specific Mortality for 240 Causes in China during 1990–2013: a systematic subnational analysis for the Global Burden of Disease Study 2013', *Lancet*, 387 (January 2016), 251–72 • 6 Karen C. Seto, Burak Güneralp and Lucy R. Hutyra, 'Global Forecasts of Urban Expansion to 2030 and Direct Impacts on Biodiversity and Carbon Pools', *PNAS*, 109:40 (October 2012) • 7 Edward Glaeser, *The Triumph of the City: how urban space makes us human* (London, 2012), p. 15.

1. Dawn of the City

1 Andrew George (ed. and trans.), *The Epic of Gilgamesh* (London, 2013), I:101ff • 2 Paul Kriwaczek, *Babylon: Mesopotamia and the birth of civilisation*, p. 80; Mary Shepperson, 'Planning for the Sun: urban forms as a Mesopotamian response to the sun', *World Archaeology*, 41:3 (September 2009), 363–78 • 3 Jeremy A. Black et al., *The Literature of Ancient Sumer* (Oxford, 2006), pp. 118ff • 4 P. Sanlaville, 'Considerations sur l'évolution de la basse Mésopotamie au cours des derniers millénaires', *Paléorient*, 15:5 (1989), 5–27; N. Petit-Maire, P. Sanlaville and Z. W. Yan, 'Oscillations de la limite nord du domaine des moussons africaine, indienne, et asiatique, au cours du dernier cycle climatique', *Bulletin de la Societé Géologique de France*, 166 (1995), 213–20; Harriet Crawford, *Ur: the city of the Moon God* (London, 2015), pp. 4ff; Guillermo Algaze, *Ancient Mesopotamia at the Dawn of Civilization: the evolution of the urban landscape* (Chicago, 2008), pp. 41ff; Hans J. Nissen,

The Early History of the Ancient Near East, 9000–2000 BC (Chicago, 1988) • 5 Gwendolyn Leick, *Mesopotamia: the invention of the city* (London, 2001), pp. 2–3, 8–9, 19ff • 6 Ibid., pp. 35ff, 50, 54 • 7 Thomas W. Killion, 'Nonagricultural Cultivation and Social Complexity: the Olmec, their ancestors, and Mexico's Southern Gulf Coast lowlands', *Current Anthropology*, 54:5 (October 2013), 569–606; Andrew Lawler, 'Beyond the Family Feud', *Archaeology*, 60:2 (March/April 2007), 20–5; Charles Higham, 'East Asian Agriculture and Its Impact', in Christopher Scarre (ed.), *The Human Past: world prehistory and the development of human societies* (London, 2005), pp. 234–63; Roderick J. McIntosh, 'Urban Clusters in China and Africa: the arbitration of social ambiguity', *Journal of Field Archaeology*, 18:2 (Summer 1991), 199–212 • 8 Jennifer Pournelle and Guillermo Algaze, 'Travels in Edin: deltaic resilience and early urbanism in Greater Mesopotamia', in H. Crawford (ed.), *Preludes to Urbanism: studies in the late Chalcolithic of Mesopotamia in honour of Joan Oates* (Oxford, 2010), pp. 7–34 • 9 H. Weiss, 'The Origins of Tell Leilan and the Conquest of Space in Third Millennium North Mesopotamia', in H. Weiss (ed.), *The Origins of Cities in Dry-Farming Syria and Mesopotamia in the Third Millennium BC* (Guilford, CT, 1986) • 10 Guillermo Algaze, 'The Uruk Expansion: cross-cultural exchange in early Mesopotamian civilisation', *Current Anthropology*, 30:5 (December 1989), 581 • 11 William Blake Tyrrell, 'A Note on Enkidu's Enchanted Gate', *Classical Outlook*, 54:8 (April 1977), 88 • 12 Guillermo Algaze, 'Entropic Cities: the paradox of urbanism in ancient Mesopotamia', *Current Anthropology*, 59:1 (February 2018), 23–54; Florian Lederbogen et al., 'City-Living and Urban Upbringing Affect Neural Social Stress Processing in Humans', *Nature*, 474 (2011), 498–501; Leila Haddad et al., 'Brain Structure Correlates of Urban Upbringing, an Environmental Risk Factor for Schizophrenia', *Schizophrenia Bulletin*, 41:1 (January 2015), 115–22 • 13 George, XI:323–6 • 14 Leick, pp.1ff, 29 • 15 Geoff Emberling and Leah Minc, 'Ceramics and Long-Distance Trade in Early Mesopotamian States', *Journal of Archaeological Science*, Reports: 7 (March 2016); Giacomo Benati, 'The Construction of Large-Scale Networks in Late Chalcolithic Mesopotamia: emergent political institutions and their strategies', in Davide Domenici and Nicolò Marchetti, *Urbanized Landscapes in Early Syro-Mesopotamia and Prehispanic Mesoamerica* (Wiesbaden, 2018) • 16 Hans J. Nissen, Peter Damerow and Robert K. Englund, *Archaic Bookkeeping: early writing and techniques of economic administration in the ancient Near East* (Chicago, 1993), p. 36 • 17 Leick, pp. 89ff • 18 Ibid., p. 106 • 19 Kriwaczek, p. 162 • 20 Ibid., pp. 161–2 • 21 Leick, pp. 139, 146, 268

2. The Garden of Eden and Sin City

1 Jean-Jacques Rousseau, *Politics and the Arts: letter to M. d'Alembert on the theatre*, trans. A. Bloom (Ithaca, 1968), pp. 58–9 • 2 Victoria E. Thompson, 'Telling "Spatial Stories": urban space and bourgeois identity in nineteenth-century Paris', *Journal of Modern History*, 75:3 (September 2003), 542 • 3 Jon Adams and Edmund Ramsden, 'Rat Cities and Beehive Worlds: density and design in the modern city', *Comparative Studies in Society and History*, 53:4 (October 2011), 722–756 • 4 Le Corbusier, *The City of Tomorrow and Its Planning* (NY, 1987), p. 244; Ebenezer Howard, *Garden Cities of Tomorrow* (London, 1902), p. 18 • 5 Jonathan M. Kenoyer, *Ancient Cities of the Indus Valley Civilization* (Oxford, 1998); R. K. Pruthi, *Indus Civilisation* (New Delhi, 2004); Andrew Robinson, *The Indus: lost civilisations* (London, 2015) • 6 Asko Parpola, *Deciphering the Indus Script* (Cambridge, 1994), p. 21; cf. Dilip K. Chakrabarti (ed.), *Indus Civilisation Sites in India: new discoveries* (Mumbai, 2004), p. 11 and Hans J. Nissen, 'Early Civilisations in the Near and Middle East', in Michael Jansen, Máire Mulloy and Günter Urban (eds.), *Forgotten Cities in the Indus: early civilisation in Pakistan from the 8th to the 2nd millennium BC* (Mainz, 1991), p. 33 • 7 Robinson, p. 47 • 8 Liviu Giosan et al., 'Fluvial Landscapes of the Harappan Civilization', *Proceedings of the National Academy of Sciences*, 109:26 (2012), E1688–E1694; Peter D. Clift and Liviu Giosan, 'Holocene Evolution of Rivers, Climate and Human Societies in the Indus Basin', in Yijie Zhuang and Mark Altaweel (eds.), *Water Societies and Technologies from Past and Present* (London, 2018); Liviu Giosan et al.,

'Neoglacial Climate Anomalies and the Harappan Metamorphosis', *Climate of the Past*, 14 (2018), 1669–86 • 9 Cameron A. Petrie et al., 'Adaptation to Variable Environments, Resilience to Climate Change: investigating land, water and settlement in Indus Northwest India', *Current Anthropology*, 58:1 (February 2017), 1–30 • 10 Arunima Kashyap and Steve Weber, 'Starch Grain Analysis and Experiments Provide Insights into Harappan Cooking Practices', in Shinu Anna Abraham, Praveena Gullapalli, Teresa P. Raczek and Uzma Z. Rizvi (eds.), *Connections and Complexity: new approaches to the archaeology of South Asia* (Walnut Creek, 2013); Andrew Lawler, 'The Mystery of Curry', Slate.com, 29/1/2013, https://slate.com/human-interest/2013/01/indus-civilization-food-how-scientists-are-figuring-out-what-curry-was-like-4500-years-ago.html • 11 Will Doig, 'Science Fiction No More: the perfect City is under construction', Salon.com, 28/4/2012 • 12 'An Asian Hub in the Making', *New York Times*, 30/12/2007 • 13 William Thomas, *The History of Italy (1549)* (New York, 1963), p. 83 • 14 Terry Castle, 'Eros and Liberty at the English Masquerade', *Eighteenth-Century Studies*, 17:2 (Winter 1983–4), 159; Stephanie Dalley, *Myths from Mesopotamia: Creation, The Flood, Gilgamesh, and others* (Oxford, 1989), p. 305 • 15 Simon Szreter, 'Treatment Rates for the Pox in Early Modern England: a comparative estimate of the prevalence of syphilis in the city of Chester and its rural vicinity in the 1770s', *Continuity and Change*, 32:2 (2017), 183–223; Maarten H. D. Larmuseau et al., 'A Historical-Genetic Reconstruction of Human Extra-Pair Paternity', *Current Biology*, 29:23 (December 2019), 4102–7 • 16 Leick, pp. 59–60 • 17 James Boswell, *Boswell's London Journal* (1952), pp. 249–50, 257, 320 • 18 Farid Azfar, 'Sodomites and the Shameless Urban Future', *Eighteenth Century*, 55:4 (Winter 2014), 391–410 • 19 Randolph Trumbach, 'London's Sodomites: homosexual behaviour and western culture in the eighteenth century', *Journal of Social History*, 11:1 (Autumn 1977), 1–33; Gavin Brown, 'Listening to the Queer Maps of the City: gay men's narratives of pleasure and danger in London's East End', *Oral History*, 29:1 (Spring 2001), 48–61 • 20 Leick, p. 59 • 21 Vern L. Bullough, 'Attitudes towards Deviant Sex in Ancient Mesopotamia', *Journal of Sex Research*, 7:3 (August 1971), 184–203 • 22 Leick, p. 264 • 23 Brian Cowan, 'What Was Masculine about the Public Sphere? Gender and the coffee house milieu in post-Restoration England', *History Workshop Journal*, 51 (Spring 2001), 140 • 24 *The Collected Writings of Thomas De Quincey*, Vol. I, p. 181 • 25 H. Brock, 'Le Corbusier Scans Gotham's Towers', *New York Times*, 3/11/1935; Le Corbusier, *The Radiant City: elements of a doctrine of urbanism to be used as the basis of our Machine Age Civilization* (London, 1967), p. 230

3. Cosmopolis

1 'Old Oligarch', *The Constitution of the Athenians*, 2.7–8 • 2 Demetra Kasimis, *The Perpetual Immigrant and the Limits of Athenian Democracy* (Cambridge, 2018), p. 22 • 3 Edith Hall, *The Ancient Greeks: ten ways they shaped the modern world* (London, 2016), introduction, chapter 3 • 4 Ibid., chapter 3 • 5 Mogens Herman Hansen, 'The Hellenic Polis', in Hansen (ed.), *A Comparative Study of Thirty City-State Cultures: an investigation conducted by the Copenhagen Polis Centre* (Copenhagen, 2000), pp. 141ff • 6 Ibid., pp. 146ff • 7 Ibid., p. 145 • 8 Stavros Stavrides, 'The December 2008 Youth Uprising in Athens: spatial justice in an emergent "city of thresholds"', *spatial justice*, 2 (October 2010); Ursula Dmitriou, 'Commons as Public: re-inventing public spaces in the centre of Athens', in Melanie Dodd (ed.), *Spatial Practices: modes of action and engagement with the city* (Abingdon, 2020); Helena Smith, 'Athens' Unofficial Community Initiatives Offer Hope after Government Failures', *Guardian*, 21/9/2016 • 9 Hussam Hussein Salama, 'Tahrir Square: a narrative of public space', *International Journal of Architectural Research*, 7:1 (March 2013), 128–38; Joshua E. Keating, 'From Tahrir Square to Wall Street', *Foreign Policy*, 5/10/2011, https://foreign-policy.com/2011/10/05/from-tahrir-square-to-wall-street/ • 10 Jeffrey Hou, '(Not) Your Everyday Public Space', in Hou (ed.), *Insurgent Public Space: guerrilla urbanism and the remaking of contemporary cities* (London, 2010), pp. 3–5 • 11 R. E. Wycherley, *The Stones of Athens* (Princeton, 1978), pp. 91–2 • 12 Judith L. Shear, *Polis and Revolution: responding to*

oligarchy in classical Athens (Cambridge, 2011), pp. 113ff; Gabriel Herman, *Morality and Behaviour in Democratic Athens: a social history* (Cambridge, 2006), pp. 59ff • 13 Shear, pp. 178ff • 14 Ibid., p. 50 • 15 James Watson, 'The Origin of Metic Status at Athens', *Cambridge Classical Journal*, 56 (2010), 259–78 • 16 Justin Pollard and Howard Reid, *The Rise and Fall of Alexandria, Birthplace of the Modern World* (London, 2006), pp. 1ff, 24–6 • 17 Abraham Akkerman, 'Urban Planning and Design as an Aesthetic Dilemma: void versus volume in city-form', in Sharon M. Meagher, Samantha Noll and Joseph S. Biehl (eds.), *The Routledge Handbook of Philosophy of the City* (NY, 2019) • 18 Dio Chrysostom, *Discourses*, 32:36

4. Imperial Megacity

1 Fikret K. Yegül, *Baths and Bathing in Classical Antiquity* (Cambridge, MA, 1995), p. 31 • 2 Richard Guy Wilson, *McKim, Mead and White Architects* (NY, 1983), pp. 211–12 • 3 Garret G. Fagan, *Bathing in Public in the Roman World* (Ann Arbor, 1999), pp. 34–5 • 4 Yegül, p. 30 • 5 Ibid., p. 32 • 6 Seneca, *Moral Letters to Lucilius*, 86:4–12 • 7 Fagan, p. 317 • 8 Janet Smith, *Liquid Assets: the lidos and open-air swimming pools of Britain* (London, 2005), p. 19 • 9 Ronald A. Davidson and J. Nicholas Entrikin, 'The Los Angeles Coast as a Public Place', *Geographical Review*, 95:4 (October 2005), 578–93 • 10 Michèle de la Pradelle and Emmanuelle Lallement, 'Paris Plage: "the city is ours"', *Annals of the American Academy of Political and Social Sciences*, 595 (September 2005), 135 • 11 Peter Ackroyd, *Thames: sacred river* (London, 2007), p. 339; *The Works of the Rev. Jonathan Swift* (London, 1801), Vol. XV, p. 62; *The Times*, 24/6/1865 • 12 *Pall Mall Gazette*, 13/7/1869 • 13 Andrea Renner, 'A Nation that Bathes Together: New York City's progressive era public baths', *Journal of the Society of Architectural Historians*, 67:4 (December 2008), 505 • 14 Jeffrey Turner, 'On Boyhood and Public Swimming: Sidney Kingsley's *Dead End* and representations of underclass street kids in American cultural production', in Caroline F. Levander and Carol J. Singley (eds.), *The American Child: a cultural studies reader* (New Brunswick, 2003); Marta Gutman, 'Race, Place, and Play: Robert Moses and the WPA swimming pools in New York City', *Journal of the Society of Architectural Historians*, 67:4 (December 2008), 536 • 15 Marta Gutman, 'Equipping the Public Realm: rethinking Robert Moses and recreation', in Hilary Ballon and Kenneth T. Jackson (eds.), *Robert Moses and the Modern City: the transformation of New York* (NY, 2007) • 16 Gutman (2008), 540; Smith (2005), p. 30 • 17 Jeff Wiltse, *Contested Waters: a social history of swimming pools in America* (Chapel Hill, 2007), p. 94 • 18 Edwin Torres, *Carlito's Way: rise to power* (NY, 1975), pp. 4–6 • 19 Fagan, p. 32 • 20 Jeremy Hartnett, *The Roman Street: urban life and society in Pompeii, Herculaneum, and Rome* (Cambridge, 2017), p. 1 • 21 Juvenal, *Satire*, III:190–204 • 22 Cicero, *Ad Attica*, 14.9; Strabo, V:III, 235; Mary Beard, *SPQR: a history of ancient Rome* (London, 2015), pp. 455ff; Jerry Toner, *Popular Culture in Ancient Rome* (Cambridge, 2009), pp. 109ff • 23 Louise Revell, 'Military Bath-houses in Britain: a comment', *Britannia*, 38 (2007), 230–7 • 24 Ian Blair et al., 'Wells and Bucket-Chains: unforeseen elements of water supply in early Roman London', *Britannia*, 37 (2006) • 25 Fagan, p. 188; Piers D. Mitchell, 'Human Parasites in the Roman World: health consequences of conquering an empire', *Parasitology*, 144:1 (January 2017), 48–58; A. M. Devine, 'The Low Birth-rate in Ancient Rome: a possible contributing factor', *Rheinisches Museum für Philologie* (1985), 313ff • 26 David Frye, 'Aristocratic Responses to Late Roman Urban Change: the examples of Ausonius and Sidonius in Gaul', *Classical World*, 96:2 (Winter 2003), 185–96 • 27 Yegül, p. 314 • 28 Matthew Kneale, *Rome: a history in seven sackings* (London, 2017), p. 40 • 29 Ibid., pp. 94–5

5. Gastropolis

1 Regina Krahl, John Guy, J. Keith Wilson and Julian Raby (eds.), *Shipwrecked: Tang treasures and monsoon winds* (Singapore, 2010); Alan Chong and Stephen A. Murphy, *The Tang*

Shipwreck: art and exchange in the 9th century (Singapore, 2017) • 2 See Krahl et al., and
Chong and Murphy • 3 Justin Marozzi, *Baghdad: city of peace, city of blood* (London, 2014),
p. 92 • 4 Hugh Kennedy, 'From Polis to Madina: urban change in late antiquity and early
Islamic Syria', *Past and Present*, 106 (February 1985), 3–27 • 5 Ibid.; Besim Hakim, 'Law and
the City', in Salma K. Jayyusi (ed.), *The City in the Islamic World* (Leiden, 2008), pp. 71–93
• 6 Marozzi, p. 92 • 7 Lincoln Paine, *The Sea and Civilisation: a maritime history of the world*
(London, 2015), p. 265 • 8 Xinru Liu, *The Silk Road in World History* (Oxford, 2010), p. 101
• 9 Nawal Nasrallah, *Annals of the Caliphs' Kitchens: Ibn Sayyar al-Warraq's tenth-century
Baghdadi cookbook* (Boston, MA, 2007), p. 35 • 10 David Waines, '"Luxury Foods" in Medieval
Islamic Societies', *World Archaeology*, 34:3 (February 2003), 572 • 11 International Labour
Office, *Women and Men in the Informal Sector: a statistical picture* (Geneva, 2002); 'Mumbai
Street Vendors', *Guardian*, 28/11/2014; Henry Mayhew, *London Labour and the London Poor*,
4 vols (London, 1861–2), Vol. I, pp. 160, 165 • 12 Omiko Awa, 'Roasted Corn: satisfying
hunger returns good profit', *Guardian* (Nigeria), 21/9/2015 • 13 Mayhew, Vol. I, p. 158 • 14
Charles Manby Smith, *Curiosities of London Life; or, phrases, physiological and social of the
great metropolis* (London, 1853), p. 390 • 15 Teju Cole, *Every Day Is for the Thief* (London,
2015), p. 57 • 16 S. Frederick Starr, *Lost Enlightenment: central Asia's golden age from the Arab
conquest to Tamerlane* (Princeton, 2013), pp. 132ff • 17 Marozzi, p. 65 • 18 Starr, pp. 167ff •
19 Ibid., pp. 37ff, 62ff • 20 Georgina Herman and Hugh N. Kennedy, *Monuments of Merv:
traditional buildings of the Karakum* (London, 1999), p. 124 • 21 Starr, pp. 28–9 • 22 Ibid., pp.
162–3 • 23 Hyunhee Park, *Mapping the Chinese and Islamic Worlds: cross-cultural exchange in
pre-modern Asia* (Cambridge, 2012), p. 77 • 24 Glen Dudbridge, 'Reworking the World
System Paradigm', *Past and Present*, 238, Supplement 13 (November 2018), 302ff • 25 Pius
Malekandathil, *Maritime India: trade, religion and polity in the Indian Ocean* (Delhi, 2010),
pp. 39ff • 26 Paine, p. 273 • 27 Ibid., p. 306 • 28 Kanakalatha Mukund, *Merchants of Tamilakam:
pioneers of international trade* (New Delhi, 2012), pp. 164–6 • 29 Dashu Qin and Kunpeng
Xiang, 'Sri Vijaya as the Entrepôt for Circum-Indian Ocean Trade: evidence from docu-
mentary records and materials from shipwrecks of the 9th–10th centuries', *Études Océan
Indien*, 46–7 (2011), 308–36

6. Cities of War

1 Horst Boog, *The Global War: Germany and the Second World War*, Vol. VI (Oxford, 2015),
p. 565 • 2 Paine, p. 332; Helmond von Bosau, *Slawenchronik*, ed. H. Stoob (Darmstadt,
1983); A. Graßmann (ed.), *Lübeckische Geschichte* (Lübeck, 2008), pp. 1–123; H. Stoob, *Lübeck*
(Altenbeken, 1984) • 3 Bosau, p. 304; David Abulafia, *The Boundless Sea: a human history of
the oceans* (Oxford, 2019), p. 424 • 4 Peter Johanek, 'Seigneurial Power and the Development
of Towns in the Holy Roman Empire', in Anngret Simms and Howard B. Clarke (eds.),
Lords and Towns in Medieval Europe: the European Historic Towns Atlas Project (London, 2015),
p. 142 • 5 Roger Crowley, *City of Fortune: how Venice won and lost a naval empire* (London,
2011), p. 66 • 6 O City of Byzantium: annals of Niketas Choniates, trans. Harry J. Magoulias
(Detroit, 1984), p. 317 • 7 M. Schmidt, *Veröffentlichungen zur Geschichte der Freien und
Hansestadt Lübeck* (Lübeck, 1933), Vol. XII, pp. 42–3; Ernst Deecke, *Der Lübeckischen
Gesellschaft zur Beförderung gemeinnütziger Thätigkeit* (Lübeck, 1939), p. 33 • 8 Rhiman A.
Rotz, 'The Lubeck Uprising of 1408 and the Decline of the Hanseatic League', *Proceedings
of the American Philosophical Society*, 121:1 (February 1977), 17ff, 24 • 9 Ibid., 31 • 10 J.
Kathirithamby-Wells, 'The Islamic City: Melaka to Jogjakarta, c.1500–1800', *Modern Asian
Studies*, 20:2 (1986), 333–51 • 11 Johanek, pp. 146–8; Athanasios Moulakis, *Republican Realism
in Renaissance Florence: Francesco Guicciardini's Discorso di Logrogno* (Lanham, 1998), p. 119
• 12 Manuel Eisner, 'Interactive London Medieval Murder Map', University of Cambridge:
Institute of Criminology (2018), https://www.vrc.crim.cam.ac.uk/vrcresearch/london-medieval-
murder-map

7. Cities of the World

1 Judith B. Sombré (trans.), 'Hieronymus Munzer: journey through Spain and Portugal', http://munzerama.blogspot.com/2017/04/hieronymus-munzer-journey-through.html • 2 Roger Crowley, *Conquerors: how Portugal seized the Indian Ocean and forged the first global empire* (London, 2015), p. 4 • 3 Ibid., p. 19 • 4 Ibid., pp. 64–5 • 5 E. G. Ravenstein (trans.), *A Journal of the First Voyage of Vasco da Gama, 1497–1499* (London, 1898), pp. 48ff • 6 William Brooks Greenlee, *The Voyage of Pedro Álvares Cabral to Brazil and India* (London, 1937), pp. 83–5 • 7 Gaspar Corrêa, *The Three Voyages of Vasco da Gama, and His Viceroyalty* (London, 1896), p. 295; Crowley, chapter 7 • 8 Ibid. pp. 131ff • 9 Ibid., p. 128 • 10 Tomé Pires, *The Suma Oriental*, 2 vols, ed. and trans. Armando Cortesáo (London, 1944), p. 285 • 11 Ibid., p. 287 • 12 Barry Hatton, *Queen of the Sea: a history of Lisbon* (London, 2018), pp. 55ff • 13 Annemarie Jordan Gschwend and Kate Lowe, 'Princess of the Seas, Queen of the Empire: configuring the city and port of Renaissance Lisbon', in Gschwend and Lowe (eds.), *The Global City: on the streets of Renaissance Lisbon* (London, 2015) • 14 Annemarie Jordan Gschwend, 'Reconstructing the Rua Nova: the life of a global street in Renaissance Lisbon', in Gschwend and Lowe (eds.) • 15 Hatton, pp. 71ff • 16 Michael Wood, *Conquistadors* (Berkeley, CA, 2000), p. 53 • 17 Georgia Butina Watson and Ian Bentley, *Identity by Design* (Amsterdam, 2007), p. 74 • 18 Anne Goldgar, *Tulipmania: money, honour, and knowledge in the Dutch Golden Age* (Chicago, 2007), p. 10 • 19 William Temple, *The Works of Sir William Temple*, 2 vols (London, 1731), Vol. II, p. 60 • 20 *The Philosophical Writings of Descartes: volume III, the correspondence*, trans. John Cottingham, Robert Stoothoff, Dugald Murdoch and Anthony Kenny (Cambridge, 1991), p. 32 • 21 Joseph de la Vega, *Confusion de Confusiones* (Boston, MA, 1957), p. 21 • 22 Ibid., p. 11 • 23 Ibid., p. 28 • 24 R. E. Kistemaker, 'The Public and the Private: public space in sixteenth- and seventeenth-century Amsterdam', in Arthur K. Wheelock Jr and Adele Seeff, *The Public and Private in Dutch Culture of the Golden Age* (Newark, 2000), p. 22 • 25 Ibid., p. 21 • 26 *The Travels of Peter Mundy, in Europe and Asia, 1608–1667*, ed. Sir Richard Carnac Temple (London, 1914), Vol. IV, pp. 70–1 • 27 Simon Schama, *The Embarrassment of Riches: an interpretation of Dutch culture in the Golden Age* (Berkeley, CA, 1987)

8. The Sociable Metropolis

1 Bryant Simon, 'Consuming Third Place: Starbucks and the illusion of public space', in Miles Orvell and Jeffrey L. Meikle (eds.), *Public Space and the Ideology of Place in American Culture* (Amsterdam, 2009), pp. 243ff; Howard Schultz and Dori Jones, *Pour Your Heart into It: how Starbucks built a company one cup at a time* (NY, 1997), p. 5 • 2 Jee Eun Regina Song, 'The Soybean Paste Girl: the cultural and gender politics of coffee consumption in contemporary South Korea', *Journal of Korean Studies*, 19:2 (Fall 2014), 429–48 • 3 Seyed Hossein Iradj Moeini, Mehran Arefian, Bahador Kashani and Golnar Abbasi, *Urban Culture in Tehran: urban processes in unofficial cultural spaces* (e-book, 2018), pp. 26ff • 4 W. Scott Haine, '"Café Friend": friendship and fraternity in Parisian working-class cafés, 1850–1914', *Journal of Contemporary History*, 27:4 (October 1992), 607–26; W. Scott Haine, *The World of the Paris Café: sociability among the French working class, 1789–1914* (Baltimore, 1998), pp. 1, 9; Barbara Stern Shapiro and Anne E. Havinga, *Pleasures of Paris: from Daumier to Picasso* (Boston, MA, 1991), p. 123 • 5 John Rewald, *History of Impressionism* (NY, 1946), p. 146 • 6 Rowley Amato, 'Brokers Are Now Opening Their Own Coffee Shops in Harlem', Curbed New York, 16/8/2014, https://ny.curbed.com/2014/8/16/10059746/brokers-are-now-opening-their-own-coffee-shops-in-harlem • 7 Markman Ellis, *The Coffee-House: a cultural history* (London, 2004), pp. 7–8 • 8 Ibid., pp. 29–32; Uğur. Kömeçoğlu, 'The Publicness and Sociabilities of the Ottoman Coffeehouse', *The Public*, 12:2 (2005), 5–22; A. Caksu, 'Janissary Coffee Houses in Late Eighteenth-Century Istanbul', in Dana Sajdi (ed.), *Ottoman Tulips, Ottoman Coffee: leisure and lifestyle in the eighteenth century* (London, 2007), p. 117 • 9 Ellis,

pp. 32–3 • 10 Ibid., p. 42; Steve Pincus, '"Coffee Politicians Does Create": coffee houses and Restoration political culture', *Journal of Modern History* 67:4 (December 1995), 811–12 • 11 C. John Sommerville, *The News Revolution in England: cultural dynamics of daily information* (NY, 1996), p. 77 • 12 Pincus, pp. 814–15 • 13 Ibid., p. 824 • 14 Ellis, pp. 157–8; Larry Stewart, 'Other Centres of Calculation, or, Where the Royal Society Didn't Count: commerce, coffee-houses and natural philosophy in early modern London', *British Journal for the History of Science*, 32:2 (June 1999), 133–53 • 15 Stewart, pp. 133–53 • 16 Pincus, p. 833 • 17 Paul Slack, 'Material Progress and the Challenge of Affluence in Seventeenth Century England', *Economic History Review*, n/s, 62:3 (August 2009), 576–603; Ian Warren, 'The English Landed Elite and the Social Environment of London c.1580–1700: the cradle of an aristocratic culture?', *English Historical Review*, 126:518 (February 2011), 44–74 • 18 Farid Azfar, 'Beastly Sodomites and the Shameless Urban Frontier', *Eighteenth Century*, 55:4 (Winter 2014), 402 • 19 Anon., *A Trip through the Town: containing observations on the customs and manners of the age* (London, 1735), p. 1 • 20 R. H. Sweet, 'Topographies of Politeness', *Transactions of the Royal Historical Society*, 12 (2002), 356 • 21 Ibid., pp. 355–74; Lawrence E. Klein, 'Coffee House Civility, 1660–1714: an aspect of post-courtly culture in England', *Huntington Library Quarterly*, 59:1 (1996), 30–51; Lawrence E. Klein, 'Liberty, Manners, and Politeness in Early Eighteenth-Century England', *Historical Journal*, 32:3 (September 1989), 583–605; • 22 Markku Peltonen, 'Politeness and Whiggism, 1688–1732', *Historical Journal*, 48:2 (June 2005), 396–7 • 23 Peter Borsay, 'Culture, Status, and the English Urban Landscape', *History*, 67:219 (1982), 12; Lawrence E. Klein, 'Politeness and the Interpretation of the British Eighteenth Century', *Historical Journal*, 45:4 (December 2002), 886ff; Warren, pp. 49ff • 24 'A Letter from a Foreigner to his Friend in Paris', *Gentleman's Magazine*, 12, August 1742 • 25 Jerry White, *London in the Eighteenth Century: a great and monstrous thing* (London, 2012), pp. 322–3 • 26 Ben Wilson, *Decency and Disorder: the age of cant* (London, 2007), p. 17 • 27 Darryl P. Domingo, 'Unbending the Mind: or, commercialized leisure and the rhetoric of eighteenth-century diversion', *Eighteenth-Century Studies*, 45:2 (Winter 2012), 219 • 28 White, p. 130 • 29 Paul Langford, 'The Uses of Eighteenth-Century Politeness', *Transactions of the Royal Historical Society*, 12 (2002), 330 • 30 [Robert Southey], *Letters from England: by Don Manuel Alvarez Espriella*, 2 vols (New York, 1808), Vol. I, p. 39; Helen Berry, 'Polite Consumption: shopping in eighteenth-century England', *Transactions of the Royal Historical Society*, 12 (2002), 375–94 • 31 Ford Madox Ford, *Provence: from minstrels to the machine*, ed. John Coyle (Manchester, 2009), p. 24 • 32 Ellis, pp. 205–6 • 33 Ibid., pp. 177–80, 212–14

9. The Gates of Hell?

1 *The Life and Opinions of General Sir Charles James Napier*, 4 vols (London, 1857), Vol. II, p. 57 • 2 Alexis de Tocqueville, *Journeys to England and Ireland* (NY, 2003), p. 106; Frederika Bremmer, *England in 1851; or, Sketches of a Tour to England* (Boulogne, 1853), p. 15 • 3 Frederika Bremmer, *The Homes of the New World: impressions of America*, 2 vols (NY, 1858), Vol. I, p. 605 • 4 Isabella Bird, *The Englishwoman in America* (London, 1856), p. 156; Paul Bourget, *Outre-Mer: impressions of America* (London, 1895), p. 117 • 5 Tocqueville, p. 108 • 6 Donald L. Miller, *City of the Century: the epic of Chicago and the making of America* (NY, 1996), p. 217 • 7 Frederic Trautmann, 'Arthur Holitischer's Chicago: a German traveler's view of an American city', *Chicago History*, 12:2 (Summer 1983), 42; Miller, p. 493; Simon Gunn, 'The Middle Class, Modernity and the Provincial City: Manchester, c.1840–80', in Alan Kidd and David Nicholls (eds.), *Gender, Civic Culture and Consumerism: middle-class identity in Britain, 1800–1940* (Manchester, 1999), pp. 112ff • 8 Miller, pp. 301ff • 9 Friedrich Engels, *The Condition of the Working Class in England* (London, 1958), pp. 61, 63, 64 • 10 M. Leon Faucher, *Manchester in 1844; its present condition and future prospects* (Manchester, 1844), pp. 67–8; John M. Werly, 'The Irish in Manchester, 1832–49', *Irish Historical Studies*, 18:71 (March 1973), 348 • 11 Miller, p. 123 • 12 Ibid., p. 136; Josiah Seymour Currey, *Chicago: its history and builders* (Chicago, 1912), Vol. III, p. 177 • 13 Miller, p. 122 • 14 Gunn, p. 118 • 15 Miller, pp.

273ff • 16 Angus Bethune Reach, *Manchester and the Textile Districts in 1849* (Rossendale, 1972), p. 61 • 17 Andrew Davies, *The Gangs of Manchester: the story of scuttlers, Britain's first youth cult* (Preston, 2008), chapter 2 • 18 Ibid.; Jenny Birchall, '"The Carnival Revels of Manchester's Vagabonds": young working-class women and monkey parades in the 1870s', *Women's History Review*, 15 (2006), 229–52 • 19 Davies, *passim*; Mervyn Busteed, *The Irish in Manchester, c.1750–1921: resistance, adaptation and identity* (Manchester, 2016), chapter 2 • 20 M. A. Busteed and R. I. Hodgson, 'Irish Migrant Responses to Urban Life in Early Nineteenth-Century Manchester', *Geographical Journal*, 162:2 (July 1996), 150 • 21 Richard Junger, *Becoming the Second City: Chicago's news media, 1833–1898* (Chicago, 2010), p. 22 • 22 Miller, p. 137; Frederic M. Thrasher, *The Gang: a study of 1,313 gangs in Chicago* (Chicago, 1936) • 23 Richard C. Lindberg, *Gangland Chicago: criminality and lawlessness in the Windy City* (Lanham, 2016), p. 22 • 24 James Phillips Kay, *The Moral and Physical Condition of the Working Classes Employed in the Cotton Manufacture in Manchester* (London, 1832), p. 72 • 25 Engels, p. 137 • 26 Zubair Ahmed, 'Bombay's Billion Dollar Slum', http://news.bbc.co.uk/1/hi/business/3487110.stm • 27 Janice E. Perlman, 'The Metamorphosis of Marginality: four generations in the *favelas* of Rio de Janeiro', *Annals of the American Academy of Political and Social Science*, 606 (July 2006), 167; Sanni Yaya, Olalekan A. Uthman, Friday Okonofua and Ghose Bishwajit, 'Decomposing the Rural–Urban Gap in the Factors of Under-Five Mortality Rate in Sub-Saharan Africa? Evidence from 35 countries', *BMC Public Health*, 19 (May 2019); Abhijit V. Banerjee and Esther Duflo, 'The Economic Lives of the Poor', *Journal of Economic Perspectives*, 21:1 (Winter 2007), table 9; World Bank, 'Employment in Agriculture', https://data.worldbank.org/indicator/SL.AGR.EMPL.ZS • 28 Hippolyte Taine, *Notes on England* (London, 1957), pp. 290ff • 29 John Burnett (ed.), *Destiny Obscure: autobiographies of childhood, education and family from the 1820s to the 1920s* (London, 1982), p. 107; Frank Norris, *The Pit: a story of Chicago* (NY, 1920), pp. 149ff • 30 Miller, p. 277 • 31 Emma Griffin, *Liberty's Dawn: a people's history of the industrial revolution* (New Haven, 2013), pp. 240ff • 32 Faucher, p. 52 • 33 John B. Jentz, 'The 48ers and the Politics of the German Labor Movement in Chicago during the Civil War Era: community formation and the rise of a labor press', in Elliot Shore, Ken Fones-Wolf, James P. Danky (eds.), *The German-American Radical Press: the shaping of a left political culture, 1850–1940* (Chicago, 1992), pp. 49ff • 34 City of Chicago, Department of Zoning and Planning, 'Vorwaerts Turner Hall, 2421 W. Roosevelt Rd: final landmark recommendation adopted by the Commission on Chicago Landmarks, September 3 2009', https://www.chicago.gov/content/dam/city/depts/zlup/Historic_Preservation/Publications/Vorwaerts_Turner_Hall.pdf • 35 Royal L. Melendy, 'The Saloon in Chicago (II)', *American Journal of Sociology*, 6:4 (January 1901), 433–4 • 36 Eric L. Hirsch, *Urban Revolt: ethnic politics in the nineteenth-century Chicago labor movement* (Berkeley, CA, 1990), p. 163 • 37 Sandra Burman (ed.), *Fit Work for Women* (Abingdon, 2013), pp. 100ff • 38 Gertrud Pfister, 'The Role of German Turners in American Physical Education', in Pfister (ed.), *Gymnastics, a Transatlantic Movement* (Abingdon, 2011); Gerald Gems, 'The German Turners and the Taming of Radicalism in Chicago', in Pfister (ed.); Gerald Gems, *Windy City Wars: labor, leisure, and sport in the making of Chicago* (Lanham, 1997) • 39 Dagmar Kift, *The Victorian Music Hall: culture, class and conflict*, trans. Roy Kift (Cambridge, 1996), p. 1 • 40 Harvey Warren Zorbaugh, *The Gold Coast and the Slum: a sociological study of Chicago's Near North Side* (Chicago, 1929), p. 3

10. Paris Syndrome

1 Caroline Wyatt, '"Paris Syndrome" Strikes Japanese', BBC News, 20/12/2006, http://news.bbc.co.uk/1/hi/6197921.stm; Katada Tamami, 'Reflections on a Case of Paris Syndrome', *Journal of the Nissei Hospital*, 26:2 (1998), 127–32 • 2 Sigmund Freud, *Life and Work: the young Freud, 1885–1900*, ed. Ernest Jones (London, 1953), p. 200 • 3 Emma Willard, *Journals and Letters from France and Great Britain* (NY, 1833), p. 30 • 4 David P. Jordan,

Transforming Paris: the life and labors of Baron Haussmann (NY, 1995), pp. 92–3; Victoria E. Thompson, 'Telling "Spatial Stories": urban space and bourgeois identity in nineteenth-century Paris', *Journal of Modern History*, 75:3 (September 2003), 540 • 5 Anon., *Ten Years of Imperialism in France: impressions of a Flâneur* (London, 1862), p. 30 • 6 Harvey Levenstein, *Seductive Journey: American tourists in France from Jefferson to the Jazz Age* (Chicago, 1998), p. 57; David Harvey, *Paris: capital of modernity* (NY, 2006), pp. 32–3 • 7 Gregory Shaya, 'The Flâneur, the Badaud, and the Making of a Mass Public in France, circa 1860–1910', *American Historical Review*, 109:1 (February 2004), 50; T. J. Clark, *The Painting of Modern Life: Paris in the art of Manet and his followers* (London, 1990), p. 33 • 8 Anna Jameson, *Diary of an Ennuyée* (Boston, MA, 1833), p. 6; Shaya, *passim* • 9 Christopher E. Fort, *The Dreyfus Affair and the Crisis of French Manhood* (Baltimore, 2004), p. 107; Honoré de Balzac, *The Physiology of Marriage*, Part 1, Meditation 3; Charles Baudelaire, *The Painter of Modern Life and Other Essays*, trans. Jonathan Mayne (NY, 1986), p. 9; • 10 Thompson, p. 532, n.34; Shaya, p. 51; Balzac, 1:3 • 11 *Ten Years of Imperialism*, preface; Susan Sontag, *On Photography* (London, 1979), p. 55 • 12 Jordan (1995), pp. 50ff, 166–7; David H. Pinkney, 'Napoleon III's Transformation of Paris: the origins and development of the idea', *Journal of Modern History*, 27:2 (June 1955), 125–34 • 13 Patrice de Moncan, *Le Paris d'Haussmann* (Paris, 2002), p. 28 • 14 Jordan (1995), pp. 186ff • 15 Colin Jones, 'Theodore Vacquer and the Archaeology of Modernity in Haussmann's Paris', *Transactions of the Royal Historical Society*, 6th series, 17 (2007), 167; *Ten Years of Imperialism*, p. 7; David P. Jordan, 'Baron Haussmann and Modern Paris', *American Scholar*, 61:1 (Winter 1992), 105ff • 16 Jordan (1995), pp. 265, 290 • 17 Ibid., pp. 198ff • 18 Donald L. Miller, *City of the Century: the epic of Chicago and the making of America* (NY, 1996), pp. 124–7 • 19 Jordan (1995), p. 274 • 20 Moncan, p. 107 • 21 Elaine Denby, *Grand Hotels: reality and illusion* (London, 1998), p. 84 • 22 Michael B. Miller, *The Bon Marché: bourgeois culture and the department store, 1869–1920* (Princeton, 1981); Meredith L. Clausen, 'Department Stores and Zola's "Cathédrale du Commerce Moderne"', *Notes in the History of Art*, 3:3 (Spring 1984), 18–23; Robert Procter, 'Constructing the Retail Monument: the Parisian department store and its property, 1855–1914', *Urban History*, 33:3 (December 2006), 393–410 • 23 *Galignani's New Paris Guide* (Paris, 1860), p. 13 • 24 Jan Palmowski, 'Travels with Baedeker: the guidebook and the middle classes in Victorian and Edwardian Britain', in Rudy Koshar (ed.), *Histories of Leisure* (Oxford, 2002) • 25 London & Partners, 'London Tourism Report, 2014–2015', https://files.londonand-partners.com/l-and-p/assets/our-insight-london-tourism-review-2014–15.pdf • 26 Pierre Larousse, *Grand Dictionnaire universel* (Paris, 1872), Vol. VIII, p. 436 • 27 Robert L. Herbert, *Impressionism: art, leisure and Parisian society* (New Haven, 1988), p. 21 • 28 Jordan (1995), p. 348; Clark, pp. 34–5; Herbert, p. 15 • 29 Clark, p. 29 • 30 Clark, p. 207; Herbert, pp. 33, 58, 66 • 31 Ibid., p. 35 • 32 Katherine Golsan, 'The Beholder as *Flâneur*: structures of perception in Baudelaire and Manet', *French Forum*, 21:2 (May 1996), 183 • 33 Herbert, pp. 50ff • 34 Clark, p. 253 • 35 Ibid., pp. 72ff • 36 Aruna D'Souza and Tom McDonough (eds.), *The Invisible Flâneuse? Gender, public space, and visual culture in nineteenth century Paris* (Manchester, 2006) • 37 Clark, p. 208; Ruth E. Iskin, 'Selling, Seduction, and Soliciting the Eye: Manet's *Bar at the Folies-Bergère*', *Art Bulletin* 77:1 (Mar. 1995), 35 • 38 Markman Ellis, *The Coffee-House: a cultural history* (London, 2004), pp. 201–11; Krista Lysack, *Come Buy, Come Buy: shopping and the culture of consumption in Victorian women's writing* (Athens, OH, 2008), pp. 19ff • 39 Anne Friedberg, 'Les Flâneurs du Mal(l): cinema and the postmodern condition', *PMLA*, 106:3 (May 1991), 425 • 40 Louis Aragon, *Paris Peasant*, trans. Simon Watson Taylor (Boston, MA, 1994), p. viii • 41 *The Notebooks of Henry James*, ed. F. O. Matthiessen and Kenneth B. Murdock (Chicago, 1947), p. 28 • 42 Rebecca Solnit, *Wanderlust: a history of walking* (London, 2001), p. 204; Mary Higgs, *Glimpses into the Abyss* (London, 1906), p. 94; Deborah Epstein Nord, *Walking the Victorian Streets: women, representation and the city* (Ithaca, 1995); Judith R. Walkowitz, *City of Dreadful Delight: narratives of sexual danger in late-Victorian London* (Chicago, 1992); Lynda Nead, *Victorian Babylon: people, streets and images in nineteenth-century London* (New Haven, 2000) • 43 Janet Wolff, 'The Invisible Flâneuse: women and the literature of modernity', in *Feminine Sentences: essays on women and culture* (Cambridge, 1990); Jane Rendell, Barbara Penner and Iain Borden (eds.), *Gender Space Architecture: an interdisciplinary introduction* (London, 2000), p. 164 • 44 Lily Gair Wilkinson, *Woman's Freedom* (London, 1914); Kathy E. Ferguson, 'Women and the Politics of Walking', *Political Research Quarterly*, 70:4 (December 2017), 708–19 • 45 Janice Mouton, 'From Feminine Masquerade to *Flâneuse*: Agnès Varda's *Cléo in the City*', *Cinema Journal*, 40:2 (Winter 2001), 3–16

11. Skyscraper Souls

1 Jason M. Barr, *Building the Skyline: the birth and growth of Manhattan's skyscrapers* (Oxford, 2016) • 2 *Architectural Record*, January–March 1899; Henry Blake Fuller, *The Cliff-Dwellers*, ed. Joseph A. Dimuro (Peterborough, ON, 2010), p. 58 • 3 Nick Yablon, 'The Metropolitan Life in Ruins: architectural and fictional speculations in New York, 1909–19', *American Quarterly*, 56:2 (June 2004), 308–47 • 4 Gail Fenske, *The Skyscraper and the City: the Woolworth Building and the making of modern New York* (Chicago, 2008), pp. 25ff • 5 Keith D. Revell, *Building Gotham: civic culture and public policy in New York City, 1898–1939* (Baltimore, 2003), pp. 185ff • 6 Merrill Schleier, 'The Empire State Building, Working-Class Masculinity, and *King Kong*', *Mosaic: an interdisciplinary journal*, 41:2 (June 2008), 37 • 7 Carol Willis, 'Zoning and "Zeitgeist": the skyscraper city in the 1920s', *Journal of the Society of Architectural Historians*, 45:1 (March 1986), 53, 56 • 8 H. Ferriss, 'The New Architecture', *New York Times*, 19/3/1922 • 9 Kate Holliday, 'Walls as Curtains: architecture and humanism in Ralph Walker's skyscrapers of the 1920s', *Studies in the Decorative Arts*, 16:2 (Spring–Summer 2009), 50; Daniel Michael Abramson, *Skyscraper Rivals: the AIG Building and the architecture of Wall Street* (Princeton, 2001), p. 191 • 10 Holliday, pp. 46ff • 11 Ibid., pp. 59, 61–2, 39 • 12 James Sanders, *Celluloid Skyline: New York and the movies* (London, 2001), p. 106 • 13 Ibid., pp. 105ff • 14 *Shanghai Star*, 11/11/2002 • 15 *Washington Post*, 24/3/2015 • 16 Deyan Sudjic, *The Language of Cities* (London, 2017), chapter 3 • 17 Alfred Kazin, *A Walker in the City* (Orlando, 1974), p. 11 • 18 'Bull Market Architecture', *New Republic*, 8/7/1931, 192 • 19 Gabrielle Esperdy, *Modernizing Main Street: architecture and consumer culture in the New Deal* (Chicago, 2008), p. 53 • 20 Lucy Fischer, 'City of Women: Busby Berkeley, architecture, and urban space', *Cinema Journal*, 49 (Summer 2010), 129–30 • 21 Sanders, p. 97 • 22 Ibid., pp. 156ff • 23 Ibid., pp. 161ff • 24 Ibid., pp. 165ff • 25 Ibid., pp. 161ff • 26 Paul Goldberger, 'Robert Moses, Master Builder, Is Dead at 92', *New York Times*, 30/7/1981 • 27 *New York Times*, 3/3/1945

12. Annihilation

1 W. H. Auden and Christopher Isherwood, *Journey to a War* (NY, 1972), p. 240 • 2 John Faber, *Great Moments in News Photography: from the historical files of the National Press Photographers Association* (NY, 1960), p. 74 • 3 Auden and Isherwood, p. 240 • 4 Richard Overy, *The Bombing War: Europe, 1939–1945* (London, 2013), chapter 1, pp. 19ff • 5 Alexandra Richie, *Warsaw 1944: Hitler, Himmler and the crushing of a city* (London, 2013), pp. 125ff; Ancient Monuments Society, 'The Reconstruction of Warsaw Old Town, Poland', *Transactions of the Ancient Monuments Society* (1959), 77 • 6 Hugh Trevor-Roper, *The Last Days of Hitler* (London, 1982), p. 81 • 7 Joanna K. M. Hanson, *The Civilian Population and the Warsaw Uprising of 1944* (Cambridge, 1982), p. 6 • 8 T. H. Chylinski, 'Poland under Nazi Rule' (Central Intelligence Agency confidential report, 1941), pp. 49ff • 9 Ibid • 10 Ibid., p. 5 • 11 Richie, pp. 133ff • 12 Hanson, p. 23 • 13 Ibid., p. 26 • 14 Chylinski, p. 10 • 15 Ibid., p. 9 • 16 Peter Fritzsche, *An Iron Wind: Europe under Hitler* (NY, 2016), pp. 144, 357 • 17 David Cesarani, *Final Solution: the fate of the Jews 1933–49* (London, 2016), p. 333 • 18 Ibid., p. 435 • 19 Ibid., p. 348 • 20 *Time*, 34:2 (1939), 45 • 21 Williamson Murray, *Military Adaptation in War: with fear of change* (Cambridge, 2011), p. 183 • 22 Stephen A. Garrett, *Ethics and Airpower in World War II: the British bombing of German cities* (London, 1993), pp. 32–3 •

23 Overy, pp. 287–8 • 24 Ibid., pp. 337, 433, 436 • 25 Ibid., p. 400 • 26 Ibid., pp. 172, 478–9 • 27 Ibid., pp. 638–9 • 28 Max Hastings, *Nemesis: the battle for Japan, 1944–45* (London, 2007), p. 320 • 29 Henry D. Smith, 'Tokyo as an Idea: an exploration of Japanese urban thought until 1945', *Journal for Japanese Studies*, 4:1 (Winter 1978), 66ff; Fujii Tadatoshi, *Kokubō fujinkai* (Tokyo, 1985), pp. 198–203 • 30 Hiroshima Peace Media Centre, 'Hiroshima, 70 Years after the Atomic Bomb: rebirth of the city, part 1 (3): "Workers labored to give the city light amid A-bomb ruins"', http://www.hiroshimapeacemedia.jp/?p=47982; part 1 (4): 'Workers take pride in uninterrupted water supply', http://www.hiroshimapeacemedia.jp/?p=47988 • 31 Ibid., part 1 (5): 'Post office workers struggle to maintain mail service in ruined city', http://www.hiroshimapeacemedia.jp/?p=48210 • 32 Grigore Gafencu, *The Last Days of Europe: a diplomatic journey in 1939* (New Haven, 1948), p. 78 • 33 Max Hastings, *All Hell Let Loose: the world at war, 1939–1945* (London, 2011), p. 170 • 34 Anna Reid, *Leningrad: the epic siege of World War II* (London, 2011), pp. 134–5 • 35 Ibid., p. 172; Reid, pp. 167ff, 182ff • 36 Reid, pp. 176ff, 233, 288 • 37 Anthony Beevor and Luba Vinogradova (eds. and trans.), *A Writer at War: Vasily Grossman with the Red Army, 1941–1945* (London, 2005), p. 151 • 38 Georgii Zhukov, *The Memoirs of Marshal Zhukov* (London, 1971), p. 353 • 39 Fritzsche, pp. 18–19 • 40 Cesarani, pp. 340ff • 41 Ibid., pp. 342, 345–6 • 42 Ibid., pp. 342, 487 • 43 Ibid., pp. 493ff • 44 Ibid., pp. 605ff • 45 Richie, pp. 193–4 • 46 Ibid., pp. 241ff • 47 Ibid., pp. 44ff, 249–50, 252ff • 48 Ibid., pp. 275ff, 305ff • 49 Ibid., pp. 591–2 • 50 Fritzsche, pp. 357–8 • 51 Reid, pp. 617ff • 52 Stanislaw Jankowski, 'Warsaw: destruction, secret town planning, 1939–44, and post-war reconstruction', in Jeffry M. Diefendorf (ed.), *Rebuilding Europe's Bombed Cities* (NY, 1990), pp. 79–80 • 53 H. V. Lanchester, 'Reconstruction of Warsaw', *The Builder* (1947), 296; Robert Bevan, *The Destruction of Memory: architecture at war* (London, 2006), p. 97 • 54 Reid, p. 639 • 55 Ibid • 56 Beevor and Vinogradova (eds. and trans.), pp. 312–13 • 57 Richard J. Evans, 'Disorderly Cities', *London Review of Books*, 5/12/2013, 27–9 • 58 Jankowski, 79ff; Jerzy Elzanowski, 'Manufacturing Ruins: architecture and representation in post-catastrophic Warsaw', *Journal of Architecture* 15 (2010), 76–9 • 59 Marian Nowicki, *Skarpa Warszawska* 1 (October 1945), cited in Magdalena Mostowska, 'Post-War Planning and Housing Policy: a modernist architect's perspective', *European Spatial Research and Policy*, 12:2 (2005), 98 • 60 Mostowska, p. 97 • 61 André Sorensen, *The Making of Urban Japan: cities and planning from Edo to the twenty-first century* (Abingdon, 2002), p. 149; C. Hein, J. Diefendorf and I. Yorifusa (eds.), *Rebuilding Japan after 1945* (NY, 2003); Matias Echanove, 'The Tokyo Model: incremental urban development in the post-war city' (2015), http://www.urbanlab.org/TheTokyoModel-Echanove.02.2015.pdf

13. Sounds of the Suburbs

1 Marshall Berman, 'Among the Ruins', *New Internationalist*, 5/12/1987 • 2 Ibid.; Francesca Russello Ammon, 'Unearthing "Benny the Bulldozer": the culture of clearance in post-war children's books', *Technology and Culture*, 53:2 (April 2012), 306–7 • 3 Conor Friedersdorf, 'When the Army Planned for a Fight in US Cities', *The Atlantic*, 16/1/2018; William Rosenau, '"Our Ghettos, Too, Need a Lansdale": American counter-insurgency abroad and at home in the Vietnam era', in Celeste Ward Gventer, M. L. R. Smith and D. Jones (eds.), *The New Counter-Insurgency Era in Critical Perspective* (London, 2013), pp. 111ff • 4 William Jelani Cobb, *To the Break of Dawn: a freestyle on the hip hop aesthetic* (NY, 2007), p. 142; https://web.archive.org/web/20110728100004/http://hiphop.sh/juice • 5 Michael Eric Dyson and Sohail Daulatzai, *Born to Use Mics: reading Nas's Illmatic* (NY, 2009) • 6 NPR interview, 'Nas on Marvin Gaye's Marriage, Parenting and Rap Genius', 20/7/2012, https://www.npr.org/2012/07/22/157043285/nas-on-marvin-gayes-marriage-parenting-and-rap-genius • 7 D. J. Waldie, *Holy Land: a suburban memoir* (NY, 2005) • 8 United States Census Bureau, *Patterns of Metropolitan and Micropolitan Population Change: 2000 to 2010* (2012) • 9 Martin J. Schiesl, 'The Politics of Contracting: Los Angeles County and the Lakewood Plan, 1954–1962', *Huntington Library Quarterly*, 45:3 (Summer 1982), 227–43 • 10 Becky M.

Nicolaides, *My Blue Heaven: life and politics in the working-class suburbs of Los Angeles, 1920–1965* (Chicago, 2002) • 11 Christopher C. Sellers, *Crabgrass Crucible: suburban nature and the rise of environmentalism in twentieth-century America* (Chapel Hill, 2012), p. 156 • 12 Laura R. Barraclough, 'Rural Urbanism: producing western heritage and the racial geography of post-war Los Angeles', *Western Historical Quarterly*, 39:2 (Summer 2008), 177–80; Catherine Mulholland, 'Recollections of a Valley Past', in Gary Soto (ed.), *California Childhood: recollections and stories of the Golden State* (Berkeley, CA, 1988), p. 181 • 13 Wade Graham, 'The Urban Environmental Legacies of the Air Industry', in Peter J. Westwick, *Blue Sky Metropolis: the aerospace century in Southern California* (Los Angeles, 2012); Martin J. Schiesl, 'City Planning and the Federal Government in World War II: the Los Angeles experience', *California History*, 59:2 (Summer 1980), 126–43 • 14 Mark L. Morgan and Mark A. Berhow, *Rings of Supersonic Steel: air defenses of the United States Army, 1950–1979, an introductory history and site guide* (Bodega Bay, 2002), pp. 105ff • 15 Robert Kargon and Arthur Molella, 'The City as Communications Net: Norbert Wiener, the atomic bomb, and urban dispersal', *Technology and Culture*, 45:4 (October 2004), 764–77; Kathleen A. Tobin, 'The Reduction of Urban Vulnerability: revisiting the 1950s American suburbanization as civil defence', *Cold War History* 2:2 (January 2002), 1–32; Jennifer S. Light, *From Warfare to Welfare: defense intellectuals and urban problems in Cold War America* (Baltimore, 2003) • 16 Kenneth Jackson, *Crabgrass Frontier: the suburbanization of the United States* (NY, 1985), chapter 11; Tom Hanchett, 'The Other "Subsidized Housing": Federal aid to suburbanization, 1940s–1960s', in John Bauman, Roger Biles and Kristin Szylvian (eds.), *From Tenements to Taylor Homes: in search of urban housing policy in twentieth-century America* (University Park, 2000), pp. 163–79 • 17 Jackson, p. 207 • 18 Tobin, p. 25 • 19 Waldie, p. 162; William Fulton, *The Reluctant Metropolis: the politics of urban growth in Los Angeles* (Baltimore, 1997), p. 10; David Kushner, *Levittown: two families, one tycoon, and the fight for civil rights in America's legendary suburb* (NY, 2009), p. 190 • 20 Josh Sides, 'Straight into Compton: American dreams, urban nightmares, and the metamorphosis of a black suburb', *American Quarterly*, 56:3 (September 2004), 583ff • 21 Richard Elman, *Ill at Ease in Compton* (NY, 1967), pp. 23–4; Sides, 588 • 22 Emily E. Straus, *Death of a Suburban Dream: race and schools in Compton, California* (Philadelphia, 2014), p. 107 • 23 Edward Soja, Rebecca Morales and Goetz Wolff, 'Urban Restructuring: an analysis of social and spatial change in Los Angeles', *Economic Geography* 59:2 (1983), 195–230; Sides, pp. 590ff • 24 Judith Fernandez and John Pincus, *Troubled Suburbs: an exploratory study* (Santa Monica, 1982); Elizabeth Kneebone and Alan Berube, *Confronting Suburban Poverty in America* (Washington DC, 2013), pp. 8ff; 'Crime Migrates to the Suburbs', *Wall Street Journal*, 30/12/2012 • 25 Joan Didion, 'Trouble in Lakewood', *New Yorker*, 19/7/1993; Graham, pp. 263ff • 26 Edward Soja, *Postmodern Geographics: the reassertion of space in critical theory* (London, 1989), pp. 197ff; Edward W. Soja, *Thirdspace: journeys to Los Angeles and other real and imagined places* (Cambridge, MA, 1996); Mike Davies, *City of Quartz: excavating the future in Los Angeles* (NY, 1990); Roger Waldinger, 'Not the Promised Land: Los Angeles and its immigrants', *Pacific Historical Review*, 68:2 (May 1999), 253–72; Michael Nevin Willard, 'Nuestra Los Angeles', *American Quarterly*, 56:3 (September 2004), 811 • 27 Timothy Fong, *The First Suburban Chinatown: the remaking of Monterey Park, California* (Philadelphia, 1994); John Horton (ed.), *The Politics of Diversity: immigration, resistance, and change in Monterey Park, California* (Philadelphia, 1995); Leland T. Saito, *Race and Politics: Asian Americans, Latinos, and whites in a Los Angeles suburb* (Chicago, 1998), p. 23; Wei Li, 'Building Ethnoburbia: the emergence and manifestation of the Chinese ethnoburb in Los Angeles's San Gabriel Valley', *Journal of Asian American Studies*, 2:1 (February 1999), 1–28 • 28 Fong, *passim*; Saito, pp. 23ff • 29 Saito, p. 23 • 30 Wei Li, *Ethnoburb: the new ethnic community in urban America* (Honolulu, 2009), pp. 103ff, 118, 153; Yu Zhou, 'Beyond Ethnic Enclaves: location strategies of Chinese producer service firms in Los Angeles', *Economic Geography*, 74:3 (July 1998), 228–51 • 31 Denise Lawrence-Zúñiga, 'Bungalows and Mansions: white suburbs, immigrant aspirations, and aesthetic governmentality', *Anthropological Quarterly*, 87:3 (Summer 2014), 819–54 • 32 Christopher Hawthorne, 'How Arcadia is Remaking Itself as a Magnet for Chinese Money',

Los Angeles Times, 3/12/2014 • 33 Robert Fishman, *Bourgeois Utopias: the rise and fall of suburbia* (NY, 1987); Joel Garreau, *Edge City: life on the new urban frontier* (NY, 1991); William Sharpe and Leonard Wallock, 'Bold New City or Built-Up 'Burb? Redefining contemporary suburbia', *American Quarterly* 46:1 (March 1994), 1–30; Robert E. Lang and Jennifer Lefurgy, *Boomburbs: the rise of America's accidental cities* (Washington DC, 2009) • 34 Jim Steinberg, '2015 a Big Year for Warehouse Development in the Inland Empire', *San Bernardino Sun*, 6/6/2015 • 35 Robert Gotttleib and Simon Ng, *Global Cities: urban environments in Los Angeles, Hong Kong, and China* (Cambridge, MA, 2017) • 36 Elizabeth Becker, '2 Farm Acres Lost per Minute, Study Says', *New York Times*, 4/10/2002; A. Ann Sorensen, Julia Freedgood, Jennifer Dempsey and David M. Theobald, *Farms under Threat: the state of America's farmland* (Washington DC, 2018); Farmland Information Centre: National Statistics, http://www.farmlandinfo.org/statistics • 37 Thomas J. Campanella, *The Concrete Dragon: China's urban revolution* (NY, 2008), chapter 7 • 38 Sellers, pp. 139ff

14. Megacity

1 Jason D. Fischer et al., 'Urbanisation and the Predation Paradox: the role of trophic dynamics in structuring vertebrate communities', *BioScience*, 62:9 (September 2012), 809–18; Amanda D. Rodewald et al., 'Anthropogenic Resource Subsidies Decouple Predator–Prey Relationships', *Ecological Applications*, 12:3 (April 2011), 936–43; Alberto Sorace, 'High Density of Bird and Pest Species in Urban Habitats and the Role of Predator Abundance', *Ornis Fennica*, 76 (2002), 60–71 • 2 Suzanne Prange, Stanley D. Gehrt and Ernie P. Wiggers, 'Demographic Factors Contributing to High Raccoon Densities in Urban Landscapes', *Journal of Wildlife Management*, 67:2 (April 2003), 324–33; Christine Dell'Amore, 'How Wild Animals Are Hacking Life in the City', *National Geographic*, 18/4/2016; Christine Dell'Amore, 'Downtown Coyotes: inside the secret lives of Chicago's predator', *National Geographic*, 21/11/2014; Payal Mohta, '"A Double-Edged Sword": Mumbai pollution "perfect" for flamingos', *Guardian*, 26/3/2019; Alexander R. Braczkowski et al., 'Leopards Provide Public Health Benefits in Mumbai, India', *Frontiers in Ecology and the Environment* 16:3 (April 2018), 176–82 • 3 Menno Schilthuizen, *Darwin Comes to Town: how the urban jungle drives evolution* (London, 2018); Jean-Nicolas Audet, Simon Ducatez and Louis Lefebvre, 'The Town Bird and the Country Bird: problem solving and immunocompetence vary with urbanisation', *Behavioral Ecology* 27:2 (March–April 2016), 637–44; Jackson Evans, Kyle Boudreau and Jeremy Hyman, 'Behavioural Syndromes in Urban and Rural Populations of Song Sparrows', *Ethology* 116:7 (July 2010), 588–95; Emile C. Snell-Rood and Naomi Wick, 'Anthropogenic Environments Exert Variable Selection on Cranial Capacity in Mammals', *Proceedings of the Royal Society B* 280:1769 (October 2013); E. A. Maguire, K. Woollett and H. J. Spiers, 'London Taxi Drivers and Bus Drivers: a structural MRI and neuropsychological analysis', *Hippocampus* 16:12 (2006), 1091–1101 • 4 Schilthuizen; Thomas Merckx et al., 'Body-Size Shifts in Aquatic and Terrestrial Urban Communities', *Nature* 558 (7/5/2018), 113–18 • 5 Karen C. Seto, Burak Güneralp and Lucy R. Hutyra, 'Global Forecasts of Urban Expansion to 2030 and Direct Impacts on Biodiversity and Carbon Pools', *PNAS*, 109:40 (October 2012), 16083–8; 'Hot Spot Cities', http://atlas-for-the-end-of-the-world.com/hotspot_cities_main.html; B. Güneralp and K. C. Seto, 'Futures of Global Urban Expansion: uncertainties and implications for biodiversity conservation', *Environmental Research Letters* 8:1 (2013) • 6 Seto et al. • 7 Christopher Bren d'Amour et al., 'Future Urban Land Expansion and Implications for Global Croplands', *PNAS* 114:34 (August 2017), 8939–44; Mathis Wackernagel et al., 'The Ecological Footprint of Cities and Regions: comparing resource availability with resource demand', *Environment and Urbanizaion* 18:1 (2006), 103–12 • 8 Scott R. Loss, Tom Will, Sara S. Loss and Peter M. Marra, 'Bird–Building Collisions in the United States: estimates of annual mortality and species vulnerability', *The Condor*, 116:1 (February 2014), 8–23; Kyle G. Horton et al., 'Bright Lights in the Big Cities: migratory birds' exposure to artificial light', *Frontiers in Ecology and the Environment*,

17:4 (May 2019), 209–14; Laurel E. K. Serieys, Amanda Lea, John P. Pollinger, Seth P. D. Riley and Robert K. Wayne, 'Disease and Freeways Drive Genetic Change in Urban Bobcat Populations', *Evolutionary Applications*, 8:1 (January 2015), 75–92 • 9 Greenspace Information for Greater London, 'Key London Figures', https://www.gigl.org.uk/keyfigures/; London gov.uk, 'Biodiversity', https://www.london.gov.uk/what-we-do/environment/parks-green-spaces-and-biodiversity/biodiversity; Secretariat of the Convention on Biological Diversity, *Cities and Biological Diversity Outlook* (Montreal, 2012), pp. 9, 24 • 10 Lucy Wang, 'How the Cheonggyecheon River Urban Design Restored the Green Heart of Seoul', https://inhabitat.com/how-the-cheonggyecheon-river-urban-design-restored-the-green-heart-of-seoul/ • 11 Claire Cameron, 'The Rise of the City Bee', https://daily.jstor.org/rise-city-bee-urbanites-built-21st-century-apiculture/ • 12 Sam Jones, 'Can Mexico City's Roof Gardens Help the Metropolis Shrug Off Its Smog?', *Guardian*, 24/4/2014; Ajuntament de Barcelona, *Barcelona Green Infrastructure and Biodiversity Plan 2020*, https://ajuntament.barcelona.cat/ecologiaurbana/sites/default/files/Barcelona%20green%20infrastructure%20and%20biodiversity%20plan%202020.pdf; Grace Chua, 'How Singapore Makes Biodiversity an Important Part of Urban Life', Citylab, https://www.citylab.com/environment/2015/01/how-singapore-makes-biodiversity-an-important-part-of-urban-life/384799/ • 13 *Cities and Biological Diversity*, pp. 26, 28; Amy Fleming, 'The Importance of Urban Forests: why money really does grow on trees', *Guardian*, 12/10/2016; International Energy Agency, *The Future of Cooling: opportunities for energy-efficient air conditioning* (Paris, 2018) • 14 Andrew J. Hamilton et al., 'Give Peas a Chance? Urban agriculture in developing countries. A review', *Agronomy*, 34:1 (January 2014), 54ff • 15 Food and Agriculture Organisation of the United Nations, *FAO Statistical Yearbook 2012* (Rome, 2012), p. 214; Francesco Orsini et al., 'Urban Agriculture in the Developing World: a review', *Agronomy for Sustainable Development* 33:4 (2013), 700 • 16 Toni Kan, *The Carnivorous City* (Abuja, 2016), p. 34 • 17 David Pilling, 'Nigerian Economy: why Lagos works', *Financial Times*, 24/3/2018; Robert Draper, 'How Lagos Has Become Africa's Boom Town', *National Geographic* (January 2015); 'Lagos Shows How a City Can Recover from a Deep, Deep Pit: Rem Koolhaas talks to Kunlé Adeyemi', *Guardian*, 26/2/2016; 'Lagos: the next Silicon Valley', *Business Year*, https://www.thebusinessyear.com/nigeria-2018/nurturing-entrepreneurs/interview; Oladeinde Olawoyin, 'Surviving the Inner Recesses of a Lagos Danfo Bus', *Premium Times*, 17/2/2018 • 18 Saskia Sassen, *The Global City: New York, London, Tokyo* (Princeton, 2001) • 19 Economic Intelligence Unit, Ministry of Economic Planning and Budget, 'The Socio-Economic Costs of Traffic Congestion in Lagos', *Working Paper Series*, 2 (July 2013), 7 • 20 A. T. Kearney, *Digital Payments and the Global Informal Economy* (2018), pp. 6, 7; Ifeoluwa Adediran, 'Mixed Feelings for Lagos *Danfo* Drivers as Phase-Out Date Approaches', *Premium Times*, 15/9/2018 • 21 *Guardian* (Nigeria), 16/7/2017 • 22 Victor Asemota, 'Otigba: the experiment that grew into a tech market', *Guardian* (Nigeria), 15/3/2017 • 23 Jack Sullivan, 'Trash or Treasure: global trade and the accumulation of e-waste in Lagos, Nigeria', *Africa Today*, 61:1 (Fall 2014), 89–112 • 24 T. C. Nzeadibe and H. C. Iwuoha, 'Informal waste recycling in Lagos, Nigeria', *Communications in Waste & Resource Management* 9:1 (2008), 24–30 • 25 'Lapido Market and Audacity of Anarchy', *Guardian* (Nigeria), 24/5/2019; Tope Templer Olaiya, 'Fear Grips Danfo Drivers Ahead of Proposed Ban', *Guardian* (Nigeria), 20/2/2017 • 26 Adediran; Ifeanyi Ndiomewese, 'Ethnic Bias and Power Tussle Surround Appointment of New Leadership in Computer Village, Ikeja', *Techpoint Africa*, 13/5/2019, https://techpoint.africa/2019/05/13/computer-village-iyaloja/ • 27 Manish Chalana and Jeffrey Hou (eds.), *Messy Urbanism: understanding the 'other' cities of Asia* (Hong Kong, 2016); Rahul Srivastava and Matias Echanove, 'What Tokyo Can Teach Us about Local Development', *The Hindu*, 16/2/2019 • 28 Matias Echanove, 'The Tokyo Model: incremental urban development in the post-war city' (2015), http://www.urbanlab.org/TheTokyoModel-Echanove.02.2015.pdf; Ken Tadashi Oshima, 'Shinjuku: messy urbanism at the metabolic crossroads', in Chalana and Hou (eds.), pp. 101ff • 29 Kisho Kurokawa, *New Wave in Japanese Architecture* (London, 1993), p. 11 • 30 Oshima; Jan Vranovský, *Collective Face of the City: application of information theory to urban behaviour of Tokyo* (Tokyo, 2016); Zhongjie Lin, *Kenzo Tange and the Metabolist Movement: urban utopias of modern Japan* (Abingdon, 2010) • 31 Echanove (2015); Matias Echanove and Rahul Srivastava, 'When Tokyo Was a Slum', Nextcity.org, 1/8/2013, https://nextcity.org/informalcity/entry/when-tokyo-was-a-slum; Matias Echanove and Rahul Srivastava, *The Slum Outside: elusive Dharavi* (Moscow, 2013) • 32 Chinmoy Sarkar, Chris Webster and John Gallacher, 'Association between Adiposity Outcomes and Residential Density: a full-data, cross sectional analysis of 419562 UK Biobank adult participants', *Lancet Planetary Health*, 1:7 (October 2017), e277–e288; 'Inner-City Living Makes for Healthier, Happier People, Study Finds', *Guardian*, 6/10/2017 • 33 Devajyoti Deka, 'Are Millennials Moving to More Urbanized and Transit-Oriented Counties?', *Journal of Transport and Land Use*, 11:1 (2018), 443–61; Leigh Gallagher, *The End of the Suburbs: where the American dream is moving* (NY, 2013); Ellen Dunham-Jones and June Williamson, *Retrofitting Suburbia: urban design solutions for redesigning suburbs* (Hoboken, 2009) • 34 Vanit Mukhija and Anastasia Loukaitou-Sideris (eds.), *The Informal American City: from taco trucks to day labor* (Cambridge, MA, 2014); Jake Wegmann, 'The Hidden Cityscapes of Informal Housing in Suburban Los Angeles and the Paradox of Horizontal Density', *Building's Landscapes: journal of the Vernacular Architecture Forum* 22:2 (Fall 2015), 89–110; Michael Mendez, 'Latino New Urbanism: building on cultural preferences', *Opolis: an international journal of suburban and metropolitan studies* (Winter 2005), 33–48; Christopher Hawthorne, '"Latino Urbanism" Influences a Los Angeles in Flux', *Los Angeles Times*, 6/12/2014; Henry Grabar, 'Los Angeles Renaissance: why the rise of street vending reveals a city transformed', Salon.com, 18/1/2015, https://www.salon.com/2015/01/18/los_angeles_food_truck_renaissance_why_the_rise_of_street_vending_reveals_a_city_transformed/; Clara Irazábal, 'Beyond "Latino New Urbanism": advocating ethnurbanisms', *Journal of Urbanism*, 5:2–3 (2012), 241–68; James Rojas, 'Latino Urbanism in Los Angeles: a model for urban improvisation and reinvention', in Jeffrey Hou (ed.), *Insurgent Public Space: guerrilla urbanism and the remaking of contemporary cities* (Abingdon, 2010), pp. 36ff

Index

penguin.co.uk/vintage